Rethinking Development and Politics

RETHINKING DEVELOPMENT AND POLITICS

ESSAYS BY PROFESSOR LORD MEGHNAD DESAI
ON INDIA, CHINA AND GLOBAL CHANGE

EDITED BY MARIKA VICZIANY

Rethinking Development and Politics: Essays by Professor Lord Meghnad Desai on India, China and Global Change
Edited by Marika Vicziany

© Copyright 2019
All rights reserved. Apart from any uses permitted by Australia's Copyright Act 1968, no part of this book may be reproduced by any process without prior written permission from the copyright owners. Inquiries should be directed to the publisher.

Monash University Publishing
Matheson Library and Information Services Building
40 Exhibition Walk
Monash University
Clayton, Victoria 3800, Australia
www.publishing.monash.edu

Monash University Publishing brings to the world publications which advance the best traditions of humane and enlightened thought.

Monash University Publishing titles pass through a rigorous process of independent peer review.

ISBN: 9781925523898 (paperback)

www.publishing.monash.edu/books/rdp-9781925523898.html

Series: Monash Asia Series.
Series Editor Professor Marika Vicziany

Design: Les Thomas

Cover image: The Psalter World Map, c.1260. (Public Domain/Wikipedia Commons)

A catalogue record for this book is available from the National Library of Australia

Printed in Australia by Griffin Press an Accredited ISO AS/NZS 14001:2004 Environmental Management System printer.

The paper this book is printed on is certified against the Forest Stewardship Council ® Standards. Griffin Press holds FSC chain of custody certification SGS-COC-005088. FSC promotes environmentally responsible, socially beneficial and economically viable management of the world's forests.

CONTENTS

Preface..vi
Introduction..ix

PART 1: GLOBAL ISSUES 1
1   Global Governance..................................... 2
2   The Possibility of Deglobalisation 20
3   The New Anti-capitalist Movement: Money and Global
    Civil Society....................................... 34
4   Trade and Global Civil Society: The Anti-capitalist Movement
    Revisited... 75
5   Globalisation and Poverty 118
6   The Political Economy of Donald Trump 131
7   Is There a Future for Social Democracy after the Crisis?....... 145
8   Globalisation and Sustainable Development 153

PART 2: INDIA AND CHINA 165
9   India and China: An Essay in Comparative Political Economy... 166
10 The Vase and the Mudpie............................. 191
11 Fifty Years of Development Thinking 199

PART 3: INDIAN ECONOMY, POLITICS AND CULTURE 229
12 The Economic Policy of the BJP 230
13 India's Triple Bypass: Economic Liberalisation, the BJP
    and the 1996 Elections.............................. 243
14 Could the Indian Economy Do Better?................. 253
15 *Hindutva*'s March Halted? Choices for the BJP
    after the 2004 Defeat............................... 262
16 Twin Troubles....................................... 275
17 *Bhagavad Gita*: Outlines of a Secular Critique..... 281

Glossary.. 294
Index... 299

PREFACE

Professor Lord Meghnad Jagdishchandra Desai has been an outstanding scholar, policy advisor and public intellectual in India, many other countries in Asia, the USA and Britain. Monash University Publishing is privileged to bring together this first volume of his unpublished and difficult-to-access publications spanning some four decades of thinking.

Lord Desai began life as a precocious child. Born in Vadodara (Gujarat) in 1940, he attended secondary school when he was only 7 years old and matriculated when he was 14. He began his Masters work at Bombay University where he met Professor Charles Whittlesey, Professor of Money and Banking at Pennsylvania University and Visiting Ford Foundation Fellow. He was encouraged to study in the US and in 1961 arrived in Pennsylvania with a Ford Foundation Scholarship. Throughout his early life, Professor Desai hated mathematics but ironically in the US he was assigned as a research assistant to Lawrence Klein who assumed that his new student was a maths buff. Thanks to Klein's personal tuition, Lord Desai quickly learned econometrics (i.e. mathematical economics and model building) and completed his doctoral thesis on the subject of 'An Econometric Model of the World Tin Economy' in 1963. He then found himself working as a Research Officer in the Department of Agricultural Economics, University of California building econometric models about the determination of milk prices.

Like many other young scholars at this time, the Vietnam War and America's involvement made Professor Desai critical of US foreign policy. This, together with the risks of being drafted into the US military in the event that he was allowed to stay, compelled him to leave the USA for a more neutral country, namely England, where he arrived to take up a lectureship at the London School of Economics (LSE) in 1965. His reading of Karl Marx, together with his left wing attraction to the Marxian inspired student movement, were also factors that convinced him to leave.

During his early years at the LSE Lord Desai was determined to shed his image of being a numbers man and authority on tin and milk. He began to familiarise himself with the lively debates that were taking place in the West about economics, Keynes, economic history, development economics and poverty. These interests were reflected in his establishing at the LSE the Centre for the Study of Global Governance in 1992. At the LSE he also befriended A. K. Sen, whose ideas on inequality influenced him as much as Marx. Despite his hatred of mathematics, Professor Desai came to love econometrics and published his study of *Applied Econometrics* in 1976 but only after publishing a book about his first love in 1973, namely *Marxian Economic Theory*. Professor Desai's introductory essay to this collection, explains in greater detail the evolution of his ideas since then.

Apart from Marx, Professor Desai's big love has been for Dilip Kumar, perhaps India's most famous film star. Born in 1922, Dilip Kumar's life spanned the turbulent years of India's independence movement – something that Professor Desai has sought to commemorate with his opening in Amritsar of the Partition Museum in 2017. In 2004 Professor Desai published *Nehru's Hero Dilip Kumar: In the Life of India*. The title of the book again reveals the close connection in Professor Desai's thinking between the world of art and politics. His great admiration for Dilip Kumar led him to Roli Books who appointed a personal editor for this work – Kishwar Desai. She subsequently became his second wife.

Lord Desai's life as a public intellectual in Europe, America and India has been reflected in his membership of many high-level policy committees, his work as a journalist for leading newspapers such as *Indian Express* amongst others and acting as a media commentator. A lesser known part of his life is his involvement with various entrepreneurial ventures as documented by Bloomberg: for example he has been a Non-Executive Independent Director of Elara Securities (India) Private Limited since 21 December 2011. By contrast, his contributions to the British Labour Party, Finsbury Constituency Labour Party and Islington South are well known and admired. In recognition of this work, he was made a life peer of St. Clement Danes in Westminster and was honoured as 'Baron Desai'. Since retiring from the LSE in 2003 he has continued there as Emeritus Professor in addition to serving in the House of Lords as a major participant in various policy debates including Brexit.

In India, his public life has focused on analysing the political and economic trends of the liberalisation of the economy that began in 1991. From about the same time, significant shifts were occurring in Indian politics with the rise of the Bharatiya Janata Party. The essays in this collection reflect his thoughts on these changes. As always, Professor Desai's personal political preferences play a secondary role to his defence of democracy. As he argued in his opinion piece in *Indian Express* on 26 June 2016 the vote in favour of Brexit was 'a strange idea for a country which is the oldest continuous polity in Europe. The notion that joining a multi-country union is a loss of independence is hard to credit. But ultimately that is the message the people have given'. In other words, whatever the electorate has decided that is what parliaments need to act on. In an age defined by strong ideological positions, Lord Desai's defence of democracy via the electoral process is unfashionable.

His many achievements have been admired with public recognition given in awards such as the prestigious Padmabhusan in 2007 by the Indian government. Numerous universities have also awarded him Honorary Doctorates, including Monash University in 2005. His long association with Monash University began in the 1980s and has included short-term lecturing and fellowship appointments, acting as keynote speaker at various Australian and international conferences, and supporting the work of scholars in the humanities and economics with suggestions about their work and that by their doctoral students. Professor Desai has been a dynamic and razor-sharp commentator on world affairs, but in a generous and humorous manner that wins friends despite the vigour of his arguments. Given the international interest in his work, it is a testament to Lord Desai's involvement with Australian public and academic life that he approached Monash University to bring out this volume.

In concluding this preface I would like to thank all the publishers who kindly agreed to allow Monash University Publishing to republish many of the chapters in this volume. The original publisher is fully acknowledged at the end of each chapter.

Professor Emerita Marika Vicziany
Editor
Director, National Centre for South Asian Studies,
Monash Asia Institute, Monash University

INTRODUCTION

This book brings together various essays I have written singly or jointly over the last thirty years. They were written for conferences, for edited collections, as single 'Working Papers' or in literary magazines (such as the *IIC Quarterly* – India International Centre Quarterly). They all relate to political economy but in a global context as well as against the background of the tensions between national strategies and globalisation.

The essays have been arranged thematically rather than chronologically. The first section relates to the theme of globalisation. Today we debate the threat to globalisation and the rise of nationalism. The election of Donald Trump has started a debate as to whether the long period of freer trade, liberal economic policy and sustained economic and political cooperation between the principal powers – G7 or G20 – is about to end. Will the Davos Man soon be a thing of the past?[1]

It is hard to remember that at the outset of the 1990s 'globalisation' was a new buzz word, a word that inspired fear and scepticism. But was there such a thing as globalisation? On the one hand there was the collapse of the Soviet Union and with it the salience of the alternative to capitalism. Suddenly we were in a unipolar world with the USA as the sole hyperpower. The world was going to be borderless; the Earth was flat; it was the End of History – titles given to oft-quoted books at the time.

I was lucky to have a perch from where to chart the progress of globalisation. At the London School of Economics, in 1991, I was able to establish a Centre for the Study of Global Governance thanks to some generous research grants. This led me to add global political economy to my extensive research portfolio. The first chapter in the present collection is a product of this Centre. It was the introductory chapter in the first edited collection of articles the Centre published.[2] This is a sort of general introduction to what globalisation means.

But very soon it became clear that globalisation was not to everyone's liking. Trade unions in richer countries could see that freer trade which had benefited them since the end of the Second World War was taking

---

1   In this respect see my recent book *Politicshock: Trump, Modi, Brexit and the Prospect for Liberal Democracy* (Delhi: Rupa Publications, 2017).

2   *Global, Governance: Ethics and Economics of the World Order*, edited by Meghnad Desai and Paul Redfern. (London: Pinter Publishers, 1995).

jobs away to Asia. Whereas earlier anti-capitalist movements were in the 'periphery' and not in the 'metropolis' (to use words from the 1960s), now the shoe was on the other foot. The Seattle meeting of the World Trade Organization (WTO) was disrupted by American trade unions and radical groups. Many misunderstood this as a progressive left wing movement but I could see that this was a defence of established privilege.[3]

What was clear (at least to me) was that the widespread enthusiasm for globalisation was fragile and depended on the perceived distribution of benefits from globalisation. This is where the essay on the 'The Possibility of Deglobalisation' comes from. It was 2003 and too early for deglobalisation to occur but the warnings were there.

The early Davos meetings also witnessed the arrival of a global protest movement, the Social Summit, which often met in parallel. The two essays co-authored with Yahia Said examine that phenomenon. The fear that rapid growth may affect sustainability is examined in the 1996 essay.

The happy saga of globalisation was interrupted by the financial crash of 2008. Paradoxically the progressive left movements were more worried than ever before. As it was, the almost two decades of globalisation along with the financial revolution, had spread benefits all around. The so-called Third World countries became Emerging Economies and the acronym BRICS[4] was invented by Jim (now Lord) O'Neill of Goldman Sachs. Welfare states had become smarter and more market friendly in the developed countries but as there was sustained growth, everyone – Left and Right – was happy. There was a convergence between Left and Right and politicians such as Bill Clinton and Tony Blair announced the emergence of the Radical Centre. The crisis brought the reality of open economies with a global capital market to the fore. Keynesian-style deficit spending was ruled as being against the dictates of the global capital markets. The crisis of 2008 forced austerity and hardships onto the developed countries. There was fear that social democratic movements would be threatened with an existential crisis. The Helsinki essay on the future of social democracy addresses that question.

I was lucky in spotting the distinct 'charm' of Donald Trump before he even won the Republican nomination. This was when he expounded his economic philosophy during the election campaign. In a world where

---

3   See my chapter 'Seattle: A Tragi-Comedy' in B. Gunell and D. Times (eds), *After Seattle: Globalisation and Its Discontents* (London: Catalyst Aldgate Press, 2000).

4   BRICS refers to the five new emerging economies: Brazil, Russia, India, China and South Africa.

austerity had become the orthodoxy and debt was a dirty word, he had a plan to repair the public infrastructure of the US. The essay on the political economy of Donald Trump is an attempt at taking Trump seriously and sees him as an unorthodox 'Keynesian' politician. As an unorthodox politician, Trump also recognises that for a developed country, globalisation has ceased to be an advantage. The economic baton has passed to Asia from the West. Few could have seen, in May 2016 when the essay was written, that he would be elected. I was glad to have sensed that here was someone unusual whatever his style.

The second section of this book traces the truly revolutionary result of the phase of globalisation. This was the rapid rise of Asia especially of China and, to a lesser extent, India. Henry Kissinger had said in the mid-1960s that if only China and India could feed themselves, the world would have no other problems. Few could have foreseen that China would achieve a double digit growth rate for over three decades and end up with the second largest GDP in the world. Asians no longer complain that they are victims of multinationals or of global capitalism. They have become competitive in the manufacturing sector and China has even taken on the IT giants at their own game with Huawei and Alibaba.

There has been a sort of informal race between China and India through the second half of the twentieth century. In the Cold War years, it was democracy versus communism. But as late as 1975 the two were equally poor despite following different political paths. In 1991, India changed its policy and became more open while China had already moved in that direction after 1979 thanks to Deng Xiaoping's initiatives.

The second section begins with an essay in the *longue durée* style comparing China and India. Another essay pursues the same theme of the possibility of catch up between India and China. As of now there is little doubt that China has marched way ahead of India. What the next few decades will show is anyone's guess.

One of the reasons for the slow progress of India has to do with the way development has been understood as a phenomenon. The theory of development itself is a product of the post-1945 years. Initially the urgent problem was seen to be South Eastern Europe. But decolonisation coincided with the rise of development economics. India was the largest open economy which posed a severe challenge for development theorists. India's problems occupied many economists, Indian and foreign. I survey fifty years of 'Development Thinking' in the essay here but it is very much India centred.

Indian debates on development even after all these years continue to bear the birthmarks of an ex-colony. There is suspicion of business, especially of foreign capital, distrust of the market and a love for government regulations and an eagerness to surrender to populist pressures for subsidies whatever the fiscal costs.

The third and last section of this collection is exclusively on the political economy of India over the last twenty-five years, i.e. since the reforms of 1991. Over the same period there has been as much change in the political situation of India as in its economic record. The rise of the BJP (Bharatiya Janata Party) was hardly on anyone's mind at the outset. The first victory of the BJP in 1996 was not sufficient for it to form the government but the arrival of the BJP was a shock to the Indian political system. Few had taken the party seriously except for its 'Hindu nationalist' ideology. I began to study its economic policy and the essay here is one of the first, if not *the* first to do so. I should acknowledge the generous hospitality of the National Centre for South Asian Studies in Melbourne which made it possible.

The BJP did finally form the government in 1998 and ruled till 2004. Its defeat in 2004 was a surprise. I discuss it here in my essay about the *'Hindutva's* March Halted?' (i.e. Hindu nationalism). The Congress-led coalition ruled for ten years but it was beginning to falter. This is the background to the essay 'Could Indian Economy Do Better?'[5] Now of course the BJP is back in power under the leadership of Narendra Modi who has tried to speed up the pace of development. But even so, the growth rate fluctuates and reforms face obstacles. The longer run outlook for India is hopeful but the short run shocks still abound.

The rest of the essays in the third section relate to India more generally. There is an essay on the perennially difficult subject of Kashmir. The last essay is an introductory attempt at my critique of the Bhagavad Gita about which I authored a book.[6] This detour from political economy was undertaken by me as a corrective to the revival of a somewhat unquestioning and irrational respect for the ancient texts. The return of the BJP has encouraged a literal interpretation of ancient 'holy' works. I want to propose a rational explanation for one such much revered text.

The book would not have been possible without the enterprise and heroic effort on the part of my friend Professor Marika Vicziany (assisted by Ifti

---

5 See my recent book *The Raisina Model: Indian Democracy at 70* (Delhi: Penguin, 2017).

6 *Who Wrote The Bhagavadgita?* (Delhi: Harper Collins, 2014).

Introduction

Arman Rashid) and her colleague Nathan Hollier and his staff at Monash University Publishing. They chased the publishers of the books and magazines where the essays were first published and unearthed quite a few of the essays I had long forgotten I had written. I am grateful to Marika's team.

Lord Meghnad Desai

Part 1

Global Issues

Chapter 1

GLOBAL GOVERNANCE

Meghnad Desai[1]

(1995)

The need of a constantly expanding market for its products chases the bourgeoisie over the whole surface of the globe. It must nestle everywhere, settle everywhere, establish connexions everywhere.

The bourgeoisie has through its exploitation of the world-market given a cosmopolitan character to production and consumption in every country. To the great chagrin of Reactionists, it has drawn from under the feet of industry the national ground on which it stood. All old-established national industries have been destroyed or are daily being destroyed. They are dislodged by new industries, whose introduction becomes a life and death question for all civilised nations, by industries that no longer work up indigenous raw material, but raw material drawn from the remotest zones; industries whose products are consumed, not only at home, but in every quarter of the globe. In place of the old wants, satisfied by the productions of the country, we find new wants, requiring for their satisfaction the products of distant lands and climes. In place of the old local and national seclusion and self-sufficiency, we have intercourse in every direction, universal interdependence of nations. And as in material, so also in intellectual production. The intellectual creations of individual nations become common property. National one-sidedness and narrow-mindedness

---

1   I am grateful to Ian Rowlands and Paul Redfern for their comments though I admit I have not done full justice to them.

become more and more impossible, and from the numerous national and local literatures, there arises a world literature.

The bourgeoisie, by the rapid improvement of all instruments of production, by the immensely facilitated means of communication, draws all, even the most barbarian, nations into civilisation. The cheap prices of its commodities are the heavy artillery with which it batters down all Chinese walls, with which it forces the barbarians' intensely obstinate hatred of foreigners to capitulate. It compels all nations, on pain of extinction, to adopt the bourgeois mode of production; it compels them to introduce what it calls civilisation into their midst, ie, to become bourgeois themselves. In one word, it creates a world after its own image.

(Marx and Engels, 1848, *Communist Manifesto*)

The collapse of the Soviet Union and the end of the Cold War without the much feared nuclear holocaust have opened out various possibilities for rethinking the international system. In one sense there is now an opportunity to get back to the ideals of the Atlantic Charter and fulfil the promise of the original United Nations concept. There has been much enthusiasm on some people's part about the end of communism, the triumph of the market economy, the emergence of the USA-led coalition as the sole surviving Great Power configuration – the package known as 'the end of history' (Fukuyama, 1992). This is the New International Order that President Bush talked about, or the New Imperialism that Douglas Hurd, the British Foreign Secretary, mentioned.

Other considerations which have led to a desire to rethink the international order are the realisation of the environmental constraints which are global rather than local, the challenge of population growth and/or world poverty, which seems incapable of any simple solution by individual countries, the growing sentiment in favour of a minimum level of human rights guarantee – against torture, starvation, discrimination. These issues have led to a search for a *global* rather than merely an international or multinational solution.

An added influence has been the globalisation of the world economy. The growing interdependence of the economies around the world through trade flows and capital flows, as well as the effects of currency and other financial speculation, is a phenomenon of the last ten years, if not even more recent.

Flows of drugs, armaments and 'hot' money, as well as the international spread of AIDS and terrorism, have been the dark side of the globalisation of the world economy. In areas of Africa and Latin America which experienced a severe decline in incomes as a result of the debt crisis of the early 1980s, this has meant flows of economic as well as political refugees; flows which have come nearer home to the Western world with the collapse of the socialist economies of Eastern Europe.

The world then presents dangers and opportunities to anyone who would reopen the question of global governance, though the term itself lacks in precision what it offers in its novelty. It is quite certain in most people's minds that *governance is not government*. It is not the ideal of one world government which is being revived (Tinbergen, 1994). But beyond that negative stance, the concept of global governance needs to be clarified, amplified and, if thought desirable, made operational. In this chapter, I hope to take a broad-ranging view of the manifold aspects of the concept of global governance, being fully aware that this will be the start and not the end of a long debate. (Many references to the existing literature are available. A good starting point is Rosenau and Czempiel, 1992.)

The Context

One way in which one can characterise the present situation is to highlight four aspects:

1. post-mural
2. post-imperial
3. post-Keynesian
4. post-industrial

These four aspects can be explained further as follows.[2]

Post-mural

This refers to the world after the fall of the Berlin Wall, the collapse of the Soviet Union, the end of the Leninist State and central planning in Eastern Europe, and the transition to market economy in all formerly central-planned economies except, at least at present, Cuba and North Korea.

---

[2] It has been put to me that I have missed out the environmental revolution as an important aspect. I take this question up later but admit that I have not integrated it completely with what follows.

This is the prospect described somewhat grandly as 'the end of history' by Fukuyama. Even without accepting the pseudo-Hegelian echoes in his thesis, we must accept that the end of the Cold War as well as the defeat of Leninism as a serious political alternative for countries to follow, are events which have reshaped the world. The world is no longer bi-polar in the old way; there is only one economic system – capitalism (Fukuyama, 1992).

Post-imperial

In 1945 the world was still divided into imperial powers and colonies. By 1990, not only the British but the French, Portuguese and Spanish empires had been unwound, as had the great Russian empire. But by the same token the problems created by the dismantling of empires are still some of the most bloody and intractable ones. The Ottoman empire left a legacy in the Middle East and the problems of the former Yugoslavia, Georgia, Azerbaijan, Angola and Mozambique are all post-imperial.

The world is also post-imperial in other senses. First, in the sense that the Eurocentric bias of much of the Cold War politics – the claim, for example, that there was peace through nuclear stalemate despite the evidence of a loss of at least 20 million lives in the wars in the non-European periphery – can no longer be sustained. At the same time the 'Third World' is no longer homogeneous. There are newly industrialising countries (NICs) which are nearly part of the Organisation for Economic Co-operation and Development OECD group, the rapid growth of their industries being already seen as a threat by the developed West.

Post-Keynesian

A significant feature of post-war life has been the ability of the governments of developed capitalist countries to ensure a high and stable level of employment, a sustained growth rate of income and consumption, and a safety net for the poor and unemployed. This Keynesian Golden Age lasted until about the mid-1970s. The oil price crisis and the subsequent stagflation undermined the attractiveness of the Keynesian path. Through the 1980s the liberalisation of financial markets and the many innovations in telecommunications, transport and electronics created a global economy. In this new regime all economies are open economies and governments find it difficult to control them. Much macroeconomic policy-making has to do with preserving credibility *vis-à-vis* financial markets. Microeconomic, supply-side, structural policies are being increasingly adopted by governments since they know that their ability to control the macroeconomy is limited.

There is still the possibility that Keynesian demand management policies may work at the multinational level, for example at the European Community (EC) level, but this requires a much stronger governance mechanism than we have found so far. Old style Keynesianism working within one country is now obsolete.

Post-industrial

The term 'post-industrial' has been much used. I want to use it here in a specific sense. For the OECD countries, especially for the USA and the EC but notably not in the case of Japan, the industrial sector, particularly the manufacturing part of it, has been shrinking both in terms of the share of GDP but much more sharply in terms of employment. While there is still much hope in developed countries of a 'revival' of manufacturing, the only serious prospect is for these 'old industrialised countries' to seek new products and services to develop if they wish to preserve the level of their real incomes. This will demand a lot of investment in people as well as in ideas (Research and Development – [R&D]) and finally in hardware of some sort or another. The reshaping of the global economy with industry moving from north-west to east and south-east will be a major influence in the context of global governance.

Global governance as a concept and as a programme needs to be defined in the context of these four 'pillars'. The two political pillars, the post-mural and the post-imperial, define the constraints on the United Nations [UN] system as currently understood. The two economic pillars run across the political ones and are reconstituting the world in a way more radical than the political pillars. Each set of pillars needs to be further elaborated in terms of its implication for global governance.

The Political Pillars

The United Nations was born in 1945 as a creature of the victorious Allies. Its presumption in starting its charter with 'We the peoples ...' was breathtaking since, at that time, imperialism of the European powers meant unequal relations between members of the UN (for example, between the UK and India who were both founding members). Soon this inequality was overlaid by the Cold War. The intersection of the metropolis/periphery divide with the East/West divide characterised much of the early troubles of the UN. As imperialism unwound itself, or was forced to unwind, the membership of the UN grew until it became a large collection of *nation states* which were unequal in size and power – economic and military – though formally equal as sovereign states. A basic inequality is that of the veto states – the permanent members of the Security Council – and the rest, though with the presence of China among the veto powers there is no one-to-one correspondence between economic power (as measured by GDP etc.) and political power. This lack of correspondence has been reinforced by the retention of its seat by Russia as the largest surviving member of the USSR and persists in a weaker form in the continued presence of the UK and France, two declining economic powers.

Thus in the growth of numbers of member states and the continued but unjustifiable retention of permanent membership status by the original allies, the UN suffers simultaneously from adapting to changing circumstances (admitting new members) and failing to adapt to changes (retention of permanent status). The unravelling of old empires during the three decades following the Second World War created the first anomaly: the collapse of communism and the relative decline of the erstwhile imperial powers creates the second anomaly. But at the end of this double decline we are left with a world in which there is no single hegemonic power, though formally the USA qualifies as the one (by and large) non-imperial, relatively non-declining economic and political power. Alone among the permanent members, it could claim to have won the battles of the Cold War without losing much. Thus, although it overreached itself and lost in Vietnam, this did not prove to be a prelude to long-term decline; or if it did, its rivals declined even further than the USA. By contrast, the UK won the Boer War but its economic decline is traced back to the same years. Despite the switch from a creditor nation to a debtor nation on foreign capital account and a stubborn deficit in its budget, the USA retains its primary status.

But precisely because of that debt and the deficit, the USA is less powerful than it used to be. Had it been the sole hegemon in, say, the 1950s, or if it had retained its economic strength of those days into the 1990s, the USA could have aspired to fulfil the role that Britain did in the nineteenth century. The vision of Franklin Delano Roosevelt in setting up the UN could have been implemented. As it was, the UN became distorted through the Cold War visions of Harry Truman and subsequent US presidents and so could not fulfil the original vision. By the time the Cold War had ended the USA was primus, but the extra height it has is marginal.

A more particular problem has been the growth of public opinion in the USA against foreign policy adventures which lead to loss of life. The 'body bag' issue – the return of the dead from wars abroad – has now meant that as a hegemon, the USA is reluctant to commit its own troops abroad. When it does do so, as in the Gulf War, it uses a military strategy that places a tremendous premium on minimising loss of human life *of its own citizens*. Previous hegemons, such as the UK, had Imperial armies – Indians, Irish, Australians, Africans – to fight alongside its own subjects/citizens and in overwhelming numbers in its foreign wars. Even then, given the less than fully democratic nature of UK politics, there was no premium on the lives of their own citizens – as the First World War showed. The new hegemon has no formal empire from which to recruit its mercenary army. This has been evident in the case of the conflict in Bosnia, where the USA has been reluctant to send troops to implement UN Security Council resolutions.

So we have the paradox of a world of unequally powerful nations, among which there is *too little inequality* to make one nation state dominant and *too much inequality* to establish a symmetrical framework of the Rule of Law. The world of nation states is neither ready for a Lockean contract for a democracy, nor for a Hobbesian Absolutist monarch. There are querulous barons of unequal size – too many for comfort – but with no one powerful enough to lay down the law.

Athwart this anomaly lies the democratic deficit, whereby the peoples or the nations are not represented directly in the UN but only the sovereign states. The only way for a nation to obtain representation is to become a nation state; hence the premium on secession and the profits of a civil war. (For the problems that this causes see Gottlieb, 1993.) It is as if the US Constitution had created only the Senate and not the House of Representatives as well (but had allowed the original thirteen states veto powers).

Along the way, in the course of the last fifty years, another important change has been the growth and spread of democracy based on universal adult franchise (UAF) and multi-party parliaments (MPP). In 1945 there were very few among the members of the UN which satisfied either requirement; over the years, both in the metropolis and the periphery and now in the East as well as the West, there is a growth of UAF/MPP democracies. Even within some of the oldest democracies there remained many inequities between one person and another. Thus women's suffrage was delayed in many countries (for example, France) till after 1945. Equal voting rights for Afro-Americans were achieved only in the late 1960s as a result of the movement for civil rights.

The success of the civil rights movement created in the USA a climate in which citizens' voluntary associations were fighting against the State for justice and their rights but, at the same time, were seeking codification of rights as an instrument for equity. Positive discrimination for blacks led to articulation of other dimensions of disadvantage due to status, gender, race, age and sexual orientation. Civil rights became an issue of human rights, not only in the USA but in other democracies. As a result, within these countries the civil society has been enriched by active intermediate associations – Non-governmental organisations (NGOs) of various description – and there is more political activity (lobbying, etc.) between elections as well as at the time of elections. This growth of NGOs has spilled over into the international arena.

The presence of these NGOs was seen very strongly at the United Nations Conference on Environment and Development (UNCED) in Rio as well as at the Human Rights Conference in Vienna, where they played a role in setting the agenda. One of the questions of global governance is the channel through which the contribution of the NGOs can be directed. There are questions about the accountability of these NGOs themselves but these questions will only be faced once these groups have some official standing.

The Economic Pillars

The combination of the decline of single-country Keynesianism and (for the present at least) the drift away from the north-western metropolitan core of the manufacturing industries towards the Far East is reconstituting the world in a different way. Thus if in politics the nation states are growing in number and in their ability to create serious problems of inter-ethnic rivalry, pan-national religious fundamentalism, regional blocs etc., the economics sphere is undermining the nation state. As political sovereignty is being reaffirmed for ever-smaller states, economic sovereignty is being undermined in even the most powerful countries.

The phenomenon which has accomplished this reconstitution is labelled globalisation. In one sense, globalisation – the increasing interdependence and integration of the separate economies of the globe – has been happening since the late fifteenth century and the beginnings of capitalism as a world system. But, over the years, there has been an ebb and flow in the pace of globalisation. The nineteenth century – say, 1815 to 1914 – saw a rapid growth of globalisation foreseen so brilliantly by Marx, as the quotation at the beginning of this chapter shows. There was the Gold Standard, as well as a single powerful capital market in London where money could be raised for projects in any part of the world, growth of trade, revolutions in transport and communications, etc. But the fifty-plus years following the end of the First World War, say from 1920 to 1975, saw a brake on globalisation. The Gold Standard ran into trouble and was abandoned by the 1930s. Tariff barriers went up. The notion of relatively autonomous national economies controllable by their governments, whether by central planning or Keynesian demand management, took hold. Trade declined, only to resume its growth in the 1960s.

It is the resumption of the pace of globalisation in the last quarter of the twentieth century that is the novel phenomenon. Its origins lie immediately in the Organization of the Petroleum Exporting Countries (OPEC) oil price rise of 1973, but the strains on the previous economic order were already apparent before that. The abandonment of the gold-dollar link in August 1971 by the USA saw the collapse of the dollar exchange standard which was a pillar of the Bretton Woods System. This in itself could be traced back to US trade deficits caused by the Vietnam War and its monetary consequences. The growth of international trade which had resumed in the 1960s and the restored state of the manufacturing economies of Japan and Western Europe, made the USA relatively less powerful as it made all the developed market economies more open. A world economy was about to reconstitute itself aside and away from the influence of national economies and their policy-makers. The Eurodollar market had already given a glimpse of what could happen. The petrodollar market brought the phenomenon to the fore.

The oil price rise of 1973 created trade surpluses in the oil exporting economies and corresponding deficits in the developed market economies of the OECD. (There were also problems for developing economies which were oil importers, but they are not germane to the issue here.) The task of recycling petrodollar surpluses fell, not to the International Monetary Fund (IMF) or World Bank or even the Bank of International Settlements (the club of central bankers), but to private commercial banks located in the financial centres of London, New York, Paris and Tokyo. Whereas during the two previous decades the flow of capital from the developed to the less developed world had been through official government-to-government channels, now there grew a flood of private commercial loans from the banks in the centre to, by and large, the governments in the periphery. The economies of Eastern Europe were brought within this nexus as much as the countries of the South.

In fact, for the first time since the beginning of the First World War, all parts of the world were being bound together in a financial network on a private commercial basis. As in the nineteenth century, some of the borrowers were governments but the lenders were private. Unusually, however, the primary 'savers' were not numerous *rentiers* but a few large holders of petrodollar surpluses.

At this juncture in the mid-1970s, the metropolitan countries were not major borrowers. They were still, by and large, Keynesians in their fiscal and monetary stance and they chose to 'print money' rather than to fund their deficits by borrowing. These policies failed to overcome the stagflation then endemic in the metropolitan countries. The failure of Keynesian policies exposed them to the monetarist critique. The stagflation was, however, only partly a macroeconomic phenomenon. Behind it lay the decline in profitability of metropolitan manufacturing industries and the search by capital for more profitable locations. Be it the north-east of the USA or the UK, deindustrialisation had arrived.

By 1979, the monetarists had won the battle. In the USA as well as the UK, monetarist policy was now official. West Germany had always been hardline monetarist anyway. The second OPEC oil rise of 1979 helped this process by making inflation a lively issue again. A deep recession during 1980–81, the deepest in the post-war period, coincided with anti-inflationary policies being put in place. The metropolitan countries emerged as borrowers of OPEC surpluses and the real interest rate, which had been negative in the mid-1970s, shot up to its highest level since records started being kept. Monetarists were also backed by a libertarian programme of deregulation and dismantling of the state sector. The deregulation of financial markets began at this time. The 1980s began with the creation of global financial markets. The Eurodollar market was now officially universalised.

Technological innovations in transport, telecommunications and information technology also allowed capital – financial as well as real – to become much more mobile. It was the same process that had started in the 1970s but it now accelerated. In the search for higher profitability, capital became footloose, as it had been in the previous century. This process was aided by the fact that in many sectors of the manufacturing industries, products had reached a mature stage in their life cycle and thus could be shifted away from the metropolitan countries for their production. The mid-1970s, which were stagflation-ridden for the metropolitan countries, were years of rapid industrialisation for a small number of Third World countries – in Asia and Latin America. These NICs or Asian tigers were the new base for the manufacturing industries which were leaving the metropolitan shores. Mobility of capital and flexible foreign exchanges undermined the ability of countries to pursue an autonomous economic policy. The academic theorising in macroeconomics reflected this by speaking of credibility as the main concern of macro policymakers – credibility *vis-à-vis* the financial markets which were now global. The fear of inflation or in other cases (for example, the enterprise risk management stance of the UK) the political infeasibility of the chosen policy stance caused a sudden efflux of funds and forced the reversal of policy. Thus France in the 1981–83 period witnessed the last attempt at 'go it alone' Keynesian reflation. After that experience, caution was urged constantly upon governments by the markets. Asset price inflations fingered into the late 1980s but the collapse of these booms in Japan and the UK in the late 1980s drove home the lesson about global interdependence.

It is now conventional wisdom that individual countries have limited economic sovereignty. Of course, the 'body' to which they have conceded this sovereignty is an abstract one – the market. Occasionally, the frustration of diminished sovereignty takes the form of railing against speculators or multinationals on the part of politicians of the metropolitan countries. But the fact of the loss of sovereignty is not denied.

The developing world has also suffered a similar loss. In their case, there was always a perception that political independence had not brought with it economic independence. The neo-colonialist spectre was always there. These countries felt more threatened by Western governments as well as by Western multinationals. But the 1970s again proved a watershed in their case. On the one hand the OPEC price rise strengthened not only the oil exporting countries but also gave hope to many other countries exporting primary products. The easy availability of commercial bank loans made many of them relatively independent of Western governments. The multinational capital was now seeking a base for manufacturing rather than merely extractive or raw material exporting activities in the Third World. The developed world was in stagflation and feeling worried about the rise of commodity exporting cartels.

In this atmosphere it was easy for the Third World to put the New International Economic Order on the agenda. The United Nations Conference on Trade and Development (UNCTAD) was able to embark on an ambitious scheme for commodity price stabilisation in the form of a common fund. The USA, for a while during the Carter presidency, took all this quite seriously and showed willingness to negotiate. There seemed to be a real possibility of reversing some of the asymmetries of the imperial order.

The 1980s proved a complete reversal of all trends. As the developed world went monetarist and real interest rates shot up, there emerged a severe debt crisis for the developing countries. Starting with Latin America, the middle-income, relatively industrialised countries – Mexico, Brazil, Chile and Argentina, as well as poorer countries such as Bolivia – got caught in the debt trap. Any hope that they would threaten the markets of the Western world with their products was postponed. Soon after, the countries of Sub-Saharan Africa were in the same trap although their debt was official rather than commercial. Their hope of enhanced primary commodity exports were dashed when primary commodity prices declined as the recession in the Western countries affected them.

With the debt trap came the IMF and the World Bank. These Bretton Woods institutions had survived the demise of the dollar-exchange standard. Although set up to be international banking institutions, they had failed to perform any such function for a long time. Thus the IMF did nothing to monitor the recycling of petrodollars or the emergence of the debt problem. Once the debt problem had created a severe liquidity crisis for the developing countries, stabilisation plans and structural adjustment programmes were imposed, respectively, by the IMF and the World Bank. These programmes advocated and got compliance with a package of exchange rate, fiscal and monetary policies, which the countries in trouble had to adopt if they were going to receive the various borrowing facilities available. Conditionality became the watchword for the developing countries as credibility was for the developed ones.

It is not the occasion to go through the details of these programmes or their appropriateness, but they led to a diminution of economic sovereignty without any doubt. The various iniquitous policies advocated by the IMF and pursued by these countries do nothing to correct the impression that the asymmetry, as between the rich and the poor, was being sanctified by the IMF, since neither the indebtedness nor the trade budget deficits of the USA came in for any strictures from the IMF. The countries of the North, with the sole exception perhaps of the UK in 1976, escaped the IMF's criticism. Thus, while the world of the 1950s and 1960s was full of inter-governmental inequalities with asymmetry of power mediated by the compulsions of the Cold War, now the relatively faceless Bretton Woods institutions, beyond even the formal debates of the UN General Assembly, had emerged as masters of the Third World. They, of course, said that they only represented economic rationality and prepared the Third World for the market order. Even so, the economic sovereignty conceded by the developing countries seemed to be less to the impersonal market than to the faceless bureaucracies of the Bretton Woods institutions.

Either way, the world has now got used to the idea that economic sovereignty is not absolute; that market forces require a certain fiscal and monetary discipline. While the role of the State remains important, having been transformed from an intervening to an enabling agent, the fact remains that this State is powerless in many ways.

Global Corporations: A New Phenomenon?

The other side of this coin is the emergence of global corporations, which are taking an active role in restructuring the world economy, and the shift of the centre of economic gravity to Asia – mainly Southeast and East Asia. The global corporation is the descendant of the multinational corporation. It is less dependent on its home base, either for its market or for tax and credit facilities. It recruits its top management globally and has multiple locations for its production.

The contrast between a multinational corporation and a global or a transnational corporation is well drawn by Henry Wendt in his book *Global Embrace*:

> In operation, multinationals tend to clone themselves in other countries, and, regardless of the degree of autonomy they grant to foreign subsidiaries, the centre of the companies remain [sic] at their headquarters in the home market. Thus companies often transplant managers and invariably alter the national identities of any foreign companies they acquire. Products are generally introduced in the home market and then later rolled into foreign markets. In organisation and outlook, the multinationals traditionally follow the colonial model.
>
> Transnationals, by contrast, locate various parts of their operation anywhere in the world it makes sense to do so. Production facilities may be located in many countries to gain proximity to local markets or in just a few locations to maximise efficiencies of scale. New products are introduced simultaneously in as many markets as possible. Design functions may be carried out in areas that are rich in human talent, or marketing may find a home in several strategic locations. Research and development, one of the most important activities of transnationals, may be located in countries with superior technologies, talented researchers and engineers, or desirable markets. (Wendt, 1993)

The reconstitution of the world economy by the transnational corporation is a recent event but one that is likely to be durable. After 75 years or more of thinking of the world economy as consisting of individual national economies, the time has come simultaneously to think of it as consisting of transnational corporations as well. Looked at in these two alternative ways, as a collection of national economies, or, as (largely) a collection of global/transnational corporations, the world economy can be seen either as a single trading area or as dominated by two or three large regional blocs – NAFTA, EU, APEC – if we adopt a nation-state perspective. Alternatively, it can be perceived as a system of conflict and strategic collaboration between large multi-product conglomerates. Technological progress shapes and reshapes the futures of these corporations as they compete in markets around the world. The rivalry and cooperation between the companies, as much as between the nations, are the warp and the woof of the global economy.

One effect of globalisation is to have shifted the centre of economic activity from the north-west (Europe and North America) to the Far East. The Asian economies are registering sustained high growth rates of income as well as exports. Japan was the pioneer in this respect in the 1960s and 1970s, but now it has been followed by what the World Bank calls the High Performing Asian Economies (World Bank, 1993). As yet, in terms of proportions of total output the numbers are small, but the trend towards 'Asianisation' of the world economy is unmistakable.

For our purposes, the interesting aspect of globalisation is the reduction of asymmetry as between countries in Asia and Europe/North America. After a century or more of economic domination by the latter, with imperial domination added on the part of some European countries, the tide seems to be turning in favour of the former colonies. History will be remembered as old inequities are recalled. The Malaysian episode in March 1994, with the Malaysian prime minister accusing the British press of moral decadence (*Financial Times*, 17.3.94), is an example of the challenge to Western values from a newly emerging economic power. The decision by the Clinton Administration to drop human rights conditionality before granting Most Favoured Nation status to China in May 1994 is another example of the shifting power balance. Many more such episodes could happen with India, Indonesia and Korea all flexing their economic muscles.

The second aspect of globalisation is that it is creating a set of powerful players in the world who are not regulated or regulatable (if there is such a word). Unlike nation states which are nominally supposed to abide by the

UN Charter and various conventions of Human Rights etc., the companies are subject to individual country regulations but no overall *global* regulation. Thus it was possible for Bank of Credit and Commerce International (BCCI) to locate in a country with weak banking supervision, and although it was caught out in the USA and the UK, the two sets of litigation were not coordinated and they took, and are taking, a considerable time to secure convictions and compensate the depositors. There is no regulation of international capital flows, although schemes have been put forward by the Nobel Laureate James Tobin to tax transactions in foreign exchange markets. The many emerging stock markets are attracting large quantities of funds from around the globe but there is no institution like the SEC in the USA to regulate these transactions.

A third and perhaps, for many people, the most important aspect of globalisation, is what Barbara Ward tried to inculcate so many years ago in the minds of the decision-makers – the realisation that the planet Earth is a unique but fragile system (Ward, 1966; Ward and Dubos, 1972; but see also Carson, 1962). Although she argued the case in the 1960s, it was only in the early 1970s that the Stockholm Conference on the environment (UN, 1972), as well as the Club of Rome report 'The Limits to Growth' (Meadows et al., 1972) reinforced her argument. The OPEC oil price rise strengthened the notion that there may be a finite limit to non-renewable resources. But again, there was a lull in the environmental policy debate until the mid-1980s. By then the hole in the ozone layer and the prospect of global warming were added to the finite resources argument. The report of the Brundtland Commission (1987), the UNCED conference in Rio and the formation of the UN Commission on Sustainable Development were the responses (Grubb et al., 1993).

The international community is aware of the problem but even now there is no global approach. The difference of perception between the North and the South about the nature, the urgency and the cure of the environmental problem remains. The asymmetry of power and the memories of historical wrongs block any convergence of interests. Besides the nations, the global corporations and the NGOs are also emerging as players in the environmental negotiations (McCormick, 1989). The Montreal protocol on the banning of CFCs and the adoption of targets on CO_2 emissions are encouraging signs that some consensual strategies can succeed. But the gap between international, that is, inter-state and global policymaking persists.

Globalisation may thus be generating a need (if not the demand) for some form of economic global governance by way of regulation.

A Global Civil Society?

The other, but more speculative, side of this coin is that globalisation may be creating a genuinely *global civil society*, albeit embryonic at present. Civil society, let us recall, in the works of Adam Smith, Adam Ferguson and Hegel, is the sphere of contract, of private interests. It is the sphere where the Invisible Hand may rule and if not, the State steps in to regulate the conflicts of private interest that the civil society cannot resolve. (The civil society is frequently taken to be the civilised society or the welfare state or the civic society. For my purposes it is the original Enlightenment connotation that is relevant.)

Within nations, indeed within kingdoms before they became nations much less nation states, the state existed prior to the civil society, in as much as the civil society presumes the right to private property and the enforcement of contractual obligations (Desai, 1986). This is the sense in which the Scottish philosophers conceived of the civil society. The State is thus prior to civil society but the growth of the private sphere modifies the State. The reason for discussing the issue here is whether the analogy of the modern state/civil society relationship can be extended to the global level. Can we, for example, draw a parallel between the UN as a proto-state and the global economy as a proto-global civil society?

The speculation can be continued further by asking whether the undermining of the nation state by the transnational corporations would weaken or strengthen the international institutions which will be involved in global governance – the UN, the Bretton Woods institutions, GATT/WTO, ILO, etc. If the globalising of the world economy is to undermine global as well as national governments, then the question of global governance will move on to a very different terrain of creating a new set of institutions analogous to the self-regulating organisations in financial markets. This will mean less than even a night-watchman state at the global level. If, on the other hand, globalisation will weaken nation states but create a need for a global governance framework (corresponding to the emergent global civil society), then again we are on a very different terrain. In this latter case, 'market forces' will strengthen global institutions and urge compliance by nation states with global rules – harmonisation of taxation, free trade, single currency, a proper global central bank, etc.

It is not possible, with the data at hand, to judge which way the balance will go. It is early days of globalisation, and the nation states are by no means powerless, either singly or in groups, when it comes to international economic issues. The completion of the Uruguay round of GATT showed how much the narrow national economic interests of the powerful can detract from the promotion of global welfare. In a truly globalised economy, trade would be market determined; we are far from that world, even now, if it is at all a realistic possibility and not just a pipe dream of neoclassical economists.

Governance

Governance, at the minimum, has to be about providing a framework of rule by which all the participating parties in the commonwealth agree to abide. It is the provision of a 'Rule of Law', a symmetric framework in which the weak as well as the strong are subject to the same rules. A second task the state has performed has been the issuance of currency and coins which are legal tender. A third, and much more recent, task has been the promotion of public well-being and, later yet, the maintenance of high employment or low inflation and the promotion of economic growth.

Can we at the present juncture envisage the possibility of even a minimal framework of law and order? The foregoing analysis has pointed out the asymmetries of power that arise from history. The political pillars sustain an unequal, undemocratic international order in which the powerful set rules for the rest but do not themselves obey the laws they promulgate. The economic pillars, however, give some hope that the asymmetries may be in the process of correction – Asianisation and globalisation being the economic forces which are the corrective ones. Economic rules and regulations, especially those that go with the grain of the market (after all, the nation state was established very much in parallel with the market economy in a mutually determining way), may be easier and early established forms of global governance. The political framework – respect for human rights, especially those of the citizens of the weaker states by the governments of the powerful ones (asylum, refugees, labour mobility, etc.) – may take longer to put into place. A United Nations with an entrenched Security Council with permanent powers armed with veto is hardly likely to be the best vehicle for a symmetric rule of law. An undemocratic General Assembly only adds to the weakness of the UN in this respect; no member government will allow the UN to champion its own citizens in defiance of the government. It may yet be that, paradoxically, globalisation may be the only hope for global governance.

References

Brundtland Commission (1987), 'World Commission on Environment and Development', *Our Common Future*, Oxford, OUP.
Carson, R. (1962), *Silent Spring*, New York, Fawcett Crest.
Desai, M. (1986), 'Men and Things', *Economics*, February.
Fukuyama, F. (1992), *The End of History and the Last Man*, London, Hamish Hamilton.
Gottlieb, G. (1993), *Nation Against State: A New Approach to Ethnic Conflicts and the Decline of Sovereignty*, New York, The Council of Foreign Relations Press.
Grubb, M. et al. (eds) (1993), *The 'Earth Summit' Agreements: A Guide and Assessment*, London, Earthscan for the RIIA.
McCormick, J. (1989), *The Global Environmental Movement: Reclaiming Paradise*, London, Belhaven Press.
Marx, K. and Engels, F. (1848), *Communist Manifesto*. Reprinted in K. Marx and F. Engels (1968), *Selected Works*, London, Lawrence & Wishart Ltd, pp. 38–9.
Meadows, D.H. et al. (1972), *The Limits to Growth*, New York, Universe Books.
Rosenau, J.N., and Czempiel E.-O. (eds) (1992), *Governance Without Government: Order and Change in World Politics*, Cambridge and New York, Cambridge University Press.
Tinbergen, J. (1994), *Global Governance for the 21st Century*, UNDP.
UN (1972), 'United Nations Conference on the Human Environment: Final Documents' (Stockholm, Sweden: 5–16 June 1972), reprinted in *International Legal Materials*, Vol. 11, No. 6, November 1972: 1416–69.
UNDP (1994), *Human Development Report*, Oxford, OUP.
Ward, B. (1966), *Spaceship Earth*, London, Hamish Hamilton.
Ward, B. and Dubos, R. (1972), *Only One Earth: The Care and Maintenance of a Small Planet*, New York, W. W. Norton and Co.
Wendt, H. (1993), *Global Embrace: Corporate Challenges in a Transnational World*, New York, Harper Business.
World Bank (1993), *The East Asian Miracle: Economic Growth and Public Policy*, Oxford, OUP.

Acknowledgement

First publication: Desai, Meghnad (1995) 'Global Governance' in *Global Governance: Ethics and Economics of the World Order*, edited by Meghnad Desai and Paul Redfern. London, Pinter Publishers, pp. 6–21. Used by kind permission of Bloomsbury Publishing Plc.

Chapter 2

THE POSSIBILITY OF DEGLOBALISATION

Lord Meghnad Desai

(2003)

Introduction

Globalisation and all that it entails has led to a large and continuing controversy. The many issues that have been raised can be listed here only briefly:

a) Is globalisation a new phenomenon or merely a repeat of the late-nineteenth-century pattern? Can we even say that globalisation is a fact or that inter-nationalisation is still the norm and globalisation is just an overhyped concept?[1]

b) Has globalisation made territorial borders irrelevant, has it made the territorial (nation) state powerless or has it enhanced national and religious conflicts (fundamentalism) and hardened state boundaries?[2]

c) Is globalisation a Western/MNC-run operation to reinforce the present inequitable divisions in the world or is it a self-organising process which no one controls and of which all are victims or beneficiaries at various times?[3]

---

1   Hirst and Thompson (1996/1999) and Weiss (1998), among others.
2   Ohmae (1990) and Weiss (1998); see Halliday (1995) on fundamentalism.
3   Many Third World authors take this view but see also the two books entitled *Globalization and Its Discontents* by Sassen (1998) and by Burbach et al. (1997).

d) Is globalisation an impossible utopian experiment to run the world on the basis of a free market system bound to be ruinous or is it a liberalising, freedom-enhancing affirmation of the merits of private property and the market?[4]

e) Has the impact of globalisation been positive or negative on work opportunities, income growth and environment and in terms of countries and ethnic groups – who has gained and who has lost?[5]

f) Is culture being homogenised and trivialised or is the full diversity of all cultures becoming available across the globe due to the diasporas spreading everywhere?

I could list many more issues on each of which the opinion is divided. My own position is that globalisation is capitalism, in a phase that is a repetition of the late-nineteenth-century pattern, but at a higher level of technology and with many more democratic state formations than we had the last time around. Thus it is a spiral, not a circle. The most important thing about globalisation is the unregulated movement of capital inaugurated by policy changes in the USA and UK in the 1970s followed by other developed capitalist countries in the 1980s and later. This free movement of capital had been stemmed by the Bretton Woods conventions and thus the Golden Age of Keynesianism is separated from the inauguration of globalisation. The new technologies of information processing, communication and transport were important ingredients in this but so was the changed climate of opinion in favour of liberal free market policies. Globalisation is a dialectical dynamic process whose good and bad effects are intertwined. It is a gale of creative destruction, to use Schumpeter's phrase. It is a process in which multinational corporations (MNCs) are as important players as states and the MNCs are beginning to behave as if they were truly global, with no national bias.[6]

We are in the early days of this new phase of globalisation and so in order to distinguish it from the earlier globalisation episode, I shall label

---

4   John Gray's *False Dawn* has argued the Polanyi thesis about the utopian nature of the globalisation experiment; the Hayekians and neoliberals have argued the libertarian case (Gray 1998).

5   Paradoxically, the complaints from the North have been as loud as those from the South: see, in no particular order of merit, Bauman (1998), Korten (1995), Greider (1997), Barnes (1999) and UNDP (1999).

6   I have argued the case of G20 as being shaped by MNCs in M. Desai 'Global governance' in Desai and Redfern (1995), *Global Governance*, London: Cassell.

it G20 (globalisation in the 20th century). At the earliest it started in the mid-1970s or at the latest after the fall of the Berlin Wall. Its nineteenth-century predecessor ('G19' hereafter) is dated loosely as starting sometime in the second half of the century and ending in 1914. It would do us no harm to take the period 1873–1914 as the length of G19. Now G19 came to an abrupt end in the First World War. The reasons for the war have been endlessly debated but I wish to pose a stark, somewhat naïve question. Was the war a way of ending G19, an endogenous response against the utopian market experiment a la Polanyi (though he himself dated the end of globalisation at the Second World War)? And what is more: could G20 come to an end due to endogenous systemic reasons and, if so, what would they be?

I am quite aware that this is a very naïve, mechanistic way of posing the question – does history repeat herself? I know she does not, not even as a farce having been a tragedy. Yet to pose the question of deglobalisation is at the same time to pose the question of the endogenous systemic limits to globalisation. What are the forces working for globalisation and what are the retarding, checking forces? Is there an endogenous dynamic to globalisation whereby it may self-destruct, much as many Marxists-Leninists thought (and still think) capitalism would?

The First Deglobalisation

The reasons for the First World War are many and there is no settled story of the causality. But there is no doubting the fact that the war put a stop to the globalised world of the nineteenth century – capital flows dried up, the gold standard broke up, trade progressively shrank, mobility became difficult due to passports etc. But what were the forces for and against globalisation in that case? What I want to do below is to mention five factors which are relevant to understanding both the First World War and its context, if not its causes, which may have resonance in this phase of globalisation.

Imperialism/Capitalism as a Cause of War

The growing international socialist movement debated and prepared for a war. It was convinced that an imperialist war would happen in Europe and in 1907 at the Stuttgart Conference the strategy to be adopted in case of a war was debated. Socialists, especially Marxists, wanted to use the First World War to further the collapse of capitalism which they thought was imminent. The new cartelised phase of capitalism with the domination of finance capital (though this was a German rather than an Anglo-Saxon concept) would, it was said, lead to territorial wars. Markets would be fought over and in that fight war would break out.[7]

Lenin articulated this thesis in 1916 in his *Imperialism*, but that was after the war had already happened. So it was not a predictive model. Hobson had thought imperialism to be irrational – a search for land rather than markets motivated by the land hunger of the aristocratic classes. Hobson was a radical Whig who had thought that free trade would bring universal peace but for the pre-capitalist elements in the ruling classes. His thesis was similar to that of Schumpeter. So, while for Lenin it was capitalism that was the cause of imperialism and war, for Hobson and Schumpeter it was imperialism as an atavistic pre-capitalist form that was responsible for the First World War. Kautsky, on the other hand, thought capitalism would see the advantages of collaboration among the imperial powers and they would form a supercartel of imperial powers (EU, anyone?).[8]

Thus imperialism led to war either as a phase of capitalism or as a form of atavistic pre-capitalist throwback. In the first case Marxism as practiced at that time led to two contradictory predictions of capitalism/imperialism as leading either to war or to a supercartel. The 1914 war seemed to vindicate Lenin (though, as I said, he had postdicted it) rather than Kautsky. But later events after the Second World War – EU, G7 etc. – seem to support Kautsky.

In as much as G20 is a new phase of capitalism (one after the highest phase which, according to Lenin, was imperialism), the question can be asked again – Is there anything about the nature of G20 that may lead to its violent end? I will come to this question below.

Nationalism as a Cause of War

The war did, after all, start with the assassination of Archduke Ferdinand by a Serb nationalist, Gavrilo Princip. The dynamics of the national movements in the Austro-Hungarian Empire as well as the Ottoman Empire on the mainland of Europe were definitely a force for instability in the pre-war period. This was imperialism as a political rather than an economic phenomenon. The Boer War had preceded the Great War as a rehearsal;

---

7   See Schorske (1955).
8   Lenin (1916), *Imperialism, the Highest Stage of Capitalism* was not published until later and Schumpeter's *Imperialism and Social Classes* was published in 1919, i.e., both after the war had finished. Hobson (1902), *Imperialism* (London: Macmillan). For Kautsky, see Massimo Salvadori (1979).

Hobson, after all, was writing in reaction to the Boer War. That too was a nationalist uprising against an imperial power. Japanese nationalism had defeated Russia in 1905 and was seen as a threat. There was an upsurge of nationalism in China and India in the first decade of the twentieth century. One of the end products of the war was the end of empires and the formation of new nation states in Europe. Nationalism put pressure on the metropolitan centre in each empire. Though the war was between these empires and no link-up took place among nationalisms across empires, nationalism was a more potent anti-imperialist force than socialism.

It could also be said that the territorial disputes which preceded the war – the two Morocco incidents of 1905 and 1911 – were not motivated by economic gain but by pure territorial atavistic aggrandisement on the part of Germany which felt left out of the imperial club.

The interest of nationalism for G20 is that it is very similar to the fundamentalism forces which are seen as a serious threat today. Also the detritus of the break-up of the Ottoman and the Hapsburg empires is still with us in the form of national and subnational conflicts – Yugoslavia, Israel/Arab wars, Greece/Turkey etc. Since 1991, the break-up of the Romanov/Bolshevik Empire has added new fragile 'nations'. They link up G19 and G20.

Trade Wars

Free trade was scrupulously practiced by the British and advocated by them. The liberal free traders believed that wars would be inconceivable in a world of free trade. But the USA and continental Europe were not fully committed to free trade and even in Britain the tariff debate was gathering pace (witness Joseph Chamberlain's defection to the Tory Party). The perception by the then richest country that it could be suffering the adverse effects of free trade has been echoed in more recent times by politicians of developed countries such as James Goldsmith, Pat Buchanan and Ross Perot. While there were no trade wars before 1914, free trade as a philosophy was eroding. The notion of empires as *zollvereins* – free trade within the Customs Union and protection against the outside – was gaining ground. Thus was Friedrich List, rather than David Ricardo, ruling the waves.

Diasporas

America had become a melting pot with many Central and East European nationalities well represented there. There was much pro-German and anti-British feeling in its politics. The Industrial Workers of the World (IWW) as a trade union owed much to the European background of many first-generation immigrants. If America did eventually enter the war albeit on the British/French side, it was as much due to diasporic pressure as not. It was the un-diasporic people, the English, who had migrated in the 1600s who finally triumphed in this choice. Elsewhere, the migration from Asia to Africa and to the Caribbean had also created large Indian and Chinese minorities in these regions.

The diasporas are again a force in G20 even more than they were in G19. They are more multi-racial and wider spread than in G19. Thanks to decolonisation and the immigration since, from the periphery to the core, diasporas are much more varied than before.

Long Waves

The theory of long waves has been popular with many who want to be able to predict long run. Kondratieff waves have long been popular. No one quite believes in regular fifty-year cycles but there may be some advantage in thinking in broad long waves terms. Thus the 1870s as well as the 1970s witnessed a change of gear for the world economy. No one believed in the 1960s that full employment could come to an end in the 1970s. The 1890s were a boom time when Eduard Bernstein was arguing that capitalism had changed its character and was no longer cyclical. In the 1990s we heard much talk of a new paradigm or eliminating boom and bust cycles. Kondratieff was wrong in locating a fifty-year cycle but the world has an uncanny habit of repeating itself, especially where it means committing errors. (For a discussion of long swings, see Mandel (1995).)

Now the Kondratieff wave started from its trough in 1873 and should have lasted until, say, the 1920s. The war interrupted the downswing of the Kondratieff wave from the mid-1890s to the 1920s. Before that the 1790–1820s period was also characterised by wars in Europe. Are we in for another interrupted downswing of the Kondratieff?

Deglobalising of G20

These issues listed above as the context of the deglobalisation of G19 will not come back exactly as before. It is a spiral, not a circle, as I said above. The context is different now and to begin with I wish to bring out the major differences in the context today.

Equity and Democracy

The big issue for G20 is the reconciliation of free movement of capital with equity. This is not merely the equity/efficiency choice of economics textbooks but has a special dimension in G20. The reasons lie in the major difference between G19 and G20.

The big difference between the two episodes of globalisation is democracy. We have not only many more states today which have parliamentary democracy and public accountability but the ethos of the late twentieth century was much more anti-elitist, much more suspicious of decisions coming down from the top, much more irreverent than was the case in the 1890s. At that time the growing population of Europe had made its presence felt as 'the mob' became an object of study. There was also an explosion of the print media, radio had just come on the scene and cable and telephones were making new forms of communications available. But now the mob has been enfranchised. The electoral process has empowered it much more than was the case a hundred years ago. The NGOs have become a parallel extragovernmental level of governance at both the national and international levels. We tend not to be impressed by these developments because they are too familiar for us. But mass democracy with universal franchise is a bigger problem for global capitalism than the growing socialist movement was in the late nineteenth century.

The consequence is that equity issues are much more prominent now than before. It is not enough to say nowadays that the market will in the long run promote welfare. It may be true and I believe it has more truth than many admit. But the twenty-five years of the Golden Age of Keynesianism gave a different version of capitalism much credibility. This version had full employment, a growing welfare state and the market was contained. Although that phase has passed and the passage away from it in the 1970s and 1980s was painful, the memory of a regulated capitalism at the national level is a very strong one. Equity-based NGO movements will seek to establish regulatory competence at the global level – Tobin taxes, world financial authority, global Keynesianism, environmental taxes or restrictions on pollution, fair trade issues before the WTO, etc. If they succeed it will lead to a globalised world which emulates the best properties of the Golden Age (although that was restricted to the OECD countries). The reconciliation of equity issues with the unregulated flow of capital is the biggest challenge to G20.

The reason why such a solution may yet be arrived at is that, unlike in G19, the costs of G20 are being felt in the North as much as in the South.

During G19, and indeed up to the early 1970s, there was asymmetry in the way the world economy operated. Crudely put, the North won every time and the South lost.[9] Now, while there is still a lot of inequality between the regions there is much less asymmetry as a result of the outflow of capital and consequentially jobs, especially blue-collar jobs, from the North to the South. Indeed for the first time since the birth of capitalism, the North is frightened of it as never before. Groups in the North – those losing from technological change – the Luddites, for example, have always protested but they have never been able to stem the tide of capitalism. Now the pain is more widespread as the free movement of capital seeks profits wherever it can, with no loyalty to the country where the MNC headquarters are. Right-wing politicians are becoming anti-globalisation as much as left-wing ones who have always been.

Equity issues centre around three considerations: job displacement, real wage erosion (both of these are North issues) and job insecurity (which is both a North and a South issue). The first reaction to job displacement was an alarmist one of 'end of work'. But in the 1990s, in the USA as well as the UK, the paradox is that rates of unemployment are lower than they have been for twenty years and yet there is a fear of job displacement. It is of course a class and a generation thing. Blue-collar jobs for men in their forties and above have been lost while jobs for women and the educated are growing. Since the blue-collar workers were the backbone of politically powerful trade unions and because they were employed in manufacturing which is also displacing itself to the South, both unions and subcontracting suppliers etc, are complaining about the impact of globalisation.

Real wage erosion is another factor where 'Are your wages determined in Beijing?' becomes the rhetorical cry. Real wages of manufacturing workers are growing less quickly than they used to and in the USA until very recently there was, if anything, decline rather than growth. This effect is well predicted by international trade theory as an effect of freer trade between labour scarce/capital rich countries with labour rich/capital scarce countries. The effect of trade is to lower the return to the relatively scarce factor. The debate is still raging amongst economists as to the effect of trade, as against technical change, in this respect. Yet again the growth of wage inequality in the developed countries has helped the educated and the young and hurt the less educated and older workers.

---

9 I use 'north' to refer to the dominance of the old European/American powers and developed countries, and 'south' to refer to the developing economies of Asia, Latin America and Africa.

But both real wage erosion and job displacement are mirror images of the positive effects of globalisation for the South, not all of it, but for those countries, which are industrialising and exporting manufacturers. Some North NGOs are countering this result by complaining about low wages in the South, but while these wages are low relative to those in the North, they are less so than they were before globalisation and they are higher than what these workers could earn in the non-tradeable or agricultural sector in their countries. So globalisation has shifted industrialisation to the South and any attempt to jack-up wages in the South will only benefit the North, which is well endowed as it is. This is one reason why many South countries are opposing the social clause discussion in the WTO.

Job insecurity is a pervasive worry. Flexible labour markets may create jobs but these jobs are not long-term ones and the anxiety about job insecurity pervades in the North and South. There is an admission that while some OECD countries can take the burden of a high level of unemployment and maintain their welfare states, this is a diminishing option. In any case, for most countries in the world this is not an option at all.

Equity issues are unlikely to lead to global coalitions but in many rich countries they could generate a backlash against freer trade (I say freer trade rather than free trade since free trade does not exist as of now) and against the larger corporations. Such a backlash would have trade union and industrial [SME] support. It will be a Right/Left alliance, which will reconstitute politics much as it did with the split in the Liberal Party in the UK when Chamberlain joined the Tories on a tariff platform. There could also be a reimposition of some controls on the flexible labour market but this conflicts with the pressure to be competitive which cannot be easily avoided by most economies. But the reaction will be country-specific rather than global. Global alliances are difficult to build up in this case because there is no commonalty of interest across countries or even within countries.

Environment and Sustainability

The environment was not an issue in G19 although the problem of greenhouse gas emission was first mooted in the 1890s. Since the publication of Rachel Carson's *Silent Spring* in 1962, and especially since the oil crisis of 1973, the questions of non-renewable resource exhaustion, biodiversity and endangered species, greenhouse gas emission and global warming and the ozone layer have come to the forefront. In the 1970s these problems failed to be addressed by governments in a global fashion. But in the 1990s, the Rio Conference, the Montreal Convention and the Kyoto Summit have attempted global solutions to these problems. This is not to say that problems have been solved but, as the Montreal Convention example shows, given the will, solutions can be found. While there is a North/South divide, especially about who will bear the costs, in terms of both economic restructuring and financial resources, there is here a potential for a global cross-national alliance which could, given sufficient strength, bring about a major regulation of economic activities worldwide. This is because these are genuinely global problems as employment and wage problems are not.

Of course there will be debate as to whether solutions cannot be found with a market approach rather than an institutional/regulatory one. Thus, tradable pollution permits may work better than any quantitative restriction on consumption of say gasoline, especially if the USA is a party to the deal. The Green Clause as proposed in WTO negotiations by the North has shown that in some matters the free market is preferable to the South, than a restriction when it is likely to be a non-tariff barrier. Thus when environmental issues interfere with trade, no global coalition is likely, at least between states. There could be a combination of some NGOs and some states which may become globally powerful but even NGOs are often split across North/South lines on issues, such as the Green Clause.

Thus neither employment/wage nor Green issues are likely to generate a global coalition powerful enough to 'stop', much less reverse globalisation; by 'stop' I mean bring about a global regime with serious restrictions on capital movements or back to a Bretton Woods regime. This is not surprising since it is difficult to find a commonalty of interest in any economic area. It is not that such topics are a zero sum game but that the drive to find positive sum solutions will dominate those that rely on a threat of zero sum or negative sum outcomes as a way of forging a global coalition. The only exception is the global warming problem and that too only if a market-based solution is rejected as politically or technically unfeasible. But at that stage deglobalisation is unlikely to come about without conflict and catastrophe.

Nationalism/Fundamentalism

This is very much a revisit to G19 but again with a difference. There are many more independent nations and many movements for nations to be recognised and given status as independent political entities, i.e. as nation states. The break-up of Yugoslavia is an instance. The Kurds, the Palestine people, the Tamil in Sri Lanka, the Kashmiris in India and Pakistan occupied Kashmir, the many struggles in Africa, are all examples of this tendency. As I said above, many of these nations are the leftovers of the dissolution of the empires at the end of the First and the Second World Wars. Some of these conflicts have been with us ever since. Greece versus Turkey and its consequent Cyprus problem is a prime example of this. When empires dissolved, the boundaries they first drew were arbitrary, as indeed the victorious nationalist movements themselves said, but now the same nationalist movements in power have to defend those imperial demarcations as legitimate. The India–China border dispute of 1962 is another example of this.

The 1990s decade has seen simultaneously a unipolar power structure at the top and an almost anarchic and uncontrollable set of conflicts at the bottom. These are mainly 'new wars' but there have also been some old wars – Iran–Iraq and Operation Desert Storm being two examples (Kaldor, 1999). NATO and G7 have tried to build up a fire-fighting capability, as was seen in Bosnia and Kosovo and East Timor, but it is of course always late and selective, as was seen in the appalling Great Lakes tragedy. The new order born at the end of the Cold War that George Bush hailed has not yet succeeded in preventing wars or mitigating their effects in time. But they have contained them geographically. Unlike in 1914, a Serbian atrocity is unlikely to cause a worldwide conflagration.

Associated with nationalism is fundamentalism, and in particular Islamic fundamentalism. It is not because there are not other kinds of fundamentalisms but the Islamic one runs across countries and has a wider global reach than, say, Christian fundamentalism (very much an American phenomenon) or Hindu fundamentalism (confined to India) or Jewish fundamentalism (an Israeli problem). Islamic fundamentalism has unsettled many countries in the Middle East and North Africa. Thus Algeria, Egypt, Iran and Afghanistan have all suffered from terrorism or domestic civil wars or worse during the 1990s. While Islamic fundamentalism has been demonised by some Western experts as a threat to the West, it is its destabilisation of Muslim countries which is remarkable. So far its capacity to cause a global crisis has been limited.

The one channel through which fundamentalism of any kind can spread is the diaspora. On the one hand the competing ethnic groups in the diaspora make a bias for one side or the other in any dispute difficult for the metropolitan countries – for instance Kashmir where the UK government is confronted by Indian and Pakistani diasporas. But the loyalty of a diaspora member is multiple and cannot be exclusively to the state where s/he has taken citizenship. This makes them suspects in any paranoia about international terrorism, howsoever unfairly. It is not just that they may strike against their new habitat but even conspiring against their birthplace can be seen to be a problem. In September 1998, the British Parliament was recalled in a special session to pass legislation, one purpose of which was to prohibit activities which might be hostile against distant countries of interest to the diaspora. This was a major restriction of civil liberties of all citizens and a retrogression from the freedoms available in the G19 days.

The tendency of nationalism/fundamentalism is to cause havoc in its backyard rather than disrupt the global flows of capital or trade. It raises the costs of doing business but more for the poor or middle-income countries than for the rich ones. It has the potential for disruption and wars in particular regions but these regions can be sealed off and the spillover of the violence prevented. This is what seems to have happened in Yugoslavia and FSU. So I do not think this force, though potent in causing local trouble, can be a force for deglobalisation.

Unipolarity

American domination of the world's international relations as well as its economy raises some anxiety. American politics can be very parochial and disregarding of the rest of the world's welfare. This happened with the League of Nations vote, with the ITO vote, and continues to be the case in most environmental disputes in which the Americans have been involved. It has been glaring in the unilateral trade war America can launch with Super 301 and its disputes with the EU regarding bananas, hormone-fed beef, genetically modified organisms etc. Congress cannot be trusted to abide by rules to which it wants all else to be subject if it perceives American interests (and these may be parochial in terms of regions within America) to be at stake. America's commitment to free trade in the post-1945 world has been maintained more by elite manipulation than by populist support. If the global regime of freer trade and unregulated capital movements is seen to conflict with American interests, a protectionist President and a similar-minded Congress can easily renege on the commitments. After all, one of the reasons for the withdrawal of the Multilateral Agreement on Investment (MAI) was the reluctance of the Congress to sign up to any deal which would impose a rule of law on America.

Conclusion

So the fragility of G20 is not from the grass roots equity movements which will no doubt fight against globalisation. Nor will it come from the ecological dangers, real though they are, which threaten the globe. The nationalist forces will cause local trouble but not coalesce to undo the global order. G20 can only be undone by the powerful and only if the powerful feel their interests threatened. It may come from the USA. This is a paradox. But recall that G19 was not destroyed from below by the forces of protest of the excluded. It was destroyed by the powerful when their interests did not agree with the global regime.

It is an elementary principle of dialectics that one must look for weakness in the strongest element of any structure.

A Post-Seattle Postscript

This paper was written and delivered on 5th November 1999, at a Conference of the European Association of Evolutionary Political Economy. Since then the WTO ministerial meeting at Seattle has ended in a shambles. As I imply above, some people in the US economy are beginning to doubt the gains from further free trade. Clinton thought more of the US Presidential election of 2000 and pressures of American Federation of Labor and Congress of Industrial Organizations (AFL-CIO) when he practically sabotaged the meeting by his aggressive insistence on labour standards. There were other anti-MNC groups at Seattle but the balance in my view was held by the powerful labour lobby defending its high-wage jobs at the cost of slowing down deglobalisation. The issue remains: will American and other multinationals buckle under such pressure or will they fight for freer trade?

References

Alexander, T. (1996), *Unravelling Global Apartheid: An Overview of World Politics*, Cambridge: Polity Press.
Amin, S. (1997), *Capitalism in the Age of Globalization: The Management of Contemporary Society*, London: Zed.
Barnes, J. (1999), *Capitalism's World Disorder: Working Class Politics at the Millennium*, New York: Pathfinder.
Bauman, Z. (1998), *Globalization: The Human Consequences*, Cambridge: Polity Press.
Burbach, R., O. Nunez and B. Kagarlitsky (1997), *Globalization and Its Discontents, The Rise of Postmodern Socialisms*, London: Pluto.

Desai, M. (1995), 'Global governance', in M. Desai and P. Redfern, *Global Governance: Ethics and Economics of the New World Order*, London: Cassell.
Gray, J. (1998), *False Dawn*, Cambridge: Polity Press.
Greider, W. (1997), *One World Ready or Not: The Manic Logic of Global Capitalism*, New York: Simon and Schuster.
Halliday, F. (1995), *Islam and the Myth of Confrontation*, London: IB Taurus.
Hirst, P. and G. Thompson (1999), *Globalisation in Question* (2nd edn), Cambridge: Polity Press.
Hobson, J.A. (1902), *Imperialism*, London: Macmillan.
Kaldor, M. (1999), *New and Old Wars*, Cambridge: Polity Press.
Korten, D.C. (1995), *When Corporations Rule the World*, San Francisco, CA: Bewett-Koehler.
Lenin, V.I. (1916), *Imperialism, the Highest Stage of Capitalism*, various printings.
Mandel, E. (1995), *Long Waves of Capitalist Development: A Marxist Interpretation*, London: Verso.
Ohmae, K. (1990), *The Borderless World*, New York: Collins.
Ohmae, K. (1995), *The End of the Nation State: The Rise of Regional Economies*, London: Harper Collins.
Richmond, A. (1994), *Global Apartheid: Refugees, Racism and the New World Order*, Oxford: Oxford University Press.
Salvadori, M. (1979), *Kautsky and the Socialist Revolution 1880–1938*, London: Verso.
Sassen, S. (1998), *Globalization and Its Discontents: Essays on the New Mobility of People and Money*, New York: The New Press.
Schorske, C. (1955), *German Social Democracy 1905–1917: The Development of the Great Schism*, Cambridge, MA: Harvard University Press.
Schumpeter, J. (1919), *Imperialism and Social Classes*, Oxford: Basil Blackwell.
Scott, A. (ed.) (1997), *The Limits of Globalization: Cases and Arguments*, London: Routledge.
UNDP (1999), *Human Development Report*, New York: Oxford University Press.
Weiss, L. (1998), *The Myth of the Powerless State: Governing the Economy in a Global Era*, Cambridge: Polity Press.

Acknowledgement

First publication: Desai, Meghnad (2003) 'The Possibility of Deglobalization' in *Globalization, Social Capital and Inequality: Contested Concepts, Contested Experiences,* edited by Wilfred Dolfsma and Charlie Dannreuther. Cheltenham, Edward Elgar, pp. 1–13. Republished with kind permission of Edward Elgar.

Chapter 3

THE NEW ANTI-CAPITALIST MOVEMENT

Money and Global Civil Society

Meghnad Desai and Yahia Said

(2001)

Washington DC, Prague, Seattle, Davos, and wherever 'the money men' meet have been the foci of protest which have mobilised a broad coalition of groups, activists and lay individuals. While they may differ on many things, they agree on one. They consider many of the recent developments in globalisation as harmful, disruptive of their communities, and destructive in the long run. Such protests have taken many by surprise both in their scope and in their intensity, and have contributed to the increased interest in civil society in recent years. The protesters rarely attack globalisation as such, targeting instead corporate globalisation, global capitalism, the neo-liberal order, multinational companies, international financial institutions (IFIs) and trade agreements. Whatever the target, however, these protests are often branded as anti-globalisation. The counter-argument is usually a defence of globalisation as helpful to the world at large in enhancing output growth by expanding trade, helping the developing countries industrialise, and affording an opportunity for the first time in human history to eradicate world poverty.

In a framework where globalisation is understood as a symbiotic relationship between global capitalism and global civil society, this chapter analyses the interactions between the two. These interactions make up what we define as global civil society irrespective of whether or not it includes the market.

Given the breadth of its subject, this chapter focuses on money and finance as a proxy for global capitalism. This simplification is permissible for three reasons:

1. Finance is the dominant force in global capitalism. Financial flows far exceed trade flows and play an ever-growing role in every market transaction. Any sizeable trade today will almost certainly include bank credits on both sides, hedges against exchange rates and commodity price fluctuations in the form of futures and derivatives, and other forms of insurance. The growth and spread of the financial services industry and the unprecedented liberalisation of financial markets can be explained by the investment needs of the new industrial paradigm. The shift to information and communication technologies requires the mobilisation of vast financial resources, and global finance is the fastest way to achieve that. Similar financial booms occurred during previous technological revolutions (Perez 2000).

2. The financial services industry is among the main promoters of global capitalism, pushing for the opening of new markets and ever deeper liberalisation. The financial services industry is more dependent than any other on the low inflation advocated by the neo-liberal orthodoxy. Currently, the industry is pushing hard for the expansion of the WTO into the area of finance and investment through the General Agreement on Trade in Services (GATS). This will significantly expand the organisation, giving it jurisdiction over two-thirds of world GDP and bringing it into areas that affect every aspect of human life.

3. As we explain below, the financial services industry has traditionally been singled out for moral condemnation. So it is today, when it represents an extreme version of global capitalism. Financial juggernauts several times larger than many countries, fat-cat investment bankers and International Monetary Fund (IMF) executives playing God, astronomical profits on both the upside and the downside of the economic cycle, and bizarre financial products seemingly useless for anything other than the enrichment of those who invent them make finance an inevitable and often convenient target for those seeking to confront global capitalism.

Money and Morality

Our analysis deals with the ways in which global civil society has responded to the many activities of the financial sector – domestic and international, private and public – as they have affected the lives of the people. Finance is organised, complicated and pervasive. It comprises bank loans and debts, bonds and share markets, central bank and IMF regulation, and new innovative services such as futures and derivatives. It operates around the globe for twenty-four hours a day from places like the City of London and New York's Wall Street.

Financial developments have been at the forefront of globalisation. But even so, the core of financial market activities is age-old: buying and selling, borrowing and lending. The world has been familiar with money, credit and exchange for millennia. There are deeply ingrained moral attitudes about money, exchange and credit which shape the response of global civil society to recent developments.

Money has long been regarded as morally questionable. It is thought to be barren, which in turn calls into question the morality of charging interest. Money is often alleged to break up established communities, leaving atomised rootless individualism in its wake. Money is said to devalue relationships by reducing them to a financial calculus; money-using societies are contrasted with 'primitive' or pre-modern societies, which are said to embody more genuine emotional relationships since they are based on barter or gifts rather than monetary exchange. The anti-money critique leads to a utopian vision in which monetary exchange is superseded and relations based on 'real' values are re-established.[1] Against this is the view that money is an enabling, liberating and helpful device which oils the wheels of commerce and brings prosperity all round.

There have always been religious and philosophical objections to monetary transactions. The ideal is the self-sufficient household, or even the self-sufficient community, based on barter. Aristotle believed that money should be limited to restoring self-sufficiency. 'Interchange of this kind is not contrary to nature and is not a form of moneymaking: it keeps to its original purpose – to re-establish nature's own equilibrium of self-sufficiency' The objection is thus more to profiting from the use of money than from money in itself. If money is barren, it should not be made to yield a return. This logic is at the heart of the medieval Christian ban on usury as well as the Koranic injunction against charging interest on credit.

It was in the eighteenth century with Bernard Mandeville, David Hume and Adam Smith that a new understanding of money emerged. Smith reversed the story about the naturalness of self-sufficiency by asserting that mankind had a 'propensity to truck, barter and exchange'. It was this

---

1 In some of this discussion we rely on Parry and Bloch (1989). The quotations from Aristotle and Simmel are taken from this source.

propensity, motivated by self-interest, that brought happiness. Smith was aggressively modernist and did not concede anything to the earlier moral discourse about the immorality of exchange. He argued that the 'system of natural liberty' guaranteed prosperity not only to some but to all: 'the Kings of primitive tribes could not have gained such wealth' (Smith in Desai 2001).

Against Smith, Marx argued that whereas in previous modes of production the purpose of money was to facilitate the exchange of commodities (C-M-C), under capitalism its purpose was to increase the quantity of capital (M-C-M).

The sociologist George Simmel saw money 'as an instrument of freedom, and a condition for the extension of individual personality and the expansion of the circle of trust; but, at the same time, as a threat to the moral order' (Parry and Bloch 1989: 3). That threat came from the transition that money facilitated from Gemeinschaft (community) to Gesellschaft (association) (Tönnies 1955), encouraging rational calculation and abstract relationships as opposed to the primacy of feelings and emotion in traditional society.

Marcel Mauss, the French anthropologist, argued that money not only dissolves bonds of community but also allows for a separation between persons and things (Mauss 1996). This is the one aspect of money which has been crucial in globalisation. According to Simmel:

> Money permits possession at a distance. Only in the form of money can profits be easily transferred from one place to another, allowing for a spatial separation between the owner and his property which 'enables his property to be managed exclusively according to objective demands while it gives its owner a chance of leading his life independently of his possessions' (quoted in Parry and Bloch 1989: 5).

The change from an Aristotelian to a Smithian view of money was not accidental. For about a thousand years before the Iberian maritime expansion of 1490s which inaugurated the modern world system, Europe was starved of precious metals. It ran an adverse balance of trade with Asia, mainly India and China, and exported gold and silver to pay for imports from Asia. Money, being scarce, was expensive and interest rates were high. But the arrival of bullion from the Iberian colonies of West Africa and South America changed that. It affected social relations, favouring Peruvian merchants at the expense of the old landed wealth. Things began to be bought and sold for money which were previously not subject to exchange. Commerce began to create more wealth than agriculture had done for millennia. Money became the gateway to modernity and capitalism.

That does not, however, mean that traditional societies did not use money or that money coincided with modernity or the frail identification of money and capitalism with the West. The use of money has been found to be very important in many traditional pre-capitalist economies. The reciprocal interdependence of non-monetary, caste-based exchange of the Hindu jajmani system – a classic example of village self-sufficiency – is a myth propagated by modern (Western) investigators who wanted to see non-monetary exchange as a feature of 'traditional' society. As Parry and Bloch say:

> What implicitly seems to underlie the misrepresentation is a deeply entrenched notion about the transformative potential of money such that its presence becomes an index of a 'modern' society, with the corollary that in a 'traditional' one it can only be of peripheral significance. (1989: 7; see especially also Fuller 1989)

Thus we can dismiss the notions that traditional societies were based on real relationships unmediated by money, and that money, like the serpent in the Garden of Eden, arrived and corrupted the innocent. Money, and our views of its good or bad effects, are therefore never context-free. Our culture – that is, the modern, post-colonial, post-imperial world as it has come to be shaped by two centuries of industrial capitalism – is shot through and through with money and its higher form, credit. Indeed, it is impossible to imagine our economy without money, though pockets of 'local money' networks survive which use labour time as units of account and even means of payment. (See Box 3.5.)

The major concerns we have, however, are not with such local pockets of resistance but with global finance and especially the ways in which global civil society has encountered the massive money flows which have become the distinguishing feature of globalisation. It is here that we encounter the contrasting views of money as barren or liberating, and it is these that we must consider in more detail. These two competing views of money and its usefulness represent the two extremes and the many possible positions between them.

At one extreme there is the libertarian view in which the market and all its works are benevolent and beyond criticism. An allied view is that, benevolent or not, the market is a self-organising process and its regulation self-defeating and counterproductive. There is the moderate view that the market is more or less self-regulating but needs an occasional correction. Then there is the view that the market is prone to failure and the state should be ever-ready to regulate it. This view easily slides into one which

Box 3.1: Civil Society and the International Financial Institutions

The message is abundantly clear. There is no confusion, dithering, or doubt:

> The IMF and the World Bank, far from bringing economic stability and reducing poverty, are destroying the environment and impoverishing people. Their calls for dialogue are just a public relations ploy and the announced reforms are cosmetic. The Bretton Woods institutions should be abolished and all Third World debt cancelled. Moreover, the entire political and economic system of global capitalism needs to be overhauled. This is to be achieved by a global movement of solidarity opposed to the neo-liberal model imposed by multinational companies, the rich countries, and their minions at the World Bank and the IMF.

This was, in short, the message delivered by Katerina Liskova, one of the leaders of the Movement Against Economic Globalisation (INPEG), the coalition of NGOs and activists which organised the anti IMF/World Bank protests in Prague in the autumn of 2000. Katerina was speaking at a panel debate organised by Czech President Vaclav Havel at Prague Castle. The 20-year-old activist delivered this defiant message flanked by World Bank President James Wolfenson and IMF Managing Director Horst Kohler. UN Human Rights Commissioner Mary Robinson was moderating this unique forum, which also included international financier and philanthropist George Soros, Jubilee 2000 founder Ann Pettifor, Filipino academic/activist Walden Bello, and South African Minister of Finance Trevor Manuel. Despite the predictability of the protesters' message, the global financial leaders seemed dumbfounded. Wolfenson just reiterated his readiness for dialogue while Kohler insisted that he also had a heart. Indeed, World Bank and IMF representatives always appear hurt and surprised when attacked by civic activists.

The International Bank for Reconstruction and Development (IBRD), also known as the World Bank, and the International Monetary Fund (IMF) emerged out of the Bretton Woods conference held in the US in 1944. They were designed as components of an international regime of fixed exchange rates which was meant to deliver growth and stability to the post-war world economy. British economist John Maynard Keynes, who believed that public intervention could improve on market outcomes, at least in the short run, was one of the founding fathers of the two institutions.

The organisations were shaped by their origins. First, they are proactive; they are supposed to combat 'market failures' on a global scale: poverty in the case of the World Bank and financial instability in the case of the IMF. Second, they tend to be elitist and undemocratic primarily because they are dominated by their founder and main donor, the United States, and because they are run by 'experts' who don't expect ordinary people to understand complex economic problems. Over time neo-liberal economists came to represent the overwhelming majority of these 'experts', reflecting both trends in the economic profession and political change in the major donor countries. US and Western domination in general meant that political considerations often prevailed over economic ones in determining World Bank and IMF policies, especially when it came to regimes which were deemed pro-Western or at least anti-communist. This continued even after the end of the cold war, as was the case with billions of IMF and World Bank dollars loaned to Russia with the aim of propping up President Yeltsin and his 'reformers'.

The combination of activism and elitism described above meant that the Bretton Woods institutions were, and continue to be, attacked from both right and left. Extreme neo-liberals who see no point in public intervention, especially at the international level, view the IMF and the World Bank as examples of 'big government'. The Meltzer Report commissioned by the Republican majority in the US Congress exemplifies this approach, albeit with some moderation (IFIAC 2000). The report is critical of the proactive 'mission creep' at the Bretton Woods institutions and stresses the potential for market distortions caused by their interventions, such as the displacement of private investment and moral hazard. Attacks from the right have increased since the two institutions, especially the World Bank, embarked on a number of reforms aimed at increasing transparency and dialogue and taking policies beyond the neo-liberal scriptures. It is because of the constant attacks from the right that IMF and World Bank officials feel hurt when they are attacked from the left.

The leaders of the IMF and the World Bank believe that they have gone out of their way to accommodate activists' concerns and point out that the institutions are constrained by the will of the member states. They blame both developed countries for holding the purse strings too tight and developing country governments for blaming the IMF and the World Bank for their own failures.

Ann Pettifor partially agrees with this opinion but she would not go as far as to blame the developing countries for the debt crisis. At the Prague Castle meeting she invited activists to direct their attention to the 'puppet masters' in the G7 countries instead of the Bretton Woods institutions. This opinion was seconded by George Soros, who believes that things would be a lot better if developed countries adhered to their commitment to allocate 0.7 per cent of their GDP to foreign aid.

The World Bank, the IMF and other international institutions are facing similar problems of content – guiding principles, mission, goals – and form – accountability and participation, checks and balances. Solving these issues in each institution separately seems inefficient if not impossible. There is a need to explore 'global' solutions such as a set of common principles, parameters, guidelines, or common structures such as an Ombudsman or appeals court. International institutions may even share an 'upper/second chamber', like the ones proposed by the Angela Wood of the Bretton Woods Project (Wood 2001), which would better represent poor countries or non-state actors. Speaking at the Prague Castle meeting, Mary Robinson congratulated Katerina on her courage and proceeded to outline such a global solution. She calls it the 'rights-based approach' and it entails cross-referencing trade and global finance rules with human rights principles and environmental norms.

Such 'global' solutions, however, require a political momentum which does not seem available at the moment. Quite the contrary: the new unilateralist US administration is likely to attempt to curtail the Bretton Woods institutions, reducing them to extensions of US foreign policy. While Walden Bello sees no problem in a tactical alliance with the extreme right against the Bretton Woods institutions, other activists would think twice before hopping into bed with the likes of Pat Buchanan. They may also heed the sombre observation raised by the South African Finance Minister Trevor Manuel, at the Prague Castle meeting. He pointed out that, without the IMF and the World Bank, only three countries in sub-Saharan Africa would have access to external financing. Time will show whether activists will be able to keep the heat on the IFIs without playing into the hands of the extreme right.

sees the market as chronically malfunctioning and hence in need of overarching control. The extreme view would be a rejection of the market and all its works and its replacement by a self-conscious democratic rule of 'Society' (Desai 2001). There is extremism at either end of the spectrum in which one celebrates the market while the other excoriates it. In between are nuanced objections, not to abstractions such as the 'market' or 'money' but to concentrations of economic power (transnational/global corporations) or to excessive income and wealth inequalities; not against 'market failures' in general but environmental degradation or racial or gender discrimination; not to flows of capital as such but to the uses to which they are put and the returns obtained and to inequalities of power in international trade. The theme common to all of these is the economic or the monetary link which unites them.

Given the Manichean division at the extremes and the multiplicity of nuanced attitudes in the middle, it is necessary to distinguish the types of money flows or trading arrangements which attract different degrees of protest. Capital flows are singled out because it is the unregulated, or at least freer, flow of capital in the last ten to fifteen years which, in our view, marks out the new phase of globalisation.

Capital Flows: Types, Impacts, Responses

The shock of globalisation and the flows of capital it sets up are not new phenomena in world history. Trade has taken place between the different continents by sea or land for millennia. Europe and Asia especially have a continuous history of trade and gold flow, which goes back to the Phoenicians. The dawn of capitalism in the 1500s introduced a new element of violence in the relationships of trade and gold flow between Europe and Africa and the Americas. Massive gold flows to Europe were forcibly extracted from the older civilisations of those continents. This sorry saga has been well mapped out by Immanuel Wallerstein in his many writings (see, for example, Wallerstein 2000).

With the industrial revolution, capital and commodity flows took very different forms and had a very different impact. Now labour could be harnessed at home and abroad without coercion; surplus could be extracted from labour made more productive by new machines. Capital began to flow outwards to the periphery as much as it flowed back in the form of repatriated profits. The periphery was transformed in the process of colonisation by the flow of industrial capital. Soon the colonies began to crave their emancipation, which to them implied their own industrialisation, and decided upon independence to pursue capital accumulation and industrial self-sufficiency. In this new context after 1945, private flows of capital from the core to the periphery dried up. Much of the capital flowed within the core. The flows from the core to the periphery took the form, for the first time in history, of massive government-to-government transfers and some smaller flows from the multilateral lending institutions set up at the Bretton Woods conference in 1944 – the World Bank and the International Monetary Fund – to the countries of what in the 1950s came to be called the Third World.

The founders of the Bretton Woods system believed that they had discovered the magic formula which would harness the creative forces of capitalism while mitigating its negative side effects. A fixed exchange-rate regime backed by the promise of IMF intervention was supposed to help everyone reap the fruits of free trade without worrying about instability. Aid facilitated by the World Bank was meant to help address issues of poverty and inequality.

The 1970s and the Petrodollar Debt

This new dispensation persisted until the early 1970s. At that juncture the first of many events occurred which began the transformation of the post-war world by what we now call 'globalisation'. The United States came off the dollar-exchange standard and the Bretton Woods system of fixed exchange rates collapsed. The quadrupling of oil prices generated a massive transfer, of up to about 5 per cent of their GDP, from the OECD countries to the oil-exporting countries. This was the largest flow in the 200 years since the industrial revolution of money from the developed countries to the (oil-exporting) developing countries. This in turn led to the recycling of petrodollars, which brought private bank loans from developed-country banks to the developing countries. This integration of the periphery into the global banking world heralded a new phase of the world economy.

The First Crisis of the 1980s

It was when international debt became a problem in the early 1980s that we may say global civil society encountered the financial world. As Marx saw 150 years ago, capitalist power relations are non-coercive in a crude physical sense. The distancing between the owner of capital and its effects on the ground further complicates the agency problem. When debt piles up and interest payments mount, the poor may starve but whose fault is it really? The borrowers – those in power in the developing countries – eagerly shift the blame to the lenders – the IMF or Western banks. The IMF and the banks accuse the borrowers of economic mismanagement. But the real reason for the debt crisis was that the developed world had decided to put its house in order, adopted monetarist policies, and began to borrow rather than print money. This led to the turnaround in the bond markets when interest rates rose from 5 per cent to 15 per cent in nominal terms and from around minus 10 per cent to plus 10 per cent in real terms.

Through the 1980s, as country after country with debt problems had to seek IMF loans and submit to structural adjustment, civil society everywhere began to realise the severe impact such flows could have on daily life. It was as if, until then, people had been insulated from the outside world of global finance whose rules were non-negotiable even to their sovereign governments. Governments tried to bear down on their people in order to repay their debts, however wisely or foolishly the money had been used, and in response to the protests of their people could only plead helplessness in the face of IMF or foreign banks. In the years since independence people had thought that their governments were on their side or could at least be brought round to their side, and had some power to better their lives, as they had been promised. Now there was a cleavage between them and their governments, which pointed a finger at a bigger external power.

It was in devising defensive responses to this new situation that civil societies began to form in many countries. Until then, there had been a unity between the state and the people, which had arisen from twentieth-century independence movements in Asia and Africa. Now the people had to articulate their voices against the state, even their own state. People began to build defensive, cross-class alliances to fight against the cutbacks in food subsidies, rises in taxes and prices, unemployment, shutdown of public facilities, pricing of previously freely available goods, and so forth (Cornia et al. 1987).

The resolution of the debt crisis of the 1980s was in one sense surprising and in another quite business-like. It took the intervention of the US government in the form of Brady Bonds (see the Glossary) to allow the banks to do what they normally do with bad debts: write them off. After much misery, much of the debt was written off, converted into equity, swapped for factories in debtor countries, or forgiven in recognition of some environmental good deed. It was painful and messy but once the write-off had been agreed by the developed country governments (which had to bear the tax burden of debt write-offs) the private commercial debt issue was resolved.

The 1990s: The Peso and the Asian Crises

The events of the 1990s were yet another phase of the movement that had started in the 1970s. Communist economies had by then collapsed and begun their transition to market economies. China had adopted market-oriented policies, albeit without renouncing socialism. Stock markets were springing up all over the emerging market economies. Developed countries had all by then deregulated capital movements. The financial markets and the foreign exchange markets were dealing in $1 trillion per day, helped by the revolution in telecommunications and information technology. The preferred form of capital flow was equity rather than debt. Foreign direct investment (FDI) flows to the Third World were soon outstripping foreign-aid flows by a factor of 4 to 1.

Two further shocks jolted the brave new world of global finance during the 1990s. First was the Mexican peso crisis in December 1994. Having followed an orthodox fiscal and monetary policy, much to the approval of the IMF, Mexico loosened the purse-strings in a pre-election year and made a risky dollar conversion of its debt. The uprising in Chiapas coincided with a transition to a new presidency, and the credibility of the peso collapsed. A massive rescue operation of $18 billion had to be organised by the IMF. A bad deflationary year followed in 1995 with much loss of output, but 1996 saw a recovery and a flow of funds back into Mexico.

The other shock was the Asian crisis of 1997 and 1998. This spread across nations previously hailed as miracle economies. Starting with the Thai baht, the currency depreciation and stock market collapse moved to Malaysia, then to Indonesia, and finally to South Korea. The Asian crisis was truly the first crisis of globalisation of the late twentieth century. It started on the periphery but spread to the metropolis via Russia. It originated in the financial sector, which is at the forefront of globalisation. Its resolution, partially at least, came when the US Federal Reserve cut interest rates three times in quick succession in recognition of the likely impact of the crisis on US stock markets.

The Asian crisis was special in that it was triggered by bank lending rather than by portfolio investments or FDI. It took place in countries with high growth rates, high savings rates and generally good macroeconomic policies. The IMF misdiagnosed the crisis as one of 1980s-style macroeconomic mismanagement. But it was a private lending crisis, not a public finance one. The policy of pegged exchange rates proved to be inconsistent with unrestricted bank lending from abroad. What seemed like risk-free lending became risky when the baht could no longer hold on to its peg to the US dollar. Since the bulk of the debt liability was in foreign currency, the domestic central bank could not help by performing its function as lender of last resort.

The Asian crisis was serious in terms of loss of output and currency depreciation. It also meant a substantial adverse impact on living standards of many people who had just recently emerged from poverty (see Box 3.2). In some countries, especially Indonesia but also Thailand and South Korea, the crisis became one of political authority. South Korea succeeded in making a transition to democracy and a peaceful change of regime, and Thailand reformed its constitution. Indonesia also went through a traumatic transition to democracy which remains fragile. The democratic deficit enhanced the need for civil society to organise resistance movements. By its clumsy intervention, the IMF seemed to be as much part of the problem as of any solution. The insistence of the Malaysian prime minister, Dr Mahathir, that controls on capital movements be revived in face of IMF opposition strengthened this impression, as in the event Malaysia did insulate itself against the worst effects of the crisis.

Calls for reform of the international financial institutions, for a new 'global financial architecture', were made in the wake of the Asian crisis during the summer of 1998. But the resolution of the immediate impact on US markets by the Federal Reserve cooled the ardour for any fundamental change among the G7 countries. No lender of last resort has been set up at the global level. The IMF escaped either bolstering of its powers or downsizing, as advocated by the Meltzer Report for the US Congress (IFIAC 2000). There were some changes in terms of greater transparency, greater accountability and wider consultation with developing countries.[2] But there was no radical reform.

Growth and Persistence of Foreign Direct Investment

Through the 1990s, despite the peso and the Asian crises, the movement of FDI to developing countries proved much less volatile than that of portfolio capital or bank lending. This has not excused FDI from criticism and its volume now exceeds that of foreign aid by between three and four times. While the large volume of turnover in the foreign exchange and bond markets – $1 trillion plus daily – attracts much attention, it is FDI which has effects at a local level and has longer-term effects on growth, employment and the environment than portfolio capital. Its spread is confined to a small

---

2 For an overview of the Financial Stability Forum and other IMF reforms, see IMF's website.

Box 3.2: The Cost of the Asian Crisis

> In East Asia, it was reckless lending by international banks and other financial institutions combined with reckless borrowing by domestic financial institutions – combined with fickle investor expectations – which may have precipitated the crisis; but the costs – in terms of soaring unemployment and plummeting wages – were borne by workers. Workers were asked to listen to sermons about bearing pain just a short while after hearing, from the same preachers, sermons about how globalisation and opening up capital markets would bring them unprecedented growth.
> (Stiglitz 2000: 1)

East Asia enjoyed an unprecedented 7 per cent GDP growth per year for the last two decades of the twentieth century. This enabled some countries in the region, namely, Hong Kong, South Korea, Singapore and Taiwan, to become the only ones to actually make the transition from Third World to First World. Following the 1997 crisis, the region's economies shrank by 4 per cent (United Nations 1999). Inflation and unemployment, hitherto virtually unknown in most of these countries, skyrocketed. Although most of the region's economies managed to recover by 1999, they remain below their potential level had pre-crisis trends persisted:

The crisis left these countries with a heavy public debt burden, forcing the governments to spend a greater proportion of GDP on interest payments.

GDP deviation from pre-crises growth trend in 1999 (%)

Indonesia	-16.6
Malaysia	-7.2
Korea	-12.9
Thailand	-14.5

Source: World Bank (2000)

The crisis left these countries with a heavy public debt burden, forcing the governments to spend a greater proportion of GDP on interest payments.

Increase in debt servicing costs as % of GDP after the crisis	
Indonesia	3.9
Malaysia	2.2
Korea	0.5
Philippines	2.1
Thailand	10.3

Source: World Bank (2000)

While most of the region's economies are growing again, the social consequences of the crisis persist. In the aftermath of the crisis, the number of people in the region earning less than $1 day increased by 10 million (18 per cent).

South Korea, which had an unemployment rate of 2 per cent before the crisis, was still reporting a rate of 4 per cent at the end of 2000, despite the fact that the economy grew by 9.5 per cent in the same year. Real unemployment is even higher, as unemployment numbers do not reflect either the percentage of people who are nominally employed but receive no salary or the 117,000 migrant workers who had to leave South Korea after the crisis. South Korea also had no unemployment insurance until the crisis. The scheme since established does not cover most of the unemployed. Real wages declined by 14 per cent in the aftermath of the crises after growing by 7.3 per cent in 1996. This, combined with inflation, led consumer spending to decline by 12 per cent, the steepest drop in South Korean history. The result of all this is a persisting increase in poverty. Before the crisis 7.5 per cent of the urban population were poor. This number jumped to 23 per cent at the height of the crises and was standing at 14 per cent at the end of 1999, despite the recovery.

In Indonesia, unemployment rose from 4.9 per cent to 13.8 per cent after the crisis. Real wages dropped by between 40 per cent and 60 per cent. The percentage of people living in poverty jumped from 11 per cent in 1996 to 20 per cent at the end of 1999, an addition of 20 million people.

In Thailand, unemployment remains at three times the pre-crisis level, despite strong recovery. Combined with a 6 per cent decline in real wages, this translates into an increased incidence of poverty of 15 per cent.

Hong Kong and South Korea are the only East Asian countries who have an unemployment insurance system. In Hong Kong unemployment rose from 2.2 per cent in 1997 to 5 per cent in 1998. At the end of 2000 it stood at 5 per cent despite two consecutive years of growth.

The cost of the Asian crisis, 1996–1999

	1996	1997	1998	1999
GDP growth rates (%) (IMF)				
Hong Kong	4.5	5.0	-5.0	2.9
Indonesia	8.0	4.5	-13.0	0.3
Korea	6.8	5.0	-6.7	10.7
Malaysia	10.0	7.3	-7.4	5.7
Philippines	5.8	5.2	-0.6	3.3
Singapore	8.0	8.4	0.4	5.4
Taiwan	5.7	6.8	4.7	5.7
Thailand	5.9	-1.7	-10.0	4.2
Unemployment as a percentage of workforce (ILO)				
Hong Kong	2.8	2.2	4.7	6.3
Indonesia	4.0	4.68	5.46	N/A
Korea	2.0	2.6	6.8	6.3
Malaysia	2.5	2.5	3.2	3.4
Philippines	7.4	7.9	9.6	9.37
Singapore	3.0	2.4	3.2	4.6
Taiwan	N/A	N/A	N/A	N/A
Thailand	1.08	0.87	3.41	3.0

Sources: Stiglitz (2000); United Nations (1999); World Bank (2000).

number of countries with high savings rates, large pools of semi-skilled labour, good governance and high levels of literacy. There is, however, no IFI which monitors FDI or polices its accountability. Within the domestic jurisdiction of all OECD countries, there are tough regulations on corporations (for example, the US Justice Department's moves against Microsoft) and regulatory bodies such as the Securities and Exchange Commission in the US and the Financial Services Authority in the UK. There is, however, no move afoot today for a global regulator of FDI. The Multilateral Agreement on Investments (MAI) was an attempt to introduce a uniform structure of rules for both domestic and foreign capital, but it did not extend to a uniform and universal regulation regime such as exists in individual OECD countries. The demise of the MAI was due as much to protests by the NGOs as to the reluctance of the US Congress to contemplate symmetric treatment of foreign and domestic capital. (See Box 3.3.)

If there has been no global move towards regulation of FDI or any serious move for the reform of the IFIs, there has been a successful single-issue movement – Jubilee 2000 – for the reduction of Third World debt. While the petrodollar debt owed to commercial banks caused serious debt default problems in the 1980s and much misery, it was resolved, as noted above, by some cancellation of debt, some payment in lieu in the form of environmental policy changes, and even some capital sales. Public debt has proved to be a much tougher nut to crack. For one thing, the World Bank, as well as the governments of developing countries who are the lenders, do not believe in writing off bad debt. What is a sound commercial practice is forbidden to public agencies. This is a peculiar example of the inflexibility of government finance.

This Third World debt arises from a small amount of intergovernmental or IFI lending to some very poor countries in the late 1980s and early 1990s, including Uganda, Mozambique and Niger. The original principal has now mushroomed into a much larger sum due to the inability of many of the debtor countries to service it, as unpaid instalments have been added and compounded. The size of the debt now bears little relation to the original amount. Debtor countries have been weakened by the collapse of primary commodity prices since the late 1970s and many local and civil wars. Individual G7 countries have taken some initiatives; the UK has been in the lead since 1990, when John Major was briefly the Chancellor of the Exchequer, and has accelerated this lead under Chancellor Gordon Brown; but the World Bank's Highly Indebted Poor Countries (HIPC) initiative has been on the table since the mid-1990s. It has been mired in inaction.

The total amounts are smaller than those in the 1980s but the debtor countries are now much poorer. It is also more difficult to persuade countries, especially the G7 which dominate the voting in the IFIs, to agree to any debt forgiveness.

Paradoxically, Third World debt, which Jubilee 2000 focused on, has little to do with globalisation. Indeed, it is the countries which cannot access the private lenders in the form of either debt or equity because they are abysmally poor that are forced into the arms of governmental or multilateral institutional lenders. Their plight is an aspect of the unequal nature of the global power structure as enshrined by the UN constitution, which gives veto power to the permanent members of the Security Council, and in the decision-making structures of the Bretton Woods institutions. The Asian crisis was a crisis of countries that had become just rich enough to be attractive to private lenders. The public-debt crisis is that of countries that are too poor to be of interest to commercial lenders and too weak to be a threat to the powerful governments which have lent them money.

Box 3.3: The Demise of the MAI

At the end of 1998, negotiations within the framework of the Organisation for Economic Cooperation and Development (OECD) for a Multilateral Agreement on Investment (MAI) were abandoned. The collapse of the negotiations was precipitated by a number of factors including a broad international campaign coordinated by Friends of the Earth, 50 Years Is Enough, and other international and local groups.

The MAI was intended to promote cross-border investments by providing a unified set of rules governing interactions between governments and investors worldwide. The rules proposed were favourable to investors, prohibiting governments from discriminating among or against them and giving investors the right to prosecute offending governments in international courts. For example, the agreement would have eliminated a government's right to place certain industries or areas of activity out of reach for foreign investors. It would have prohibited the imposition of local content or other performance requirements committing foreign investors to purchase a certain proportion of their outlays from local suppliers or to create local jobs. It would have allowed investors the freedom to move money in and out of countries without restrictions and prohibited any form of expropriation.

The negotiations, which were taking place largely unnoticed since 1995, began to attract unwanted attention after the Asian crisis of 1997. The crisis left both governments and activists with little appetite for further financial-market liberalisation. Disagreements among G7 countries were also on the rise. The US wanted to maintain the right to persecute companies investing in Cuba or Iran. France wanted to protect its film industry from Hollywood. Hungary wanted to preserve employee and management-centred privatisation schemes. In the end it was France's withdrawal from the process which sealed the MAI's fate.

Activists succeeded in amplifying and leveraging government disagreements up to the point of defeating the MAI.

The critical method employed by anti-MAI campaigners was education and information. They provided in-depth analysis of the proposed agreements and their possible environmental, social and political implications. They published glossaries explaining obscure legal and trade terms and provided real-time coverage and analysis of the negotiating positions.

This was probably the first time such negotiations were conducted in the spotlight of public attention. It presented a radical break from the tradition of conducting negotiations among technocrats away from public scrutiny, providing only a doctored summary of concluded agreements to the public and parliaments at the ratification stage.

One may agree with the technocrats' contention that the popularised version of the MAI draft agreements and the analysis of their impact by NGOs are not scientifically accurate or that many of those involved in the debates were not qualified to pass judgement on such matters. This is changing rapidly, however, and many activists today have access to high-quality research on economic issues. The campaign against the MAI was, however, a breakthrough in terms of democratising international trade negotiations by providing the public with an alternative opinion; forcing politicians to scrutinise the proposed agreement; and requiring the technocrats to be more transparent and to defend their positions to a sceptical public.

The MAI negotiations also witnessed increased cooperation/coordination between NGOs and governments trying to alter or stop the agreement altogether. France used NGO arguments against the agreement in both domestic and international deliberations. The government-commissioned Lalumière Report, conducted in the summer of 1998, relied heavily on NGO testimony to justify France's reservations (Friends of the Earth 1998a).

The MAI defeat was a temporary and, some would say, a pyrrhic victory for civil society. Most groups involved in the campaign would have preferred to see an alternative agreement which would regulate foreign investments in ways that protect the environment, labour, human rights and indigenous cultures. Many wanted to see multinational corporations and financiers brought under national or international jurisdiction. An international agreement on investment is necessary to avoid a race to the bottom among governments in their quest for foreign investments. Faced with the choice between a dangerous treaty and an even more dangerous lack thereof, campaigners, unable to come up with a comprehensive alternative, opted for the latter. They leveraged the nationalism of individual governments to derail the whole process.

> Offering suggested changes to the MAI is a trickier issue. Whereas it is important to eliminate the MAI's worst features in case the agreement goes forward, but [sic!] eliminating those sections alone would not result in an acceptable agreement. Good rules on investment would include binding language on investors' responsibilities for the environment, workers and human rights. Therefore, signalling any support for the MAI in exchange for textual changes can be dangerous because the agreement as a whole is fundamentally unbalanced in favour of investors. (Friends of the Earth 1998b)

The issues covered under the MAI are back on the table again through the General Agreement on Trade in Services (GATS) in the framework of the WTO. GATS covers a much wider area of activities than investment alone and is already the target of intense opposition from activists worldwide (see for instance the World Development Movement URL). Will they be able to advance an internationalist alternative or will they ally themselves with protectionists to derail the whole process as they did with the MAI?

Anti-capitalism: An Overview

Throughout the forty or so years following 1945, there was a vibrant anti-capitalist movement, in the form either of orthodox Leninist communist parties or of democratic socialist parties. Feminist and civil rights movements were added to this worldwide. The focus everywhere was the state because the state was seen as an instrument of control over capital or over the unequal power structure. Political parties of the left were part of this broad protest movement even when they were in office, as were the trade unions which supported these parties. The 1960s saw a big explosion of these movements across Western Europe and in the USA at a time when 'capitalism in one country' was perhaps performing at its best in terms of full employment and growth. The 1970s saw a worsening of economic performance, with stagflation and a deepening of the crisis of the state, but also of resistance against it. But even in the 1970s the various national movements were separate; only the environmental movement forged global interconnections. It was the changes in the 1970s and in the 1980s discussed above which shattered the logic of capitalism or socialism in one country and began to shape the new global economy not as an ecological ideal but as an economic reality.

The anti-capitalist movement of the 1960s and 1970s was wounded if not defeated by the structural changes which capitalism underwent in the 1980s in the developing countries. The collapse of the Soviet Union demoralised the Leninist left and shut down many communist parties. There was instead a growth of NGOs, many of them concerned with development or ecological issues. Other movements, like the women's movement and human rights campaigns, survived the neo-liberal onslaught of the 1980s. They have now emerged as the opposition to globalisation in the 1990s and beyond. Their numbers are larger, both individually and in their memberships. They are more globally networked. They are also less connected with political parties. In the following sections these movements are analysed in terms of their stances on the financial effects of globalisation.

The last ten years have witnessed historic changes in the world system. The state socialist countries of Europe have transformed themselves into fledgling democracies and fragile market economies. Across OECD countries, social democratic parties in office or out of it have rethought their old philosophies and abandoned any desire for state ownership or control of capital. A system of countries each pursuing 'capitalism in one country' with weak articulation through trade has changed into one with strong articulation through international capital flows, inter-country, inter-corporate competition, flexible exchange rates and converging long-term interest rates through global bond markets. Governments have suffered a narrowing of their scope for fiscal discretion. Stock markets have grown in size and numbers across the world. The logic of globalisation is one of unregulated global flows and a single bond market, although that logic is as yet far from realised.

Civil Society and Global Finance: Four Responses

Interactions between civil society and global capitalism take place at two friction points. At one point, society is reacting to market encroachment on both personal and public spaces: consumerism, atomisation, the erosion of public services, and nation state models of democracy. At the other, society is reacting to socio-economic consequences of capitalism such as poverty, inequality and instability.

At these friction points the anti-capitalist movement raises two corresponding sets of questions:

1. What are the boundaries of the market? How are they determined and enforced?
2. Can the market be trusted to produce just and stable outcomes or does it require external intervention? How would such intervention be carried out?

These questions, although as old as capitalism itself, have gained in relevance over the past twenty years, providing an impetus to the anti-capitalist movement. The reasons for this renewed attention are set out below.

First, there is a perception that liberal democracy is lagging behind neo-liberal economics or even being threatened by it (Mittelman 2000). The neo-liberal reforms rammed through during the 1980s by right-of-centre governments in the West and by the IMF in the East and the South, the inexorable encroachment of the market into the public sphere, the unchecked reign of multinational corporations, and the apparent inability of national leaders to challenge any of the above has given the anti-capitalist movement a new angle of attack.

Second, the abandonment of nation state–based answers to the contradictions of capitalism, be they the welfare state in the North or state-sponsored development or superpower patronage in the South, is generating pockets of extreme poverty in both rich and poor countries. While overall levels of prosperity are increasing, the situation at the bottom of the socio-economic ladder has actually been deteriorating. The widening gap between rich and poor, both within and between countries, is increasingly difficult to conceal, justify or sustain.

The anti-capitalist movement has changed in tandem with its target. In the era of state capitalism the focus was on the state. Some wanted to capture it, others to reform it, and yet others just wanted it out of the way. Today, attention is shifting to the corporation as the main target of the anti-capitalist movement. Some strands of the movement against corporate globalisation would even call for protecting and strengthening the territorial state while others demand solutions that require the creation of a global welfare state. To be sure, the state, especially in the G7 countries, remains an important target for many movements. There is a growing awareness, however, of the limitations of state power under globalisation.

The movement against global capitalism falls into four groups: isolationists, supporters, reformists and alternatives. As with all such classifications, no movement, campaign or event can be allocated solely to any one of the categories. Many shift from one to the other depending on the issue, event or time frame in question.

Isolationists

In addition to remnants of communist and Stalinist groups, isolationists include some environmental groups such as Friends of the Earth, who tend to be more radical in their economic than in their ecological agenda; think tanks and groups promoting national solutions to Third World development issues, such as Focus on the Global South; anti-globalisation groups such as the International Forum on Globalisation, Global Exchange, and 50 Years Is Enough; local social movements such as the Landless Workers Movement in Brazil (MST); individuals such as Walden Bello and Noam Chomsky; and media outlets such as *Le Monde diplomatique*.

The isolationists represent the only global civil society response to global capitalism which openly claims to be anti-globalisation. The isolationists call directly or indirectly for the abolition of the existing global economic order. Walden Bello says:

> Indeed, I would contend that the focus of our efforts these days is not to try to reform the multilateral agencies but to deepen the crisis of legitimacy of the whole. I am talking about disabling not

just the WTO, the IMF, and the World Bank but the transnational corporation itself. And I am not talking about a process of 're-regulating' the TNCs but of eventually disabling or dismantling them as fundamental hazards to people, society, the environment, to everything we hold dear. (Bello 2000)

Other isolationists are less categorical. Many call for 'economic diversity' (Friends of the Earth 2000), presumably allowing for certain elements of global capitalism to continue in some areas. The demands they advance, however, can hardly be compatible with a functioning market economy, particularly given their objection to such concepts as economic growth or comparative advantage.

Isolationists treat globalisation and global capitalism as synonyms. They oppose globalisation in most of its manifestations, promoting instead deglobalisation (Bello 2000) or localisation (Hines 2000) which entails:

- *economic subsidiarity*: trade should be minimised, goods should be produced as closely as possible to the site of consumption;
- *political subsidiarity*: states and local communities should be re-empowered at the expense of transnational corporations and international organisations, decisions should be taken as closely as possible to where they take effect; and
- *self-sufficiency*: resources for investment should be mobilised locally, reliance on foreign investment should be minimised.

In their blanket opposition to the IMF and the World Bank, left-wing isolationists find strange bed-fellows among their right-wing rivals and supporters of global capitalism. To quote Bello on this subject:

The motivation of the incoming Republicans in criticising the IMF and World Bank lies in their belief in free-market solutions to development and growth. This may not coincide with that of progressives, who see the IMF and World Bank as a tool of US hegemony. But the two sides can unite behind one agenda at this point: the radical downsizing, if not dismantling, of the Bretton Woods twins. (Bello 2001)

On the specific issues of global finance, the isolationists hold the following positions.

Public debt. Third World debt is a direct consequence and responsibility of Western powers, banks and international lending institutions. Loans were knowingly made to corrupt and/or incompetent Third World leaders for political reasons, for example to ensure loyalty during the cold war or to perpetuate a relationship of dependence. Lending was also used as a beachhead to secure access for transnational corporations. Hence, all Third World debts should be written off. Moreover, given the real transfers[3] from the Third World to the rich countries caused by unfavourable terms of trade and interest payments and outright looting in colonial days, the debt relationship should be reversed. In the future, Third World countries should avoid borrowing altogether and rely on their own resources for investments.

Short-term capital flows. Equity investments, derivatives and foreign exchange transactions are all part of a global casino. On the upside, they only enrich Western speculators; on the downside, they cause widespread suffering to working people both in the North and in the South. Speculators often get bailed out by the IMF and other rescue programmes. They may even benefit from crises, as did George Soros, attacking the European Union's exchange rate mechanism and the Thai baht.

Short-term capital flows are inherently volatile and destabilising. The responsibility for financial crises such as those in 1997–98 lies squarely on the shoulders of Western speculators and their private-sector counterparts in the afflicted countries. It also lies with the IMF, which forced the emerging economies to liberalise their capital markets in the first place. Post-crisis IMF interventions bail out speculators while aggravating the effects on working people. Countries should have the option to introduce currency and exchange controls and opt out of the global capital market altogether.

Long-term foreign direct investments. Foreign investments benefit only the multinational corporations that make them. They serve to perpetuate the exploitation of the poor and destroy the environment. Consequently, structural adjustment programmes and other liberal reforms aimed at encouraging foreign investments are part of the same conspiracy:

DEBT⟶ DEBT CRISIS⟶ STRUCTURAL ADJUSTMENT
⟶ OPENING TO TRANSNATIONAL CORPORATIONS

Self-reliance and self-sufficiency are the only way forward. This is the unifying slogan which brings together the isolationists in the Third World

---

[3] Adverse terms of trade meant that Third World countries over many years sold relatively cheap raw materials to industrialised countries in exchange for relatively expensive manufactured goods.

with protectionists in the North by shielding national favourites, such as state-sponsored manufacturing industries, in the developing countries and sunset industries, such as the car industry, in developed ones.

Supporters

Civil society responses to global finance in the 'supporters' category include no movements and very few NGOs. They consist mainly of organisations, groups, media outlets, think tanks and individuals lobbying on behalf of business, be it an individual company, an industry or private enterprise in general. Examples of supporters include the Centre for Civil Society in India, the Chamber of British Industry in the UK, the American Enterprise Institute in the US, the *Economist,* the *Wall Street Journal,* the Meltzer Commission and Thomas Friedman.

Although attention is usually devoted to instances when the interests of civil society collide with those of global capitalism, the interactions between the two are not always negative. Civil society may benefit when market expansion takes place at the expense of authoritarian regimes, fundamentalism or autarky. Capitalism can also be more just and efficient than such alternatives as feudalism or central planning. This is the main rationale behind civil society responses which are unequivocally supportive of global capitalism in its current form. Supporters are indeed the most influential of the civil society responses to global capitalism.

Since they occupy the two extreme ends of the spectrum, it should come as no surprise that supportive responses to global capitalism often coincide with isolationist positions. For diametrically different reasons both are dismissive of reforms and global governance proposals aimed at mitigating the negative consequences of global capitalism. The most important point of agreement among them is the equation of globalisation and global capitalism. As Thomas Friedman says:

> The driving idea behind globalization is free-market capitalism – the more you let market forces rule and the more you open your economy to free trade and competition, the more efficient and flourishing your economy will be. Globalization means the spread of free-market capitalism to virtually every country in the world. Globalization also has its own set of economic rules – rules that revolve around opening, deregulating and privatising your economy. (Friedman 2000)

Global capitalism, according to its supporters, is not only the best way to prosperity: it is the only way. 'There Is No Alternative' (TINA) is an often-repeated argument to this end. TINA does not only mean that anyone who refuses to open up to global capitalism will be left behind; it also points to the perils of rolling back global capitalism. Supporters claim that if governments and international organisations succumb to anti-capitalist sentiments and try to rein in global capitalism, then globalisation as a whole will be rolled back, leading inevitably to results similar to those encountered when the previous era of globalisation came to an end early in the twentieth century, namely, war, fascism and communism.

Supporters not only bristle at all forms of anti-capitalism but also reject most reform proposals. According to the supporters, all the injustices and inefficiencies attributed to global capitalism are not a result of too much market but of too little. Government interference of all kinds, including protectionism, welfare provisions, corruption and incompetence is, according to them, responsible for the plight of the poor. The *Economist* (2000) states:

> Governments are apologising for globalisation and promising to civilise it. Instead if they had any regard for the plight of the poor, they would be accelerating it, celebrating it, exalting it...

Supporters attack the World Bank and the IMF for even listening to NGOs, let alone engaging them in any serious deliberations. Many of them are actually opposed to these and other international institutions as examples of interventionist big government. On the specific issues of global finance, the supporters hold the following positions.

Public debt. Most of the burden of Third World debt is the responsibility of corrupt and incompetent governments. Cancelling it will not help these countries but may actually hurt them if it is seen as rewarding bad government. Government lending in the future should be kept to a minimum and used mostly as an instrument of foreign policy. Even international lending institutions should try to stay out of the debt market. The Meltzer Report (IFIAC 2000), for example, recommends that the World Bank use grants rather than loans, but these should be disbursed through private service providers instead of being handed to governments.

Short-term flows. Short-term flows, be they loans, portfolio investments, foreign-exchange transactions, derivatives or other exotic instruments are all part of the proper functioning of market mechanisms. Derivatives, for example, help distribute risk in a way that best reflects market realities and the preferences of individual market participants. Crises attributed to short-term flows, such as the Asian crisis, always have their roots in government interference, in this case Asian crony capitalism and subsequent IMF intervention. The answer is, therefore, always more liberalisation.

Long-term foreign direct investment. FDI is the best way to match savings and investments worldwide. It allocates financial resources to their most productive use, promotes the best technologies and produces the most-needed products and services. Moreover, FDI is the best way to transfer know-how and technology, business prowess and even democratic culture. FDI is the only way for the Third World to catch up.

Not only is it self-defeating for countries to place any restrictions on foreign investment; they should do their utmost to attract it. This is done through neo-liberal reforms including deregulation, privatisation, small government, balanced budgets and tight money. The pain and dislocation caused by these policies are all justified by the expected benefits.

Reformists

The majority of movements, organisations and campaigns active in the area of global finance are reformist. They include the bulk of the labour movement and associated think tanks such as the Institute for Policy Studies; development organisations such as Oxfam and World Vision; watchdogs such as the World Development Movement and the Bretton Woods Project; issue-specific campaigns such as Jubilee 2000 and Action pour une Taxe Tobin d'Aide aux Citoyens (ATTAC); and individuals such as George Soros and Ann Pettifor. Even James Wolfenson, the head of the World Bank, could be included in this category.

Reformists comprise a broad category ranging from NGOs dedicated to monitoring the IMF to those IMF employees who are serious about reform. The reformists aim 'at partial change to try to offset current injustices and inequalities' (Cohen and Rai 2000: 2). Unlike the isolationists, movements demanding cancellation of Third World debt or IMF reforms are not pursuing a radical new social order.

The reformists pursue variations on the 'social democratic' agenda for the global era. Their aim is to maintain the advantages of the capitalist model while mitigating its excesses through re-regulation and redistribution. As the largest US trades union states:

> We need a global New Deal that establishes new rules to temper the excesses of the market; promote sustainable egalitarian growth; and assure the rights of working people everywhere are respected. (AFL-CIO 1998)

The reformists view themselves as the only true defenders of globalisation. They believe that both isolationist calls to reverse the process and supporters' insistence on 'ultra-liberal' forms of global capitalism are bound to derail globalisation, with tragic consequences. According to reformists, globalisation can succeed only if it is civilised and made more democratic, equitable and stable.

Reformists propose a variety of global governance solutions to address this task. These proposals are usually built around reforming or augmenting existing international institutions or establishing new ones.

The reformists advance a set of global governance initiatives such as the Tobin tax (explained below) or regulations for multinational corporations, which may actually require a global state to implement. John Cavanagh says:

> Some scholars such as Walden Bello, argue that developing countries would be better-off with no international financial institution rather than the IMF because this would allow local and national governments and citizens groups more autonomy in pursuing alternative development strategies. However, in an era of global capital, we would ideally have international financial institutions that could help reduce volatility and contagion in ways that can not be accomplished through nation states. An International Bankruptcy Authority has already been discussed. In addition, a number of scholars have proposed the creation of a new Global Financial Authority or a Global Central Bank. (Anderson and Cavanagh 2000)

On the specific global finance issues the reformists hold the following positions, although given the wide range of groups in this category the positions listed here are not all encompassing:

Public debt. Both developed and developing countries share the responsibility for the debt overhang and should share the burden of its resolution. For example, countries should be compensated for failed structural adjustment programmes or World Bank projects, which would offset some of their outstanding obligations. Debt should be cancelled for the poorest countries. The burden for the rest should be reduced to a level where it does not jeopardise their ability to provide basic human services. An International Bankruptcy Mechanism should be established to deal with debt cancellation and restructuring in situations when countries are no longer capable of meeting their debt obligations (Anderson and Cavanagh 2000).

Both lenders and borrowers should ensure that lending proceeds through an open and transparent process to avoid misuse through corruption or incompetence. Civil society should be involved in all stages of the process.

Short-term flows. The position of the reformists on short-term flows is close to that of the isolationists. Instead of dismissing these flows out of hand, however, the reformists seek solutions which would reorient them from speculation to long-term investment. Countries should have the option to impose 'speed bumps' and other defensive measures based on internationally agreed criteria. The IMF should not pursue the opening up of the capital account in member countries but should leave that to the discretion of governments. In case of crises, rescue packages should be aimed at minimising the negative impact on the real economy as opposed to bailing out reckless investors.

At the global level, proposals to tame short-term flows range from strengthening existing regulations to the establishment of a global lender of last resort/central bank and a Tobin tax. Named after the Nobel Prize-winning economist James Tobin of Yale University, such a tax of anything between 0.05 and 0.25 per cent levied on all foreign-exchange transactions would act as a deterrent to speculative transactions. The ATTAC platform claims that:

> Even fixed at a particularly low rate of 0.05%, the Tobin tax would gather close to 100 billion dollars a year. Collected, primarily, by industrialised countries, where the largest financial centres are located, the sum could be redirected to international organisations for activities aimed at fighting inequality, promoting education and public health in poor countries and food security and sustainable development. This kind of mechanism would put sand in the gears of speculation. It would feed the logic of resistance, give citizens and nations back some room to manoeuvre and in particular it would show that politics can be restored to its proper place. (Platform of ATTAC 1998)

Long-term foreign direct investment. Few reformists would deny the benefits of foreign investment. Like the supporters, the reformists believe that foreign investment is the best way to allocate capital to its most productive uses. It is also the only way for poor countries to catch up with the rich given the difference in savings rates.

As discussed above, the reformists promote solutions which would redirect short-term flows to longer-term investments. The reformists, however, reject the link between neo-liberal structural adjustment policies and the flow of investments. Indeed, they reject neo-liberal structural adjustment policies because of the pain they cause to the poorest in society, their 'one-size-fits-all' approach, and the fact that they have not even been proved to promote growth or investment.

The reformists also emphasise the need to augment private investments by public funds to achieve development goals. According to the ICFTU (2000), for example, public investments by both national governments and IFIs should be targeted at social protection, primary education, health care and employment.

Alternatives

The anti-capitalist protests in Seattle 1999, Washington 2000 and Prague 2000 were driven by the alternatives. Alternatives exist both as organisations – for example, the Zapatistas, Adbusters and Reclaim the Streets – and as 'submerged net-works' which come to the fore only around certain campaigns or exercise resistance through a particular lifestyle, such as INPEG (see Box 3.1), which existed only for the purpose of organising the Prague protests, or alternative money (LETS) groups (see Box 3.1). Alternatives are wary of leaders but there are alternative spokespeople such as Naomi Klein and Subcomandante Marcos. (See Box 3.4.)

Instead of aiming to transform or reform global capitalism, the alternatives are concerned with reclaiming 'things' from the encroaching market and creating space for alternatives. They are concerned with the political and cultural consequences of capitalism as much as they are with its economic and environmental costs. They perceive the encroachment of the market into the public space as a threat to democracy, which takes the form of 'corporate censorship' in the North and human rights abuses in the South (Klein 1999).

The fact that the alternatives comprise broad coalitions means that it is difficult to pin down their agenda or even what they stand for. But instead of being a weakness, the lack of a 'little red book' is translated into an advantage, ensuring mass appeal, especially among the young.

> It's not the last gasp of the old left, or the resurgence of the new right. It's not protectionism, or even anarchism. It's something entirely different; something fresh being pieced together from the shards of old ideas, and glued with new solutions for a new age. (Kingsnorth 2000)

Box 3.4: The Zapatistas

The story of the Zapatistas' uprising is a textbook example of the relation between the local and the global in civil society today. The Zapatista Army for National Liberation burst on to the international stage when it seized several towns and villages in Mexico's poorest state of Chiapas on 1 January 1994. The insurgency coincided with the launch of the North American Free Trade Agreement and made a mockery of Mexico's planned celebration of joining the First World. The armed stage of the uprising lasted for only twelve days but it succeeded in drawing international attention to the plight of Mexico's indigenous population and forced the government to give serious consideration to their demands.

The desperate insurgency had every chance of being drowned in blood or joining the long list of forgotten ethnic conflicts. Instead the Zapatistas succeeded in tapping a vast transnational network of civic activists who provided it with visibility, protection, legitimacy and support. Naomi Klein says:

> The Zapatista uprising was a new way to protect land and culture: rather than locking out the world, the Zapatistas flung open the doors and invited the world inside. (Klein 2001)

The Zapatistas brought networking to a new level. Their ideas, which spread initially through word of mouth, dominate the Internet. According to Naomi Klein, there are at least 4,500 Zapatista websites based in 26 countries. There is a Zapatista cottage industry selling 40 kinds of T-shirts, baseball caps, posters and Mayan dolls. Zapatista gatherings – Encontros – both in Mexico and elsewhere are attended by thousands of activists from all over the world. Their latest event, the Zapatour, in which the movement's masked leaders toured the country promoting their cause, culminated with a 150,000-strong rally in Mexico City.

One of the secrets behind the Zapatistas' success is their ideas as formulated by the movement's eloquent non-leader Subcomandante Marcos. These ideas go far beyond the immediate demands of the Mayan communities to articulate an alternative global vision. Marcos is inviting the millions 'stoodup' by globalisation to unite behind the Chiapas Indians by defining the 'savage capitalism of the end of the 20th century' as the common enemy. Anyone who feels disenfranchised by global capitalism can join the Zapatistas by doing whatever they can wherever they are.

The Zapatistas are sceptical both of cosmetic reforms and of 'fascist' nationalist solutions. Indeed they are sceptical of any ready-made alternatives, promoting instead a 'revolution which makes the revolution possible'. Their main goal is to create the democratic space in which alternative social proposals can compete and coexist with each other as long as they are just. Marcos says, describing the revolution:

> It will be, primarily, a revolution which is the result of the struggle on different social fronts, with many methods, within different social forms, with different degrees of commitment and participation. And its results will be, not a party, organisation or alliance of victorious organisations with its specific social proposal, but a chance for a democratic space in order to resolve the confrontation among diverse political proposals. This democratic space for resolution will have three fundamental premises which are inseparable historically: democracy, in order to decide upon the dominant social proposal, liberty in order to subscribe to one or the other proposal and justice in which all proposals should be enclosed. (Don Durito 1995)

This ambiguity combined with the movement's aversion to hierarchy and classical concepts of leadership make it ideal for the alternatives. Indeed, these ideas are the closest thing to a 'manifesto' for the alternative stream of the anti-capitalist movement. Klein says:

> I may never have made the pilgrimage to Chiapas, but I have watched the Zapatistas' ideas spread through activist circles, passed along second- and third-hand: a phrase, a way to run a meeting, a metaphor that twists your brain around. Unlike classic revolutionaries, who preach through bullhorns and from pulpits, Marcos has spread the Zapatista word through riddles. Revolutionaries who don't want power. People who must hide their faces to be seen. A world with many worlds in it. A movement of one 'no' and many 'yesses'. (Klein 2001)

Many of those who made the 'pilgrimage' to Chiapas went on to play a critical role in the major anti-capitalist protests in Seattle, Prague and Davos. Zapatista slogans, ideas, non-hierarchical methods of organisation, irreverence, humour and romanticism are omnipresent in alternative anti-capitalist events. Indeed it is hard to say today who needs the other more, the Zapatistas or the alternatives.

Box 3.5: The Other Alternatives

Civil society responses to global capitalism extend beyond protests and lobbying to 'practical' alternatives. In the area of money and finance such alternatives include LETS schemes and other money alternatives, micro-lending and Grameen banking, and socially responsible investment. These alternatives can be isolationist, reformist, supporter or alternative in nature depending on their compatibility with global capitalism. They also vary in spread and success.

According to Project LETS (see website) there are around 500 LETS schemes and networks in 36 countries. The average size of these schemes is 50 to 60 participants although larger ones can have thousands of participants.

A typical example of LETS schemes is Ithaca Hours, based in the small university town of Ithaca, New York. One Hour is equivalent to $10 or one hour of work. The core of the system is a bi-monthly tabloid in which people and businesses that accept Ithaca Hours advertise their products and services. Each advertiser receives Four Hours so that s/he can purchase other peoples' products. The currency is limited to a 20-mile radius and payments can be made in both dollars and hours. The scheme involves about 2,000 participants (Lietaer 2001). Since LETS currencies are usually based on the exchange of labour hours, most LETS schemes are community-based, although this is changing with the advent of the Internet. Formalised LETS schemes are usually political rather than practical in nature. Environmental sustainability, anti-consumerism and efforts to promote community cohesion and culture are among their main motivations. Formalised LETS schemes are trying to carve out space away from the market and as such could be designated as alternative.

The most prevalent forms of alternative money, however, are neither political nor formalised. Money shortages due to state failure or neo-liberal reforms may force millions in developing and transition countries to seek alternatives to money. In the former Soviet Union people augmented barter arrangements originally developed to deal with the shortage economy to handle the tight money of shock therapy. Such arrangements involve the exchange of both goods and services, including labour hours. Rather than being an alternative to market relations such arrangements are part of the new market economy in these countries.

The Grameen Bank extends loans as small as $50 to the poorest people in rural Bangladesh. The loans are given without collateral. The main clients are women whom the bank deems more likely to spend the money wisely and to repay it on schedule. The bank relies on community and peer pressure to ensure repayment. As such it uses social capital in the form of community relations and gender as a substitute for collateral and as a way to reduce lending costs. Grameen banking and similar forms of micro-lending have been extremely successful, reaching 14 million people in December 1999, a growth of 82 per cent in two years (Empowering Women with Microcredit 2000). The success of Grameen banking has prompted aid agencies, international lending institutions and commercial banks to emulate it in other countries. Originally, Grameen banks were all NGOs. Micro-lenders today are divided between NGOs, who have predominantly a social/environmental agenda, and banks. Grameen banking and other forms of micro-lending are firmly anchored within market structures. They could be designated as reformist since they correct a market failure by extending lending to the poorest people who are usually shunned by commercial banks.

Socially responsible investing (SRI) is the most successful of the practical alternatives. Indeed, it is becoming so commonplace for pension funds – the largest portfolio investors – to demand SRI from their fund managers that it is gradually becoming the norm rather than the alternative. In 1999 over US$2 trillion was invested in socially responsible ways, accounting for 13 per cent of assets under management in the United States. This represented a growth of 45 per cent over the 9 per cent figure for 1997 (Social Investment Forum 1999). The numbers are expected to grow especially since SRI funds are proving to be as profitable as, if not more so than, traditional ones. SRI is also spreading into Europe, albeit at a slower pace. The introduction of regulation in the UK requiring pension funds to disclose SRI policies has provided a needed boost.

Socially responsible investing in the US in 1999
- Screening: $1,232 billion
- Community investing: $5.4 billion
- Shareholder advocacy: $657 billion
- Screening and advocacy: $265 billion
  (Social Investment Forum 1999)

> British SRIs are estimated to have £45 billion under management. There are several varieties of SRI, from passive screening of companies according to certain criteria to the active use of corporate governance mechanisms to inject environmental sustainability and labour and human rights standards into corporate policies. SRI could be described as supportive because it takes place within the framework of global capitalism, using its existing tools and mechanisms. One could say that SRI proves that market mechanisms such as corporate governance are the most efficient way to produce desired public goods without government intervention.

The alternatives do not necessarily seek to overthrow capitalism and are definitely not interested in gaining power. They seek instead to defend a 'way of life' and thus, place a strong emphasis on cultural issues. It is not surprising that their protests look more like cultural happenings than political action. Indeed, the alternatives' grasp of popular culture is one of their main strengths.

The alternatives have a schizophrenic relationship to globalisation. On the one hand, by espousing many isolationist ideas they appear anti-globalisation; on the other hand they are fiercely global in placing a strong emphasis on solidarity or, as Reclaim the Streets puts it: 'The resistance will be as transnational as capital'. The alternatives are also the most technologically savvy of all the resistance movements, which further ties them to globalisation.

There are parallels between the alternatives of today and the radicals of the 1960s. For example, the radicals brought together emancipatory and rights politics of the 'old' and the life politics of the 'new' social movements. The alternatives reproduced this link in the form of the Longshoremen providing protection to the anti-sweatshop student demonstrators in Seattle. The radicals and the alternatives are also similar in their emphasis on popular culture and forms in general. But there are also differences between the two: chief among them is that the 'authority' being challenged today is the corporation, not the state.

Alternatives do not have a particular position on global finance issues. Instead they espouse a mixture of isolationist and, to a lesser degree, reformist ideas.

Table 3.1: Civil society responses to global finance

Legend: ● PREDOMINANT (P) · ◐ SIGNIFICANT (S) · ○ TO SOME EXTENT (E)

	Organisation					Activity					Position			
	Individual	NGO/Group	Movement/Network	Think tanks/Academia	Media/Website	Inform/Educate	Lobby	Mobilise	Serve	Riot/Celebrate	Rejectionist	Supportive	Reformative	Alternative
ATTAC			S	P		P		S					P	
Bank Information Center		P				P	E	S			P		S	
Bankwatch		P				E	S	P			P		S	
Bello, Waldon	P					P		S			P			
Bretton Woods Project		S		P		P	S						P	
Centre for Civil Society				P		P		P				P		
Corporate Watch		P				S		P			S		P	
Don Durito (Subcomandante Marcos)	P						P	P			S			P
Economist					P	P	P	S				P	S	
Fifty Years is Enough		P						P			P			
Financial Times					P	P	S					S	P	
Focus on Global South				P		P		S			P			
Friedman, Thomas	P					P	S					P	S	
Friends of the Earth		S	P				S	P			P		S	
Global Exchange			P	S		S		P			P			
Grameen Bank		P				S			P				P	
INPEG			P				S			P				P
Institute for Policy Studies				P		P	S	E			S		P	
International Forum on Globalization		S	P			P		S			P			
Ithaca Hours			P					S	P					S
Jubilee 2000			P			E	S	P					P	
Klein, Naomi	P					P		S						P
Landless Peasants Movement (MST)		P						S	E	P	S			P
Le Monde diplomatique					P	P		S			P			S
Meltzer Commission				P		P	S					P		
Nader, Ralph	P							P			P			
OneWorld.net					P	P		S			S		P	E
Oxfam		P				E	S	P					P	
Reclaim the Streets			P					S		P	S			P
Ruckus Society		P							P	P				P
Social Investment Forum		P				S	E		P			P	S	
Stiglitz, Joseph	P					P	S						P	
Wall Street Journal					P	P	S				P			
Wolfenson, James	P					E	S		P			S	P	
World Development Movement		P	S			S	E	P					P	
Zapatistas (EZLN)			P					P	E	P	S			P

● PREDOMINANT ◐ SIGNIFICANT ○ TO SOME EXTENT

Conclusion: The Total Is More Than the Sum of the Parts

Civic responses to capitalism are as old as the system itself. Reactions to money are even older. Isolationists, supporters, reformists and alternatives existed previously in various forms. Most of the time, governments and markets confronted or ignored them when they could not co-opt them. Lately, the individual responses have been coming together, creating something larger than the sum of its components. In Seattle and Prague, myriad individuals, organisations, movements, ideas and methods came together to deliver a message so powerful that it took everyone by surprise.

Seattle and Prague, however, are only the most visible expression of global civic responses to capitalism. The various responses are actually working together all the time.

The alternatives lend mass appeal and visibility to what would otherwise be marginal isolationist and reformist movements. They also create the space where the various responses come together. The isolationists with their militancy and radical demands keep the issues alive and sharpen the debate. The ultimate winner from these synergies are the reformists, who eventually fill the gap between the supporters and the isolationists with constructive solutions.

Civic responses to global capitalism are also coming together across regions despite supporters' claims to the contrary. The Zapatistas not only were saved by global solidarity; they are also the inspiration for alternatives worldwide. IMF and World Bank reforms are influenced by demonstrations in Turkey, Nigeria and Argentina as much as they are by riots in Prague and Washington. The Jubilee 2000 campaign would not have achieved what it did had it not been a truly global movement.

What is it that brings Ann Pettifor, Katerina Liskova, George Soros and Walden Bello together to dress down the heads of the World Bank and the IMF?[4] Why would the leaders of the Bretton Woods institutions subject themselves to such public upbraiding? After all, activists were championing Third World issues before Katerina was born. Soros made his millions even earlier, totally unaware of Bello and his fellows in the national liberation

---

4   Katerina Liskova is one of the organisers of the Prague World Bank/IMFD protest. Ann Pettifor is the founder of Jubilee 2000 campaign to cancel Third World debt. Walden Bello is a radical Filipino academic and anti-capitalist activist. Gorge Soros is a financier and philanthropist. The four participated in a meeting held at Prague castle together with the heads of the IMF and World Bank hosted by Czech President Vaclav Havel (see Box 3.1).

movement. Twenty years ago most anti-capitalist activists did not even know who the leaders of the Bretton Woods institutions were, and if they did they wouldn't have dreamt of sitting with them at the same table.

It could be that for the first time in decades the bottom rung seems to have dropped from the global social ladder, that along with overall prosperity there are more and more pockets around the world where people seem to have nothing to lose. Regardless of where they are, people are terrified by widening disparities. Many are all too aware that the Zapatista insurrection and Landless Peasant Movement land occupations are comparatively benign outbursts by those left behind, that unless something is done we can expect more violent eruptions with unpredictable consequences.

It could be that even those enjoying the fruits of prosperity are feeling less and less in control of their lives. It is, after all, frustrating to get virtually identical economic policies no matter whom you vote for and to watch your elected representatives facilitate or at best stand by helplessly as markets devour precious public space.

Maybe the whole thing is just a successful public relations stunt by the alternatives who are deftly mixing pop culture and information technology to lend a sheen of novelty and broad appeal to tired slogans. The new anti-capitalist movement may just be giving a new form to an old idea. Like its predecessors, it is unlikely to succeed in terms of defeating global capitalism (after all, supporters are the most influential of the civic responses to global capitalism) but it may just transform it.

Given the cacophony of voices behind it, the message from Seattle and Prague may be neither coherent nor constructive. It is more like an alarm, a shout of protest and despair. But it is loud enough that corporations, international organisations and governments can ignore it only at their peril.

References
AFL-CIO (1998). 'US Workers Addressing the Global Crisis' (Executive Council Statement). Monterey, California (14 October).
Anderson, Sarah and Cavanagh, John (2000). *Bearing the Burden: The Impact of Global Financial Crisis on Workers and Alternative Agendas for the IMF and Other Institutions.* Washington DC: Institute for Policy Studies. http://www.ips.dc.org.
Bello, Walden (2000). Excerpt from a talk delivered at a series of engagements during the demonstrations against the World Economic Forum in Melbourne, Australia, 6–10 September. http://www.focusweb.org.
Bello, Walden (2001). 'Is Bush Bad for the World Bank?' January. http://www.corpwatch.org.
Cohen, Robin and Rai, Shirin (2000). *Global Social Movements.* London: Athlone.
Cornia, Giovanni Andrea, Jolly, Richard, and Stewart, Frances (1987). *Adjustment with a Human Face.* Oxford: Clarendon Press.

Desai, M (2001). *Marx's Revenge: The Resurgence of Capitalism and the Death of Statist Socialism*. London: Verso.
Don Durito of the Lacandon Errant Knight for whom Sup Marcos is shield-bearer (1995). *Durito IV: Neoliberalism and the Party-State System*. Mexico: Zapatista Army of National Liberation, 11 June. http://www.eco.utexas.edu/faculty/Cleaver/chiapas95.html.
Economist (2000). 'The Case for Globalization'. 21 September.
Emerging Markets Companion (1996–9). *Brady Bond Primer*. http://www.emgmkts.com/research/bradydef.htm.
Empowering Women with Microcredit (2000). *Microcredit Summit Campaign Report*. http://www.microcreditsummit.org/campaigns/report00.html.
Friedman, Thomas (2000). *The Lexus and the Olive Tree; Understanding Globalization*. New York: Anchor. http://www.lexusandtheolivetree.com/globalization.htm.
Friends of the Earth (1998a). *MAI Update*, October. http://www.foe.org.
Friends of the Earth (2000). *Towards Sustainable Economies: Challenging Neoliberal Economic Globalisation*. 1 December. http://www.foei.org.
Friends of the Earth (1998b). *Licence to Loot: The MAI and How to Stop it*, http://www.foe.org/international/loot.html.
Fuller, C. J. (1989) 'Misconceiving the Grain Heap: a Critique of the Concept of the Indian Jajmani System', in Jonathan Parry and Bloch, Maurice (ed.), *Money and the Morality of Exchange*. Cambridge: Cambridge University Press.
Hines, Colin (2000). *Localisation: A Global Manifesto*. London: Earthscan.
ICFTU (International Confederation of Free Trades Unions) (2000). 'Securing the Conditions for Reducing Poverty and Achieving Sustainable Growth'. Statement by the ICFTU, TUAC, and ITS to the Spring 2000 meeting of the IMF and the World Bank in Washington DC.
IFIAC (International Financial Institution Advisory Commission, 'Meltzer Commission') (2000). *Report* (March). http://www.house.gov/jec/imf/ifiac.htm.
IMF (International Monetary Fund). http://www.imf.org.
Jubilee 2000. http://www.jubileeplus.org.
Kingsnorth, Paul (2000). 'Seeds of the New in the Prague Autumn'. *The Ecologist*, 30/8: 44–5.
Klein, Naomi (1999). *No Logo: Taking Aim at the Brand Bullies*. New York: Picador.
Klein, Naomi (2001). 'The Unknown Icon'. *Guardian* (3 March).
Lietaer, Bernard (2001). *The Future of Money*. London: Century.
Mauss, Marcel (1996). *The Gift: Forms and Functions of Exchange in Archaic Society*. London: Cohen and West.
Mittelman, James (2000). *The Globalization Syndrome, Transformation and Resistance*. Princeton: Princeton University Press.
Parry, Jonathan and Bloch, Maurice (1989). 'Introduction: Money and the Morality of Exchange', in Jonathan Parry and Bloch Maurice (ed.), *Money and the Morality of Exchange*. Cambridge: Cambridge University Press.
Perez, Carlota (2000). 'Technological Revolutions and Financial Capital', paper presented at 'The Other Canon Conference', Oslo.
Platform of ATTAC (Action pour une Taxe Tobin d'Aide aux Citoyens), 3 June 1998. https://www.attac.org.
Project LETS. http://lentils.imagineis.com/letslist.
Reclaim the Streets. http://www.reclaimthestreets.net.
Social Investment Forum (1999). *1999 Report on Socially Responsible Investing Trends in the United States*, November. http://www.socialinvest.org/areas/research/trends/1999-Trends.htm.

Stiglitz, Joseph (2000). 'Democratic Development as the Fruits of Labor', Keynote Address, Industrial Relations Research Association, Boston, January. Taken from Anderson and Cavanagh. http://www.ips.org.
Tönnies, Ferdinand (1955). *Gemeinschaft und Gesellschaft* (Community and Association) (trans. Charles P. Loomis). London: Routledge and Kegan Paul.
United Nations (1999). *World Economic and Social Survey*. New York: United Nations.
Wallerstein, Immanuel (2000). *The Essential Wallerstein*. New York: New Press.
Wood, Angela (2001). *Structural Adjustment for the IMF Options for Reforming the IMF's Governance Structure*. Brettonwoods Project (January). http://www.brettonwoodsproject.org/briefings/reform/sapimf.html.
World Bank (1998–1999). *World Development Report: Knowledge for Development*. New York: Oxford University Press.
World Bank (2000). *East Asia: Recovery and Beyond*. Washington, DC: World Bank.
World Development Movement. http://www.wdm.org.uk/campaign/GATS.htm.

Acknowledgement

First publication: Desai, Meghnad and Said, Yahia (2001) 'The New Anti-Capitalist Movement: Money and Global Civil Society', in *Global Civil Society 2001* (Yearbook), edited by Anheier, Helmut K., and Glasius, Marlies. Oxford, Oxford University Press, pp. 51–78. Republished with kind permission of Oxford University Press.

Chapter 4

TRADE AND GLOBAL CIVIL SOCIETY

The Anti-capitalist Movement Revisited

Yahia Said and Meghnad Desai

(2003)

Introduction

Thousands of people attended the rally which marked the launch of the Third World Social Forum (WSF) in Porto Alegre, Brazil on 22 January 2003. It was the same crowd that has perfected the art of turning desperation into hope, fear into cheer, and chaos into purpose at anti-capitalist riots throughout the world. However, we suggest in this chapter that something was amiss in Porto Alegre, that the 'movement of movements' is in danger of losing its dynamism and taking a dogmatic and ultimately self-defeating turn.

The formidable-looking Brazilian paramilitary policemen and women were on the side of the demonstrators – eager to assist and protect at every step. There was no chance of tear-gas and clubs. Brazilian authorities and businesses, including the state-owned oil multinational Petrobras, did not limit their support to words. They also footed much of the estimated US$3.5 million bill (Osava 2003). Klaus Schwab, founder and President of the World Economic Forum, had 'just one word for Porto Alegre: We are the same' (Mekay 2003).

Why were there no signs of resistance from 'the system' to this event, which is meant to represent the climactic expression of a movement out to destroy it? Why is the political and business establishment so keen on supporting the 'rabble'? (Temel-Kuran 2003)

In this chapter we will argue that three developments have been taking place in the anti-capitalist movement, especially the part of it that focuses on the global trade regime: success, institutionalisation and radicalisation.

After a moment of hesitation following the September 11 attacks in the US, the Global Justice and Solidarity Movement, as some of its followers like to call it, continued its meteoric rise. Millions around the globe took part in anti-capitalist protests and social forums. National and coordinated international campaigns succeeded in reversing privatisation plans in Peru and El Salvador. The movement also claimed a success when South Africa won the battle with multinational pharmaceuticals over the compulsory licensing of AIDS drugs. Most importantly, however, the movement succeeded in undermining the legitimacy of the Washington consensus: the neo-liberal economic orthodoxy which captured national and multilateral policymaking throughout the 1980s and much of the 1990s.

Part of the movement's success stems from the adoption of some of its rhetoric, if not spirit, by nationalist leaders and business elites on both sides of the North-South divide. Chavez and Chirac, Mugabe and Mahathir[1] have tried to attach themselves to the movement, with various degrees of success. Their goal is to leverage the movement's power and legitimacy in their struggle with domestic and foreign opponents.

Some in the movement are ready to accept these new allies. The newly elected Brazilian President Luiz Inacio Lula da Silva and Hugo Chavez were leading attractions at the WSF, which also featured three ministers from Chirac's Gaullist government. Some Asian activists spoke warmly of Mahathir's tough rhetoric, downplaying his authoritarian tendencies. 'How on earth', wonders Naomi Klein (2003), commenting on the reception accorded to Chavez at the WSF, 'did a gathering that was supposed to be a showcase for new grassroots movements become a celebration of men with a penchant for three-hour speeches about smashing the oligarchy?'

The coming together of anti-capitalist activists and nationalist capital and politicians is in part a sign of the movement's radicalisation: a predictable reaction to the advent of the Bush administration in the US and its policies, especially since the September 11 attacks. Susan George (2003a), vice-president of ATTAC France, speaking at the WSF states that the 'rich and powerful have apparently concluded...that hundreds of millions of people in the world today are superfluous'. Samir Amin (2003), one of the

---

1   Hugo Chavez, President of Venezuela; Jacques Chirac, President of France; Robert Mugabe, President of Zimbabwe; and Mahathir Muhammed, Prime Minister of Malaysia.

main organisers of the WSF, speaks of 'Washington neo-Nazis' who need to be confronted before 'September 1939'.

Along with the acceptance/collusion with national capital/nationalism, there seems to be a general sense of resignation among activists to the impossibility of reform. As Argentina's Mothers of the May Plaza put it: 'Another world is possible, only with revolution and socialism' (Cockroft 2003). In Porto Alegre and elsewhere, activists repeatedly stated that they have given up hope of transforming the international trade regime and its main institution, the World Trade Organization (WTO). Efforts to make the WTO more transparent and accountable, work towards improving market access for Southern products, and campaigns aimed at injecting environmental, social and labour considerations into the trade regime are giving way to an agenda centred around rolling back international treaties and organisations and returning power to the nation-state.

By seeking to 'Derail the WTO', the activists seem to have misinterpreted the major changes in the international arena resulting from the ascent of the neo-conservatives in the US and the September 11 attacks. The activists seem still bent on fighting a Washington consensus which no longer exists. The US administration has no particular commitment to the WTO or any multilateral institution. Globalisation and global institutions are tolerated only if they serve the interests of US and mature industry corporations associated with the Republican Party. If it is impossible or difficult to agree on rules that benefit the US, then it is better for them not to have any.

A trade regime without rules is unlikely to be more just than one governed by the WTO. Indeed, in the absence of a global set of rules economic superpowers will seek to carve up captive markets by constructing regional trade blocs. Indeed, the US administration is already pursuing such a strategy in the Free Trade Area of the Americas (FTAA) and bilateral negotiations with Chile, Singapore, Jordan and Australia. Activists are aware of this strategy but do not seem to draw the logical conclusions from it regarding their WTO strategy. Most activists calling for the abolition of the WTO suggest that a new organisation should be built from the ground up to replace it. We have yet, however, to see a detailed proposal for such an alternative or a convincing explanation why that would be more effective than a reformed WTO. Advocates of the abolition of the WTO seem implicitly opposed to global trade in principle: a position few activists would care to embrace.

Civil society movements have not always taken an uncompromising stance on international trade, indeed historically many have been pro-trade.

The next section will address some theoretical and historical aspects of civil society movements on trade. It will be followed by an outline of the various positions on trade issues today. These positions will then be illustrated with the examples of the WTO and FTAA. We will also explore strategies and methods employed by the various strands in the movement in specific campaigns and activities. We will conclude by addressing the challenges and opportunities facing the movement today.

Trade and Civil Society: Theoretical and Historical Aspects

Trade has been a major plank of the global social justice movement. The WTO is seen by many as the driving force of globalisation, and free trade is blamed for many ills: environmental damage, commodification of subsistence crops and consequent food insecurity, falling commodity prices, inequality and inequity in the global distribution of income, and so forth. There are demands for fair trade, for special treatment of the least developed countries, especially in help with negotiations at WTO meetings. But, unlike in the case of money and finance, which we surveyed in Chapter 3 of this book, there are few religious objections to trade. While there are some 'anti-trade fundamentalists' (Hines 2000), even they are only against international trade, that is, trade across national boundaries.[2] This is because some sort of exchange, whether based on money or barter, is endemic to all societies. It is also more or less axiomatic that trade benefits all parties. The dispute arises about the distribution of the gains from trade; the inequality of gains from trade is often blamed for the inequalities of income and wealth in the world today.

Trade and Comparative Advantage

The counter-argument from the days of the classical economists has always been that, far from being a cause of inequality, trade is 'an engine of growth' and that economies which are open and trade in a free environment thrive, as demonstrated by the experience of the rich developed countries. At issue is the theory of comparative advantage, which was the linchpin for

---

2   There is an age-old objection to movement of food grains far from their place of origin. Famines were blamed in pre-modern and early modern days on inter-regional movements of food grains. The Physiocrats in the eighteenth century were the first to argue for the unimpeded, toll-free movement of food grain across France; hence the expression 'laisser-passer'. See for an insight into this Rothschild (2001). The idea of 'food miles' indicates that resistance persists in some to food trade even within countries.

Ricardo's argument for free trade and the reason for the triumph of classical economics in the nineteenth century.

Classical economics started as a reaction against the mercantilist system, in which politics dominated markets and national interest was supreme. Adam Smith in his *Wealth of Nations* (Smith 1776/1993) questioned the efficiency of the mercantilist system. Ricardo in his *Principles of Political Economy and Taxation* (Ricardo 1821/1992) made resource efficiency (though he did not call it that) an objective in place of the national interest. Here indeed is the first separation in economic theory between the interests of the state and those of its citizens, even of civil society.

This theory of comparative advantage holds that if two countries – England and Portugal, in Ricardo's much cited example – are capable of producing two commodities – wine and cloth – then each should specialise in producing, and exporting to the other country, that commodity which it can produce more cheaply, *even if it could produce both commodities more cheaply than the other country*. By that specialisation, both countries will benefit from the optimal use of resources. Later neoclassical economists added that consumer welfare will be enhanced in both countries as goods will be cheaper if countries specialised along the lines of comparative advantage.

A History of Trade Activism

What converted an abstract and unrealistic theory into practical politics was civil society agitation in the nineteenth century on behalf of free trade and against the corn laws, which imposed a tax on food grain imports into Britain. Ricardo's theory became a weapon in the hands of the Anti-Corn Law League, which succeeded in having the corn laws repealed and British agriculture 'globalised'. It was a classic redistributive struggle in which the workers and capitalists challenged the power of the landed aristocracy. In the particular English context of the 1840s, consumers were largely the urban workers and their families, so this movement also acquired a class character, which is why Marx supported free trade against protection (Desai 2002). The Anti-Corn Law League raised money and set up machinery across England and Wales to increase voter registration, which then enabled it to get MPs elected who would vote down the corn laws. Established in 1839, it succeeded within seven years and the corn laws were abolished in 1846. The Anti-Corn Law League represents the first civil society movement on a trade issue, though pro–free trade.

Despite its triumph in Britain, Ricardo's theory had several features which have made it controversial ever since it was first propounded. First, in theory, free trade operates between countries, but the politics of international relations is absent. Thus, many critics point out that when Ricardo wrote about trade between England and Portugal the Methuen Treaty between the two countries had already relegated Portugal to a subordinate status. Also, by specialising in an industrial commodity – cloth – England could reap the advantages of dynamic increasing returns to scale, while Portugal would be confined to a commodity in which there were diminishing returns and few innovations. Of course, in that case cloth would become cheap over time but not wine; thus, the terms of trade – the ratio of the price of wine to that of cloth would move against England and in favour of Portugal. But later, a terms-of-trade pessimism developed among economists, and the Singer-Prebisch thesis held that over time the country producing the agricultural commodity would see its terms of trade decline (Prebisch 1950). This was because the demand for the primary commodity was income-inelastic as well as price-inelastic (that is, the price of primary commodities and the level of income have little or no impact on the demand for that commodity). Thus, with growing world incomes the demand for primary commodities did not keep pace. Moreover, the markets for primary commodities were competitive; and so, as output increased due to the introduction of new land or better techniques, the price of the primary commodity declined; but this decline in price did not lead to higher demand. Manufactures, on the other hand, it was averred, were produced under oligopolistic conditions and their prices were determined on a cost-plus mark-up basis. Hence, the price of the manufacture would not fall but stay constant or rise while that of the primary commodity would fall. Thus trade would heighten the inequalities between the two rather than narrow them. (The Singer-Prebisch thesis did not go unchallenged. See Spraos 1983 for a response.)

Second, in theory goods move but factors do not. Trade imposes restructuring on the domestic economy – for example, complete as opposed to partial specialisation – but the theory takes no account of the short-run human costs while emphasising the long-run welfare gains. When one industry has to be shut down while another expands, then workers bear the burden of unemployment and the costs of re-skilling. Politicians are concerned with immediate or short-run losses and not willing to sacrifice their voters for the sake of long-run gains. Thus, tariffs and protection have always had much more political support than free trade. Even in England, the classic free trade country, there was a move against free trade in the early twentieth century after the franchise had been extended.

Free trade in fact operates through the inter-state (so-called international) system. Free markets filter through the power system. The theory of comparative advantage sets out the limits of specialisation on theoretical grounds, but power relations between states define the actual limits. In practice, the international trading system has been an uneasy compromise between mercantilism and free trade. When there has been a hegemon – Great Britain in the nineteenth century and the USA post-1945 – championing free trade, then the balance between mercantilism and free trade has edged towards the latter. But even here there has always been a gap between the hegemon's rhetoric and the practice. Thus, Great Britain's shipping acts in the nineteenth century stipulated that British exports should be transported exclusively in British ships, and the USA today protects its agriculture and other sectors.

Free trade theory was denounced as an English ideological plant to harm continental economies. Friedrich List (1837/1966) as well as many American economists of the mid-nineteenth century argued that free trade might be suitable for rich and developed England, but Germany and America needed protection. The *Zollverein*, established in 1833, was a customs union comprising Prussia and other German states. It combined free internal trade with tariff barriers against imports, rather like the European Union today. List began the anti–free trade movement by giving it a developmentalist edge.

This also helped to radicalise the anti-colonial struggles in India, where nationalists saw free trade as part of an imperialist strategy to keep India de-industrialised. A distinction was drawn between the interests of domestic capital/state and foreign capital/state, which turned the discourse against free trade. Classical economic theory had contrasted the interest of the civil society (consumer) with that of the state in attacking mercantilism. With List the contrast was between the rich/developed/metropolitan state and the poor/underdeveloped/colonial state. The interests of civil society in the poor/colonial state were to be identified with those of the state.

There are problems of trade in manufactured goods where production is determined by the status quo in comparative advantage. Until the middle of the twentieth century, most manufacturing industries were located in OECD countries and exported to developing countries. Developing countries as they started industrialising by import substitution methods encountered the criticism that they were ignoring comparative advantage. Nationalists in developing countries dealt with this criticism in Listian fashion by championing the interests of domestic against foreign capitalists regardless of any harm done to the interests of consumers (Box 4.1).

Box 4.1: Actors in International Trade: Classes and Interests

The conflict that trade generates within a country, as in the corn law agitation in nineteenth-century Britain, or across countries, as in contemporary movements, can be analysed in a schematic way by delineating the principal actors and how their interests may combine or clash. In the original Anti-Corn Law League debate, the 'actors' were:

(a) manufacturers/capitalists/shopkeepers;
(b) industrial/urban workers;
(c) landlords;
(d) farm/rural workers;
(e) consumers;
(f) civil society.

The story is that (a) and (b) combined to defeat (c). The (d) element was not enfranchised and played little part in the debate. The then government consisted of MPs elected by (a) and (c). Usually it is only (a) and (c) that feature in the argument but governments are also part of the action as signatories to treaties such as the WTO. In neoclassical economists' interpretations of the free trade argument, consumers (e) are the most important group as against industrial producers, (a) and (b) together with agricultural producers (c) and (d). In the neoclassical story free trade benefits (e) by providing cheaper goods and hurts (a) and (b) or (c) and (d) in the short run due to competition; but the long run effects are beneficial to all by improving resource allocation and allowing higher levels and perhaps a higher growth rate of output and income. Of course, consumers can also be seen as civil society, but to keep the notation clear we label civil society separately as (f).

Under Friedrich List's analysis we have to add the foreign counterparts to the six actors above. Label them (A) to (F). In what follows the rich country is denoted by lower-case letters and the poor country by upper-case letters. Thus (A) would be the local (poor country) manufacturer and (a) the English (rich country) manufacturer. List saw the battle as between (a) and (A). From the two sets of interest groups (a) to (e) and (A) to (E), we can map the location of various protest groups as identified with one or other cluster. Thus the anti-colonial struggle for tariffs took the interests of (A) and (B) to be pitted against those of (a) and perhaps (b). During his visit to England for the Round Table Conference of 1930, Gandhi tried to win over the Lancashire mill workers who had been adversely affected by his insistence that Indians bought only Indian cloth. Thus he was aware of the harm to the interests of (b) but sought international solidarity between (b) and (B).

Today we have to add a further dimension: capital is mobile and 'foreign' capital could be hiring domestic workers. In this case the interests of (a) and (B) combine to harm (b) as well as possibly (A). Thus, in attacking foreign direct investment for employing cheap labour and taking jobs away from the home country (as argued by some AFL-CIO groups in Seattle), the interests of (b) are pitted against (B) but blamed on the tendency of (a) to compete with or even align with (A). Farm subsidies by the US or the EU help (d) in these areas but hurt (e) and, via dumping, (D). In denouncing multinational corporations, protesters identify the villains as (a) foreign capital; but often (A) domestic/poor country capital is no better than foreign capital, say in health and safety risks, environmental damage, or gender discrimination.

Another new element resulting from globalisation is the capacity of civil society movements to forge international or indeed global alliances. In this respect alliances of rich-country and poor-country anti-trade groups do have some confusing clashes of interests which if not resolved can lead to contradictions between anti-trade movements in theory as well as in practice. If we characterise the Anti-Corn Law League as a combination of (a), (b), and (f) against (c) and (d), today we have the possibility of combinations of (f) and (F) championing individual or groups of countries against others i.e. aligning with any permutation of (a) to (e) and (A) to (E).

Thus from the simple alliances of (a) and (b) versus (c) and (d), or even (a) and (b) versus (A) and (B), we have (a) and some (B) versus (b) and some (A) and some (B). We have antagonism of (c) and (d) towards (C) and (D). The anti-trade movement may then represent an alliance of (f) and (F) or some sections thereof against workers in poor countries (B) and in favour of workers in rich countries (b) just because they don't like the rich-country capitalists (a). The movement against trade in food may hurt poor-country farmers (D); but silence on trade distortions such as EU and US farm subsidies benefits rich-country farmers (c) and workers (d) but hurts (C) and (D). Being anti-trade is no longer simply being anti-rich and pro-poor.

For many years the General Agreement on Tariffs and Trade (GATT), set up after the Second World War, tolerated this deviation from free trade as long as the offending countries were poor and not exporting their goods to rich country markets. But with the Uruguay Round concluded in 1993 things changed. Developing countries which had successfully acquired industries that could compete in export markets wanted greater access to rich country markets. Rich countries in their turn were eyeing the newly emerging markets where there were potential consumers of their products. Thus, the context of international trade negotiations began to change and a long series of negotiations resulted in the Marrakech Agreement and the upgrading of GATT to the WTO.

But with freer movement of capital the old comparative advantage is changing. New developments in Internet, transport, and communications technology are making the dispersal and fragmentation of the production process not only possible but profitable, and industries are relocating from North to South. This leads to the charge that capital is footloose and that it is employing/exploiting cheap labour, that American wages are being determined in Beijing, and so on. It is in this context that the WTO is suddenly emerging as the villain of the piece since these developments in global production relocation coincide with the establishment of the WTO. Of course, not all developing countries have experienced successful industrialisation or acquired an ability to export manufactures. Thus, within the old solid South there are divisions between those whose interests lie in greater access to foreign direct investment and OECD markets, and those who are left outside this process. The latter, mostly in Sub-Saharan Africa, are exporters of primary products and suffer from the inequities of agricultural export subsidies in OECD countries, which in turn dump their surplus primary products on the developing countries. These countries have a genuine complaint about the tardiness of the WTO in tackling this distortion in the world trading system. They also receive little foreign direct investment and hence do not benefit from the globalisation of world manufacturing.

Thus, there are several strands to the modern anti-trade movements and some of them are mutually contradictory. There is resentment of developed-country domination in industrial markets but also fear of footloose capital employing cheap foreign labour and hurting rich-country workers. There is concern about the falling prices of primary commodities of the Third World but also support for farm subsidies in rich countries. There is a sentiment against the environmental consequences of global growth led by free trade, which could deny the poor countries the capacity to export and enrich themselves in exactly the ways that rich countries have done until now. In some cases the interests of the different elements in the anti-capitalist coalition are inconsistent with one another.

Positions on Global Trade

In Desai and Said (2001) we divided civil society responses to global capitalism into Supporters, Reformers, Isolationists and Alternatives. Both Isolationists and Supporters believe that globalisation and global capitalism are one and the same and that they are reversible. They believe that globalisation entails the gradual erosion of the nation-state and the expansion of the rule of the market into every sphere of life. Isolationists think that globalisation should therefore be resisted and reversed. In its place they promote values of self-sufficiency and self-reliance and seek a return to the national liberation states. Supporters believe that globalisation and global capitalism are the only way to combat poverty and totalitarianism and should therefore be embraced wholeheartedly by all and sundry. Reformers believe that there is more to globalisation than capitalism. The state, according to Reformers, is not eroded but transformed, working under new constraints of 'overlapping sovereignties'. They do not believe that globalisation could or should be reversed; instead, they call for it to be humanised. Alternatives reject the entire conceptual framework and are more concerned with carving out spaces where alternative paradigms can co-exist. Over the past three years, due to the resurgence of the new group we call the Regressives (see below) and the weakening of Reformers, many activists are being pushed into Isolationist positions.

Today, in contrast to Seattle in 1999, there is a near (if not always declared) consensus within the movement on an agenda of abolishing the WTO and most other international trade initiatives. In this chapter we use a revised classification of civil society positions on trade to reflect these changes (see also Tables 4.1, 4.2 and 4.3).

Supporters advocate a strict interpretation of trade theories. This group, comprised mainly of academics and officials at international organisations, believe that even without equity or redistributive mechanisms trade liberalisation will benefit everyone by improving productivity. An example of the supporters' argument is a recent call by Nicholas Stern, the World Bank's chief economist, for developing countries to open their markets, even if this was not reciprocated by the developed countries, since liberalisation benefits the liberaliser (Luce 2002). What's good for business is good for everyone.

Supporters, who also include industrial lobbies, especially those associated with new industries, in addition to some of the main liberal media such as the *Economist* and the *Wall Street Journal*, are a declining minority today. 'Even the staunchest partisans of free trade suspect it is an idea whose time has not just come but gone' (Caldwell 2003).

The Supporters' ranks have been dwindling due to defections to the *Regressives*, who claim to adhere to the same orthodoxy but make an exception for their, usually rich-country, governments and corporations. According to this group, globalisation can work only under the leadership of hegemonic superpower(s). Since the well-being of the world community is dependent on the well-being of the superpower(s), they should be allowed to break the rules of free trade when those clash with their national interests. What is good for the superpower(s) is good for everyone.

Civil society Regressives are exemplified by some of the think tanks and mature industry lobbyists associated with the current US Administration. Some of them are ardent supporters of market liberalisation and free trade. As such, it would be hard for them to openly attack the WTO. Nonetheless they occasionally bemoan the organisation's unwieldy nature, which they attribute to its consensus mechanism and the resulting 'disproportionate'

Table 4.1: The new layout

	Globalisation is	Position on globalisation	Position on global trade
Supporters	Capitalism minus the state	Should be defended at all costs. The alternative is fascism.	Good even if unequal. The problem is in the inter-state system. Support the WTO.
Regressives	Capitalism plus the state	On our terms or deglobalisation	Good if on our terms. Same for WTO.
Isolationists	Capitalism minus the state	Deglobalisation	Inherently bad. Re-empower the state. Abolish the WTO.
Reformers	Capitalism plus transformed state	Should be humanised	Can and must be made more equitable. WTO reform, national and international redistributive policies.
Alternatives	Less capitalism and less state	Space for alternatives to compete and coexist	Neutral, the problem is with states and corporations

Table 4.2: Positions on trade agreements

	Isolationists	Reformers	Supporters	Regressives
	(e.g. Bello, Hines, Wallach)	(e.g. Oxfam, WDM, Greens, most Third World governments)	(e.g. academics, USTR Zoellick, European Commission)	(e.g. The Heritage Foundation, the rest of the US Administration, France, Italy)
Agreement on Agriculture (AoA)	Take food out of the WTO	Scrap Western subsidies and barriers. Allow poor countries to erect barriers when necessary.	Eliminate all barriers	Keep barriers when in the our national interest
New areas (investment, government procurement, competitions, trade facilitation)	No expansion to new areas	No expansion before addressing outstanding issues	Expand while dealing with outstanding issues	Expand with no restrictions as long as it is to the benefit of our companies
TRIPS (intellectual property and health)	Abolish	Should allow for preferential treatment of poor countries and national emergencies	Should have allowances only for emergencies such as health (both production and import)	Full global protection of intellectual property rights with the exception of our national emergencies
GATS (services)	Abolish	Should not extend to critical public services and public goods	Expand short of ill-defined areas necessary for the exercise of government	Expand as long as it is to our benefit
FTAA	Abolish	Abolish/amend	Support but not at the expense of WTO	Promote as alternative to WTO
Fair trade	Too little too late	At least something	May be trade-distorting	Trade is fair

Table 4.3: Civil society responses to global trade

	Organisation					Activity					Position				
	Individual	NGO/group	Movement/network	Think tank/academia	Media/website	Inform/educate	Lobby	Mobilise	Serve	Riot/celebrate	Supportive	Regressive	Isolationist	Reformative	Alternative
Action Aid		●				○	◐	●						●	
American Enterprise Institute				●		●		◐			●	◐			
ATTAC			●	◐		○	◐	●					◐	●	
Bello, Walden	●					●		◐			●				
Christian Aid		●				○	◐	◐	●					●	
Corporate Europe Observatory			●			●	◐	○					●	◐	
Economist					●	●	◐				●			◐	
Emergency Committee for American Trade		●					●	◐			●				
Financial Times					●	●	◐				●			◐	
Focus on Global South				●		●		◐					●	◐	
Food First		◐	●			●	○	◐					●	◐	
Friends of the Earth		◐	●				◐	●					●	◐	
GATS Watch					●	●		●					●	◐	
Global Trade Watch (at Public Citizen)					●	●		●					●		
Hemispheric Social Alliance			●					●					◐	●	○
Heritage Foundation				●		●	◐				●	◐			
Institute for Agriculture and Trade Policy				●		●							●	◐	
International Chamber of Commerce			●				●				●				
International Confederation of Trades Unions (ICFTU)			●			○	●	◐						●	
International Federation for Alternative Trade			●			○	◐	●						●	◐

	Organisation					Activity					Position				
	Individual	NGO/group	Movement/network	Think tank/academia	Media/website	Inform/educate	Lobby	Mobilise	Serve	Riot/celebrate	Supportive	Regressive	Isolationist	Reformative	Alternative
International Forum on Globalization			◐	●		●		◐					●	◐	
International Gender and Trade Network			●			●	○	◐					●	◐	
Klein, Naomi	●					●		◐							●
OneWorld.net					●	●			◐				◐	●	○
Our World Is Not For Sale			●				◐	●			●				
Oxfam		●				○	◐		●					●	
Peoples Global Action			●					●			●				
Polaris Institute				●		●		◐					◐	●	
Public Citizen		●				○	◐	●					●		
Rand Corporation				●		●	◐				●	◐			
SalAMI		●						◐		●			◐		●
Terraviva (of Inter Press Service)					●	●		◐					◐	●	○
Third World Network			●	◐		◐		●					◐	●	
Trade Justice Movement			●					●						●	
Trade Observatory (previously WTO Watch)					●	●		●	◐				◐	●	
Trans Atlantic Business Dialogue			●				●				●				
Transnational Institute				●		●	◐	◐					◐	●	
Via Campesina			●					◐	●				◐	●	
Wall Street Journal					●	●	◐				●	◐			
World Development Movement		●				◐	○	●						●	

● PREDOMINANT   ◐ SIGNIFICANT   ○ TO SOME DEGREE

influence of Third World nations (Wolf 2002). Yet it is revealing that most of their strategic advice to the Administration is focused on bilateral treaties and negotiations. In the extreme case, the Heritage Foundation completely ignores the WTO in its trade strategy advice to the administration (O'Driscoll and Fitzgerald 2002).

Indeed, the US Administration's policy towards the WTO is similar to that towards other multilateral initiatives. While Trade Representative Robert Zoellick is pursuing a 'positive agenda' at the organisation, the rest of the Administration and Congress are busy sabotaging it.[3] The introduction of 30 per cent steel tariffs in 2001 and the US Farm Bill which substantially increases farm subsidies are recent examples of new trade barriers erected by the Administration. The US recently backtracked on commitments made during the WTO Ministerial Meeting in Doha in 2001 on allowing developing countries to import unlicensed medicines to protect public health. These commitments were critical in obtaining developing country governments' agreement for the launch of a new round of negotiations. Such acts significantly undermine the prospect for the new round. In recent years the EU has won five cases against the US at the WTO. The US is, however, refusing to implement the WTO judgments, thus further undermining the system (Lamy 2003). On the other side of the Atlantic, France and Germany are engaged in similar tactics of pushing for WTO expansion while stonewalling on the Common Agricultural Policy (CAP). CAP subsidies amount to US$50 billion annually. If they are left unchanged until 2016, as suggested by a recent Franco-German agreement, they will further undermine the prospect of success at the current Doha Round of trade negotiations. Regressive politics (on both sides of the Atlantic) have more to do with industrial lobbying than with demands by farming communities and labour to which they are sometimes attributed.

The implicit double standard of this approach and the fact that its proponents are now in power not only in the US but also in many European counties is behind the radicalisation of activists on the other side of the trade debate. Even reformers are beginning to embrace *Isolationist* positions. The critical plank of the Isolationists argument is that it is almost impossible to make global trade work for the poor. They view trade as a Trojan Horse through which multinationals and their political

---

3   US Trade Representative Robert Zoellick is one of few multilateralists within the current US Administration. He could be described as a Supporter under our framework. As such his positions are often at odds with the general policy thrust of the Administration and the Republican majority in Congress.

representatives spread their power. The results are a loss of jobs in the North, poverty and loss of sovereignty in the South, and environmental degradation all round. What is good for the corporation is bad for everyone.

> Once upon a time, empires were built through direct conquest. Armies plundered their way across continents, claiming lands and resources for king and country, justifying their acts as 'bringing the light of civilisation to the savages of dark continents'. These days such invasion has lost its primary appeal, but the equivalent gains are routinely achieved through different, and more efficient, means, which those in power prefer to call not open theft but 'open markets'. (Mittal 2003)

Many Isolationist groups are united in the Our World is Not For Sale (OWINFS) network, which brings together such groups as Public Citizen, Focus on the Global South, Friends Of the Earth (FOE) International, and Food First. Isolationists call explicitly or implicitly for the abolition of the WTO and other international trade initiatives. As Lori Wallach of Public Citizen explained at the WSF, the goal is to 'Derail the WTO'. Ronnie Hall, Trade Program Manager at FOE, says that it is her 'personal' opinion (though not that of the organisation) that the WTO should be abolished. Kevin Danaher of Global Exchange calls himself an abolitionist (WSF 2003). Aye Aye Win of Dignity International was critical of this approach, describing the mood at the WSF in these terms:

> If you want a big cheer from the crowd, it's clear what the speakers should do: smash neo-liberalism to pieces, condemn foreign debt, demonize the enemy, the TNCs, the IFIs, and to round it off call for their abolition. A deafening applause is guaranteed. That's exactly what we are witnessing at the big conferences and seminars here. (Win 2003)

The Isolationists promote two alternatives to the current trade regime: the re-empowerment of the nation-state and the development of an alternative global regime from the bottom up. The alternative regime they call for, however, is defined in quite broad terms for the time being. Examples include *Another World is Possible: Popular Alternatives to Globalization at the World Social Forum* (Fisher and Ponniah 2003) or the new International Forum on Globalization report *Alternatives to Economic Globalization: A Better World is Possible* (IFG 2002). Following is an excerpt from the editors' synopsis of the report:

Written by a premier group of thinkers from around the world, Alternatives to Economic Globalization is the defining document of the antiglobalization movement. The culmination of a three-year project by the International Forum on Globalization, whose members include Ralph Nader, David Korten, John Cavanagh, Lori Wallach, and Jerry Mander, it presents both a sober critique of globalization as well as practical, thoughtful alternatives. The authors assert ten core requirements for democratic societies, including equality, basic human rights, local decision making, and ecological sustainability, and demonstrate how globalization undermines each. Offering specific strategies for reining in corporate domination, they address alternative systems for energy, agriculture, transportation, and manufacturing; ideas for weakening or dismantling the WTO, World Bank, and IMF; and rebuilding economies that are responsive to human needs.

The main themes of these proposals are state control over food, water and public services, localisation and subsidiarity, re-regulation and 'weakening or dismantling' of multi-lateral economic institutions, and establishment of new structures which put people before profits.

The *Reformers*, once the broadest camp, embracing not only activists but also many mainstream politicians and representatives of new industries, are in the retreat, squeezed between superpowers that would rather see no rules than any which may inhibit their freedom of action and activists who also seem to have given up on the reform/institution-building agenda at the global level. The main claim of the Reformers is that international trade can, as the theory predicts, bring broad benefits to everyone provided mechanisms and rules are put in place at regional, national and international levels to ensure optimal and equitable outcomes. Conversely the lack of such rules would not only entail deepening inequality but also may threaten globalisation as such.

The main reformist groups are represented in the Trade Justice Movement (TJM), a coalition which involves groups like Oxfam International, Action Aid, The World Development Movement (WDM) War on Want, and others. Box 4.2 illustrates the debate between reformers and isolationists. There is some overlap between the Isolationists and Reformers; they are united in their opposition to the expansion of the WTO into the new areas such as investment. However, even here Reformers see an opportunity to address outstanding issues at the WTO and other global forums while

Isolationists view it as part of a strategy to derail the WTO and return power to the nation-state.

> For the movement against corporate-driven globalization, derailing the 5th Ministerial or preventing agreement on the launching of a new comprehensive round would mean not only fighting the WTO and free trade to a standstill. It would mean creating momentum for a rollback of free trade and a reduction of the power of the WTO. This is well understood by, among others, the *Economist*, which warned its corporate readers 'globalization is reversible'. (Bello 2002)

Another plank of the Reformist framework is the incorporation of labour and environmental standards in the trade regime:

> The key issue we are addressing here is the worker's human rights, which are clearly defined, such as the right to organize and bargain, and freedom and protection from forced labor, child labor and discrimination...The problem we have had with the WTO in recent years, is that they are saying 'these issues have nothing to do with us', that workers' rights are not trade issues. (Seneviratne 2003)

Such demands are not only difficult to pursue at the WTO, but some Southern activists view them either as a way to legitimise the WTO or as another attempt to discriminate against Southern producers. Moreover, the radicalisation of the movement means that, instead of the painstaking work needed to bridge such differences, compromise is being achieved on the basis of the lowest common denominator of deglobalisation.

The polarisation of the debate and the retreat to comfortable old dogmas means that less space is available for the *Alternatives*. The Alternatives are the foot soldiers of the global justice and solidarity movement. Young and with a keen eye for popular culture and new technology they speak globalisation's language. In the tradition of the 1960s radicals, the Alternatives have a deep distrust of authority, be it political or economic. They are not likely to be found in traditional organisations and NGOs. At the WSF they did not even have the particular passes necessary to attend most of the 1,400 workshops. The Alternatives not only account for the bulk of the participants at riots, demonstrations and social forums but they are also responsible for the most creative ideas at these events: guerrilla gardening (digging up tarmac to plant trees), Marcus's mask (hiding one's face to identify with the faceless victims of global capitalism), white overalls

Box 4.2: The 'Rigged Rules and Double Standards' Debate

When Oxfam decided to discontinue its Fair Trade business on pro bono advice from management consultants McKenzie and Co., it replaced it with a two-pronged strategy. On the one hand it continued to provide technical assistance to small developing country exporters in accessing Northern markets. On the other it started an ambitious advocacy campaign on trade issues. The campaign is based at the MakeTradeFair.com website. It includes education, advocacy and lobbying. The campaign's flagship document, Oxfam's first major foray into the area of trade advocacy, met a maelstrom of criticism from the Isolationist camp.

The debate, which centred around Oxfam's 'Rigged Rules and Double Standards' report (Oxfam 2002a) began at the Second World Social Forum in Porto Alegre in 2002 between Oxfam on the one hand and a number of groups and individuals including Colin Hines, Focus on the Global South and Food First on the other. It highlights the differences between the Reformers and the Isolationists. The debate was quite animated and continued in the media and online long after the publication of Oxfam's report. By the time of the Third Forum, however, there was no debate at all, since the great majority of participants including many Oxfam people sided with the Isolationists on most points (WSF 2003).

The Oxfam report, which exemplifies Reformist thinking on the issue of trade, is centred on the proposition that international trade can be beneficial to the poor. Indeed, it argues that trade, as in the example of East Asia, has already lifted as many as 400 million people out of poverty. The problem, however, is that international trade rules today are 'rigged' for the benefit of rich countries and their corporations. Moreover, rich-country governments preach free trade to the developing countries but do not practise it themselves. Finally, even when developing countries are benefiting from trade, the benefits are skewed towards large suppliers and intermediaries at the expense of the poor as a result of inadequate policies pursued by these countries' governments and the multilateral organisations. The report proposes access for poor-country products into rich-country markets: agriculture and textiles in particular should be a major thrust of the campaign for a fairer international trade regime. The report does not promote market access as a panacea and stresses that it should be coupled with domestic policies to ensure an efficient and equitable distribution of the gains from trade. Oxfam also believes that focusing on market access is a useful strategy aimed at exposing the hypocrisy of developed-country leaders who do not practise what they preach.

> International trade can work for the poor or against the poor. Just as in any national economy, economic integration in the global economy can be a source of shared prosperity and poverty reduction, or a source of increasing inequality and exclusion. Managed well, the international trading system can lift millions out of poverty. Managed badly, it will leave whole economies even more marginalized. (Hobbes 2002)

Opponents of the report attack it on several fronts. First, they argue that market access, far from providing benefits to the poor in the South, aggravates commodity export dependency. According to this argument, underdeveloped countries get locked into a pattern of exporting low value added products to rich countries and importing expensive manufactured goods and services. Growing efficiency and productivity means that the relative value of poor country exports is constantly declining, thus condemning these countries to immiserisation in the long term no matter how much they succeed in expanding their exports (Prebisch 1950). Variations of this theory cover agricultural and natural commodity exports as well as exports of labour intensive products, a phenomenon known as the fallacy of composition (UNDP 2003).

Second, opponents of the report believe that by negotiating for market access Third World governments will be forced to make concessions in other areas. Finally, they argue that focusing on market access is a dangerous diversion from the efforts which should focus on derailing the WTO.

Box 4.3: The Fair Trade Movement

In the aftermath of the Second World War some church organisations marketed handicrafts made by refugees as a way of helping them gain economic independence. Many fair trade groups trace the beginnings of the movement to that period. Alternative Trade Organisations (ATO) spread in the 1960s to market handicrafts and agricultural commodities purchased in the Third World at 'fair' prices.

The ATOs' main argument is that many poor country producers and especially small farmers and cooperatives are not getting a fair price for their products due to the difficulties they face in gaining access to rich-country markets and to finance. The big difference between the retail price in the developed world and the income that these producers receive for the fruits of their labour is, ATOs argue, unfairly appropriated by various intermediaries in both rich and poor countries.

ATOs set out to correct this imbalance by direct trading: purchasing products at higher prices and selling them in rich-country markets, thus circumventing the traditional distribution channels. Many of these organisations combine direct trading with the provision of technical assistance to their suppliers in everything from management to production techniques and market access. They also campaign on all matters related to fair trade. As such ATOs are a unique hybrid of for-profit organisations and NGOs.

Oxfam was a pioneer of fair trade in the UK in the 1960s. In the US the first ATOs included 10,000 villages and Equal Exchange. Many ATOs are based in Third World countries working to protect the rights of disadvantaged producers.

With the growth of the fair trade movement and increased awareness of the issues involved, especially among rich-country consumers in the 1980s and 1990s, many of the twentieth-century fair trade groups began to coordinate efforts across borders and work towards establishing common and certifiable fair trade standards. In 1989 the International Federation of Alternative Trade (IFAT) was established, which claims to represent 160 groups in 50 countries of which two-thirds are based in the Third World. The various local groups also coalesced into national organisations which in turn established the Fairtrade Labelling Organization International (FLO) in 1997.

- The FLO is an umbrella organisation which issues the 'Fairtrade' label to qualifying products based on a set of standards applied to both producers and traders. Compliance is monitored by a network of inspectors and an auditing process. There are different sets of requirements for traders and producers. Traders must:
- pay a price to producers that covers the costs of sustainable production and living;
- pay a premium that producers can invest in development;
- partially pay in advance when producers ask for it;
- sign contracts that allow for long-term planning and sustainable production practices. (http://www.fairtrade.net.)

For producers, the requirements are different for small holders and cooperatives and for organisations dependent on hired labour. There are minimum progress requirements and specific standards for the various products. The requirements cover social, economic, organisational, labour and environmental issues.

Most products covered by FLO are food commodities such as coffee, sugar and cocoa; but the organisation is beginning to address manufactured products starting with footballs. The member organisations cover a much wider selection of products.

Coffee is one of the main fair trade commodities and shows both the success and limitations of the movement. Despite rapid growth since 1973, when the first batch of fair trade coffee was imported into the Netherlands, it accounts for only 2 per cent of the total coffee market (Oxfam 2002b). Even some of its most avid proponents admit that fair trade coffee can be targeted only at the top end of the market. Moreover, by paying a premium price the fair traders may be sending the wrong signal to a market which is already suffering from excess supply. On the other hand, fair trade buyers are lending a helping hand to some of the most disadvantaged communities in the world in a context where little effort is being made by national governments or multilateral organisations to address the issue of over-supply and the need to shift to other crops. Finally, the example of the fair trade movement is creating an incentive for large coffee buyers to address the issues at hand.

(heavily padded protesters who can withstand police truncheons), critical mass (cyclists who obstruct automobile traffic by riding in large numbers), the pink march (which succeeded in penetrating the heavily fortified World Bank/IMF meeting venue in Prague by looking unthreatening) and the controversial black block (anarchists who do not shy away from using stones and occasionally fire-bombs to attack riot police).

The Alternatives are also the driving force behind 'submerged networks' which surface around certain campaigns, such as SaIAMI, which organised the riots against the Summit of the Americas in Quebec in 2001. SaIAMI is a direct action network. Its first activities coincided with the Multilateral Agreement on Investments. It is also known for its non-violent blockade of the Montreal Conference on Economic Globalisation in May 1998.

Other submerged networks exercise resistance through the promotion of a particular lifestyle such as the Fair Trade movement (Box 4.3). The network in this case comprises of consumers who choose to pay premium prices for fair trade products (or boycott those viewed to be in violation of ethical trade norms) in addition to those who are involved in organising Fair Trade schemes.

Instead of aiming to transform or reform global capitalism, the Alternatives are concerned with reclaiming 'things' from the encroaching market and creating space for alternatives. They are concerned with the political and cultural consequences of capitalism as much as with its economic and environmental costs. They perceive the encroachment of the market into the public space as a threat to freedom, which takes the form of 'corporate censorship' in the North and human rights abuses in the South (Desai and Said 2001).

Alternatives do not represent a distinct set of positions on the issues of trade. They could thus be viewed as a particular form of global civil society, rather than a particular take on globalisation. That said, in a debate where one is expected to take sides between Western governments and corporations on the one hand and Third World leaders and industries on the other, the Alternatives have no favourite. This may explain why some of them felt so uncomfortable with certain aspects of the World Social Forum in Porto Alegre.

> For some, the hijacking of the World Social Forum by political parties and powerful men is proof that the movements against corporate globalization are finally maturing and 'getting serious'. But is it really so mature, amidst the graveyard of failed left political projects, to

believe that change will come by casting your ballot for the latest charismatic leader, then crossing your fingers and hoping for the best? Get serious. (Klein 2003)

In the following sections we address issues which illustrate the civil society position on trade described above.

The World Trade Organization (WTO)

The WTO is at the heart of most civil society campaigns on trade issues. Established in 1995, it is one of the youngest multilateral organisations. It is simultaneously one of the smallest in terms of staff and bureaucracy yet one of the most influential in terms of impact on peoples' lives worldwide.

For its staunchest opponents, the WTO embodies everything that is wrong with global capitalism and superpower hegemony: a one-size-fits-all tool aimed at prising open Third World markets for the benefit of rich-country-based corporations. One of the organisation's most loathed features is the finality of its mandate: once a market is open it cannot be closed again.

For its proponents, the WTO is the most democratic of the multilateral organisations, including the UN. It is, they argue, the only place where Costa Rica can lodge a complaint against the US and win, as was the case with underwear import restrictions (WTO Appellate Body 1997). WTO proponents view the irrevocable nature of market opening as a strength, imparting certainty to global markets by removing the threat of ad hoc government intervention.

The debate about the WTO focuses on two main issues: governance and mandate.

Governance

On governance, the WTO's opponents argue that, despite the 'one nation, one vote' and consensus systems, the so-called Quad countries (US, EU, Canada and Japan) and their corporations dominate the WTO agenda:

- The so called 'Green Room' negotiations involving the Quad countries and a selected group of others are where consensus is forged in secret, with the remaining countries left to join the consensus.
- Mini-Ministerials are often organised involving the Quad countries and a selected list of invitees. These meetings are unofficial and are therefore unreported.

- The Quad countries use their political and economic muscle to force concessions from Third World leaders. This was the case with the US using the 'war on terrorism' rhetoric at the Doha Fourth Ministerial meeting in November 2001 (TWN, http://www.twnside.org.sg).
- The negotiations are packaged in rounds: bundles of issues specifically for the purpose of horse-trading between the various issues. Some activists argue that this makes for further pressure on poorer nations (WDN, http://www.wdm.org.uk).
- The influence of corporations and the coordination between Quad governments and multinationals is seen by many, including the WTO's new director Dr Supachai, as problematic (WDM, http://www.wdm.org.uk).
- The WTO has built-in mechanisms which are aimed at rendering the process of market liberalisation irreversible. Once agreement is reached there is very little room for individual countries to revisit certain issues or reinstate barriers, regardless of circumstances. Even existing exemptions, on grounds of health and safety for example, are quite difficult to exercise, as was revealed during the dispute over generic AIDS drugs.
- The WTO's dispute-settlement mechanism, which adjudicates on violations of signed agreements, is specifically designed as an enforcement rather than an arbitration mechanism. The panel's decisions can be reversed only by consensus, rendering them virtually impossible to appeal. However, even detractors of the system admit that it is the right mechanism if the goal is the promotion of market liberalisation (US Senate Finance Committee 2000).

There are other, more prosaic reasons why Third World leaders cannot exercise their full rights within the WTO. Many cannot afford having a full-time representative in Geneva. Some lack the qualified staff and the resources to field representatives to several simultaneous meetings.

WTO proponents concede some of these charges and call for increased 'technical assistance and capacity building [for developing country governments] to be better equipped to participate in the multilateral trading system'. The WTO head considers this one of 'four pillars' which would help successfully conclude the current round of WTO negotiations

(Panitchpakdi 2002). Other shortcomings are attributed to the imbalances in the inter-state system rather than the organisation itself.

Developing-country governments, especially India, Brazil and South Africa, are displaying ever more skill in using WTO mechanisms to defend their interests. There are several Third World blocs within the organisation aimed at pooling resources and coordinating negotiating positions, including the thirty-country-strong African Bloc, the Like-Minded Group which includes almost all Third World countries, and the Cairns Group which includes both poor and rich agricultural commodity exporters. Third World governments are leveraging divisions in the Quad group as well as support and pressure from civil society to pursue their goals (see below). The Doha Fourth Ministerial (the first after the failed meeting in Seattle) was a demonstration of this new-found confidence, although it resulted in only limited achievements for developing countries in the shape of a commitment to address the issues deemed critical by these countries before embarking on a new round of negotiations at the upcoming Fifth Ministerial in Cancun. Although no progress has been made so far on any of these issues, governments and activists both seem to have identified elements in WTO procedure from which they can attack the organisation:

> If derailing the drive for free trade at the 5th Ministerial is indeed the goal, then the main tactical focus of the strategy becomes clear: Consensus decision-making is the Achilles heel of the WTO, and it is the emergence of consensus that we must prevent at all costs from emerging. (Bello 2002)

Mandate

Campaigns around the Agreement on Agriculture (AoA), the General Agreement on Trade in Services (GATS), Trade-Related Aspects of Intellectual Property Rights (TRIPS), and the new areas of investment, government procurement, trade facilitation and competition policy provide an illustration of the ongoing debate over the WTO's mandate.

According to activists, by limiting the nation-states 'policy space' the WTO denies developing countries essential tools of development. These countries claim to need preferential treatment to be able to catch up, while the WTO rules are not even equal. Trade in sectors where developing countries are most competitive – agriculture and textiles in particular – is not being liberalised by the rich. At the same time, developed countries press for liberalisation in sectors where trade mostly flows from North to

South, such as intellectual property, services and investment. The WTO also limits governments' freedom to protect small producers, to the benefit of large multinationals which are also predominantly based in the North. The activists use data showing poor countries losing anything from $100 billion to $300 billion a year due to imbalances in the global trade regime (Oxfam 2002a).

WTO defenders argue in response that, if developed countries are dragging out liberalisation in certain markets like agriculture and textiles, it is their consumers who will be the primary losers from such protectionism. They point out that discretionary policy tools such as import substitution and the promotion of infant industries, which were used by many developing countries under GATT, at best were ineffective and at worst promoted patronage and corruption. The main rejoinder from WTO proponents, however, is that the question is not whether the poor are losing out under the current trade regime but whether they would be losing more without the WTO (Bello and Legrain 2000–1). The debate over the impact of the WTO on development is ongoing and has fuelled demands to conduct an economic impact assessment before any further trade negotiations rounds are launched (Martin Khor speaking at WSF 2003).

The Fourth Doha Ministerial Meeting of the WTO in 2001 launched a new round of negotiations, dubbed the Doha Development Round, to replace the Millennium Round, which failed to materialise at the Seattle 1999 Ministerial. Doha is a compromise whereby developing countries agree to the expansion of the WTO mandate into new areas in exchange for redress of their concern over issues from previous rounds.

Outstanding Issues

Agreement on Agriculture

Developing countries are demanding the elimination of agricultural subsidies by developed countries, including the US$50 billion dispensed annually by the EU Common Agricultural Policy (CAP). They are specifically concerned with export subsidies which have direct bearing on their domestic markets as well as tariffs which prevent access for their products. The US supports this approach (in words if not in deeds, in view of the recent adoption of the Farm Bill) and is proposing across-the-board reductions in its own tariffs and subsidies. The EU, however, is baulking at compromise due especially to resistance from France. Recent agreement between the German and French governments to postpone any changes to CAP until

2016 has been met with indignation across the board. The deadline set at Doha for reaching an agreement on these issues was missed.

Isolationists dismiss the AoA and demand that agriculture and food in particular be taken out of the WTO remit. According to the isolationists, free trade in agriculture inevitably leads to the promotion of export crops at the expense of subsistence agriculture, which amounts to discrimination against small farmers and leads to environmental degradation and hunger (OWINFS, http://www.ourworldisnotforsale.org; Food First, http://www.foodfirst.org). Reformers are campaigning for the elimination of developed-country subsidies and other barriers while allowing developing countries some leeway to ensure food security and the protection for small farmers and indigenous people (see below).

Implementation

Rich countries which were supposed to eliminate tariffs and quotas on textiles over ten years by 2005 have left most of them in place until the last minute. Developing countries are demanding that the rich start reducing tariffs in this area immediately. The US, as part of its 'positive engagement' policy, is proposing drastic reductions not only in textiles but in industrial tariffs across the board. The deadline for reaching agreement on implementation issues has not been met. Reformers support the developing country position in this respect. The Isolationists dismiss this approach as a gimmick designed to allow the developed countries to present their fulfilment of their long-standing obligations as a concession and give the Reformers a sense of achievement (Bello 2002).

Special and Deferential Treatment

The WTO offers a number of avenues to take special consideration of the development needs of its poorer members. Those include longer implementation periods and technical assistance both during negotiations and at the implementation stage. Agreements usually have mechanisms whereby developing countries can negotiate certain exceptions to satisfy their policies. The developing countries are demanding more flexibility in designing policies which they deem essential for development. The US and the EU are willing to consider such flexibility provided developing countries agree on 'graduation' criteria (Korea, an OECD member, is still benefiting from developing-country exceptions). No agreement was reached on these issues within the deadline set at Doha.

Both Isolationists and Reformers agree that developing countries should be allowed freedom in choosing development strategies and certain forms of protectionism which were employed successfully by developed countries, including late developers in East Asia (Oxfam 2002a).

Trade Related Aspects of Intellectual Property Rights (TRIPS) and Public Health

One of the few tangible achievements of the Doha meeting for developing countries was the agreement in the final declaration 'that it is important to implement and interpret the TRIPS Agreement in a way that supports public health – by promoting both access to existing medicines and the creation of new medicines'. This is done either by allowing countries to manufacture needed drugs without having to obtain a licence (compulsory licensing) or by importing generic unlicensed drugs from third countries (parallel importing) (WTO 2001). Negotiations were supposed to take place to clarify the modalities for making use of this exception especially by countries that did not have their own pharmaceutical industry. The negotiations broke down when the US backtracked on the principles agreed at Doha and sought to limit the number of diseases to which the exception would apply. Pharmaceutical companies that are behind the US trade representative's change of heart claim, not without some justification, that a blanket exception could be open to abuse by manufacturers of generic drugs, including those based in South Africa and India (Alfeld and Hofheinz 2003). The deadline was missed in this case as well. Activists of all persuasions have no love for TRIPS, especially when it comes to medicine.

New Areas

While there are disagreements among activists on the outstanding issues, there is an almost unanimous rejection of proposals for WTO expansion into new areas. Apart from previously mentioned strategies of reforming or abolishing the WTO, opposition to expansion is based on the activists notion of the market limits and the optimal level of policy space which should reside at the nation-state level.

Market limits are based on an understanding of what is tradable. Can public goods be left to the market or should they remain fully under state control? Should these goods, in principle, also be tradable internationally? Even if there is no principled objection to either, should they be subject to international trade under the present system?

The tradability of utilities and public services is a thorny issue since these usually include social costs and benefits which are not reflected in their market value. Markets for such services have therefore a higher risk of failure, the consequences of which can be more devastating than in other sectors of the economy. A collapsing health-care system is more dangerous than a collapsing automotive industry.

Beyond the issue of market failures and externalities, however, public services and utilities tend to have emotional, cultural and political dimensions which sit uneasily with market relations, let alone foreign control. 'Services are the public tangible manifestation and expression of our shared values as citizens. How we choose to heal our sick, teach our kids, protect our water, connect to one another through transport and communication are expressions of our collective vision for society' (Klein 2000). 'Water', as a banner in Porto Alegre exclaimed, 'is Life. It cannot be bought and sold' (WSF 2003). Finally, poor countries and poor people depend on the free or nearly free provision of these services for their survival, much more than their more fortunate counterparts.

One of the main complaints about the WTO compared with its predecessor, the GATT, is its impact on domestic *policy space* – an issue which arises from its targeting of non-tariff barriers. Environmental and safety regulations and other domestic policies have often been successfully contested through the WTO as trade-restricting. The famous image of protesters dressed in turtle suits in Seattle is related to one example of the WTO reaching into environmental regulations. The activists were protesting a WTO ruling in favour of Asian shrimp exporters who successfully contested a US environmental regulation which prohibits the import of shrimp farmed in ways which harm sea turtles (WTO 1998). There are many other examples of such rulings, including the well-known case when Europe was penalised for banning the import of US hormone-treated beef (WTO 1997).

The expansion of the WTO remit into new areas of services, investment, government procurement competition policy, and trade facilitation will further limit the scope of domestic policy. This is one of the main reasons why many in the Third World view the WTO as a new form of colonialism (Romapu 2003). The New Areas are at the heart of most WTO campaigns. These are not strictly trade issues, but any coverage of the WTO that did not address these issues would be incomplete. The discussion of the Multilateral Investment Framework also provides an update on the Multilateral Agreement on Investment campaign covered in Chapter 3 in this book.

The Multilateral Investment Framework (MIF)

Objections to the MIF are not dissimilar to those raised against its defeated predecessor, the Multilateral Agreement on Investment (MAI; Desai and Said 2001). It reduces government's regulatory discretion and grants foreign investors unprecedented legal rights. Activists question the agreement's capacity to increase foreign direct investment. Some even question the link between investment and development (TWN, http://www.twnside.org.sg). Activists would like to see an agreement which improved regulatory control over multinationals, but believe that such an agreement is unlikely to emerge within the WTO framework. The agreement, according to its detractors, would establish a false equality between the developed and the underdeveloped, which is inconsistent with affirmative action principles. Finally, unlike trade, investment flows only from North to South, which means that the agreement will largely benefit the developed countries and their corporations.

A workshop on the 'WTO Investment Issue' was organised in Geneva on 18–21 March 2003 by the Third World Network, Oxfam International, WWF, Public Services International, Center for International Environmental Law and Institute for Agriculture and Trade Policy. The workshop issued a statement signed by fifty groups calling on governments to drop investment from the agenda for the upcoming WTO ministerial in Cancun (Khor and Yen 2003).

The defenders of the MIF argue that the agreement will not necessarily restrict regulatory space but make it more transparent. Rules and transparency will promote investment and lead to development (WTO, http://www.wto.org).

General Agreement on Trade in Services (GATS)

The GATS has been in effect since the establishment of the WTO in 1995. It is a rolling agreement which aims to open up ever more areas of services, a market estimated at US$5 trillion, to WTO rules. GATS in theory should cover 'everything that you cannot drop on your foot' (WDM 2002) with the exception of services associated with the direct exercise of government. This exception is, however, circumscribed by the proviso that these services are not offered on a commercial basis.[4] As Susan George (2003b) puts it in *Red Pepper*, 'All human activities are to become, in the fullness of time, profit-oriented commodities that can be invested in and traded'.

---

4 For example, a government's right to exclude government-owned postal services from the GATS remit is limited if those services are provided on a commercial basis.

Its proponents argue that GATS covers only sectors which governments agree to include; moreover, governments are entitled to place exemptions on sectors which they offer for opening. For example, India has opened its tourism sector but maintained certain restrictions including the requirement that foreign operators act through local subsidiaries. Malaysia opened up its insurance sectors but maintained a 51 per cent limit on foreign ownership (Lal Das 2003).

GATS is currently undergoing a request-offer round which was supposed to end in April 2003. Countries are exchanging lists of sectors which they want included in GATS. There are also demands to lift previously established restrictions such as the ones listed above. Once a country offers the opening of a sector or a lifting of restrictions to any WTO member, it is obliged to open it to all under most favoured nations (MFN) rules.

Unlike goods, services can cross borders in a variety of ways. GATS also covers four modes of delivery of services:

1. cross-border supply, such as banking via wire transfer;
2. consumption abroad, for example studying in a foreign country;
3. commercial presence, for example the establishment of a hotel as part of an international chain; and
4. presence of natural persons such as a construction crew travelling to another country to participate in a project.

Of most interest to many developing countries is Mode 4, which covers provision of services through the movement of physical persons. Developed countries have, however, diluted the potential of Mode 4 by invoking exceptions on grounds of security. Mode 3, on the other hand, is more interesting for developed countries. It covers the provision of services through movement of legal persons and could offer a back-door introduction of the MIF.

The sectors most targeted for inclusion into GATS or further liberalisation are utilities, transport, tourism and financial services. Thanks to an energetic bipartisan (reformist-isolationist) campaign against it, GATS expansion does not seem to be justifying the activists' worst fears. To judge from the sectors offered for opening by the EU, health, education and water will remain outside reach of GATS as far as Europe is concerned (OWINFS, http://www.ourworldisnotforsale.org).

Bypassing the WTO: From NAFTA to FTAA

Corporations and the neo-conservatives who serve them are not waiting for the WTO to pursue the opening of new markets. There is a cascade of multilateral, regional and bilateral arrangements through which liberalisation is being pursued in ways which are more radical than ever envisaged under the WTO.

While the GATS negotiators debate whether trade in water itself should be liberalised or whether it is 'environmental services' such as water treatment and supply which should be opened to competition, the World Bank has already succeeded in privatising water and utilities in several Third World countries. Trade officials who reject linking the liberalisation of services with privatisation of health and education (WTO, http://www.wto.org.) have been pre-empted with the introduction of fees for education and health care under the Bank's conditionality, a process which is correctly viewed as a first step towards privatisation.

The FTAA includes radical versions of GATS and the other new agreements on investment and government procurement.

> Our objective with FTAA is to guarantee North American companies the control of a territory that goes from the Arctic Pole all the way to Antarctica, free access to the whole hemisphere without difficulties or obstacles for our products, services, technology, and capital. (US Secretary of State Colin Powell, quoted in Mittal 2003)

Finally, bilateral treaties such as the one between the US and Chile or British Petroleum (BP) and Turkey go even further than the FTAA in placing multinational corporations above the law. These treaties lack even the few monitoring and control mechanisms that are available in a multilateral framework like the WTO. For example, the agreement between the Turkish government and the Baku-Tbilisi-Ceyhan Pipeline Consortium led by BP exempts the pipeline from obligations under any current or future Turkish law that may threaten the project's profits, including environmental, social and human rights legislation. The only Turkish law not superseded by the agreement is the Constitution (Baku Ceyhan Campaign 2002).

Negotiations for the establishment of FTAA were launched at the first Summit of the Americas in 1994. It was then conceived as a trade alliance encompassing all 'democratic' states in the hemisphere, that is, excluding Cuba. The FTAA seeks to expand to the entire continent the model of the North American Free Trade Agreement (NAFTA), which brought together the US, Canada and Mexico in 1993. The FTAA is seeking a mandate almost identical to that of the WTO, including the new areas of government procurement, competition policy, trade facilitation, and investment. FTAA by design is meant to 'improve upon these [WTO] rules and disciplines wherever possible and appropriate' (FTAA, http://www.ftaa-alca.org). FTAA, like NAFTA but unlike the WTO, is likely to incorporate some labour and environmental provisions.

> Essentially, what the FTAA negotiators have done, urged on by the big business community in every country, is to take the most ambitious elements of every global trade and investment agreement – existing or proposed – and put them all together in this openly ambitious hemispheric pact. (Barlow 2001)

Like the WTO Doha Round, FTAA negotiations are supposed to be completed by 2005. Like the WTO, they have been bogged down in the face of fierce resistance by civil society and, to a lesser degree, governments in most Latin American countries. Like the WTO, the FTAA requires consensus to be approved, which is inspiring optimism among its opponents about its chances of success.

The FTAA seems to attract more vociferous opposition and from a broader set of actors than the WTO. Few of the treaty's opponents seek to improve it, focusing instead on preventing it from ever coming into force. One reason may be the NAFTA track record and the damage attributed to the treaty in the US and Canada but especially in Mexico. Unlike the WTO, NAFTA is directly associated by its opponents with the loss of manufacturing jobs in the US and Canada and the devastation to small-scale agriculture and indigenous livelihoods in Mexico. Global Exchange attributes the loss of 766,000 jobs in the US to NAFTA (Global Exchange NAFTA FAQ, http://www.globalexchange.org/ftaa/faq.html) while Food First claims that 600 Mexican farmers are forced off their lands every day due to the treaty (Mittal 2003; see also Chapter 8). Moreover the maquiladora jobs[5] created by NAFTA along the US-Mexico border are notoriously unstable and underpaid. Flagrant labour and environmental abuses are attributed to the operators of factories established specifically to service the US and Canadian markets. Environmental degradation along the US-Mexico borders attributed to NAFTA has

---

5   'Maquiladora': these are foreign-owned factories in Mexico that import components and assemble them for export. Jobs created in such factories were supposed to stop migrant labour from leaving Mexico and moving into the US.

prompted the establishment of 'Border XXI', a binational border environmental plan to address air and water problems (US Trade Representative, http://www.ustr.gov/regions/whemisphere/ftaa.shtml). Another explanation for the vociferous opposition to the FTAA is fear of being overwhelmed by the USA. More than any of the other regional and international alliances, the FTAA will be dominated by the USA, which accounts for 75 per cent of the hemisphere's GDP.

The campaign against the FTAA has evolved since 1997 into the focal point of anti-capitalist and, over the past year, anti-war activities in the hemisphere. Hundreds of groups have joined forces in myriad activities, predominantly trades unions in the US and Canada and peasants organisations in Latin America. The organisation which best represents the movement is the Hemispheric Social Alliance (HSA). A network of networks, the HSA involves multi-sectoral national and regional networks such as the Common Frontiers (Canada), the Quebec Network on Hemispheric Integration, the Alliance for Responsible Trade (United States), the Mexican Action Network on Free Trade, the Chilean Alliance for Just and Responsible Trade, and the Brazilian Network for Peoples Integration. It also involves sectoral networks such as the hemispheric coordinators of the labour sector (ORIT) and the peasant sector (CLOC). The HSA claims to unite groups representing more than 45 million members.

The HSA organised among others the first Peoples' Summit in Santiago, Chile, in April 1998 parallel to the second official Summit of heads of state of the Americas. It has been a visible presence in almost every major activity targeted at NAFTA/FTAA and the WTO in the Americas. The HSA elaborates and updates its own alternative agenda to the FTAA in *Alternatives for the Americas*. The latest version of the document was drafted in December 2002. *Alternatives for the Americas* covers topics on the official agenda, such as investment, finance, intellectual property rights, agriculture, market access, services and dispute resolution. It also addresses issues of human rights, sustainability, environment, labour, immigration, the role of the state, and gender, which are either ignored or addressed inadequately at the negotiations. The main guiding principle of the document is set out in these terms:

> Trade and investment should not be ends in themselves, but rather the instruments for achieving just and sustainable development. Citizens must have the right to participate in the formulation, implementation, and evaluation of hemispheric social and economic policies. Central

goals of these policies should be to promote economic sovereignty, social welfare, and reduced inequality at all levels. (HSA 2002)

Strategy

Most civil society groups involved in trade issues pursue a mix of strategies in varying proportions. Most seek to multiply their impact by being involved in overlapping regional, thematic and international networks.

Inform and Educate

The movement on trade issues has developed by leaps and bounds since Seattle. The various groups have almost real-time access to the minutiae of trade negotiations: secret or public, within the WTO or the other treaties. Secret documents are regularly leaked by sympathetic government negotiators and trade bureaucrats. Information is extracted skilfully through parliaments and freedom of information tools. One recent leak in this context is an EU document listing the services which the EU would request for opening under GATS from various countries (WDM, http://www.wdm.org.uk).

Groups have their own experienced cadre of trade experts and lawyers. They also draw on resources from academia, the civil service, and international organisations, especially the UN. They provide almost real-time analysis of the available information, evaluate negotiating positions and scenarios, and recommend countermeasures.

Outcomes are passed on to the public, parliaments and friendly negotiators in digestible, actionable, and campaignable form through websites such as Global Trade Watch (Public Citizen), Trade Observatory (Institute for Agriculture and Trade Policy), The Third World Network Information Service on the WTO and MakeTradeFree.com (Oxfam).

Special tools and information packages are produced for the various audiences including briefs, step-by-step talking points, frequently asked question lists and guides for MPs, their constituents, trade negotiators and government officials. Some groups produce and commission in-depth research papers, reports and monographs and conduct workshops for activist policymakers and experts, and organise speaking tours.

Lobby

Groups target multiple levels in their lobbying including parliament, government, negotiators and international organisations. Groups have become adept at using fissures among the various establishment actors: MPs, trade officials in the capitals, trade negotiators, ambassadors and WTO employees. Activists are also quick to exploit tensions between the various actors: EU, US, Japan, Like Minded Group and Cairns Group.

Movement–Third World Government Cooperation

There are numerous examples of cooperation between NGOs, think tanks and UN agencies on the one hand and Southern governments on the other. Cooperation includes designing both negotiating strategies and domestic policies aimed at maximising benefits or reducing adverse effects of trade liberalisation, and improving the bargaining position of the South at the WTO.

One organisation active in this field is Martin Khor's Third World Network (TWN). An example of TWN's projects is the Asia Pacific regional consultation which was organised in Colombo, Sri Lanka, on 17–19 April 2003. The consultation dedicated to the WTO/TRIPS Agreement and Access to Medicines was attended by about seventy government officials, health-related NGO representatives, health professionals, and international trade and intellectual property rights experts. It was organised jointly by the Health Action International-Asia Pacific, Sri Lanka Ministry of Health, and the World Health Organization (South East Asia Regional Office). The main conclusion of the meeting was that TRIPS, despite its adverse impact, does provide flexibilities for governments to safeguard public health. Governments were advised on policies to utilise these flexibilities based on, among other things, the experience of the North.

TWN closely monitors WTO developments and issues regular research and strategy papers for the benefit of Southern delegations and NGOs. Most recently it issued a guide to Southern countries' delegations on handling GATS negotiations (Lal Das 2003). The guide author, Lal Das, is a former Indian representative at GATT.

The Southern and Eastern African Trade Negotiations Institute (SEATINI) is another organisation providing support to Southern governments at the WTO, with a specific focus on Africa. SEATINI is 'dedicated to strengthen Africa's capacity to take a more effective part in the emerging global trading system and to better manage the process of Globalization'. It is an affiliate of the International Southern Group Network (ISGN). It draws on academic, NGO, legal and trade negotiations resources from governments, UN agencies, academia and the WTO itself. SEATINI organises regular meetings and advises African policymakers on negotiating positions and trade policies. It conducts research on trade-related issues and runs an Advisory Clinic which provides ad hoc online assistance to African trade negotiators (SEATINI, http://www.seatini.org.).

Conclusions

The anti-capitalist movement has racked up some impressive advances over the past four years. No longer a ragtag army of romantic activists, the movement has evolved into a well-informed and organised political force to be reckoned with. It has chalked up impressive victories, reversing some privatisation and liberalisation policies in Latin America and restraining the fervour of free traders in Europe. Most importantly, it dealt a severe blow to its main target: the Washington consensus.

The movement may yet fall victim to its own success. Its meteoric rise has attracted some nasty fellow-travellers in the guise of nationalist leaders, Third World multinationals and old left gurus. They are threatening to hijack the movement and blot out its most attractive features – openness, cosmopolitanism, informality and popular appeal.

The movement is also at risk of falling into the old trap of investing too much stock in the ability of great national leaders to deliver the goods of justice and equality. Historically these leaders did not justify this trust. They turned into tyrants, or sold out, or provided convenient targets for the forces of global capitalism.

While boosting the positions of Southern leaders and multinationals may contribute to levelling the global economic playing field, these actors are no more committed to global justice than their opponents. Indian and South African pharmaceutical companies produce generic drugs for profit and not out of concern for those dying of AIDS and malaria. More ominously, however, the exclusivist nationalism which comes with some of the newly found allies is threatening to contaminate the movement: 'The Forum's place as a focus for what I would call the new global solidarity is being put in question by those who seek to not only give it national but nationalist character' (Waterman 2003).

A catastrophic success scenario may materialise if the nationalists succeed in using the movement to 'derail the WTO'. At a time when multilateralism is under siege, destroying the only international organisation which has the potential to hold superpower(s) to account is not what one would expect from a global justice and solidarity movement.

Dismantling the WTO won't solve the problems of injustice in the global trading system. Quite the opposite: it may lead to an even less equitable and more hegemonic globalisation. It will hand an easy victory to the movement's worst enemies: unilateralist neo-conservatives, rusty old industries, and politicians who are trying to go back in time. Without the constraints of the WTO they will be free to muscle their way into any market through bilateral and regional agreements like the much maligned NAFTA. It will be a pyrrhic victory like the one chalked up by the music industry when it shut down Napster, only to push music swapping into distributed networks with no single reference point.

Global justice needs global solutions which national leaders, no matter how enlightened, cannot deliver. Present tensions between the negotiators of North and South on how to safeguard the environment and protect labour without jeopardising development will be swept aside. If the painstaking work needed to build a just global trade system is abandoned as futile, unity can be based only on a lowest common denominator agenda of deglobalisation. The progressive answer to one-size-fits all, elitist institutions which serve corporate interests is democratic multilateral institutions that serve the causes of development and equity, in addition to a robust movement that holds governments, businesses and international organisations to account. Given the sophistication of the tools at the movement's disposal and its growing political clout, it is no longer sufficient for it be engaged in a purely negative purpose. Drawing up utopian plans to return to the anti-colonial state or, further back, to the state of nature does not amount to building an alternative future.

The movement has matured to the point where it has both the ability and the obligation to get down to the painstaking business of institution (re)building. Fixing GATS or the MIF so that they put people before profits, hold the rich and powerful to account, and protect nature is neither easy nor glamorous but it has to be done.

Delivering an hour-long litany of worn conspiracy theories at the end of the World Social Forum, Noam Chomsky almost managed the incredible feat of putting a full stadium of jubilant young people to sleep. Mercifully, he was followed by his exact opposite: Arundhati Roy was quiet, powerful, cryptic and accessible. She spoke of the twin evils of liberalisation and nationalism. She called on activists to lay siege to the empire, mocking it with their culture and joy instead of confrontation. By the end of the speech the crowd was ecstatic. Despite its young age this is a sophisticated movement, which we hope will not be content with tired old slogans and idols. Activists are seeking sophisticated answers to the issues of globalisation. They should be prepared to do the hard work necessary to find them.

References

Editor's note: URLs were correct at the time of first publishing but may no longer be correct.

Alfeld, Haiko and Hofheinz, Paul (2003). 'End the Squabble'. *Wall Street Journal*, 14 March.
Amin, Samir (2003). 'Confronting the Empire'. Contribution to WSF. 22–7 January http://www.forumsocialmundial.org.br/dinamic.asp?pagina=conf_samir_amin_ing.
Baku Ceyhan Campaign (2002). 'Oil Companies Colonise Turkey: MAI by the Back Door?' Press Release. 30 August.
Barlow, Maude (2001). 'The FTAA and the Threat to Social Programs, Environmental Sustainability and Social Justice in Canada and the Americas' http//www.stopftaa.org.
Bello, Walden (2002). *The Oxfam Debate: From Controversy to Common Strategy.* http//www.maketradefair.com.
Bello, Walden and Legrain, P. (2000–1). 'Should the WTO be Abolished?'. *The Ecologist*, 30/9.
Caldwell, Christopher (2003). 'Free Trade is Running Out of Time'. *Financial Times*, 1 April.
Cockroft, James (2003). 'Report on Porto Alegre 2003', 25 March. http://www.forumsocialmundial.org.br/ dinamic.asp?pagina=bal_cockcroft_ing.
Desai, Meghnad (2002). *Marx's Revenge: The Resurgence of Capitalism and the Death of Statist Socialism.* London, New York: Verso.
Desai, Meghnad and Said, Yahia (2001). 'The New Anti-Capitalist Movement: Money and Global Civil Society'. In Helmut Anheier, Marlies Glasius, and Mary Kaldor (eds), *Global Civil Society 2001*. Oxford: Oxford University Press.
Fisher, William F. and Thomas Ponniah (eds) (2003). *Another World is Possible: Alternatives to Globalization at the World Social Forum.* Basingstoke: Palgrave Macmillan.
FLO (Fairtrade Labelling Organization International) http://www.fairtrade.net.
Food First http://www.foodfirst.org.
FTAA (Free Trade Area of the Americas) http://www.ftaa-alca.org.
George, Susan (2003a). 'Corporations Domain and Crisis in the International Financial System'. Contribution to WSF. 22–27 January. http://www.forumsocialmundial.org.br/dinamic.asp?pagina=conf_susan_george_in.
George, Susan (2003b). 'How GATS Could Affect Your Life'. *Red Pepper*. January.
Global Exchange. NAFTA FAQ http://www.globalexchange.org/ftaa/faq.html.
Hines, Colin (2000). *Localization: A Global Manifesto.* London: Earthscan.
Hobbes, Jeremy (2002). Speech at WTO Symposium. April.
HSA (Hemispheric Social Alliance) (2002). *Alternative for the Americas.* Ottawa: HSA.
IFG (International Forum on Globalization) (2002). *Alternatives to Economic Globalization: A Better World is Possible.* San Francisco: Berrett-Koehler.
Khor, Martin and Yen, Goh Chien (2003). 'NGOs Call on Governments to Drop Investment Issues at WTO Cancun Meeting'. *TWN Information Service on WTO Issues*. March.
Klein, Naomi (2000). Speech at WDM's GATS campaign launch, November. http://www.wmd.org.uk.
Klein, Naomi (2003). 'Cut the Strings'. *The Guardian*, 1 February.
Lal Das, Bhagirath (2003). 'Services Negotiations in the WTO: Requests And Offers'. *TWN Information Service on WTO Issues*, 25 February.
Lamy, Pascal (2003). 'Come on America, Play by the Rules!'. *Wall Street Journal*, 3 March.

List, Friedrich (1837/1966). *The National System of Political Economy*. New York: Kelly.
Luce, Edward (2002). 'Poor Nations Urged to End Trade Barriers'. *Financial Times*, 29 November.
Mekay, Emad (2003). 'Interview with Klaus Schwab'. *TerraViva*, 27 January.
Mittal, Anuradha (2003). 'Open Markets or Open Plunder'. *TerraViva*, 27 January.
O'Driscoll, Jr, Gerald P. and Fitzgerald, Sara J. (2002). *Trade Promotes Prosperity and Security*. Washington, DC: Heritage Foundation.
Osava, Mario (2003). *TerraViva* (official newsletter of the WSF), 22 January.
OWINFS (Our World is Not For Sale) http://www.ourworldisnotforsale.org.
Oxfam (2002a). *Rigged Rules and Double Standards: Trade Globalization and the Fight Against Poverty*. London: Oxfam.
Oxfam (2002b). Coffee Report. http://www.maketradefair.com.
Panitchpakdi, Supachai (2002). 'From Doha to Cancun and Beyond'. Speech at the General Assembly of the Swiss Bankers Association, 22 September.
Prebisch, Rudiger (1950). *The Economic Development of Latin America and its Principal Problems*. New York: United Nations.
Ricardo, David (1821/1992). *The Principles of Political Economy and Taxation* (ed. Donald Winch). London: Dent.
Romapu, Mina (2003). TWN activist speaking at WSF.
Rothschild, Emma (2001). *Economic Sentiments: Adam Smith, Condorcet, and the Enlightenment*. Cambridge, MA: Harvard University Press.
SEATINI (Southern and Eastern African Trade Negotiations Institute) http://www.seatini.org.
Seneviratne, Kalinga (2003). 'Interview with Guy Ryder, Head of the International Confederation of Trades Unions (ICFTU)'. *TerraViva*, 24 January.
Smith, Adam (1776/1993). *An Inquiry into the Nature and Causes of the Wealth Of Nations*. Savage, MD: Rowman & Littlefield.
Spraos, John (1983). *Inequalising Trade? A Study of Traditional North/South Specialisation in the Context of Terms of Trade*. Oxford: Clarendon Press in cooperation with UNCTAD.
Temel-Kuran, E. (2003) 'Report from Porto Alegre'. *Milliet*, 24 January.
TWN (Third World Network) http://www.twnside.org.sg.
UNDP (United Nations Development Programme) (2003). *Making Global Trade Work for People*. London: Earthscan.
United States Senate Finance Committee, Subcommittee on International Trade (2000). *Testimony of Lori Wallach Regarding the WTO Dispute Settlement System: Powerful Enforcement of Unbalanced, Extensive Regulations Without Basic Due Process Protections*, 20 June.
United States Trade Representative FTAA http://www.ustr.gov/regions/whemisphere/ftaa.shtml.
Waterman, Peter (2003). 'Reflections' http://www.forumsocialmundial.org.br/dinamic.asp?pa gina=balan_waterman2003in.
WDM (World Development Movement) (2002). *Trade in Services: MP Briefing*. http://www.wdm.org.uk.
Win, Aye Aye (2003). 'Righting Global Wrongs: No Simple Solutions'. *TerraViva*, 27 January.
Wolf, Charles (2002). 'The WTO Controversy: Exaggerated Fears and Unrealistic Hopes'. *Straddling Economics and Politics: Cross-Cutting Issues in Asia, the United States, and the Global Economy*. Arlington, VA: Rand Corporation.
WSF (World Social Forum) (2003). Notes from WSF proceedings by Yahia Said who attended the Third WSF in Porto Alegre, Brazil, 22–7 January.

WTO (World Trade Organization) http://www.wto.org.
—— (1997). *EC Measures Concerning Meat and Meat Products (Hormones) Panel Report*.18 August. Geneva: WTO.
—— (1998). *United States – Import Prohibition of Certain Shrimp and Shrimp Products: Report of the Panel* (WT/DS58/R). Geneva: WTO.
—— (2001). *Final Declaration: Fourth Ministerial Meeting*. Doha. November.
WTO Appellate Body (1997). *United States – Restrictions on Imports of Cotton and Man-made Fibre Underwear*. 10 February. WTO.

Acknowledgement

First publication: Said, Yahia and Desai, Meghnad (2003) 'Trade and Global Civil Society: the Anti-capitalist Movement Revisited', in *Global Civil Society 2003* (Yearbook), edited by Kaldor, Mary; Anheier, Helmut & Glasius, Marlies. Oxford, Oxford University Press pp. 59–85. Republished with kind permission of Oxford University Press.

Chapter 5

GLOBALISATION AND POVERTY

Meghnad Desai

(2003)

Introduction

Broadly speaking my view is very positive on globalisation. I think that globalisation is the only way that mass poverty will be cured and no better way has been found yet. I recall my days as a graduate student in the '50s and early 1960s. I had just started practising economics and there was a great debate about the prospect of developing countries ever getting rid of poverty. It used to be said by Paul Baran and Andre Gunder Frank that if developing countries depended on capitalism they would never get rid of poverty because monopoly capital hinders development of the Third World. So the only way the Third World could develop was by rejecting capitalism and taking on socialism. The *Political Economy of Growth* that Paul Baran wrote is very good and people should read it if only to remind themselves of what that thesis was about. Baran's argument was based on pessimism about the possibility of growth in developed countries because he and others believed that developed countries would suffer from secular stagnation and if they suffered from secular stagnation the forces of monopoly capitalism would not allow rivals to exist and come into the world markets. Markets would be restricted, competition would be deleterious and so developed countries would keep developing countries out of that market.

When you think about this period you will also note that it was not only economists who were pessimistic. Politicians were also pessimistic about developing countries ever getting out of poverty. I remember Henry

Kissinger saying if only China and India could get rid of the problem of food supplies we could then proceed to tackle other problems. No one in the 1960s would have believed that China or India would have developed as they are today. My argument is that not only was the Baran thesis wrong, but that he was already wrong in his own day because by the late 1950s secular stagnation was not the story in the capitalist countries. Rather sustained growth was the story.

What really happened in the second half of the twentieth century was the defeat of the Leninist model as an alternative path of development for all developing countries. This model bit the dust, although the Leninist political programme survives in China, Cuba and North Korea. But the story of China is a quite remarkable example of first having tried the Leninist economic model and then abandoning it in the late 1970s and latching onto a different path and achieving spectacular success. Asia has had spectacular success. The fact that northeast Asia and Southeast Asia have achieved such remarkable growth is amazing. I am old enough to remember when people had not seen 5 per cent growth rates. Now growth rates can be 8 or 9 per cent. First Japan did it, then Korea in the 1970s. We were all in denial saying it was due to American defence aid and it would all collapse. But it did not collapse, it went on and on. What is remarkable about that is that Asia has shown that capitalism is a game that any country can play. There are no cultural restrictions. This is not a Max Weber model of Protestantism or anything like that. Anyone can do this. One of the merits of the capitalist model is that anyone can play the game and win. And therefore to think within cultural paradigms where capitalism is only a Western game is all gone now. The success of Asia has defied that Eurocentric logic – the first example being the astonishing development of Japan.

I need not go into all this in great detail because I have written a book about this – *Marx's Revenge*. The most remarkable thing about the twentieth century is that Italian and German fascisms were defeated. Remember that fascism was the first system to try planning. Unfortunately, they got bad press so we have forgotten all that. The Germans had five-year plans with private and state enterprises. Fascism was defeated first. Then after the Second World War communism was defeated. So by the end of the twentieth century there is only one mode of production left and that is capitalism. Even if you have different varieties of capitalism, still there is only the capitalist mode of production.

Asia's Achievements

Another remarkable thing about the history of Asia, especially from 1970 onwards, is the extraordinary reduction of mass poverty. The figures for China, Taiwan, Korea, Thailand, Malaysia all show real success stories. The stories in the Philippines, Indonesia and India are not that good, but Sri Lanka has a good story to tell. Given that much of the world lives in Asia the reduction of poverty in Asia in absolute numbers must be the largest reduction ever in human history. From the mid-1970s onwards, a number of Asian countries saw that they had to have an open economy policy. This does not have much to do with either free markets or free trade as such. What is relevant is that it was about pursuing policies that were profit friendly and not profit reducing. The contrast between India and Korea is not that the state did not intervene – they interfered in both countries, but in Korea the state was a smart state and went with the market and encouraged industries and firms that were competitive. They got subsidies but they were monitored to ensure competitive performance and the only point of competitive performance was to produce exports. In contrast, India was not export oriented. It only catered for the home market and foreign trade pessimism ruled.

Again, all of the eastern European economies that we used to read about all had massive amounts of investments. If you go back and read the Reports of the Economic Commission of Europe, every year eastern Europe was growing healthily and all the GDP calculations showed impressive growth. But what was actually happening in eastern Europe was that they produced output which they did not have to sell abroad. They did not have to satisfy what Marx called, the law of value. As a result, many economic activities such as producing concrete and steel buildings ignored the markets. No economic value was being generated. Economic value is not a matter of engineering. What you had in the German Democratic Republic was a system without economic value. As a result, when Germany was unified, the entire capital stock of the GDR could not be sold to anybody. It was a complete pile of junk. As this dramatic example shows, it is possible to pursue policies, as India has, to merely generate output and create nothing but junk.

The open economy context in East and Southeast Asia was very different. What happened was that the trigger of globalisation was released when capital movements became possible across countries in a reasonably unregulated fashion. Capitalist firms realised that if they were going to realise adequate profits they had to relocate their companies. The relocation of industries from the industrial North to the developing South started in the 1970s and accelerated in the '80s and '90s to the extent that we have now redrawn the map of manufacturing. The old developed countries are witnessing a decline in the share of manufacturing in terms of output and employment. Manufacturing is no longer the leading sector in many developed countries and manufacturing employment is growing, if anywhere, in the developing countries.

Globalisation and Industrialisation of the South

If you recall in the late 1960s there was a conference of the United Nations Industrial Development Organisation in Santiago, Chile. They had set a target that by 2000 the South's share of manufacturing export should be 25 per cent and very few people thought that that was possible. Even in the 1980s people were very pessimistic about this. But now there is a remarkable resurgence of manufacturing exports from the South and it happened not by South-South cooperation that also used to be fashionable. South-South cooperation is not useful. Beggars cannot sell things to each other, to put it bluntly. The key was developing countries getting access to the markets of developed countries. The way East Asia and Southeast Asia reduced their poverty was by having access to the markets of the West and selling things that the West could not make itself at prices that the people could afford. This has happened to many mature industrial products that have migrated to the South from the North. North capital and South labour are creating a whole new manufacturing industry in the South and that is very much a part of globalisation. This has been made possible by other aspects of globalisation such as the IT and communications revolution, satellite technologies, cheaper transport and the faster movement of money.

Globalisation has made possible the relocation of production processes. At the same time it has also made possible the fragmentation of the production process so that very frequently an entire product is not made in the same location. Much of the success of the 1950s and '60s, especially the Japanese success story, had much to do with recognising this principle. In the 1950s and '60s people used to believe in economies of scale. Steel factories were integrated and they would try to own their own mines and steel marketing. For example, there used to be something called US Steel – a very powerful corporation – it defeated President Kennedy in his attempt to regulate their price-fixing powers. Now there is no US steel in the US because the Japanese discovered that you do not have to locate everything in the same place. You can have just-in-time inventories and you can have completely displaced branches and assemble different manufacturing components. In no single location in Europe is a car made; cars are made in different locations and then put together. What that does is that it keeps the high value added, high knowledge intensive parts of the production process (design and engineering) in the West and the more routine part of the production processes in the South. So if you are wearing a pair of Nike shoes, only 10 per cent was made in a single country and much of what you pay for is design. You are paying for those little holes on the Nike shoe through which your feet can breathe etc. And you buy the Michael Jordan image because Michael Jordan is endorsing a product. You are buying a dream, an abstract commodity. What globalisation has made possible is the production of a tremendous amount of abstract commodities in which, to some extent, the North has an advantage but you still need the routine production of the kind that happens in the South.

Poverty and the Welfare State

It is very hard for me to understand people who go on about globalisation. There was nothing like this possible in the 1950s and '60s. There was no way we thought that this kind of industrialisation was possible then. And what is also interesting is that in the West poverty came down, in a substantial sense, only after WWII. If you look at what happened to living conditions in the inter war years, it is quite amazing how poor people were. In the North poverty was tackled under the Keynesian regime. You had relatively sustained full employment and good growth. But at that stage the participation in the labour force was quite limited. Core poverty was tackled through the State. What we find in the North is that State action was regarded as the way of dealing with poverty by creating a Welfare State. Through the State, people who were out of employment got part of the surplus via government taxation.

Two things have happened since then. That strategy cannot work in a developing country as they cannot afford to establish a Welfare State. Moreover, if you are poor you cannot afford to be unemployed. If you are unemployed, you starve to death. So in a developing country you need to have anti-poverty strategies that depend on creating work and creating skills for that work. Developed countries are also finding after the Keynesian boom that they also cannot afford the Welfare State that they used to have. They can't afford it partly because their own employment structures have been transformed by globalisation. Their unskilled workers no longer have the lifetime employment they used to have in manufacturing because those manufacturing jobs have moved away. Their workers are having episodic employment experiences, they are not having any continuity of employment. At the same time, they are living longer. What the Welfare State used to do is take your own income and redistribute it over your lifetime. What the Welfare State did not do, at least in Britain, is take from the rich and give to the poor. It took from the poor while they were young and working and gave it to them when they retired, or in between during unemployment episodes which were very infrequent. This is what British studies show.

Today, that model breaks down because people are living far too long after retirement and even the savings they are setting aside during their working lives will not be enough to finance their retirement. So suddenly ageing becomes a problem and all Welfare States are facing this crisis of how to tackle poverty and retirement. And they have found exactly the same answer that developing countries have found – it has to be a work related, poverty reduction strategy. You can no longer have poverty reduction done through the State unconnected with work. To say that the UK government is going to help them out of poverty means that they have find work and give them some subsidies and tax cuts, in order to enhance their take home pay. They will give back their tax payments in some form or another, as long as they stay in work. So suddenly, across the world the strategy for poverty reduction has become identical because of globalisation and increased longevity. Even in the heyday of Keynesian policy, people were complaining that poverty was not being tackled. There was a rediscovery of poverty in the 1960s in the US and UK. Even then they found that there was relative poverty. What we have found about poverty reduction is that it is very difficult to design massive redistributive programmes that can effectively tackle poverty in any meaningful sense. Again, we have been forced to rethink our alternative strategies even in developed countries because while they remain capitalist, the nature of capitalism has changed even within our lifetimes. So the developed countries are feeling much more subjected to global competition than ever before.

Migration and Stabilisation

What do we do from now on? It is a paramount duty for developed countries not to obstruct the process of globalisation; not to adopt restrictive trade policies. Ideally I would like to see the abolition of all agricultural subsidies in Europe and in the USA. Each cow in Europe per day gets a subsidy of US$2.25. This is above the poverty line that the World Bank applies to the poor in developing counties i.e. the poor are defined as those that live below US$2 per day per capita. According to this definition, even the European cow is above the global poverty index. The smallest American cotton farmer gets US$100,000 for an industry which should not exist at all – why does America need to grow cotton when there is perfectly good cotton grown in the Third World? But much more than that the European Common Agricultural Policy by dumping abroad is a serious cost to Third World agriculture. There is no point in Lionel Jospin, the former PM of France, talking about Tobin taxes when if he really does want to redistribute wealth he should stop his own agricultural subsidies. Many anti-globalising movements should really be marching in the streets against agricultural subsidies. I have been quoted as saying that the Common Agricultural Policy is a crime against humanity and I stick by that.

The same applies to industrial products. There has to be continuous liberalisation of trade. Some of the things that happened at Seattle at the WTO meeting were a protectionist backlash against the growth of trade. The American Trade Union Movement was very much against the admission of China into the WTO because they could see that this would mean the displacement of their jobs. What developed countries have to be ready for is the restructuring of manufacturing towards more R&D intensive, more knowledge intensive manufacturing and more service activities that are more value adding.

These are the two primary problems that developed countries need to face. But in addition to removing agricultural subsidies and expanding markets for manufacturing, there is a third thing which is increasingly important. This is the more controversial question of the movement of people. With globalisation we have accepted that one of the distinguishing marks of globalisation is the freer movement of capital across the world. It is not a complete freedom of movement for capital; many restrictions remain but by and large all the OECD countries have completely liberalised capital markets. And there are more and more countries of the Second and Third World that have capital liberalisation policies. I have nothing against that and I am very sure that the volatility that goes with such capital movements can be lived with.

But the movement of capital is not the only movement we need. It is quite remarkable that in the nineteenth century when we had the phenomenon of globalisation, there was also a lot of movement of people. Today we have forgotten that between 1914 and 1945 the world became deglobalised and we started thinking within the boundaries of the territorial state. Today we think of economics within the territorial state; we think of welfare as taking place within the territorial state. We have forgotten that that was not the way the world normally functioned. The territorial state was a very short, peculiar period in European history. During the nineteenth century people moved across international boundaries quite a lot; one-third of the population of Europe moved to north America and Australia. When you think of one-third being displaced, you realise that that fundamentally changed the prospects for poverty reduction. People who moved across state boundaries clearly moved because they knew their conditions would improve. They suffered a horrible passage across; when they got there they had no entitlements; they had no welfare payments; they had to work their way up; practically nothing was given except admission to the US. But if not to them, by the second generation they had achieved a remarkable living standard that they could not have enjoyed had they stayed in Europe. And we forget how much poverty reduction occurred by people moving away from where they are stuck.

In the post-1945 period we think of poverty as those people over there. Whereas in the nineteenth century it is quite possible for the poor to say this place is a hopeless place I am going to get up and go somewhere with better job prospects. We know that there is a lot of movement within countries but in the nineteenth century there was a lot of movement across countries. A lot of people from the Indian subcontinent moved to Malaysia and to the Caribbean and to Florida. A lot of Chinese moved to Southeast Asia, to the west coast of America and a lot to Australia until in the beginning of the twentieth century Australia stopped Asian immigration.

In the new phase of globalisation, migration is going to be the biggest topic in the next ten to fifteen years. We have already noticed that people have taken the initiative on their own to travel across state boundaries; they are taking enormous risks to move to where there is prosperity. And country after country has to deal with immigration problems. By and large developed countries are making a total hash of it. We have all decided that we are not going to admit economic refugees because they are dirty people who want to make themselves better off. How absurd it is to try to make yourself better off – you should stay where you are! We don't necessarily want to give them foreign aid but we certainly don't want them here. This is what is happening today in countries already full of economic refugees.

We are also trying to deal with another consequence of globalisation – the asylum seekers. We have decided to have some asylum seekers; we will take some but not all. We have decided to put restrictions on the number. There is a simple reason for it. As Nigel Harris points out in *The New Untouchables* when we created the Welfare State during the First World War it guaranteed it would look after the welfare of its citizens. The emergence of the Welfare State coincided with the emergence of the territorial state. By creating a category of citizen, it also created a category of foreigners that did not exist in the nineteenth century. Today's State will look after its citizens but not after foreigners. The nation-state was invented to stop the movement of people. The nation-state also had aspirations to stop people leaving – hence the debate about the brain drain. The problem is that welfare does not come packaged with the territorial state; it travels with people. We have to understand that there is going to be a need to match the free movement of capital with the free movement of labour. There is no reason in logic why people who accept the free movement of capital cannot accept the free movement of people.

Lots of arguments have been used to think of welfare in terms of territorial states. The 'good people' or progressives in the territorial state (NGOs, bishops etc) have a view that they should only admit people to whom they can give the full welfare entitlements. But because we can't afford too many like that we don't want too many foreigners to come in. There is great resistance to diluting the conditions of citizenship – they just don't want the people to be there. Lots of countries are trying to restrict the access of asylum seekers that they are by treaty bound to admit. They are using a whole range of arguments to do this – you are not a genuine asylum seeker, you are an economic refugee and so on.

The nineteenth century approach was very different. The nineteenth century said you can come in if you want to but you need to go through an intermediate passage until you get full citizenship. It was a bit like the 'Green Card' today: you are welcome to come and live in America but you are not a citizen; you pay the tax but you do not get a full entitlement to welfare. You only get a full welfare entitlement when you become a citizen.

I would like to propose that countries should adopt 'Green Card' strategies. Some people would argue that the conditions are very harsh but they are actually kinder than the strategies we are adopting now. What we want to say to people who want to come in is, yes you can come but you get no welfare benefits at all. I would only make an exception for the children of new arrivals. There should be full child benefits but adults should not get any. Adults know what is good for them; they have chosen to come here. After perhaps five or ten years they would get full citizenship rights. It is actually a cruel strategy to adopt but in terms of redistribution, it is much kinder than saying don't come, stay out there because we can't afford you. Even with this strategy, there are all sorts of cultural problems, but the economic problems are also interesting.

The major economic problem is that if these people are going to work and we want them to work, our labour market structures are very exclusionary and they will be undermined by an influx of people. Most particularly our minimum wage legislation will be affected. This is the dilemma. Ronald Dworkin, a distinguished advocate of human rights, gave an example of a case in a New York bakery with someone working sixteen hours a day. He asked the audience what people thought about this. They were all horrified. But it turned out that the immigrant could not get a job in most regulated industries; he could only get a job in an unregulated industry. He could only get a job where he had to work for sixteen hours. For him this was the only humane passage out of poverty into work for an immigrant because everywhere there was regulation and restrictions on people coming in and getting jobs.

We do have to think very seriously about the nature of the labour market structures we have adopted for a certain era of capitalism when we thought only about the territorial state in which there was a privileged membership for citizens and no membership for outsiders. We clearly want to make many more people better off and one way we can do this is to have an intergenerational shift in benefits by saying you can come into this country to work and your children will be better off but you won't be entitled to benefits.

This is a very cruel way of putting it but I think that short of that we will have considerable problems with labour migration in the world. A lot of the developed world, having come through a development process, is now essentially taking away the ladder for other people who have come later. And I don't think it is going to benefit the developed world. One reason is that the age structures in developed countries are already such that they either cannot afford their pension system or their welfare state, and the clear demographic projections in Britain and Europe (I am sure Australia as well) show a dependency ratio of aged people that is already of such proportions that all the needed welfare cannot be financed by the welfare state.

There are obviously some other solutions whereby you can extend the working life of the workforce or dilute their pension entitlements, but another solution is to import people. And calculations have been made about this for the European Union. It has been estimated that the EU needs to import some 100 million people over the next fifteen years in order to keep up its current economic output. The EU was so shocked by this study conducted by the UN Department of Social and Economic Affairs that the EU refused to have the report circulated. They were worried about the impending demographic crisis. It can be shown that there are certain cruel but kind ways of dealing with immigration that are mutually beneficial – not in the immediate short run but in the intermediate and long run. But there has been no political leadership that has been able to explain this to the citizens of the developed countries; nor have the people who have argued for mass poverty reduction in the World Bank and UNDP taken this option. Because everyone is thinking of countries as separate little blocs and they can only deal with poverty by getting the money out there but not moving the people.

The argument that people have been the most immobile factor of production and everything else can move is a complete fallacy. All world history shows that people do move. And different countries will solve this problem in different ways. The Americans have an interesting strategy of getting skilled people into the country in generous quantities. They also get unskilled workers illegally across the Mexican border. If you look at the American population figures she has a growing population both in terms of internal reproduction rates and net migration unlike Europe that has a stagnant or declining population and severe restrictions on immigration. Sooner or later Europe will have to do something about this, perhaps adopting a strategy similar to the Americans. But strategies will be different according to the relative economic strengths and weaknesses of the economies.

My own view is that this is something that needs a global examination of some kind through the WTO or ILO; the world will have to reach a decision of some sort over the next fifty years to deal with the mass movement of people. In principle asylum seekers are temporary stayers. There is some evidence in the UK with Kosovo and Afghanistan that asylum seekers have been temporary and many have returned home. One can be generous to these, knowing that they want to go back and one might only admit them on the basis of temporary migration. But so far as economic refugees are concerned, we do not need to be more generous to them. Let them bear the costs of migration and have no costs bearing on the citizens. Of course citizens will carry the indirect cost of such economic refugees but in return they will also have some benefits from that migration in terms of a more youthful age profile and increased economic productivity.

Globalisation has provided a remarkably great opportunity for tackling mass poverty. There is one exception to this – Africa as a continent has not benefited as much as Asia. Partly this has to do with commodity prices. Another feature of modern industry is that commodities have become 'weightless' – they use less raw material and are lighter and artificially manufactured materials are used. So primary commodity prices have been on a secular decline through the last twenty-five years. Another problem has been the failure to create the nation-state and coherent political societies or governance. This is a major contrast between Asia and Africa. It is not a problem to do with corruption or authoritarian vs. democratic systems. It is really a question of the difference between a responsive state and an unresponsive state. The Asian state in a variety of forms has always responded and paid back to its citizens some of the fruits of development. That connection between the state and the people has been there in the case of Malaysia and China for instance. In both Malaysia and China the ruling parties have been in touch with the grassroots and have been able to deliver some development. But that has not been the case in Africa. Except for the first few years after independence there has been an extraordinary failure of the rulers to respond to the citizens. Why this is true is very complex but one thing is certain – this has nothing to do with globalisation. Globalisation has ignored Africa rather than ruined it whereas globalisation helped Asia because Asia was able to create a successful polity. We will have to think about how Africa can be brought into globalisation.

Bibliography

Baran, Paul (1960) *The Political Economy of the South*, New York: Monthly Review Press.
Desai, Meghnad (2002) *Marx's Revenge: The Resurgence of Capitalism and the Death of Statist Socialism*, London: Verso.
Frank, Andre Gunder (1965) *Capitalism and Underdevelopment*, New York: Monthly Review Press.
Harris, Nigel (1997) *The New Untouchables*, London: I B Taurus.

Acknowledgement

This is the text of a speech delivered by Lord Desai to a public lecture in Melbourne, Australia, on 11 December 2003. The lecture was hosted by the Monash Asia Institute, the Monash Institute for the Study of Global Movements and the Productivity Commission. Lord Desai's visit to Australia was made possible by the Australia South Asia Research Centre at the Australian National University, Canberra.

Chapter 6

THE POLITICAL ECONOMY OF DONALD TRUMP

Meghnad Desai

(2016)

Trump the Unorthodox: A Figure Who Surprises

Donald Trump will be the Republican nominee for the 2016 US presidential election. He has come this far fighting, or perhaps disregarding, widespread disbelief, as well as undisguised contempt on the part of the elite of both main US parties and almost the entire liberal community. But he won the primaries and has caught the imagination of millions of people, garnering their votes.

Let us move a step on and imagine that Trump wins the election and takes over from Barack Obama in 2017. What sort of president would he make? More particularly, what will his economic policy be? How will he be able to fulfil the many promises he has made? Here again, dire predictions are being made about the economic consequences of a Trump presidency. Most commentators see him going on a fruitless journey, promising the moon and not even delivering cheese.

This report explores the possible outcomes of the unorthodoxy of Trump's economic thinking and asks whether he may surprise us. After all, odious political views have coexisted with successful unorthodox economics in the past. During the Great Depression of the 1920s and 1930s, European fascist parties in Germany and Italy were the first and very successful Keynesians.

Trump has been careful not to articulate a complete and consistent economic philosophy. Tactically this is shrewd – he is a moving target and difficult for his critics to shoot at. He is not a fool as many say he is. Nor is he confused or self-contradictory. His is a studied stance intended to sow confusion in the minds of his opponents. Trump has made promises to create jobs, restrict immigration, build a wall along the US-Mexico border, and reverse the 'drain' caused by trade, particularly in respect of China.

The Republican nominee is a mercantilist and a protectionist. (This is a hallowed American tradition: until the end of the Second World War the US was a protectionist nation.) He has said things financial market experts view as beyond the pale, such as reneging on debt and talking down the dollar. But memories are short. Most people believe a strong dollar has been a permanent feature of US economic policy. But they forget the volatility in the dollar's value in the two decades after the US exit from the dollar exchange standard in August 1971, which ended the Bretton Woods system and inaugurated flexible exchange rate markets. As John Connally, Richard Nixon's Treasury secretary, told European leaders, 'The dollar is our currency and your problem'.

Trump's Cavalier Stance on Public Debt

Trump has been cavalier in his statements about debt – as to its size, buying back and/or reneging on it; about trade – US repudiation of its international obligations; about immigration and the expulsion of illegal immigrants; and about renouncing Obama's policy on the environment. He has been rude about Muslims, Mexicans, Hispanics more broadly, and women.

This sort of right-wing populism is not new. But it has rarely had popular resonance to the extent that Trump has provided it with. Previous rightwing presidential candidates such as George Wallace in 1968 were antiblack Americans, given that Hispanics and Mexicans then had a negligible presence in the US. Easy contradictions can be pointed out in Trump's rhetoric. But there is much agreement about the malaise that has given him a willing audience.

The American middle classes have suffered in relative terms in the four decades since the first oil shock of 1973. These are the people who feel they have lost out from globalisation (which can be used as a portmanteau term for freer trade, liberal immigration policies, fiscal discipline in the matter of obeying the message of the bond markets, independent central banks, and the pursuit of inflation targeting as a central policy).

But here is the first contradiction. Since the deprived sections of the American middle class span white, black and Hispanic households, can Trump gain by focusing on white grievances and alienating black and Hispanic voters?

Normally one could summarise the Republicans' stance by saying that they favour lower income and corporation taxes, especially for the better-off; constantly worry about the size of the public debt and the budget deficit; and express anxiety over growth in public spending, especially entitlements for the less well-off.

Trump, however, has based his campaign on appealing to blue-collar manual workers and the growing number of unemployed in those regions dominated by failing manufacturing industries. He has railed against 'the system', including the large banks and international corporations, which has advocated and benefited from globalisation at the expense of American workers. He has shown hostility to international free trade and has advocated boosting public spending to counteract some of the impact on American workers.

This blurs the traditional distinction with the Democrats, who would like, but have been unable, to increase taxes on the rich and spend more on benefits. With Democratic primary contender Bernie Sanders' message having gained significant traction, the policy of the Democratic nominee (which, almost certainly, will be Hillary Clinton) may swing more to the left, against Wall Street (using that as a portmanteau term for corporate tax deductions, lax regulation, shunting the tax liability to tax havens abroad, high corporate salaries and bonuses).

British Referendum Benefits for Candidate Trump

The British decision to leave the European Union will help Trump in a number of ways. The right-wing populist and xenophobic thrust that was a feature of the UK Leave campaign is very much in his style.

He may enjoy the tough attitude towards globalisation and trade treaties. The idea that a nation should not be bound by previous commitments is his message too.

There is also confirmation of the Trump style of campaigning and presenting serious issues in simplified binary form. Liberal critics have sought to contrast his somewhat boorish approach to international relations with Europe's more subdued style of politics.

Now one of the oldest European polities has gone his way.

The shock of 'Brexit' has weakened sterling relative to the dollar. The uncertainty created by the UK decision is one of the factors dissuading the Federal Reserve from an immediate increase in interest rates. Bond yields have dropped to their lowest level in recent years.

Trump should benefit from this as his stance would be fiscally unorthodox, taking on debt and spending on infrastructure.

Even if the pound rallies moderately after the arrival of a new British prime minister, nervousness in sterling and bond markets may continue. Trump can use this to his advantage.

Theresa May, the new British prime minister who took office on 13 July, has appointed Boris Johnson, the larger-than-life former mayor of London, as foreign secretary. Johnson has frequently been compared to Trump in his demeanour, appeal to a cross-party spectrum and approach to national issues (including hostility to the EU). Like Trump, Johnson has ascended the political firmament in unlikely fashion – and is capable of springing surprises from a variety of directions.

Businessman as President

The first thing to remember about Donald Trump is that he is a businessman, and a very successful one. He has a hand in real estate, television, casinos and other entertainment products. He is the first business person (and seasoned television performer) to run for president and be a nominee of a major political party since the emergence of Ross Perot in 1992, a Texas businessman who ran as an independent and garnered 19 per cent of the popular vote.

Other nominees and contestants may have made their money in business, but usually entered politics and competed for the presidency only some years after being successful in the business world. Mitt Romney, who contested the 2012 presidential election, worked in the management consultancy and private equity industries before entering politics in 1994. George H. W. Bush was an oil industry executive. Barry Goldwater, the Republican nominee in 1964, had a background in business, as did Wendell Wilkie, who ran against Franklin D. Roosevelt in 1940.

Trump has had no schooling in politics. He has been in the public eye for decades as a businessman and a public personality. The implication is that his economics may derive more from his daily experience and knowledge than other candidates, who require expert advice on economic issues. This has been clear in his very unorthodox attitude to debt. As a businessman who has amassed a fortune, he views debt not as a burden but as a tool for doing business.

Thus, while the economic programme of Paul Ryan, the speaker of the House of Representatives, has focused on tackling the size of the public debt above all else, Trump does not see debt in the same light. He knows that you have to end up richer than when you started. If debt is necessary to achieve that goal, so be it. It is easy to deplore this attitude towards debt. Yet we have to remember that, since September 2008, many rules of orthodox finance have been broken.

Bankrupt banks and financial institutions have been bailed out using taxpayers' money while the ruling politicians have eschewed a sufficient fiscal boost to the economy to benefit the excluded middle. Federal actions such as the 2008 Troubled Asset Relief Program (to acquire 'toxic' assets and equity from beleaguered financial institutions) have channelled money to the few but denied it to the many. The deprived middle classes have seen rules being broken and the guilty being rewarded rather than punished.

Quantitative easing may now be sold as merely an enhanced version of open market operations, but it has broken all the previous rules in its extent and scope. Monetarists told us that monetising public borrowing was unsound and could lead to inflation.

In the US and the UK, not to mention Japan, central bankers have been printing money with scant regard to previous rules and orthodoxies. There has been little response in terms of inflation. The Federal Reserve and Bank of England have taken interest rates to near zero, while the European Central Bank and Bank of Japan have driven them into negative territory. The main beneficiaries of these policies have been asset owners and large borrowers, including big companies, who still refuse to invest but profit from the availability of cheap credit to increase their asset values. 'Joe public' has got nothing out of this departure from orthodoxy, hailed as innovation.

If Trump takes the view that he wants to borrow to create jobs with infrastructure investment, it would be hard to mount too strong or moralistic a protest. The long recession has heightened income inequalities. Bank and corporate bonuses have soared; wage income has not. Trump could argue that orthodoxy has much to answer for. His critics have also displayed amnesia about American history. We are told how, ever since Alexander Hamilton was Treasury secretary in the late eighteenth century, financial probity has been the rule for the US. This is fanciful history.

Critics need to revisit the period between the destruction of the Second Bank of the United States by Andrew Jackson, then president, in September 1833, and the creation of the Fed eighty years later.

Box 6.1: The Men behind Trump's Economic Policy

Sam Clovis – Policy Director
Professor of economics at Morningside College, activist for the Tea Party movement. Holds a Ph.D. in public administration from the University of Alabama. Responsible for shaping many campaign policies, involved in most of its domestic and foreign policy proposals. In 2014, he ran for Republican nomination for Senate in Iowa and then as state treasurer.

Larry Kudlow – Economic Adviser
Working with Trump on tax plan with Moore (see below). Syndicated television talk show, long history as a political commentator, first as a liberal and then a conservative. Columnist for a range of newspapers, and a distinguished scholar at the Mercatus Center of George Mason University, Virginia. Former Reagan administration official, chief economist at Bear Stearns.

Arthur Laffer – Economic Adviser
In campaign background, may re-emerge. Policy co-chairman, with Kudlow, of the Free Enterprise Fund: 'the pre-eminent lobbying force in Washington for the passage of legislation that will promote economic growth, lower taxes, and limited government'. Member of Reagan's Economic Policy Advisory Board in 1981–89.

Paul Manafort – Campaign Chairman and Chief Strategist
Senior partner in consulting firm Davis, Manafort, and Freedman. Largely responsible for messaging and communications. Gained control in April over expanded $20 million campaign budget, hiring decisions, advertising and media strategy. Track record of advising Republican presidential contenders: Ford, Reagan, Bush senior and junior.

Steven Mnuchin – Fundraiser
Heads campaign's fundraising as national finance chairman. Yale-educated banker, film producer and political fundraiser, former partner at Goldman Sachs. Set up hedge fund Dune Capital Management. Former chair of OneWest Group, formed from failed housing lender Indy Mac in 2009, sold to CIT Group in 2015.

> **Stephen Moore – Economic Adviser**
> Economics writer and political analyst. Working on Trump tax plan. Founded Club for Growth, a conservative organisation with a tax-cutting agenda, in 1999, president until 2004. Former member of *Wall Street Journal* editorial board, and a distinguished visiting fellow at the Heritage foundation, a conservative American think tank.
>
> Other advisers with an economics, business or financial background include Carter Page, foreign policy adviser, who is founder and a managing partner of Global Energy Capital, and George Papadopoulos, senior policy and economic adviser to former Republican presidential contender Ben Carson. John Mashburn, campaign policy director, has worked on budget and appropriations bills in Congress. Kent Gray, Illinois state director, is a former executive assistant to the Illinois Comptroller.

The Politics of American Credit

Throughout the nineteenth century, American credit abroad was not sound. The battle over joining the gold standard after the American civil war, particularly the struggle of farmers who suffered from the resulting deflation as against the East Coast corporations, has planted a permanent distrust of banks and bankers in the American political psyche.

More recently, in 1971, the US unilaterally reneged on a promise to buy gold at $35 an ounce, destroying the Bretton Woods system of monetary management. The US has a dubious record in terms of financial responsibility and Trump has many precedents to cite.

Trump is pragmatic about trade. Like any businessman, he would like a captive market, even though he may mouth platitudes about competition. He wants to capture as many of the gains from trade as possible. If this requires trade restrictions or exchange rate devaluation, then he would not be against using these instruments.

Again, what matters to him is not dogma but success – the bottom line. Trump does not agree with the argument that free trade leads to mutual advantage for both parties and is optimal for each. More to the point his core supporters do not agree with this view either. It has not been part of their life experience.

This may be for cogent economic reasons – the 1973 oil price shock, the migration of manufacturing abroad in search of cheap labour, a strong dollar. But Trump and his core support cannot accept that they should be helpless as a result of external factors. Their instinct is to use the levers of political power to regain control.

Again, while free trade is 'first best' and freer trade is better than protection, practice has always departed from theory. US and European Union protection of their respective agricultural sectors generates much resentment in emerging economies. The Doha Round of World Trade Organization talks aimed at lowering trade barriers has been stuck for years because of developed country resistance to developing countries demanding similar protection for their farmers.

At least this is what Xi Jinping, China's president, and Narendra Modi, the Indian prime minister, tell the US. Now Trump complains about China not playing by the rules. But this is just a sign that the US is no longer as dominant in international trade – in manufacturing at least – as it was in the 1960s and 1970s. Even the EU has complained about the US in the Transatlantic Trade and Investment Partnership negotiations.

The Politics of American Deficits

Despite the homilies about budget deficits, in practice both Democrats and Republicans have presided over deficits. Ronald Reagan, viewed as a paragon of Republican virtue, in the 1980s spent money in an almost Keynesian fashion, running a deficit in each of his eight years in office.

The country's debt to GDP ratio, which had fallen to 31 per cent by 1974, had reached 50 per cent by the end of Reagan's presidency and rose above 60 per cent in 1992. With further deficits under George H. Bush and Bill Clinton, it peaked at 65 per cent in 1996, subsequently declining to 55 per cent in Clinton's second term.

George W. Bush ran a budget deficit in each of his eight years as president. The debt to GDP ratio was 67 per cent in 2008. Then, as has happened in other countries, output growth reversed and debt continued to rise. The debt to GDP ratio rose steadily from 67 per cent in 2008 to 101 per cent in 2013 after the 2008–09 recession, and was around 102 per cent in 2014 and 2015.

Table 6.1: US is the world's largest debtor economy
Net international investment position of the largest debtor countries, 2014–15

	Largest debtor economies			
	NIIP ($bn)		NIIP (% of GDP)	
	2015	2014	2015	2014
US	-7,357	-7,020	-41	-40.5
Spain	-1,065	-1,208	-88.8	-87.3
Brazil	-799	-723	-26.6	-50.1
Australia	-689	-553	-56.3	-25.9
Italy	-475	-799	-26.2	-33.1
France	-416	-508	-17.2	-17.9

Source: IMF, Eurostat, OMFIF calculations

The Long Tradition of Raising Public Debt

The US budget has been in surplus in only twelve years since 1946 – four years under Harry S. Truman (1947–49, 1951); three years under Eisenhower (1956–57, 1960), and four years under Clinton (1998–2001). The only other year in which the country ran a surplus was 1969, Nixon's first year in office.

Trump would not be the first US president to run a deficit and increase debt. All he would need is a pliant Congress. Republicans attribute the deficit during the Reagan years to winning the Cold War, and the Bush deficit to the September 2001 attacks on New York and Washington (and the subsequent war on terror). Trump has to find a headline-grabbing theme for his deficits. He will then be in good and safe company.

The US has run a persistent current account deficit for more than twenty years, rapidly increasing its net foreign debt. At end-2015 US liabilities were almost $7.36 trillion, equal to 41 per cent of GDP. This has risen from under $800 billion, or 9 per cent of GDP, in 1997. Countries with large external debts and/or current account deficits should, in theory, face downward pressure on their currencies and rising costs of borrowing, encouraging them to adapt their monetary, fiscal and regulatory policies and ultimately rebalance domestic and foreign demand.

America's stable and attractive domestic financial and political environment and deep liquid markets, however, have meant the US has been able to draw in reserves, investments and other sources of long- and short-term capital from around the world. Along with its role as the main reserve currency-issuing country, these factors make the US a special case, allowing it to borrow heavily, at cheaper rates, while maintaining a strong currency.

Trump's Choices

If Trump ran serial budget deficits or increased the debt, this would be the norm rather than the exception.

Of course, the key to keeping the debt to GDP ratio under control is to work on the denominator as much as restricting the numerator.

But it could be argued that the US has under-borrowed, if anything. The country's infrastructure is badly in need of repair, while its total infrastructure investment needs have been calculated at $3.63 trillion. These needs include surface transport (almost $2 trillion), waterways and port ($131 billion), electricity ($736 billion) and airports ($134 billion).

US infrastructure is old. There is some urgency here. The 2014 dirty water crisis in Michigan state, where high levels of lead were found in the drinking water, provides a painful reminder of infrastructure neglect.

US Wage Stagnation

The other problem is flatness of wages (average hourly compensation of production/non-supervisory workers in the private sector) over the last forty years.

Between 1973 and 2014, productivity grew by 72.2 per cent and wages by 9.2 per cent, according to the Washington-based Economic Policy Institute. Only 15 per cent of the additional growth generated since the 1970s has accrued to workers. The rest has contributed to corporate income.

This has been as much a redistribution induced by policies that have deregulated financial markets, lowered taxes and increased deductions for corporations as a result of competition from cheaper labour in emerging economies.

The Secret of Trump's Appeal

Trump's core supporters want an unorthodox economic policy because the orthodox policy has not brought benefits to many middle-class voters who now feel alienated and disenfranchised. These supporters blame Washington because they see the malaise as the result of a deliberate policy choice, justified on the grounds of 'sound economics' or 'benefiting the wealth generators'. Sanders has concentrated on corporate privileges (Wall Street), while Trump has focused on creating jobs and shutting down foreign trade to help American workers.

Changing the climate of free and open trade may not be as easy as Trump thinks. International treaties cannot be changed or reneged on that easily. (The Paris climate agreement, which Trump has denounced, has built-in safeguards against unilateral withdrawal by any country.) But there may be a synergy in his desire for large infrastructure projects (such as the wall along the border with Mexico) and further tackling the US infrastructure deficit, a long neglected priority.

Members of Congress like spending the money that comes to their constituencies. 'Shovel-ready' projects could generate demand for workers lacking the education levels to take jobs in the services sector but who could take on manual jobs.

Of course, sentiment against the liberal globalisation orthodoxy has been rising around the world. We see the rise of right-wing nationalist parties in Europe, as well as anti-capitalist leftist extremist parties. It may be that, as in the past, the boom cycle of globalisation may yield to a rise of 'deglobalisation' as a result of the 2008–09 crisis and persistent low growth and deflation. If so, Trump will face less hostility internationally than many orthodox observers expect.

Reviving Infrastructure: Lessons from Eisenhower

A model for Trump to follow is Eisenhower's approach to infrastructure investment. The Interstate Highway System – the network of highways, turnpikes and motorways that still covers America – was built during the 1950s. Eisenhower initiated these projects in a sustained fashion. Arthur F. Burns was his chief economic adviser between 1953 and 1956, and went on to serve as chair of the Federal Reserve in the 1970s.

Burns was a conservative and a compassionate person as far as his economic beliefs were concerned. He was not a Keynesian in respect of his economics, but his advice led to the best public capital spending years the US has enjoyed. Gross public investment peaked at around 7 per cent per annum during the Eisenhower administration and has not reached those proportions since.

Eisenhower did this while pursuing a prudent fiscal policy, bringing the debt to GDP ratio down to 53 per cent in 1960 from 72.7 per cent in 1952 (the last year of the Truman administration). Public works spending in these years exceeded that during Roosevelt's 1933–38 New Deal. These were also years of full employment (with a mild recession in 1957) and sustained growth, keeping tax revenues buoyant.

The 'baby boom' had given the US a young and growing population that placed few demands on health infrastructure. Welfare spending was modest and would remain so until Lyndon Johnson's 'Great Society', a series of programmes aimed at eliminating poverty and racial injustice. Income growth prevented the debt to GDP ratio from rising.

As an icon of prudent public finance, Eisenhower beats Reagan, Bush and the rest of Republican presidents hands down. He pioneered a public-private initiative in the way the Saint Lawrence Seaway – a network of locks, canals and channels linking the US and Canada – was financed.

Attracting Sovereign Funds to Finance US Infrastructure

Trump could initiate a second large-scale public capital spending programme by taking advantage of low interest rates and borrowing to meet the need. Following the Saint Lawrence Seaway example, he could even tap sovereign funds to finance his proposals. After all, the total infrastructure deficit, estimated at $3.63 trillion, is just 19.6 per cent of GDP.

A capital spending programme at 5 per cent of GDP would amount to around $900 billion. This much could be borrowed as a sound principle of public finance. Sovereign funds as well as pension funds would be attracted if the US borrowed with long maturity, fixed coupon bonds. If sustained over four years, the borrowing would address the entire US infrastructure gap. It is difficult to estimate the number of jobs it would create, but it cannot be negligible.

If Trump undertook such a bold investment programme, he could meet most of the promises he has made without provoking a trade war with China. He may yet want to adopt an aggressive stance for the sake of popularity. But he may equally choose to live with a Congress that would not let him effect a major protectionist move.

What Trump May Achieve

Trump is an unorthodox person in respect of his politics and is promising to be one in terms of his economics too.

There has been paralysis in the G7 and G20 international forums in terms of bold fiscal policy. There may have been a time to hold back on fiscal spending (as in the UK) immediately after the steep rise in the deficit and debt in the first few years following the financial crisis. Borrowing is defensible for investment purposes at all times.

Monetary policy – quantitative easing – took up the task of easing the pain of the recession and helped 'zombie households' and 'zombie companies' survive.

But following years of QE, monetary policy has reached its limits. Negative interest rates have become the latest problem. Companies are using cheap money for share buybacks or other ways of pursuing asset bubbles. Little of the money has been channelled into reviving the economy, raising wages or driving inflation back to the target level of 2 per cent.

In this climate, rather than seem helpless in the face of insurmountable problems, a bold unorthodox policy would remove obstacles to growth.

Technical progress – for example, artificial intelligence or driverless cars or robots – will only take care of the skilled when it comes to jobs. The many unskilled manual workers who used to enjoy a high and rising standard of living have lost out over the last forty years. American unemployment rates remain low, but there is still much dissatisfaction over wages. Household debts have risen.

Capital Spending will Boost Job Growth

A bold policy of capital spending on infrastructure projects will increase the job opportunities precisely for those workers who need it and revive the economy. A policy of sustained capital spending will raise income and its growth rate.

These indirect/multiplier effects are difficult to estimate, but they can only be positive. This itself may reduce the debt to GDP ratio to a level lower than it would have been were the debt incurred because of a shortfall of tax revenues below current spending. If Trump adopts such a policy, he may yet turn out to be a Keynesian, despite himself.

Ultimately, an American president with an economic plan to enact requires a compliant Congress that accommodates budget proposals and provides the sought-after extension of the debt ceiling.

This depends on whether Trump has coat tails that will carry Republicans into the two houses and maintain the party's majority – and whether the Republicans themselves have an appetite for Trump's unorthodox policies. None of this is guaranteed. If Trump wins in November, those who fear his actions should pray for four years of legislative gridlock. This would not be a propitious outcome, for the US and the world – and we must hope that it is not the best on offer.

Acknowledgement

First publication: Desai, Meghnad (2016) 'The Political Economy of Donald Trump', Report, Official Monetary and Financial Institutions Forum, 20 July 2016, pp. 7–22. Republished with kind permission of the OMFIF.

Chapter 7

IS THERE A FUTURE FOR SOCIAL DEMOCRACY AFTER THE CRISIS?

Meghnad Desai

(2009)

The deepest financial crisis in the last eighty years has come and almost gone. But in the midst of this crisis of global capitalism, socialist and social democratic parties have not been at the forefront of the efforts for the rescue and reform of the system. In France and Germany, the Left is in retreat. In the UK, while the Labour Party is in power, it is widely expected to lose the election when it is held next year. It is the case that Gordon Brown can rightly claim to have initiated the recapitalisation of banks in the UK which was then copied by other countries. The recent victory of PASOK in Greece apart, the European Left does not have much good news. Obama could be said to be as far 'left' as US Presidents go, though even he in the context of his own party is a centrist.

In rescuing the system from its double crisis of financial system dysfunction and real economy recession, the answers have been uniform across the European Left and Right. Merkel and Sarkozy, as well as Brown, have adopted the policy of restoration first and reform later. Obama has done the same.[1] The prospect is of better regulation of the financial system, perhaps greater competition or even the return to the old structures – Glass-Steagall

---

1 For a comment on how mild the Obama reforms are see Jeff Madrick 'They Did Not Regulate Enough and Still Don't', *New York Review of Books*, November 5–18, 2009, Vol LVI, number 17, pp. 54–7.

   Even mildly radical reform such as the restructuring of the auto industry to make it more 'green' or adapt electrical or hydro powered cars has not been pursued even as a lot of money has been given to the car industry by Obama.

as they are labelled – of separation of retail banking from investment banking. The European Commission has put its emphasis on greater competition and enforcement of its code against state aid. In industrial restructuring the approach is again of restoration and handing back ownership to the original owners as and when the time comes. Capitalism has come to stay, bloody and battered but bandaged with tender care by governments of the Right and Left.

Thus it is clear that even more so than the prospect of electoral victory or holding of office, there is a singular lack of a viable alternative vision around which the Progressive parties could coalesce. Even after reminding the world 'we said so', radical debates have not proposed a viable scheme which would deliver a better future.

What Then is the Future of the Left?

My contention is that the Left has lost because of a failure to comprehend the working of capitalism. The twentieth century was the century of the Left, both of the Leninist anti-democratic Left and the social democratic Left. The Leninists were very influential in arguing that capitalism was in one of its terminal crises and would disappear soon ushering in the possibility of socialism. As we celebrate the twentieth anniversary of the destruction of the Berlin Wall, we note that, North Korea and perhaps Cuba apart, there are no regimes still subscribing to that idea. In my book *Marx's Revenge* (MR) I have labelled this as Socialism Outside Capitalism (SOC).

Social democracy began with a critique of capitalism, but, rather than rejecting it, tried to humanise it. In much of the developed world, in Western Europe especially, it succeeded beyond its expectations. The last great crisis of capitalism in the 1930s gave social democracy its opportunity, and the war solidified its democratic mandate. Social democracy delivered socialism within capitalism (SwC) successfully – welfare state, trade union rights, guaranteed incomes if unable to work, as well as, more recently, human rights, gender rights and the freedom to pursue a lifestyle of your choice. As many of the OECD countries become multiracial, it is the social democrats who have led the attempt at welcoming the newcomers and allowing them to settle in their new countries with dignity. Status equality has now been guaranteed in the developed economies although income equality remains elusive.

But SwC was always predicated upon the nation-state captured by social democracy being able to direct the economy. This in turn required that the national economy be not strongly integrated with the rest of the world. This was a capitalism where we had an archipelago of national economies loosely articulated. But by the 1990s we arrived at a new phase of globalisation with much greater integration of the economies and consequently much less control of the nation-state over the domestic economy. The global flows of capital both direct and via portfolio movements across many stock markets, the explosion in global trade and the much slower yet significant upsurge in global movement of people created a situation in which the ship of the economy had to be steered at high seas, with much less control in the hands of the State.

Although social democracy always claims to be internationalist, its structures and even more so its ideology did not get out of the archipelagic world of many national economies run by the separate nation-states. There was no global social democratic vision to match the global phase of capitalism. Where has the Socialist International been in the recent crisis? The market moved globally and the politics did not catch up. The failure of the Left is not accidental; it is systemic. It is a failure of theory – the worst failure imaginable for anyone on the Left.

There is also a somewhat academic point to be made *inter alia*. This is that the Left never developed its own economics/political economy. It did not quite embrace Marxian economics (such as it was). It adopted neoclassical economics with the emphasis on market failure at the micro level and Keynesian economics at the macro level. (Scandinavian countries had an older tradition of macroeconomics thanks to Wicksell and the Stockholm School of economics.) The ideas about state intervention and capturing the 'commanding heights' of the economy were derived from the war time experience during 1914–18 and corporatism and planning in a mixed economy from the fascist economies – Italy and Germany – during the 1930s. Thus market failure at the microeconomic level, Keynesian underemployment analysis at the macro level plus State ownership of the commanding heights defined the distinctive social democratic approach to economic policy. All three aspects required State intervention and the Left was confident that it could deliver its promises if it controlled the State.

During the 1980s, state intervention in the industrial economy lost its appeal. State-owned companies became loss making and were a burden of the budget while other more urgent needs were claiming priority. In any case, thanks to the new technologies of transport and communication, it became more profitable to relocate the manufacturing industries to Asia and Latin America. The industrial working class shrank across the developed economies. Trade unions representing workers in manufacturing and mines and transport declined in numbers and strength. They had been the bedrock on which social democratic parties had been built. Without the 'commanding heights', social democracy was left with administering the public sector services with white collar unions, and began to face questions of consumers' choice in public services which had already been the fact in private sector. This led back to orthodox neoclassical economics. The issue was no longer the correction of market failure but to mirror the market in publicly provided services.

Globalisation also imposed constraints on the conduct of macroeconomic policies which made them more orthodox. This move started with anti-inflation policies with the dominance of central bank rather than treasury, and, after much debate among economists, a consensus developed that governments had to inspire credibility in their conduct of macroeconomic policies by making medium term commitments and avoiding surprises and sudden changes. The distinctive political economy the Left had fashioned for itself out of neoclassical economics – market interventions with taxes and subsidies and an aggressive fiscal stance to guarantee full employment – began to lose out to the compelling logic of the ideology of liberal markets.

The best social democracy could do was, *faute de mieux*, to adapt to global capitalism and combine a progressive social policy with a liberal economic policy. The label 'New Labour' or 'Third Way' may have been British but European social democratic parties had converged on this message in their own separate trajectories, with Sweden in the vanguard decades before UK. In doing so, social democracy lost its previous critical reservations about how the system had in-built failures; it did not update its theory to match the new phase of globalisation. When the system did break down, it had no remedy of its own. The electorate knew this. The Right could do the job of restoring the system just as well as the Left. Merkel and Sarkozy were singing a similar tune to Brown.

Perhaps it is worth mentioning that while social democracy prided itself on a vibrant culture of ideas, it thought that the Right was unthinking and blinkered and only represented 'old money'. But there was a thinking revolution on the Right during the 1960s and '70s. The dividing line was no longer 'Free Market' versus the State as between the Right and the Left. The Right used state power to restructure the industrial economy and privatised much state capital. It also gave power to central banks to control inflation. More crucially the Right facilitated the change from state ownership to state regulation of industries and public utilities. The Left was caught napping and had to scramble to get even in the battle of ideas.

What Is to Be Done?

The most serious challenge to the Left is to understand yet again how capitalism works. Why even as it fails, it revives itself, albeit with a lot of help from the nation-state. The State is the lender of last resort when the financial system is in difficulty. This however assumes that the liabilities are in terms of the domestic currency which the State can print in any amount. But as the case of Iceland shows, when the liabilities of the financial system are in terms of foreign currencies and its assets have gone toxic, even the State may not have the (foreign exchange) resources to bail the system out. The State can go bankrupt. This is a lesson familiar to Third World countries and was indeed learned bitterly in 1997 during the Asian crisis, but developed countries did not know it till now. As some EU and EEA countries faced bankruptcy, the IMF had to come to their rescue. The IMF, which in the 1980s and '90s was left with only the Third World to look after, has now become important for developed countries as well. In the phase of global capitalism, the individual nation-state is not powerful enough to stand on its own without outside help. In the latest crisis, the G7/G20 has shown that intergovernmental coordination has been for the time being both necessary and sufficient along with national intervention to manage the crisis. This however may not be the case the next time around.

The Crucial Question for the Left

Is capitalism a fully self-adjusting system which has cycles and crises but no end-point?
 Or
Is capitalism a hopelessly crisis-ridden system where the system cannot be trusted to run itself without extensive state control?
 Or
Is capitalism a system which most of the time works with cycles and crises and but only occasionally needs extensive, though internationally coordinated intervention?

The first way is that of laissez faire politics, the second of the old social democracy. If the present crisis has shown the validity of the third way of looking at capitalism how should the Left think about it?

Rethinking Economics

Academic economics has been in a bad repute recently. The models of mainstream macroeconomics about market rationality have been much mocked and quite rightly. But the issue is why did 'practical' men and women take such ideas so seriously. Academic economists often, if not always, only talk among themselves and know all the unstated qualifications to what they say to each other. But policymakers and politicians did swallow such ideas and did not know the unstated qualifications being made. What is more is that while many people rightly criticise academic economics for neglecting economic history and the history of economic ideas, why did the practical people fall into this trap as well?

Thus while recent macroeconomics may have ruled out crises (though the actual case is more nuanced as Robert Lucas argued in his essay in the *Economist*, 6 August, 2009), there are a number of well-known ideas in economics which predict cycles and crisis. Marx, Wicksell, Schumpeter and Hayek are four names which come to mind besides Keynes whose ideas are enjoying a revival. [Keynes in fact never went away. It is his policy nostrums which have helped to contain the present crisis thanks to 'built-in' stabilisers; the extra fiscal stimulus provided by governments of the Right and the Left was also thanks to his ideas. Keynes had no remedy for bank failures. Here it was Milton Friedman and Anna Schwartz's study of the Great Depression which told us that the Fed then had failed to provide sufficient liquidity to keep the banks going. This time around Ben Bernanke and Mervyn King were not going to repeat that mistake.]

The idea that capitalism is never, fully permanently stable but subject to recurrent cycles and crises used to be common knowledge, not just on the Left but among the business people as well. There was until the mid-1970s a flourishing subject area about business cycles taught in economics departments. We need to revive that part of economics. Even where economists knew the theory of markets working perfectly on their own, as in the case of Wicksell, Hayek and Schumpeter they asked as to why in that case there were cycles. In more recent times, Richard Goodwin of the University of Cambridge and the University of Sienna devoted himself to that topic. Charles Kindleberger wrote lucidly about crashes in his book *Manias, Panics and Crashes* and Hyman Minsky provided a theory of financial meltdowns. All this literature should be known to practical people and even more so to those who want to reform capitalism.

No one should be carried away with the claims of modern economists that they can provide the tools to 'eliminate boom and bust'; the best that economists can do is to moderate the effects of wrong policy which exacerbates such booms and busts.

It is not a mystery why the crisis happened. We have to lay aside ideas about greedy bankers and newfangled financial instruments having 'caused' the crisis. Every crisis had greedy bankers, and financial innovations have happened ever since cheque clearing was first mooted. These new elements may cause surprise but should not obscure the real reasons.

It was Knut Wicksell who first theorised about rises caused by bank lending. [Marx had a theory of cycles based on the movements in wages and profits. But there were few banks in his day. I have dealt with his theory in *Marx's Revenge*]. Wicksell said that if the rate at which investors can borrow (the market rate) is below the rate which they can earn from their investment (the natural rate), then there will be a cumulative upward movement in the economy. If the natural rate is below the market rate then there will be a cumulative downturn. To this Hayek added the caveat that at some stage the banks panic that they have over-lent and suddenly jack up the market rate. At this point the boom collapses and the long downturn begins.

What is Wealth?

But there are some other old fashioned ideas which need reviving. Since the housing bubble has been at the centre of the crisis and indeed house ownership has been a major political selling point, we need to ask why people are led to believe that a house represents wealth. Most houses are bought on a mortgage and for a number of years the house mortgagee owns a small part of the equity in the house. But even if that were not the case why is the house an asset? What is the *value* of a house?

Note that I say value not the price of a house. We have had people surprised that the price of their house has plummeted and they face negative equity. But the house stands as usable as it was before the price fell. How does a house lose wealth without any physical change? If I buy a car or a refrigerator I know that its second-hand price will be much less than the price I paid at purchase time. But with a house we all expect that the longer we hold on to it the higher its price would be. Houses are like pensions; they come in handy in old age.

None of the above discussion is predicated upon ignoring the many problems capitalism creates and with which we are familiar. But somehow the world seems to have voted for capitalism rather than any of the alternatives which were on offer during the twentieth century. The instincts of democratic politics are to rank the welfare of our own nation's citizens above that of others. Is there a cosmopolitan vision which we can cultivate to match the global phase of capitalism and if we can, how do we implement it?

Acknowledgement

This chapter was presented as a speech at The Foundation for European Progressive Studies and The Kalevi Sorsa Foundation Conference, Helsinki, on 6–7 November, 2009.

Chapter 8

GLOBALISATION AND SUSTAINABLE DEVELOPMENT

Meghnad Desai

(1997)

Globalisation is a new buzz word, a cliché, a new term to frighten the children. Its champions say that it has altered all economic relations, marginalised the nation-state, given unregulated and highly mobile capital the upper hand over labour and over governments, and that it is ushering in a borderless world. Its detractors say that it is globaloney or gobbledegook to say these things. Globalisation is not new: it is merely a throwback to the nineteenth century or, indeed, merely another chapter in the saga of the world systems built up by capitalism since the fifteenth century. Economists point out that, despite all the hype about globalisation, interest rates diverge even between OECD markets, and that domestic savings still correlate highly with domestic investment which they should not if there was a global market and that national policies still have a significant role to play. Political economists on the Left especially discount globalisation by saying that it is merely internationalisation, that there is no truly global firm but only multinationals, based in a few advanced countries, parading falsely as global.

There has been, however, a fundamental change in the world economy as I shall explain below (see also Desai 1995). First, capitalism is alive and well and pervading all over the globe except for a very small number of countries – Cuba and North Korea – which still retain fully a Leninist character with central planning and a command economy. Leninism, as a variant of socialism, is dead and gone, after occupying a pivotal position as an alternative to capitalism (Desai 1992). Capitalism has a variety of formations across the world, from Anglo Saxon to Scandinavian, to Asian/Confucian to European social corporatist. But even as debate continues about the role of the State one thing is clear: successful State intervention, as in the Asian case, has to be capitalist friendly, i.e. profit enhancing. Call it managing the market, but it is a market friendly way of intervening that we have all come to accept as the limit of intervention, as against the Fabian or the Leninist versions which were market hostile and sought to control and divert the market from its uncontrolled dynamic flow.

The defeat of socialism at the level of a single country, and indeed even the demise of Keynesianism in one country, has led to a search for new limits to global capitalism on the Left. There is no global state nor a global working class ready to take on global capital. May not the ecological crisis define the limits to global capitalism? people ask, half in hope and half in desperation. What with global warming and exhaustible non-renewable resources and the hole in the ozone layer, could it not be that global capitalism will run into its contradictions with the ecosphere? Sustainable development becomes the new cry.

The purpose of this paper is to damp down this speculation. I shall argue that the globalisation process is more robust than people think and that markets remain powerful instruments even in the face of the environmental problem. At the same time I argue that globalisation, for the first time in 200 years, challenges the hegemony of the North *vis-a-vis* the South and that only a structural adjustment in the North, as drastic as the South has experienced during the last twenty-five years, will save the North.

I argue these points in the context of the now widely accepted, but loosely defined, notion of sustainable development. The following section questions the precision of the concept of sustainable development and gives examples of where the market has worked in an eco-friendly way. It then goes on to describe globalisation as a process with some asymmetric effects on the North and the South and shows that the North will have to alter its ways drastically to survive global competition.

Can Sustainable Economic Growth be Measured?

Sustainable economic growth (SEG) has not been defined rigorously and, given the fuzziness of the concept, it is difficult to see how it can be defined in a satisfactory operational way. The Brundtland Commission definition, which mentions leaving the world for our grandchildren as we would like to find it, essentially evokes the Hicksian definition of income (Brundtland 1987; Hicks 1939). Income is the maximum sustainable level of consumption, given a set of interest rates and price expectations such that the value of the stock of assets is the same at the beginning of the period as at the end. (Hicks's definition is discussed in further detail in the Appendix to this chapter.)

Thus income is an *ex ante* forward-looking concept. It depends crucially on expectations of prices and interest rates over the period where you are desiring to measure income. It starts with an initial valuation of the stock of assets (given their existing prices) and it relies on the possibility of computing the expected value of the stock at the end of the period. In addition, it must be borne in mind that this concept of income pertains to the individual. Aggregating it over individuals is not just a technical problem: it is a general equilibrium problem.

Hicks, when discussing this concept, confessed that he did not think income thus defined was measurable. This is so even if all the commodities – consumption goods as well as assets – are marketable and have deep markets which can determine prices. The principal reason is uncertainty. Even if we take a conventional (not Keynesian) view of uncertainty, the longer the period over which projections have to be made, the more unreliable the measure would be. Thus at the minimum, there would be multiple values of income over the same future period. There is no unique value of income that could be sustainable.

Since SEG is the ratio of income over the value of assets, i.e. a growth rate, there will be multiple rates of SEG. If we compound this problem with variables for which there are no markets and no prices, for which there are not even estimates of current levels of physical stocks, the multiplicity will obviously increase. Also implicit in the notion of value of assets are prices of each type of commodity which goes into the total capital stock. Now for conventional marketed commodities, prices purport to measure relative substitutability under conditions of competitive equilibrium. If we deviate from competitive equilibrium conditions, even in this case of conventional commodities, prices fail to signal relative substitutability.

When we come to components of the ecosystem, the notion of substitutability, say, among the species or of one non-renewable resource for another, is itself in dispute. Are we willing to trade an endangered species for more clean air or less global warming? (Desai 1995).

Thus even excluding the ecosystem, to compute income over the next fifty years will not give us a unique answer. If we add the ecosystem, the concept is impossible even to define.

Of course, gross national product (GNP) is nothing like this Hicksian concept. It is an *ex-post* measure of marketed outputs (or incurred expenditures or money incomes) with marginal adjustment for non-marketed (but in principle *marketable*) outputs (Desai 1993).

Thus it is premature, if not dishonest, to speak of SEG as if we knew what it is or should be – whether, in terms of gross domestic product (GDP) growth, the rate should be high, low, positive, zero or negative. GDP is such an imperfect measure (as indeed the Greens always remind us) that any amount of environmental damage could be associated with the same growth rate of GDP. Negative GDP growth can often be more damaging than a positive rate. The total amount of environmental deterioration is determined by the particular mix of production processes and products as well as consumption patterns (including residential location) and working habits. Thus it may be enough to change processes or products rather than reduce GNP or its growth rate in some sense.

Given the pervasive uncertainty about the future as well as the indeterminate nature of our knowledge of the present levels of natural capital of all types, what is to be done? One strategy would be to exercise caution just in case our worst fears were justified. Since, if they are, in the event, not justified, we (or our grandchildren) are alive to adjust to the higher consumption path. If they are true, then the cautious strategy may prolong human life on the planet a bit longer.

But being cautious is not an operational recipe. Cautious in what – in targeting high growth or in taxing energy? Although market prices are myopic, there is no guarantee that not following market prices will lead us to correct prices (or price paths) since no unique correct prices exist, *even in principle*. The longer the time period over which we project, the less unique such prices (or price paths) will be. Thus over the very short run, market prices may be the *least unsatisfactory alternative* available because the only guarantee of market prices is that they will change in the light of changes in the immediate circumstances. In a dense fog with very low visibility, the only thing you can do is to take one extra step at a time. (By market prices, I mean the prices corrected for such externalities as are perceivable at present.)

Market Prices as Appropriate Green Signals

Thus it may be interesting to examine the role of market prices, knowing full well that these prices are not perfect competition prices and that they have to be supplemented by taxes and subsidies. Let me outline five examples when market pricing led to desirable outcomes, whether intended or not, as well as examples when taking a decision in defiance of the market led to ecologically undesirable outcomes. These are:

1. *Nuclear Energy*: Only when the UK government decided to privatise the electricity industry, nuclear energy was subjected to the market test and revealed to be expensive as well as dangerous. Only in countries with state subsidies (e.g., France) does nuclear energy survive. The ecological danger posed by nuclear power stations in the former USSR is grave and a lot of money (US$100 billion) may have to be expended to decommission these power stations. These costs have to be made more public.

2. *Oil Shock*: The 1973 quadrupling of oil prices led to a steady diminution of the use of energy per unit of GDP in the OECD countries. Of course, this adjustment took time and the short-run reactions took the form of a recession, but in the medium term, energy economy did occur. I doubt whether such economising could have occurred via a conference declaration or an intergovernmental coordination effort.

    I should also mention that the forecasts made in 1972 by The Club of Rome and many others, underestimated the scope for substitution of scarce material as well as the augmentation of supplies of such scarce material. Thus the oil price today is lower in relative terms than it was before 1973.

3. *The Debt Rescheduling Problem*: At the beginning of the 1980s, the problem of the Third World debt burden became prominent. But by the end of the 1980s, Latin American countries, which had contracted their debt with private commercial banks, had successfully tackled their debt burden by securitising the debt. The debt was floated on the market, and some of it was settled for as little as 10 cents on the dollar.

    The official debt of Sub-Saharan African countries has been more difficult to reduce. Despite the Trinidad conditions announced by the UK prime minister three years ago, there is still no debt forgiveness on the part of governments. Thus the market found it easier to tackle debt than governments do.

4. *The DM/OM Exchange Rate*: The fixing of the exchange rate, as between the Deutschmark and the Ostmark on the reunification of Germany, is an example of the market defying political decisions which imposed enormous extra burdens on the reunification process. A market based approach would have been much easier. The problem of poverty in East Germany could have been tackled separately.

5. *The US Gasoline Price*: The US is a high energy consumer, in large part due to its failure to price gasoline in the way it is set in Western Europe. The lack of courage to tax gasoline in the US is doubly damaging – it fails to tackle the budget deficit and is environmentally damaging.

I do not mean to imply that markets are perfect, but that often they are quicker to act, although not without side effects, to accomplish certain environmental economies or produce developmental outcome. There will be a need to intervene in the market to correct externalities, but it would be better to take care to pursue incentive compatible market intervention rather than one that goes against market signals. In any case neither governments nor markets can overcome the problem of uncertainty and the impossibility of correct forecasts.

Globalisation

What has happened in the last few years to alter the balance in favour of the market has been the renewed dynamic growth of capitalism. Confounding the prophecies of its imminent or eventual demise through much of the twentieth century – by Lenin, by Schumpeter, and many others – capitalism is still a vibrant dynamic system. It has also globalised in recent years. While capitalism has always been international, indeed 'a world system' in the words of Immanuel Wallerstein,' it is only recently that technological innovation and institutional deregulation has made the system truly global. Manuel Castells has defined globalisation 'as an ability to act in real time on a planetary scale'. Financial markets are truly global in this sense. Direct foreign investment is also globally mobile, but it is by sourcing and sub-contracting using electronic devices (email, fax) that instant changes in plans can be implemented. Thus a Western airline can have its global reservation plans carried out in India due to the availability of good software. A New York corporation can get its accounts processed every day in Galway in Ireland, exploiting the time difference and availability of cheaper skilled labour.

The process which led to globalisation began as early as 1973 after the oil shock, but could be said to have accelerated during the 1980s. The most important aspects of it today are that on the one hand it has made the world more symmetric as between North and South. It has also led to a fragmentation of the South into rapidly developing regions and those still left behind.

The picture of the world economy in the 1960s and 1970s was one where the North and its trans-national corporations (TNCs) dominated/exploited/robbed the South. The South was thought of as passive, dependent and exploited. There was much pessimism, for example in the works of Baran, Frank and others, about the possibility of rapid economic growth in the South (Baran 1960; Frank 1967). Although this image persists in some people's discourse, even to the extent of a refusal to believe that growth has occurred, the reality is very different today. Today, for example, there is a lot of worry in the North about competition in the manufacturing sector from the Asian countries and pessimism about the possibility of generating full employment or about financing the welfare state (Reich 1992; Goldsmith 1995). Fifteen years ago, no one anticipated that the manufacturing industry of South Korea, Taiwan, Malaysia, Indonesia, China or India, would be seen as posing a threat to the industrialised North. Some of these fears have crystallised around the Uruguay Round of GATT and the ratification of the GATT treaty. There is now suddenly an attempt to impose a social clause or an environmental labelling as part of GATT. The rapidly industrialising countries of the South view this as a cynical ploy to impose non-tariff barriers to their exports.

At the same time, the South is no longer homogenous. East and Southeast Asia are industrialising rapidly and South Korea will soon join Japan in the OECD. South Asia is also undergoing an economic liberalisation process and becoming fully integrated with the global economy. Latin America has come out of its debt-ridden state and is resuming its industrialisation. It is a middle income region, and Mexico has already entered OECD. (None of this is meant to ignore the inequalities of income distribution in these countries but these were present as much during the phase of relative autonomy pursued by the South as is the case now. In some cases, inequalities may even improve, as is the case in South Korea and Taiwan.)

Sub-Saharan Africa is still left in the classic category of South, though even here, Southern Africa as a region may grow rapidly now that apartheid has been removed.

Against this background, I wish to argue that globalisation is a process that is not necessarily hostile to sustainable growth and that indeed it should be harnessed for the purpose. Policies which further globalisation should be supported and those blocking it (e.g., protectionism) should be resisted (Goldsmith 1995). Especially important here is the near certainty that globalisation will force certain harsh structural adjustments on the North that will have the welcome effect of cutting consumption levels and increasing savings. Let me explain.

One major problem that confronts the developed countries of the North is that of restoring full employment levels. The rate of unemployment has trebled during the 1980s relative to the 1950s and 1960s (Layard, Jackman and Nickell 1993). Since the 1970s, although per capita GDP has risen, unemployment has also gone up – hence the jobless growth, as it was called by the Human Development Report, 1993 (UNDP 1993). The only exception to the experience of jobless growth is Japan, which managed to increase employment as well as income, so that its unemployment rate stayed low (it did go up, however, in the recent recession).

One reason for jobless growth and for the frustration of the governments in tackling the problem of employment is the globalisation of the world economy. This has meant the loss of autonomy on the part of nation-states to determine their economic policy. In this sense 'Keynesianism in one country' is dead. This is not because governments are no longer able to affect employment but because the determinants of employment are no longer what they used to be. It is no longer lack of effective demand which determines the level of employment. Globalisation has shifted both the demand curve and the supply curve of tradeable goods and services. Thus any amount of exports can be sold as long as the economy is competitive. The competitiveness of the economy is determined by the rate of productivity growth which itself depends on the rate of investment and the speed of innovation.

The example of Japan is instructive in this respect. The Japanese economy invests more than 30 per cent, maintains a high speed of innovation by fostering domestic competition among its large conglomerates and thus, productivity growth is high. But Japan also practices the creation of a large number of jobs in the non-tradeable sector. These are low productivity/low wage jobs.

The tradeable sector is now increasingly the wealth-creating sector but not a job-creating sector. The challenge facing the developed West is to raise its investment rate by saving and investing more. It has also to maintain a high rate of productivity growth in its tradeable sector to go on creating wealth. But, at the same time, job creation in the non-tradeable sector poses a challenge not only in terms of the number of jobs which have to be created, but also because of the difficulty of the inequality of wages as between the tradeable and the non-tradeable sectors. To some extent this requires a transfer of surplus from the tradeable to the non-tradeable sector. This can be done either by differential pricing of the non-tradeable goods and services (to the extent that they can be priced) – I have discussed some of these problems in Desai (1994). Now one conclusion to which this analysis leads is that countries of the North, facing these problems of persistent unemployment, will have to:

1. raise their savings rate and to do this reduce the level and change the pattern of their consumption;
2. shift taxation from employment (payroll taxes of various kinds) to consumption, especially of natural resources;
3. and increase investment in non-material capital such as education, health and training.

It is not too much then to say that the impact of this effect of globalisation will be positive on the environment. This may be one of those dialectical contradictions, the unintended effect of human actions.

Conclusion

Globalisation has often been demonised. My purpose here is to point out that by forcing structural adjustment in the North, it may yet lead to benevolent effects on the environment.

Appendix

Hicks's definition was given in his 1939 classic *Value and Capital*. It may be useful to quote it here for future reference:

> The purpose of income calculations in practical affairs is to give people an indication of the amount they can consume without impoverishing themselves. Following out this idea, it would seem that we ought to define a man's income as the maximum value which he can consume during a week, and still expect to be as well off at the end of the week as he was at the beginning. (*Value and Capital*, p. 172)

Hicks goes on to explain that this forward looking definition of income has to be supplemented, adding that this measure of income depends upon the expectations concerning future prices and interest rates. Having considered these problems, he argues 'By considering the approximations (ie, for interest rates and prices (MD)) to this criterion (the definition quoted above (MD)), we have come to see how very complex it is, how unattractive it looks when subjected to detailed analysis. We may now allow a doubt to escape us whether it does, in the last resort, stand up to analysis at all, whether we have been chasing a will-o'-the-wisp' (op. cit., p. 178).

Even if these problems were overcome, this only pertains to the income of a single individual. At this level, income is equivalent to the *sustainable level of consumption*, assuming zero growth in the stock of wealth. But this income is subjective as it is conditional on expectations. It is also easy to take interest rates and prices as given when speaking of a single individual. But when we speak of many individuals or the economy as a whole (national or global), this assumption is no longer tenable. What is sustainable for an individual is not necessarily so for the economy.

Related to this issue of endogeneity of interest rates and prices is the problem of reconciling the subjective expectations of different individuals since, by the definition above, the sustainable level of consumption (i.e., income) is conditional on expectations, and there is no simple way of aggregating over the subjective expectations of different individuals. In the SEG context, think of either the present and the future generations or even the rich and the poor.

The answer, of course, has been to ignore all these complications in national income accounting and pretend that the *ex-post* measure of goods and services produced (which is what GNP is) is the same as the *ex-ante* welfare theoretic measure of income. This is often more a hindrance than a help. Thus the problem of properly measuring the depreciation of capital in order to derive a net national product from gross national product is important, even for the *ex-post* measurement of income, regardless of welfare implications. In this way the proper accounting of used up 'natural capital' is important. What it does not do is deal with the issue of future generations and sustainability.

References

Baran, Paul A. *Political History of Growth*. New York: Monthly Review Press, 1960.
Baranzini M. and A. Cencini (eds). *Marxs, Hayek and the Demise of Official Keynesianism*. 1996.
Brundtland G. H. *Our Common Future*. Oxford: Oxford University Press, 1987.
Desai, Meghnad. 'Greening the HDI?' in A. MacGillivray, ed. *Accounting for Change*. 1995.
Desai, Meghnad. 'No Easy Jobs', *New Statesman and Society*, 22 July, 1994.
Desai, Meghnad. 'Income and Alternative Measures of Well Being', in D. G. Westendorf and D. Ghai,
Monitoring Social Progress in the 1990s. Aldershot: Avebury, 1993.
Desai, Meghnad. 'Is Socialism Dead?' *Contention*, Winter 1992, 1.2, pp. 143–58.
Desai, Meghnad and Redfern P. (eds). *Global Governance: Ethics and Economics of the World Order*. London: Frances Pinter, 1995, pp. 6–22.
Frank. A. G. *Capitalism and Underdevelopment in Latin America*. New York: Monthly Review Press, 1967.
Goldsmith. J. *The Trap*. London: Macmillan, 1995.
Hicks. J. R. *Value and Capital*. Oxford: Clarendon Press, 1939.
Layard R., Jackman R. and Nickell S. *Unemployment*, Oxford: Blackwell, 1993.
Reich. R. *The Work of Nations*. New York: Alfred Knopf, 1991.
UNDP. *Human Development Report*. New York: Oxford University Press, 1993.
Westendorf. D. G. and Ghai. D. (eds.) *Monitoring Social Progress in the 1990s*. Aldershot: Avebury, 1993.

Acknowledgement

First publication: Desai, Meghnad (1997) 'Globalization and Sustainable Development', in Gupta S.D., Choudhry N.K. (eds) *Globalization, Growth and Sustainability*. Recent Economic Thought Series, vol. 58. Springer, Boston, MA; pp. 231–242. Reproduced with kind permission of SNCSC.

Part 2

India and China

Chapter 9

INDIA AND CHINA

An Essay in Comparative Political Economy

Meghnad Desai

(2005)

Introduction

India and China are two of the oldest and still extant civilisations. For Europeans, they were legendary seats of immense wealth and wisdom right up to the eighteenth century. Somewhere between the mid-eighteenth century and early nineteenth centuries, both of these countries became, in the European eyes, bywords for stagnant, archaic and weak nations. For China, this happened between the adulation of Voltaire and the cooler judgment of Montesquieu; in India's case, it was the contrast between Sir William Jones's desire to learn things Indian and James Mill's dismissal of Indian history as nothing but darkness.

The twentieth century brought nothing but a deepening of the perception of the two countries as bywords for misery and the perceptions were not too far behind actual conditions of the two countries. For one thing they were, and remain, the two most populous countries. In 1820, they had a combined population in excess of half a billion and by 1900, it reached 700 million. Within the twentieth century, their population had trebled. But they were also two of the poorest countries, typically thought of as locations of famine, disease, backwardness and superstition, of women with bound feet and men with long pony-tails in China, untouchables beyond the pale and myriad gods with many heads and limbs in India.

In the mid-twentieth century, particularly in the 1960s, the fortunes of these two countries seemed to have reached their nadir. They were independent republics supposedly launched on their path of development, but both suffered devastating famines. China's famine was hidden, perhaps more from China's own ruling classes than from its people or the world, but it had followed swiftly upon the debacle of the Great Leap Forward, a memorable piece of policymaking by fantasy. A double harvest failure in 1965 and 1966 brought India to its proverbial knees in terms of foreign policy and dependence on US food aid. These two countries were 'basket cases' in the then fashionable terms of international diplomacy.

In the span of less than forty years, we are discussing China and India not as failures nor for their ancient wisdoms, but as dynamic modern economies. The *Economist* has to write editorials to tell the world not to be afraid of China's economic power. American legislators pass laws to prevent their businesses from outsourcing work to India's software and telecommunication services. China ranks as the second largest economy in terms of gross domestic product (GDP) in purchasing power parity (PPP) dollars. Together the two countries account for 19.2 per cent of gross world product – China 11.5 per cent and India 7.7 per cent. This is still below their share of world population 37.5 per cent – with China 21 per cent and India 16.5 per cent.

National income estimates covering a long period are, by their nature, broadly indicative rather than precise.[1] Angus Maddison, to whom the profession is indebted for making these calculations his lifetime work, gives the shares of gross world product and population of China and India for two earlier dates in the twentieth century as follows.

Table 9.1 succinctly describes the course of the two economies over the twentieth century. They start with the share of income below that of population. Over the previous century they had slightly different trajectories. India's per capita income is estimated to have grown from M$533 in 1820 (Maddison dollars [M$] or 1990 international dollars) to M$673 in 1913 while China's per capita income declined from M$600 in 1820 to M$552 in 1913. But during the first half of the twentieth century, both countries saw a decline in their per capita incomes – India from M$673 in 1913 to M$619 in 1950 and China from M$552 in 1913 to M$439 in 1950.[2]

---

1   Beyond this vague assertion I do not intend to go into statistical measurement problems.
2   Dharma Kumar (1998), who independently made comparative estimates of India and China over the early twentieth century, arrives at not dissimilar estimates. She puts India's per capita income as US$60 in 1952 and China's as US$50 (at current prices).

Table 9.1 says two things: India and China both suffered a declining per capita income and a rising population during the first half of the twentieth century, but India was slightly better off than China between 20 per cent[3] and 40 per cent.[4] By 1998 this was reversed. Both countries were better off, but China was much better off than India. China's per capita income was M$3117 while India's was M$1760. Thus, while India roughly trebled its income, China increased it sevenfold. In earlier periods, China, while more populous than India, was not noticeably richer. In terms of GDP, the two economies were of roughly similar size. The ratio of China's GDP to India's was 1.18 in 1918; 1.08 in 1950; but in 1998, it was 2.28.

Table 9.1 Share of world output and population

Year	Share of world product (%)		Share of gross world population (%)	
	China	India	China	India
1913	8.9	7.5	26.4	17.0
1950	4.5	4.2	21.1	14.2
1998	11.5	7.7	21.0	16.5

Source: Maddison (2001).

Therefore, one theme of this chapter is the contrast between the economic performance of China and India and its proximate causes. But there are also a lot of similarities between the two, both in the path to modernisation and, as we shall see later, the future prospects for their economies. There are also political similarities and contrasts between the two, both as to their twentieth-century history and twenty-first century challenges.

Historical Legacies

Political Legacy
While both India and China have a long history, their histories are very different. China has been by and large a stable, centrally run state throughout its history with limited periods of instability and lack of a single authority. India's history has been exactly the reverse. The periods when a single king or political authority ruled over even the major part of India's territory

---

3   Kumar (1998).
4   Maddison (2001).

can be counted on the fingers of one hand. In China's case there was a deep desire for unification of the country as a driving force of nationalism in the twentieth century. But it was called reunification. Thus at the onset of the Second World War, China was divided, and Jonathan Spence (1999) expresses the drive for nationalists as follows:

> The solidification of such a group of new states, that is, war lords, KMT [Kuomintang], communists and Japanese enclaves, would return China to the situation that had prevailed before the Qin conquests of 221 B.C., during the so-called Warring States period when ten major regimes controlled the country among them; or it might bring a recurrence of the shifting patterns of authority and alliances that typified China's history from the third to sixth century A.D., and again from tenth to the thirteenth.[5]

In India's case, there never was any authority which has ruled over all of India; indeed, not even the British or even the present Indian government. India has been an idea in world culture for millennia, but its borders had been fixed only in the late nineteenth century sometime after the British gave up on Afghanistan and drew the Durand line. Kings have ruled over much of North India – the Maurya and Gupta dynasties just before and after the BC/AD division. The Mughals could be said to have ruled over much of India between the years of Akbar's maturity in 1570 and Aurangzeb's death in 1707. Their empire extended to Kabul but did not take in all of South India. The British could be said to have ruled over two-thirds of India between 1857 and 1947, with the remaining third being ruled by native princes under their paramountcy but not direct rule. In 1947, India was partitioned and thus even what is now called India is not what Nehru in 1946 wrote about in *The Discovery of India*.[6] Indian system of kingly power was not so much like a pyramid, but like a multi-tiered cake. It was flatter and while there was a top and a bottom plus layers in between, the power of the top king over his vassals below was not absolute. Loyalty, though owed by the lower tiers to the top, was always negotiable and there had to be some give and take.[7] The British were perhaps the first rulers to try a more absolute and hierarchical structure of power under the limitation of oversight by a democratic Parliament back in London.

---

5   Spence *et al.* (1999, p. 426).
6   Nehru (1946) and Keay (2001).
7   Inden (2000).

Yet in one sense it was British rule which gave India its definitive territorial extent, fixed its boundaries and gave it a structure of provinces and central government with an administrative 'steel frame'. The British gave India their language, which facilitates even today India's access to global markets, as do the legal system of property rights and Western orientation of its elite. India's independence movement was critical of the economic ruin the British had caused – deindustrialisation, drain of treasure, deskilling and diversion of agriculture into commercial crops away from food crops, and so on. But India began to acquire railroads and modern industry in the 1850s – a quarter of a century earlier than China. More foreign capital per capita was poured into India than in China; in 1913 India had US$6.9 per capita foreign capital while China had US$3.7.[8]

There is, however, another much less mentioned benefit that India derived from British rule. Of course, it might have been better for India to have never suffered foreign rule, but to have been united under a native king or republic. But between 1500 and 1800, India had several foreign trading companies vying for control – the Portuguese, the Dutch, the French, the Danes, and of course, the English. As a counterfactual of history, it is possible to imagine what we call India today and take it for granted as a single country being made up of several different 'countries' in the west, south, east and north with different foreign languages being spoken along with local languages. Thus the Tamils could have been French speaking and the Maharashtrians Portuguese speaking and so on. Thanks to the religious wars of Europe in the seventeenth century and British victories in European wars in the eighteenth century, India ended up with a single foreign power, and thus the idea of India as a single country developed with its modern nationalism. This is not entirely fanciful since Southeast Asia with a population and extent not dissimilar to India's was ruled by the Dutch (Indonesia), the French (Indochina) and the British (Burma, Malaysia and Singapore) with Thailand being independent. What is more, the hegemonic political ideology of the nationalist movement – liberal democracy – was also borrowed from the foreign rulers. The India we talk of today is a nineteenth-century product in more than one sense.

China, by contrast, never suffered foreign rule over majority of its territory. There were foreign concessions in ports and later in interior towns extracted by several foreign powers in circumstances that the Chinese found humiliating. But it had not suffered classic imperial rule until 1931 when

---

8   Maddison (2001, p. 99).

the Japanese invaded Manchuria and later in 1937 when they occupied large chunks of eastern and central China.[9] Yet China's attitude to foreigners was and is much more hostile than India's. The removal of foreigners, especially the reversal of concessions, became a driving force for China. For India, the hostility to things foreign, except perhaps for foreign private capital, melted like snow in spring soon after independence. If anything, India in its early days after independence sought foreign capital from public rather than private sources and from a variety of countries rather than merely its old colonial masters. China after 1949 relied on one country, the USSR, and soon came to regret its connection. China's problem, unlike that of India, was the multiplicity of foreign powers gnawing at its sides with no single hegemonic ruling ideology as India had had with liberal democracy from Britain. It had the Germans, Japanese, Americans, French and British jostling not so much for rule over Chinese minds as over their cash boxes. There was some missionary input, more than in India, but eventually China had to forge its own ideology of modernity. It had to struggle to confront Confucianism against Western ideologies – liberalism, fascism and communism.

These historical legacies shaped both the politics and economics of the two countries. For India, the problem was in achieving unity in diversity and in accommodating various languages and religions in a political structure, so as to give its centre enough power to maintain its territorial integrity but its regions enough room to develop their diversities. India had a problem of articulating a single vision of Indian nationhood since it had been a nation only since the mid-nineteenth century and even this was asserted against by the foreign rulers who saw India not as a single nation but a motley collection of races and religions.[10] India thus chose a federal polity with a strong centre able to alter state boundaries, split up states or create new ones. India even so is a soft state in Myrdal's famous description where the government has to work consensually and exert control sparingly and, that too, only against serious threats to national integrity.[11] India's fear is a break up of its territorial unity as had happened in the Partition.[12]

---

9   I am treating the Manchus as not being foreign, though many Chinese at the beginning of the twentieth century emphasised that they wanted to remove the Manchu empire and establish a Chinese republic.

10 Desai (2000).

11 I have learned a lot about federal structures and federalism in India while co-supervising Katherine Adeney (see Adeney, 2003).

12 Myrdal (1968).

China has always had a vision of itself as a nation. Through much of its history, there has been a strong central power, and China has been run as a unitary polity. Indeed, Sun Yat Sen and his Communist supporters viewed the prospect of federalism as akin to feudalism.[13] The theme of reunification in early-twentieth-century China meant recentralisation of authority. China has its minorities, but it is viewed and indeed views itself as a country of the Han people – a solid homogenous mass. While there are differences between Mandarin and Cantonese, the language is the same for an overwhelming majority of the Chinese. China is thus a unitary hard state which can pursue a single goal with determination and mobilise maximal resources in its achievement. It has ever been thus, be it in building the Great Wall or the system of grand canals, or in recent times in the Great Leap Forward.

There was a further advantage of being a unitary state which has often not been recognised. As Kent Deng has said in a recent survey of Chinese economic history:

> a basic structural factor – namely, that for most of the time most of China had a nationwide market, a single government (which was active in maintaining food supply, famine relief, and price control), a standardized written language, a uniform calendar and a system of weights and measures, a dominant Confucian code of conduct, a nationwide transport network, and the mechanisms for social mobility and inter-regional migration ... China could claim to have been a proto industrialized country by the 13th century and indeed has been considered by many scholars to have been a prime candidate for a capitalist revolution which it missed.[14]

But anticipating somewhat later themes, strong states can also be brittle states, while soft states are difficult to smash and break since they are pliable. India has through its history been ruled by many authorities and sometimes none, but it has had a social stability which is remarkable. In India's case the enveloping unity was provided by the Hindu social structure, especially the caste system, which determined the basis on which interregional mobility could be conducted. Indeed the caste system proved to be so powerful that even among the Muslims and Christians a caste hierarchy took root and

---

13   Spence *et al.* (1999).
14   Deng (2000, p. 6) surveys this literature. There has been a similar though less extensive discussion among Indian historians as to whether India could have had its own capitalist revolution (see Habib, 1971).

developed. While the concept of the Asiatic Mode of Production (AMP) is much derided nowadays, its essence was about a society in which the state was epiphenomenal and the peasant society went on impervious to changing rulers. India was throughout its history like that.[15] China, on the other hand strong as it was, became subject to spasmodic breakdowns which lasted several years. Within the modern period, we have had the Taiping Rebellion (1851–64), the Boxer Uprising (1900) which eventually led to end of empire (1911) and four decades of warlordism, and more recently the Cultural Revolution (1966–76). Even the Tiananmen incidents of 1989 are more a sign of brittleness than of strength.

Economic Legacy

Both India and China were a highly urban civilisation by the eighteenth century, though of course the bulk of the population lived in rural areas. China was much advanced in science and technology, with gunpowder, printing, paper and paper currency as its inventions. China's scientific and technological achievements are known to us thanks to the monumental efforts of Joseph Needham.[16] India was known for its mathematics and its philosophy. The Chinese gave the world the wheelbarrow and bureaucracy; India gave the world the zero, decimals and Buddhism. Both were major exporters of fine textiles, silks and muslins; their ships sailed around the world and indeed dominated the seas till 1500. After that the Chinese withdrew from the seas and while the Indians continued, the powers that be in Delhi or Agra had no need for a navy. It was the kingdoms in South India which were maritime adventurers. As they declined in power under the Mughals, Indian shipping began to be conducted increasingly on a private basis rather than a state sponsored one. The control of the seas passed to a series of Western European countries. Yet China and India remained economically vibrant till the late eighteenth century.

China had a higher productivity in its agriculture, the iron tipped plough having been in use at least half a millennium before it made its appearance in India. Thus Needham attributes the animal drawn plough to the period of the Warring states, while Habib says that the iron plough came to India in the first century AD.[17] Chinese irrigation systems were bigger and better

---

15 See O'Leary (1989) for a critique of the Asiatic Mode of Production (AMP). Also see Habib (1983) for a sympathetic account of Marx's views on India, and Deng (2000), who sees the AMP as a useful concept.

16 Needham *et al*. (1954).

17 Needham *et al*. (1954) and Habib (1995).

than any in India.[18] Thus Maddison's estimate of M$600 per capita income for China and M$533 for India in 1820 is roughly the right sort of relative difference.

The difference was made up in the next 130 years. By 1950, India had caught up with China, as we saw earlier, in the per capita as well as total income estimates. In output per person employed, Maddison shows India at M$1377 in 1950 and China at M$1297. The story is that in the nineteenth century India did enjoy a rising per capita income. This is not uncontroversial, as everything else about British impact on India. But it is consistent with much data.[19] India was a land surplus rather than a labour surplus country in the nineteenth century with a population of about 200–230 million, that is, one-fifth of the current level, and much the same amount of land. It became for a while an agricultural exporter rather than industrial exporter, but still managed a trade surplus. By the late nineteenth century, India began to acquire modern infrastructure and industry, not large relative to its population, but large relative to other countries. India is in this sense an early industrialising country. In 1945, it was the seventh largest industrial country by volume of output.

But their history drove both China and India to define industrialisation rather than economic development as their prime goal. Even within industrialisation, the strategy was one of concentrating on basic goods such as steel and machinery – 'Department I goods' in Marxian terminology – rather than consumer and low-tech goods. Both countries were inspired by the example of the USSR and its planning achievements. They both sought independence of foreign capital and self-sufficiency.

The contrast between the two was most stark in agriculture. Being vast territories there is a similar diversity in the eco-agricultural make up of regions in both countries. But China's central rule meant that a uniform revenue collection system and land ownership pattern prevailed especially while the central power was effective. India by contrast had different legal patterns of revenue collection and different land tenures as a result of a lack of central authority reinforced by British experimentation with Ryotwari, Zamindari, Mahalwari and the like. Land reform was a straightforward issue of changing ownership of large landholdings across China as far as

---

18 Oriental Despotism, a notion begotten by Wittfogel from Marx and Engels's AMP, was supposed to be good at hydraulic projects. Be that as it may, the abandoned city of Fatehpur Sikri is a monument to how a Mughal king built a city where he failed to provide water supplies.

19 See Heston in Kumar and Desai (1983).

the Communists were concerned. They were also committed to it as soon as they could become the sole powers. In India land reform was a maze of regional complexity and the Congress Party was not a revolutionary organisation. Land reform thus became a state/provincial subject rather than a union/central policy issue. Thus India added legal and economic variation to the eco-agricultural one.

Development Paths

Differences between China and India appear much greater from the current vantage point than they would have in 1973 or even 1983. Each has gone through two broad phases, which I characterise in this section.

Taking Nationalism Seriously – Mistakes and Learning

Both countries feared foreign domination and considered development as synonymous with industrialisation. Both considered the State as the engine and the driver of growth and suspected the private sector's initiatives. The ideology forged during the long march to independence – Marxism, Leninism, Maoism in China and Gandhism in India, plus an amalgam of social and liberal democracy in India shaped the response more than economic realities warranted. One man ruled the roost though his closest associates did not share his beliefs as much as they said they did while he was still around. Mao for China and Nehru for India laid down the path from which each country had to deviate, if only because the path led to a blind alley.

For China the first period lasted from 1949 to 1978; for India from 1947 to 1980. China learned quickly thanks to Deng Xiaoping. India did not have a Deng. Blood proved much thicker than pragmatism in matters of economic ideology. India began a half-hearted change in 1980 when Mrs Gandhi abandoned self-sufficiency as an ideal and took a big loan from the international monetary fund (IMF). But that loan and subsequent hard currency borrowing were frittered away. India could be said to have wasted ten years in a half-hearted liberalisation, which hit the buffers in 1991 when the country nearly went bankrupt.

Living in the Modern World and Adapting to It

In the second phase, each country forgot the lessons it had thought it had learned from its history, xenophobia, fear of foreign trade and foreign capital, distrust of private initiative and decentralisation. Each adapted to the rhythm of the world economy rather than sail against the wind. Being large vessels, they have a bit more freedom of manoeuvre than small countries. They misused the freedom in the first phase and corrected themselves in the second phase. Their comparators would be two smaller countries both with a colonial past – South Korea and Taiwan who did not go through a two-phase path. After 1960, South Korea single-mindedly pursued growth with spectacular results. Taiwan had a similar colonial background to Korea's but it also had the influx of the Guomindang elite, which transformed property rights in Taiwan and achieved what it could not on the mainland – a successful growth strategy.

The comparison between the two pairs of countries is revealing. In 1950 China and India had per capita incomes of M$439 and M$619, while South Korea and Taiwan had M$770 and M$936. By 1999, the numbers were: China M$3259, India M$1818, South Korea M$13,317 and Taiwan M$15,720. Let me examine the two phases in some detail.

The First Phase

Both China and India saw a development of Department I goods – steel, cement, machine-making equipment – as pivotal to their growth strategies. India had at this time a viable world-class textile industry which it chose to stifle in its search for an employment-intensive growth strategy meant to favour small-scale and low-tech firms over large-scale industrialised firms. India diverted resources from the production of domestic consumption goods, especially of the machine-produced variety, to the production of investment goods by the industrial sector and consumer goods by small-scale industries. However, its savings rate was not significantly raised and the growth rate remained modest. China seems to have concentrated its industrial efforts also on the basic goods sector initially, but after the first three or four years switched to an all-round emphasis on heavy as well as light industries. Apart from the aberration of backyard steel furnaces in the Great Leap Forward phase, it was not saddled with a small-scale industry strategy. But China had a more successful resource mobilisation strategy than India did. India's Second Five-Year Plan (1956–61) ran into a resource constraint by 1958. China on the other hand ran into the evils of overweening ambition in launching the Great Leap Forward. There seems to have been a slowdown in China in the 1960–65 period, whereas in India it came in the second half of the 1960s after the Third Five-Year Plan (1961–66).

China managed its agrarian reform better than India. Starting from a higher level of productivity, China went on to transform not only the tenurial relations in agriculture but also the production conditions. Thus abolishing of landlords and forming cooperatives and then communes changed not only the distribution of surplus, but also its size. India concentrated on changing the tenurial relations by abolishing zamindari and intermediaries and redistributing the surplus. Reform was of course different across regions as the polity dictated. But India did little to change production conditions – land pooling, technology used or labour deployed. These changed in India in the 1960s with the advent of the Green Revolution, where a combination of foreign knowledge, domestic subsidies and rural private initiative brought a capitalist revolution to the Indian countryside. Despite this, China's lead in agricultural productivity remained to the end of the first phase and indeed increased, when in the second phase, China moved to a more private initiative system.

But above all, China did very well by human development. Long-run calculations of Human Development Index (HDI) have been made by Nicholas Crafts. For China and India he has estimates for 1950, 1973 and 1992 (Table 9.2). The World Bank's Human Development Report (HDR) has over the various years published trends in countries' HDIs from 1960 onward. Its methodology has evolved over the years and so the estimates have also been revised even for earlier years. Using the 1997 HDR and the 2002 HDR we can see the trend up to 2002. The HDR estimates start in 1960 and are not strictly comparable to Crafts' estimates, but they are close enough.

Table 9.2 Human development indices, 1950–2000

	1950	1960	1973	1980a	1980b	1992	2000
China	0.163	0.248	0.407	0.475	0.554	0.594	0.726
India	0.160	0.206	0.289	0.296	0.434	0.439	0.577

Sources: Crafts (1997) for 1950, 1973 and 1992; United Nations Development Programme, *Human Development Report (HDR)* (1997) for 1960 and 1980a; and *HDR* (2002) for 1980b and 2000.

Thus we see that despite having similar HDIs in 1950, China had left India behind by 1973, even with similar per capita incomes. Over the fifty-year period, while the HDIs are not strictly comparable, China enhanced its HDI four-and-a-half times while India did so only three-and-a-half times. Taking the estimates for 1950, 1980b and 2000, we see that in the first thirty years, China advanced much faster – by three-and-a-half times – than in the last twenty years – only by a third more. India on the other hand took its HDI up two-and-three-quarter times between 1950 and 1980 and again by a third in the next twenty years. Some writers have argued that the slowing down of China's advance in human development was due to the disbanding of the communes and with it the downgrading of the health care facilities available to all.[20] On the other hand, the closer a country's HDI comes to the limit of 1.0, the harder each step becomes. Whichever way we look at it, China has done much better in human development than India.

While there may be an argument about the state of health care facilities in China after the Deng reforms were launched, it is in other dimensions that China kept on doing well. Its emphasis on education for all from early on paid handsome dividends, while education remains a blot on India's record. Here again the centralist versus federal polity makes a lot of difference. Social conditions differ immensely across India in terms of caste structures, religious influence and superstitions. Hinduism is not an egalitarian religion even in theory and Islam, at least in India, is not so in practice.[21] It is only when you go south where the influence of Christian missions was felt and social movements against the caste system were successful in the early twentieth century that you witness an improvement in human development statistics. India continues to pay a heavy price for its neglect of education, especially as it concerns women.[22]

The first phase, despite the differences in approach to agrarian transformation and human development, altered the relative positions of China and India from what they were in 1950, but not by much. By 1978, per capita income of China was M$979 and of India M$966. China had caught up with India over the thirty years, but not dramatically surpassed it. Agricultural productivity per worker was almost identical in 1975 in the two countries – China 2.3 and India 1.9 (relative to the United States =

---

20   Dreze and Sen (1989).

21   The distinguished French anthropologist Louis Dumont has celebrated India's inegalitarianism in his *Homo Hierarchicus* as well as other books (see Dumont, 1980).

22   The usual exception in India is of course Kerala, which shows what can be achieved even in a democratic society by committed public action. Kerala has had the benefit of a democratically elected Communist government ever since the mid-1950s. But historically Travancore Cochin, which was the native state in what became Kerala, had higher literacy rates even by the 1940s than its surrounding British India districts. Matriarchy and Christianity plus an enlightened ruler played their role here.

100).²³ One may ask why this was so. Why is it that China did not do much better than India despite its revolutionary effort in industry and agriculture and its immense achievements in education and poverty reduction. There are two responses to that question.

One, of course, is that it did. China's income doubled while India's only went up by 50 per cent. Of course, China had suffered from the ravages of foreign and civil war through the fifteen years since Japan's invasion of Manchuria in 1933. So its per capita income in 1950 was below its potential. But even then we must acknowledge that China's growth was not smooth. While it was rapid, China's growth suffered from the tendency of Mao to take immense risks and plunge the economy into catastrophes. I am personalising the problem because Mao was a dominant influence in China to an extent that Nehru never was. This is where a totalitarian system can differ from a democratic one. It can accelerate growth and mobilise immense resources, but if the direction is wrong it can also crash and waste an awful lot of resources in a short period of time. But added to that, the political culture of China has been long used to such imperial power, while India has been a much less commandable polity. Thus Mao plunged China into the Great Leap Forward as well as the Great Proletarian Cultural Revolution (GPCR), with the structure of centralised and personalised power which led to the catastrophic famine of 1962. China paid a price for this in terms of death, starvation and wasted resources in abandoned projects. Much human capital, of both university teachers and students, was revalorised during the GPCR.

India, by comparison, had its muddle and mess but no great discontinuities in its development experience. It had a multiparty system and even within the Congress Party had antagonistic factions, which could mobilise opposition to Nehru. Even before his death, Nehru was forced to abandon his preferred policy of cooperatives in agriculture by the farmers' leader Charan Singh, but then besides Nehru no one else in the Congress took cooperative agriculture seriously and had done nothing about it since the Agrarian Reforms Committee of the Congress proposed it in 1949. The Second Five-Year Plan had to be modified due to resource shortages, but the Third Five-Year Plan kept to the same basic strategy. During the 1960s, India went through what was known (in a Maoist parody) as the Three Twos – death of two prime ministers, two harvest failures and two wars. There was a policy reversal in agriculture when the High Yield

---

23 Maddison *et al.* (2002).

Variety programme was adopted. In addition, rural and regional political bosses asserted their hold over the Congress Party and displaced the urban Westernised elite after Nehru's death, but they in turn were displaced after 1969 when Mrs Gandhi regained control of the Congress. India also had to devalue its currency and felt the heat of the US and World Bank disapproval. Yet the economic strategy did not (sadly) change. The crisis of slow growth came in 1975 when in face of popular unrest, Mrs Gandhi was driven to suspend democracy and declare the Emergency. But that did not last long, proving yet again that India cannot be commanded by centralised and personalised power.[24]

The Second Phase

It was China, after 1978 under the influence of Deng, that accelerated, leaving India far behind. In the next thirty-five years China's per capita income more than trebled while that of India merely doubled. The logic of compound growth rates is pitiless, and China's per capita income is now almost double that of India. How did China do this?

China did this paradoxically by adopting a much more 'capitalist road' or Bukharinist strategy[25] than any other communist regime (the former Yugoslavia included). What is more, China adopted a road that India could always have adopted; indeed, this was possible right after independence except that no one, not even the Indian capitalists, were advocating greater import of foreign capital, opening up the economy to an export orientation, with Special Export Zones (SEZs).[26] While India went on restricting its large native capitalist class after independence, China had to practically reinvent its own bourgeoisie after 1978. Indeed according to a newspaper story cited by Dharma Kumar,[27] China, which had invented an examination system for the selection of bureaucrats in the mists of time, approached India in the 1980s to seek its guidance about conducting examinations for its civil servants on the lines of the Union Public Service Commission (UPSC) exams in India.

Of course, China's policy revolution was not seamless and Deng had to struggle to establish his hegemony. There is a debate among China scholars about the fang/shou (stop-go) cycle in Deng's reforms between 1978 and

---

24   Desai (1975).
25   For those old enough to recall these arcane labels.
26   In China's case, the SEZs are not all that different from the foreign concessions in ports which were so much resented before 1949.
27   Kumar (1998).

1989.[28] But once established, his control over policy was absolute; the political culture's habit of obedience to emperors helped.[29] Deng transformed agriculture by introducing the Family Responsibility System – privatisation Chinese Communist style. He then took on the industrial sector and opened it up to foreign capital while making room for the growth of village and local enterprises. He left the public sector enterprises untouched but slowly brought modern methods of fiscal and financial control to China. China had to introduce property rights and contract laws which India has had since Macaulay in British times.

India meanwhile also started to jettison some of its own orthodoxies, but the personality in power was still the same. Mrs Gandhi abandoned the fetish of national self-sufficiency and began to borrow abroad, from the IMF to begin with. She, however, changed little else in the dirigiste logic of Indian economic policy. The collapse of India's textile industry was symptomatic of the malaise. Within thirty-five years of independence, India had managed to bankrupt its once globally competitive industry. Freed from the constraint of food grain availability thanks to the Green Revolution, India did not manage to apply to its industrial sector the lessons learnt in its agricultural revolution – that is, to use foreign knowledge, rely on the dynamic private sector and deploy subsidies selectively. Instead, foreign borrowing was used to ease the consumption constraint in the public sector and to cushion lossmaking public enterprises. Ian Little and Vijay Joshi (1994) argue in their book on Indian economic reforms that Indian policymaking alternates between five-year spurts of radicalism then quiescence, flaring up under political or economic pressures.[30]

India really changed course only after the shock of 1991 when it was nearly bankrupt and had foreign reserves which would cover only two weeks' imports. But in changing the same personalities were involved as in the old dirigiste regime. Manmohan Singh as Finance Minister was crucial to the reform, but he was no Deng and neither was Narasimha Rao, who was prime minister 1991–96. Indeed, by 1994, India began to reveal its reluctance about economic liberalisation. Ever since, India has been reforming its economy, but in a much more embattled way than China. Given the nature of the political culture, reform can only be introduced by broad

---

28 See Baum (1994) and Shirk (1993).
29 After all, the establishment of Imperial authority had to go through such transition periods throughout Chinese history, but to support that claim will take me too far away from my theme as well as my competence.
30 Joshi and Little (1994).

consent, and all the potential losers (many of whom are in power) have to be bribed (sometimes literally so) to advance matters.

Thus, while China has received a lot of foreign capital, India has not. By 1998, Maddison's calculations show that foreign direct investment (FDI) per capita in China was US$183 and in India US$14. Even if a lot of China's FDI was due to the Chinese diaspora, it only shows the failure of India to attract its own diaspora to invest, in spite of a lot of trying. Indeed, India has sought portfolio capital more than FDI since suspicion of foreigners remains strong, not only among India's politicians but even more among its capitalists. There has been some change for the better in the five years under the government of the Bharatiya Janata Party (BJP) and its National Democratic Alliance, but there is a long way to go.[31] There are other more usual reasons for the difference in economic performance. For one, China's savings rate is almost 50 per cent of GDP, nearly twice that of India. Indeed given the higher savings rate in China plus the FDI influx, the growth rates are less far apart than should be the case. India averaged 5.5 per cent in the 1980s and around 6.5 per cent in the 1990s. Even at 7–9 per cent, China's growth rate implies inefficient use of capital barring gross measurement errors. Or it could indicate sharply diminishing returns to capital, but I doubt that given that a lot of FDI embodies the latest knowledge.

The reason may be that in both countries there is a large public sector where enterprises are seriously loss making. Both countries are wedded to Soviet-style emphasis on inputs rather than outputs and accumulation for its own sake. India had begun to shed some of these traits and has always had a smaller public sector than China. So the waste of resources by malinvestment[32] is larger in China. In both countries, there is also a budget deficit which is out of control; perhaps more so in India due to the exigencies of democratic and coalitional politics, as well as weak central control over provincial budgets.

The two countries have mobilised savings through their financial structures, but the mobilisation has left the financial sectors in fragile states. Nonperforming assets in the banking systems as well as the nonbank financial sector (international trade and investment corporations in China) indicate a problem ahead. India has failed to impose arm's-length regulatory regimes free of politics and the result has been fraud and corruption in

---

31 For recent restructuring efforts in the organised private sector in India, see Forbes, N. (2002) in *Doing Business in India: What Has Liberalisation Changed?* (ed. by Krueger, 2002).

32 An old fashioned Hayekian word.

equity market-related activities – Unit Trust of India (UTI), stock market scams of Harshad Mehta, and so on.

It is difficult to predict whether a combination of budget deficits, domestic debt and financial sector weakness will cause a major crisis in either country. Both have managed to run their external accounts fairly well. Their reserve positions are healthy, exchange rate policy – pegged to the dollar in China and a dirty float in India – are prudent. India has moved faster to full capital convertibility in recent years while financial sector reforms have yet to be fully undertaken. China has not moved as far with convertibility but its peg to the dollar may cause problems if the dollar weakens to any significant extent. India's foreign liabilities are more weighted toward the short run and portfolio end, while China has a larger FDI flow. The Asian crisis reminded us that even sound macroeconomic performance is no guarantee against a run on the currency if the markets suspect a mismatch between internal and external balance. Here it is India which is more fragile than China.

Speculations and Counterfactuals

I now turn to some very broad and highly speculative considerations. Having looked at China and India over the years since 1820 against a longer background, it is worth exploring a longer future. What follows is even more my own view than what has been said so far. In a *longue durée* perspective, the present strong relative position of China can be attributed to the radical changes there since 1978, thanks to Deng. Of course the foundations laid in the first phase wherein China doubled its per capita income obviously helped. But the similarities in their respective per capita incomes in 1980 merely reflects the longer history of the two countries. *A priori*, there is no reason why China should have opened such a large distance in such a short period of time. This is especially so because as I have already remarked earlier, China adopted a policy which it was always possible for India to adopt. Indeed anyone looking at the two countries at any time between 1950 and 1975 could have thought that India had a better capitalist infrastructure as well as commercial culture than China had. The diasporas of both China and India have always been adept at commercial activity so there is nothing in Chinese or Indian culture as such which could make a difference. The difference arises out of the political and institutional differences inside the country and these are very much short run and changeable.

Can China Combine Capitalism with One Party Rule?

China appears to have been able to separate the political institutions of a Leninist state with single party dominance from its economic imperative of state ownership of all means of production. This is unique in the political economy of modern times. The transition is not yet fully complete as there is still a lot of central control over economic life and a large state-owned sector. It would be a bold person who could predict how far China could go in this separation. Thus could one have a fully capitalist or even a largely capitalist economy with a Leninist state? This is not the same as market socialism but more like state capitalism, although the word has now been much maligned in the polemics on the left. When Lenin spoke of state capitalism, he had the German war economy during the First World War in mind – a private ownership economy run in a centralised fashion.[33] The Chinese version of state capitalism could in the limit amount to private diffuse ownership with single party monopoly of political power. Is this feasible or likely?

Normally we associate rise of democracy with a prosperous middle class with plenty of 'bourgeois' elements. A private ownership economy is bound to require a lot of economic freedom and as we are all crude materialists in this matter, we associate economic freedom with political liberties. While there is some opening out in the direction of separation of powers in some local jurisdictions,[34] it is difficult to envisage separation of powers in the absence of multiparty democracy with free elections and a possibility of change of the party in power. China's experiment is thus one of the most interesting episodes in modern political economy. Will China be able to sustain one-party rule with a private enterprise economy? Is state capitalism feasible in peaceful post-revolutionary times?

The implicit Chinese answer seems to be that if the Chinese Communist Party (CCP) delivers on fast and sustained economic growth while restructuring the economy continuously in a capitalist direction, then the CCP monopoly on political power will become feasible with limited concessions such as separation of powers but no party competition. Marxian and every other political economy says that this is not easy, even not possible.[35] Economic freedom will spill over into demands for political freedom. Even authoritarian governments – that is, noncommunist dictatorships – have been

---

33 Desai (2002a).
34 For example, SEZs in China such as Shenzen.
35 See Moore (1971) and Desai (2002a).

unable to sustain a monopoly on political power with developed capitalism. Leninist state formations in Europe collapsed along with their economic forms. Apart from China, only North Korea and Cuba remain as major non-capitalist economies and non-liberal democratic polities. Can China defy the so-called laws of historical materialism (or even cross section growth regressions of new political economy) and avoid the transition to democracy?

One particular problem in this respect relates to the legal framework. While civil and political liberties can be curtailed, once you grant property rights certain liberalising consequences inevitably follow, as any eighteenth-century political economist will tell you. Thus, the Communist Party *qua* contractor or buyer and seller of property cannot be above the law. There has to be accountability and auditing, legal sanctions and punishments for non-delivery or non-performance. From this requirement follows the need to have law courts and a legal profession which enjoy a certain degree of immunity from the perennial habits of communist parties to bully if not liquidate all those who disagree with them. An independent legal profession needs further freedoms of speech and association and so on. It is this compulsion to establish a rule of law which will be crucial for China. In a fascinating and detailed study of the growth of the rule of law in China, Peerenboom makes the following observation:

> In the end, however, a transition to democracy is likely to be necessary to overcome the [Communist] Party's legitimacy deficiencies, to address accountability issues, and to reduce growing social cleavages. It is possible that over time the Party could stave off extinction by transforming itself into a Social Democratic party. The Party could well gain support of its citizenry if in the next decade it is able to reduce corruption to a tolerable level and to sustain economic growth while dealing with such pressing problems as SOE [state-owned enterprise] reforms, reform of the banking and financial sectors, and the need to establish a social security system and to clean up the environment. It could further broaden its appeal by gradually relaxing its grip on society and allowing citizens greater, albeit still limited, freedom of speech, assembly, and association. In short, it could adopt a more communitarian approach. If it does not, and elections are held, it could very well lose out to the party that does adopt such an approach, all else being equal.[36]

---

36   Peerenboom (2002, p. 572–3).

This is a tall order for any country much less China. Indeed India itself has not eliminated corruption nor reformed its banking and financial sectors. But people will tolerate corruption if they can throw the corrupt out of office, even if this exit is only through a revolving door. Democracies coexist with all sorts of imperfections and can indeed even withstand a lot of misery unlike authoritarian regimes, as the fate of the USSR in face of the stagflation crisis of the 1970s showed in contrast to Western economies. What Mrs Thatcher could do to the British economy, Brezhnev, Chernenko or Gorbachev could not. So China does not have to make things perfect if it can only grant bourgeois freedoms to its people. If not it has to be better than the most perfect democracy. Can China find its way out of this paradox?

My interim answer to this is that the odds are stacked against China being able to do this. Not that it is impossible or even unlikely but the odds are not favourable. There is one major reason for this, for which I appeal to Chinese history. This is China's inability to handle dissent and defiance of central rule without a lot of damage. The episodes of the Taiping and Boxer Rebellions in the Imperial era and GPCR, as well as the 1989 troubles which were not confined just to Tiananmen, show that China is fragile if not brittle when it comes to dissent. In the next ten years, China will be adjusting to economic restructuring in response to the demands of the World Trade Organization (WTO), as well as facing up to global media exposure due to the 2008 Olympic Games. It will be an open invitation to human rights movements and Falun Gong to expose the regime to international scrutiny. Moscow's experience of the 1980 Olympic Games proved crucial in the way the Soviet Union collapsed. What about China?

I expect China to survive as a powerful economy, but after a short period of political turbulence on the lines of the Taiping Rebellion or GPCR. China will be forced to make a political transition as profound as the Eastern European states did with their economies. The final shape will be a more democratic China, but it may not necessarily be a liberal democratic Western-type regime. There are after all living examples of 'less-than-liberal' democracies – Singapore, Taiwan, Malaysia – which China can follow. You can have a multiparty democracy with a single party dominance as in Mexico and Japan, and India till 1989. One can also have dual power as in Iran, with the Ayatollahs vying for control with a democratically elected power. There are many choices on the way to a full transition to liberal democracy.

Can India Catch Up with China?

India has problems about delivering strong, focused government pursuing a single objective with total commitment. Its great achievement is to have constructed the world's most populous democracy against all the odds – illiteracy, multiple languages and religions, racial and social heterogeneity. There have been spurts of committed action – in the mid-1950s when the Second Five-Year Plan was formulated, in the early 1970s when Mrs Gandhi pursued her anti-poverty programme, in the mid-1980s when Rajiv Gandhi pushed the import liberalisation policy harder, the early 1990s with Narasimha Rao and Manmohan Singh liberalising the economy, and finally in the last five years when the reform process has been kept up rather than reversed as many had feared. The average growth rate has gone up from 3.5 per cent in the 1970s to 5.5 per cent in the 1980s and now to 6.5 per cent in the past decade.

India has also achieved another miracle relative to many post-colonial societies. It has maintained its territorial integrity, unlike for example Pakistan. It has not had a civil war, unlike Nigeria or Sri Lanka, and while multiethnic federations such as the former Yugoslavia and the USSR have broken up, India has not. This has absorbed resources as India has had to fight subnationalisms in the northeast Nagaland, in Panjab with Khalistan, and in Kashmir with international subversion added to internal dissension. It has had communal strife between Hindus and Muslims, Hindus and Sikhs, between caste Hindus and Untouchables/dalits and so on. It has also faced class-based revolts in Telangana in the 1940s, in West Bengal, Andhra Pradesh and Bihar with the Naxalites. Through all this it has survived as a democratic open society based on consensus and debate. Life is about more than per capita income and its growth.

For India any hope of growing faster depends on less government rather than more, on harnessing the private sector entrepreneurial talent which has always been there but was stifled for a long time. This requires a less interventionist government but also a better regulatory regime. India's bane is the politicisation of all aspects of economic life and the difficulty of constructing an arm's-length regulatory regime free of political interference. This is because of and despite its democratic politics.[37] Thus even after a major stock market fraud or the mishandling of Unit Trust of India (UTI) customers' investments, there has been little by way of punishment.

---

37   Desai (2002b).

Indeed, a large number of financial scandals have thousands of victims but no culprits convicted.[38] One cannot expect a flourishing private enterprise culture in the absence of trust and effective regulation. Thus a black economy, smuggling and criminalisation of financial markets flourish. Depoliticisation of the economy, therefore, remains a challenge. This is the same challenge as the more frequent complaint about control of the budget deficit, because the deficit is due to the compulsions of consensual politics with a coalition government and weak powers over regions.

What then are the chances for India that we may see a strong effective government emerge at the centre with effective fiscal control over its own budget as well as the budgets of states and an ability to depoliticise regulatory structures? Herein lies the deep dilemma of the Indian polity. India was set up after independence as a federal polity because of the awareness of the first generation of leaders of the difficulty of holding the various linguistic and religious groups together. Indian nationhood was defined as unity in diversity. But lately a new, more Unitarian construction of Indian nationhood has been advanced by the forces of *Hindutva* nationalism. Thus far, it has been muted in its approach, but is also quite successful. If in the forthcoming months and years the Unitarian approach were to be pursued harder and if it was to be electorally successful, then India may emerge simultaneously as a nonsecular, majority Hindu polity with single party dominance by the BJP and its parivar. The advocates of *Hindutva* often cite Israel as their ideal example.

Historically, modernity in India was supposed to come with a secular and perhaps even socialist society. This was certainly Nehru's ideal, as well as practice, and at least the rhetoric if not practice for the two Gandhis. But the events of the last ten years or so raise the serious possibility that modernity in India will come with a Hindu or religious rather than secular as well as a capitalist dispensation. It is conceivable that such a Unitarian nationalism may accelerate growth by following a more liberal policy. But it is also likely to lead to greater social disharmony. Of course a majoritarian rule of the largest religious group is possible with non-discrimination of the minorities, but in the Indian context and given the history, it is not very likely.

---

38 See *India Today* (2003) for a recent list.

Conclusion

My own view is that India will remain a soft state, a consensual polity, and it will not be capable of sustained growth at the sort of rates which China has attained. To stay a stable, peaceful society, India has to be a muddle and a mess. It is a miracle that proceeding in the way it has done, it has come as far as it has done, trebling its per capita income. But there will not be growth convergence between China and India.[39] India and China will both remove poverty in their midst and cease to be bywords for misery that they had become for 150 years after 1820. China will again become a viable Great Power; India may become just a Great Democracy.

References

Adeney, Katherine, 2003, 'Federal Formations and Consociational Stabilisation: The Politics of Identity Articulation and Ethnic Conflict Regulation in India and Pakistan' (Ph.D. dissertation; London: University of London).

Baum, Richard, 1994, *Burying Mao* (Princeton, NJ: Princeton University Press).

Crafts, Nicholas, 1997, 'The Human Development Index and Changes in Standards of Living: Some Historical Comparisons', *European Review of Economic History*, Vol. 1, pp. 299–322.

Deng, Kent G., 2000, 'A Critical Survey of Recent Research in Chinese Economic History', *Economic History Review*, Vol. LIII, No. 1 (February).

Desai, Meghnad, 2002a, *Marx's Revenge: The Resurgence of Capitalism and the Death of State Socialism* (London: Verso).

Desai, Meghnad, 2002b, 'Democracy and Development: India 1947–2002', presented at the K. R. Narayanan Lecture (Canberra: Australia South Asia Research Centre, The Australian National University).

Desai, Meghnad, 2000, 'Communalism, Secularism and the Dilemma of Indian Nationhood', in *Asian Nationalism*, ed. by Michael Leifer (London: Routledge).

Desai, Meghnad, 1975, 'Contradictions of Slow Capitalist Development', in *Explosion in a Sub-Continent*, ed. by Robin Blackburn (London: Viking Penguin).

Dreze, Jean, and Amartya Kumar Sen, 1989, *Hunger and Public Action* (Oxford: Oxford University Press).

Dumont, Louis, 1980, *Homo Hierarchicus* (Chicago: University of Chicago Press).

Forbes, Naushad, 2002, 'Doing Business in India: What Has Liberalization Changed?' in *Economic Policy Reforms and the Indian Economy*, ed. by Anne O. Krueger (Chicago: The University of Chicago Press).

Habib, Irfan, 1995, *Essays in Indian History: Towards a Marxist Perception* (New Delhi: Tulika).

Habib, Irfan, 1983, 'Marx's Perception of India', *The Marxist*, Vol. 1, No. 1 (July–September) and reprinted in Irfan Habib, 1995, *Essays in Indian History: Towards a Marxist Perception* (New Delhi: Tulika).

Habib, Irfan, 1971, 'Potentialities of Capitalist Development in the Economy of Mughal India', *Enquiry*, New Series (Winter).

---

39 Except unless China has a long breakdown in its transition to democracy.

Heston, Alan, 1983, 'National Income', in *The Cambridge Economic History of India, Volume 2, c.1757–c.1970*, ed. by Dharma Kumar and Meghnad Desai (Cambridge: Cambridge University Press).
Inden, Ronald B., 2000, *Imagining India* (London: Hurst, 2nd edn).
Joshi, Vijay, and I. M. D. Little, 1994, *India: Macroeconomics and Political Economy, 1964–1991* (New Delhi: Oxford University Press).
Keay, John, 2001, *India: A History* (London: HarperCollins).
Krueger, Anne O., ed., 2002, *Economic Policy Reforms and the Indian Economy* (Chicago: The University of Chicago Press).
Kumar, Dharma, 1998, 'The Chinese and Indian Economies, 1914–1949', in *Colonialism, Property and the State*, ed. by Dharma Kumar (New Delhi: Oxford University Press).
Kumar, Dharma, and Meghnad Desai, eds, 1983, *The Cambridge Economic History of India, Volume 2: c.1757–c.1970* (Cambridge: Cambridge University Press).
Maddison, Angus, 2001, *The World Economy: A Millennial Perspective* (Paris: Development Centre Studies, Organization for Economic Cooperation and Development).
Maddison, Angus, D. S. Prasada Rao, and W. F. Shepherd, eds, 2002, *The Asian Economies in the Twentieth Century* (Cheltenham, UK: Edward Elgar Publishing).
Moore, Barrington Jr, 1971, *Social Origins of Dictatorship and Democracy* (London: Allen Lane).
Myrdal, Gunnar, 1968, *Asian Drama: An Inquiry into the Poverty of Nations* (New York: Pantheon).
Needham, Joseph *et al.*, 1954, *Science and Civilisation in China* (various volumes) (Cambridge: Cambridge University Press).
Nehru, Jawaharlal, 1946, *The Discovery of India* (Calcutta: Signet Press, 1st edn).
O'Leary, Brendan, 1989, *The Asiatic Mode of Production: Oriental Despotism, Historical Materialism, and Indian History* (Oxford and New York: Basil Blackwell).
Peerenboom, Randall, 2002, *China's Long March Toward Rule of Law* (Cambridge: Cambridge University Press).
Shirk, Susan L., 1993, *The Political Logic of Economic Reform in China* (Berkeley: University of California Press).
Spence, Jonathan *et al.*, 1999, *The Search for Modern China: A Documentary Collection* (New York: W.W. Norton and Company, 2nd edn).
United Nations Development Programme, *Human Development Report* (various years) (New York and Oxford: Oxford University Press).
Wittfogel, Karl A., 1957, *Oriental Despotism: A Comparative Study of Total Power* (New Haven, CT: Yale University Press).

Acknowledgement

First publication: Desai, Meghnad (2005) 'India and China: An Essay in Comparative Political Economy' in *India's and China's Recent Experience with Reform and Growth*, edited by W. Tseng and D. Cowen, Procyclicality of Financial Systems in Asia. London, Palgrave Macmillan, pp. 1–22. Republished with kind permission of Palgrave Macmillan.

Chapter 10

THE VASE AND THE MUDPIE

Meghnad Desai

(2009/2010)

Forty years or so ago, Henry Kissinger observed wryly that if only India and China could feed themselves, all the world's problems would be solved. As usual, he was wrong. India and China have solved the problem of growing enough food grains, even if India has not quite managed to feed everyone. However, most of the world's problems are still to be solved. Ironically, the basket cases of Kissinger's time in the 1960s are the new hope for a world mired in the aftermath of a severe recession and financial crisis. In Copenhagen, the possibility of a global compact depended on whether China and India would play ball with G1 – the USA. Every other country just disappeared off the scene, almost like children frightened when they see their parents quarrel.

China and India are two of the world's oldest civilisations and have been in roughly the same form for the last 4000 years or so. China has also been a single state for most of that time while India became a nation-state for the first time in 1947.[1] However, they began their journey towards becoming modern nations simultaneously in the late 1940s. For the first twenty-five years after that, each had a strong ideological bias in their development strategy. China had Mao's version of the Bolshevik developmental state with drastic land reforms and forced industrialisation that plunged the economy into the worst famine it had faced, when 20 million Chinese people died. Yet, despite that, China in 1975 was more pro-poor in its development and had become a significant military power as well. India had a milder social

---

[1] I have discussed this in greater detail in *The Rediscovery of India* (Penguin India, 2009).

democratic version of the Soviet disease, thanks to Jawaharlal Nehru. It, too, began to industrialise but the land reforms it undertook were mild. Nehru's major achievement was making India a democracy. His economic legacy was a low-growth rate, which his ideologically tougher daughter took still lower. The poor were sorely neglected. However, India too, like China, emerged as a nation with nuclear capability. In short, if the choice was guns or butter, both India and China were in no doubt: the choice was guns over butter.

* * *

Mao's death in 1975 gave his old associate Deng Xiaoping the chance to make a 180-degree turn in development strategy. Marxist/Maoist ideologue that he was, Deng soon became a pragmatic realist. He foresaw the sclerosis of the Soviet Union and the vibrancy of Taiwan and Hong Kong in achieving a high level of income. So he reversed the commune system and inaugurated private land leases. He also opened the economy to foreign investment and later gave the domestic private sector its head by establishing Special Economic Zones where capitalism could flourish.

The result was spectacular: three decades of double-digit growth. China – potentially, if not actually – has now come to be regarded as the world's second-largest economy. This goal has been achieved by following a path well laid down by Japan and then South Korea – the Standard East Asian Developmental model, as it were. This involves over-saving and under-consumption, export orientation and directed industrialisation, a model first perfected by Japan in the 1960s and 1970s when it was regarded as a miracle economy. In the 1970s and 1980s, South Korea followed the same path.

In 1975, India and China had a roughly equal per capita income.[2] Now, thirty-five years later, China's GDP stands at US$4.33 trillion while India's is US$1.22 trillion. With similar populations, China's per capita income is three-and-a-half-times that of India. The gap is only partially explained by the contrast between a democratic and a totalitarian polity. India did not change its path drastically till 1991, though some hesitant steps were taken by Rajiv Gandhi during his early years as prime minister. Like Deng, it was Dr Manmohan Singh, steeped in the orthodoxy of the muddled

---

2   I have surveyed the 500-year-old parallel history of the two economies in my 'China and India' in the IMF collection, *China and India Growth and Reform Processes*.

Nehru-Gandhi ideology of state-led development, who was able to escape the old mould. This was perhaps also due to the accident that, for the first time in twenty-five years, India had as prime minister someone who was not also a member of the Nehru-Gandhi dynasty.[3]

For India, moving to a more liberal market-oriented regime was not as much of a shock as a return to the earlier days of development. In the ninety years between 1857–1947, India had acquired a modern industrial structure and a lively entrepreneurial community, the largest in any colonial country. However, the nationalist movement was in an anti-capitalist phase in the 1930s, thanks to the Great Depression. After independence, Nehru neglected – if not distrusted – the private sector while his daughter was positively hostile to it. India, thus, wasted forty years after independence reinventing the wheel. The result was the low 'Hindu' rate of growth until 1980, which only marginally improved in the 1980s.

* * *

As we examine the economic and political dimensions of their growth, the question often asked now is about the future trajectory of the two countries. Let us first take a look at the economy. Most analysts simply project the recent trends into the indefinite future and this makes China speed ahead of India, as well as every other nation in the world. But history, one must remember, is not linear. If nothing else, the latest crisis, as well as the trajectory of these two nations over the last sixty years, should warn us against this fallacy. Again, the experience of Japan shows us that growth engines can slow down and stagnate. Thus we need to take care in projecting future growth scenarios.

In political futurology, many analysts see China as making a necessary transition to a Western-style liberal democracy.[4] This is based on the same crude version of economic determinism that used to be capsulated as Windmills – Feudalism, Watermills – Capitalism. The idea is that economic growth leads to the growth of a middle class that demands democracy. Or

---

3   I have argued that had Lal Bahadur Shastri lived and been prime minister for longer, India may have transited to a better model of development sooner. *The Rediscovery of India*, op. cit.

4   See my debate with Will Hutton, 'Does the Future Really Belong to China', in *Prospect Magazine*, no. 130, January 14 2007, https://www.prospectmagazine.co.uk/magazine/doesthefuturereallybelongtochina.

an assumption that, without democracy, China cannot progress much further. Again, if anyone wants to doubt such crude determinism, one only has to look at India, which adopted democracy before growth.

Let us set both these simple models aside. In a sense, both India and China will face severe challenges at home and abroad and each will require leadership of a high calibre to meet them. The three issues that need to be addressed, therefore, are: Is there a capacity for reform within the system? Is the economic growth sustainable? Can we take political stability for granted?

* * *

Since it has to be consensual, a persistent problem that plagues India is the slow pace of economic reform. Even if we grant that the latest election results indicate the end of the era of political fragmentation and the possibility that a stable Congress-dominated coalition will rule for the next ten years, the high hopes entertained by many – especially abroad – that sans the Left, the UPA will charge ahead with liberal reforms has been belied. The fact is that in India, the entire political system – not just the Congress – has a moderate left bias and a fear of the market. Few leaders are willing to openly admit that the growth experience of the last eighteen years has been good for the country as a whole, even for the poor. This is why, even though liberal reform is urgently needed, it has to take place by stealth in the guise of technical improvements, or in a halting manner.

India's rural economy has 60 per cent of the population but produces only 20 per cent of output. Low productivity translates into endemic poverty. The need is to industrialise faster with large factories that can employ 10,000 or 20,000 workers, as in Malaysia and China. Only then will the rural under-employed get round-the-year jobs that can use their unskilled or semi-skilled manual labour. This requires land to be freed for building large factories and a reform of the labour laws that makes hiring and firing more flexible in large establishments. Presently, the difficulty of these issues in factories of 100 employees and above has led to a proliferation of small high and medium-tech industrial establishments outside the organised sector. India's manufacturing sector has stagnated at around 25 per cent in its share of the GDP.

Vitally needed reforms of labour law and land markets, needed to speed up industrialisation and growth, will not be easy to deliver. Tata's experience in

Singur, West Bengal, illustrated this vividly: the Left-Right labels do not work any longer. Parties in power want change, but opposition parties are against change. With coalition politics still the norm at State and central levels, obstruction is easier to accomplish than change. This will remain a challenge for India until a clear mandate for change is won by some political party.

China's problem, on the other hand, is a combination of timidity and the overbearing power of its leadership. Even where the system needs change and the leadership can see the need, it is too cautious to make it lest it leads to yet another Tiananmen. The issue of some sort of pluralism – let alone democracy – haunts the leadership. It is not that China needs to move fast forward to liberal democracy. Its need is for pluralism and tolerance of dissent. Even inner party democracy remains a tough nut to crack.[5] China has many paths for greater pluralism – Singapore, Malaysia, Korea and Japan themselves offer many models of limited pluralism. Even Iran, with the control of the theologians over the parliamentary democracy, would be an apt model for the Chinese Communist Party to study. With increasing episodes of dissidence and the ever-present threat of the internet, Chinese leadership is showing less than its usual command over its polity.

* * *

Both India and China managed to weather the recession very well with only a slight slowdown in growth rate of GDP. Between the two, China's reflationary package was larger than any other country's and concentrated mainly on infrastructure. China had to redirect its economy away from exports since its markets in the OECD countries were in recession. It needs to shift away from an over-saving/under-consumption model to a better balance between domestic consumption and exports. Yet, when devising its reflation strategy, China chose the easy way out of concentrating on infrastructure since the pace can be dictated from above. This has led to excess capacity in the steel, cement and other capital goods sectors. Along with China's insistence that it will not revalue its currency, this also shows that there is a great deal of conservatism in China's economic management.

---

5   See 'Democracy in China: Control Freaks', *The Economist*, 19 December 2009– January 2010.

Again, China's growth strategy is excessively capital intensive. With around 50 per cent of saving and another 5 per cent in FDI, China achieves 10–11 per cent GDP growth. India saves around 35 per cent plus a small amount of FDI 2–3 per cent achieves 8–9 per cent growth. Thus China's Incremental Capital Output ratio is nearer five while India's is four. In this respect, China is reminiscent of the USSR, which had an input-driven model of growth and which collapsed. China's growth will not collapse, but unless it becomes more efficient in the use of resources, it may find it difficult to keep the growth rate up.

India has a domestic market-led growth model and it is also driven, by and large, by its private sector (though few in Delhi will admit this.) [China's capitalist class to a significant extent comprises the cronies of the Communist Party who have been sold public property at throwaway prices.] India is also equipped with a better macroeconomic policy since it is not excessively risk averse. India's problem is that the government is still a large borrower and a burden on the domestic savings. This leads to high interest rates and corporations find it difficult to raise money cheaply. However, divestment is proceeding far too slowly and it will again be some time before the budget deficit is back under control.

By and large, the Indian state does many things it should not (own banks and industrial enterprises) while not doing what it should. Thus its investment in primary and secondary education and public health lags behind even Third World averages. This is due to an elite preference for state enterprises where jobs are well paid and secure and also a weakness in governance as education is split between the centre and the states, and excessively politicised at each level. India has a demographic dividend relative to China but it may yet dissipate it due to its failure to get the state out of what it should not and into plugging urgent gaps in the human resource infrastructure.

* * *

India has survived twenty years of a fragmented political party system, which led to short-lived unstable governments mixed with some episodes of stability. Now with the UPA back into power, although still in a coalition, India has learnt to live with this somewhat costly but inclusive model of democracy. The slow growth of the first forty years after independence has built up massive demands from the many excluded non-elite groups. The more numerous of these groups – OBCs and dalits – have taken to the electoral path to get their share of the public resources. The result has been Mandal and further demands for positive discrimination in entry to higher education and government jobs. Yet there are still the numerically small but excluded communities, mainly in tribal areas where arid or hilly regions make agriculture unsustainable. It is in these areas that the Naxalite movement has gained strength. The challenge to the Indian democratic system is that its inclusive model has to reach beyond the electoral mode and find ways of re-enfranchising communities numerically too weak to work the electoral system for a defence of their own interests. They have been deprived of access to collective common property by the established system even sometimes under the excuse of development, not to say, socialism.

India is not faced with any threat of a Balkanisation. There are movements for the new states to be created, new identities to get recognition. But all this is routine democratic politics. At its birth, the founding fathers of India had a rigid Unitarian model in mind for the country and although that mould has been broken many times, India refashions itself again and again like a clay pot that can be smashed and moulded again after being made into a mud pie.

China, on the other hand, has the appearance of super-stability. The Communist Party's authority seems unchallenged and there is no organised domestic opposition, except perhaps among the minorities of Tibetans and Uyghurs and the Falun Gong. Yet the system is fragile in its own perception. The 1989 Tiananmen Square uprising has not been forgotten and the preparations for the 2008 Olympics involved excessive repression of the Falun Gong and many others.

Yet one must point out that in the last quarter of the past century, we have seen excessively stable regimes fall apart – in Iran, and Romania and indeed the entire Eastern European system. When these super-stable states face a crisis they have no internal mechanisms for affecting a change of direction. China's system has shown itself to be excessively cautious and conservative. It is in this respect, somewhat like a Ming vase, strong but brittle. Once smashed the system may take some time to remould. While this may not be very likely, its possibility cannot be dismissed in any attempt at a prospective analysis. After all, Mao destabilised the system during the Cultural Revolution, which cost China ten years of political chaos. Previous episodes, such as the Taiping and the Boxer Rebellions are also reminders that China goes through phases of chaos before returning to equilibrium. India, by contrast, is always in a state of perpetual, though mild, dis-equilibrium.

The chances are that China and India will still be around a hundred years from now, richer and better in terms of the well-being of their people. They may also be similar to what they are now as unified polities – one democratic and other led by a single party. But that may not be as certain as we think today.

Acknowledgement

First publication: Desai, Meghnad, 'The Vase and the Mudpie' in *India China Neighbours Strangers*, *India International Centre Quarterly*, vol. 36, no. 3/4, Winter 2009 / Spring 2010, pp. 172–179. Republished with kind permission of *India International Centre Quarterly*.

Chapter 11

FIFTY YEARS OF DEVELOPMENT THINKING

Lord Meghnad Desai

(2011)

When remembering how the Institute of Social Sciences [New Delhi] began in the mid-1980s, I thought of the famous Eleven Theses on Feuerbach: philosophers have hitherto only interpreted the world in various ways, the task, however, is how to change it. Of course the man who wrote it, the only way he could change the world was by writing another interpretation of the world. And the world must never neglect ideas. Ideas are very powerful instruments to change the world. What I'm going to do is I'm going to tell you my life story.

In 1958 I began to study development when I started doing my MA. And of course Professor D. T. Lakdawala was one of my teachers and I always associate the Institute with the name of Dr Lakdawala who was its first chairman. I'm just going to take you very rapidly through the way our whole thinking on development has changed in these last fifty years. In a broad way, it has gone from thinking about *things* to thinking about *people*. One very core idea of development is a very simple one: it says people are poor; they are really meant to be rich, or people are poor today but they were rich in a previous era or some golden age because there was large surplus which somebody has robbed them of. Now, in a sense, development is a creature of colonialism and independence from colonialism. Because the people who thought about development articulately were not so much the classical economists who were thinking about growth in a different way in the eighteenth and nineteenth centuries but people who are, as it were, living with a contrast between the poor countries and their rich masters. So one of the first ideas (in fact lots of ideas or a clutch of ideas) is the very basic idea that people are poor because there is a pot of gold sitting somewhere and if you could only get that pot of gold and distribute it, everybody would be rich. I think it's wrong but a very powerful idea and that is where the idea of 'drain' comes from. One of the first ideas of development that Dadabhai Naoroji developed was the idea of drain; there is a drain of surplus from India and because of that drain [taking wealth or resources] away it's not helping in development. Of course there were lots of drains going on even within India. I think that the Maharajas were probably draining away more surplus than the British were. Anyway there is an idea that people are poor because some people are rich and the only way for the poor people to become better off is to take surplus from the rich people. That idea I think will never ever leave us because emotionally it is a very powerful idea. Bangladesh was set up on the proposition that East Pakistan was poor because West Pakistan was robbing it and if East Pakistan would get rid of West Pakistan, Bangladesh would become Sonar Bangla. But it doesn't happen that quickly, it takes a few decades before you can realise that growth comes by raising productivity of the present generation of workers and not by living off past accumulations.

I'm going to tell you why this powerful idea is not correct. It is very popular in Africa – that Africa has been robbed and plundered. Let me go back roughly to around about the Second World War, longer than fifty years ago. There was, after the Great Depression, a real pressure on colonial powers to do something about their people, the people they were ruling over. They were really frightened. The Soviet Union had happened; they were worried about rebellion and revolution. Radicalism was in the air. A number of colonial powers adopted ameliorative policies. Now they have been completely forgotten but the first thinking on development was done by colonial officers. Furnivall who was an officer in Burma wrote a book on plural societies and Birken in Indonesia, called the Dutch/Netherlands East Indies, first argued that there is a dualism among the poor countries. There are some urban, Westernised, organised centres and there is also a large rural impoverished society. The idea was basically that poor countries were fragmented and rich countries were integrated.

Then there was an idea, which again became unfashionable because it came from colonial powers, that basically people were poor because their culture encourages laziness. A very, very strong idea, and to put it in a more sophisticated way, it says the supply curve of labour in poor countries is backward sloping; if you pay these guys two square meals a day, they will stop working. When a certain break happened in the Second World War and independence came, surprisingly the thinking in development was very much generated by Western economists. By 'Western' I don't mean just capitalist Western but communist Western as well because they both were Western thoughts. One was of course influenced by Keynes. Keynesian economics had triumphed and people thought that Keynesian economics could be used to solve the world's problems. In Keynesian economics the idea of growth had not at all been part of economics; it was only in the post-war period that growth became a subject of academic study. Roy Harrod, who was a student and biographer of Keynes, gave lectures in the London School of Economics (LSE) in 1949 titled 'Towards a Dynamic Economics' in which he put forward the first growth theory. His theory in that respect was extremely mechanical and very macroeconomic. It says, what is the percentage savings rate of a country? Look at the capital output ratio and divide the savings rate with the capital output ratio and that will give you the rate of growth of the economy. That is one formula, you can write it in various ways. In a sense there is absolutely no behaviour there, the idea is that there is a constant savings rate and there is technological capital output ratio and, Voila! You divide one by the other and you get the growth rate. If you go back and read the draft frame of India's First Five-Year Plan, which actually is the first official development document written down in the world, it is very much imbued by that spirit.

The story goes that K. N. Raj, fresh from the London School of Economics, went to work for the Planning Commission. Of course the ambition of the Planning Commission was great; the National Planning Committee had been established by Subash Chandra Bose and Nehru was the chairman of that and it had decided that in the first decade after independence they wanted to increase income or wealth by six times – just in one decade. Then they themselves realised it to be a little bit ambitious, they decided, maybe two to three times will do. Even to double income in a decade requires a 7 per cent growth rate per annum. K. N. Raj had to hesitantly tell the prime minister that even 5 per cent would be rather hard to achieve and perhaps they should plan for a slightly lower growth rate. Prime Minister Nehru got very angry and said, 'Young man, why are you so pessimistic? You've been imbued by Western economic thinking, you don't realise that people have great possibilities', and all that. Luckily, Nehru was not Mao Tse Tung. Mao Tse Tung was seriously mad and wrecked the Chinese economy spectacularly in trying to surpass Britain in one decade.

It caused a huge famine in which 30 to 40 million people died. Nehru afterwards calmed down and decided that the young man's words may have some truth in the matter and the growth rate was going to be much less. But in a way what the First Five-Year Plan was in India was a collection of the late colonial projects and schemes which had not yet been finished, plus a bit of Keynesian economics. It was drafted by the brother of C. D. Deshmukh, I'm told. He may have been an ICS officer, I don't remember. It is a very coherent document.

In any book on development thinking that anybody wants to write, India itself will play a part, both as an exemplar and as a contributor of ideas. India became a laboratory of development thinking both by Indians and by non-Indians. Anyway, it began to be really clear to the people that the capital output ratio was a given technological constant and that was that. Another version of this idea was developed in the Second Five-Year Plan, and that was the Mahalanobis model. Mahalanobis on his own, without reading any economics, discovered a planning model which was written for the Soviet Union. It is a two or four sector growth model with capital output ratios and all that. Then it became possible to describe the economy in certain input-output tables. Input-output tables got larger and larger. It is very interesting that everybody thought that economy is something like a machine which could be described fully by a set of numbers or a set of formulae. And to get growth you just have to get those numbers right. It was thought to be very left wing to believe in input-output analysis and very right wing (when I was young) to believe that Indian agriculture needed more resources. It was thought to be seriously right wing to say that in the Third Five-Year Plan the allocation for agriculture should be higher than in the Second Five-Year Plan. One was thought to be an American agent if you said that. Anyway, slowly it began to be clear that development is a slightly more complex idea. At least a multi-sectoral approach was needed. In India a notion of surplus labour was developed and the idea that surplus labour was a resource, it was a kind of hidden savings in the economy. If you could only mobilise surplus labour and put it to work then growth will occur. But surplus labour was out there in the villages and growth was happening in the cities through industries because industries were always in the cities and people were always in the countryside. So how do you move people from the countryside to the cities and how do you feed them and so on? W. Arthur Lewis, the first non-white professor of economics in UK and later on a Nobel prize winner had this article in 1954 'Economic development with unlimited supplies of labour' which became a classic. The idea was we have these people sitting in the countryside, eating but not producing anything matching how much they eat because they are surplus. So you take them, you transfer them somehow to the cities and they will get into factories, but they had to carry the lunch pack with them, i.e. the food they were eating had to follow them. Of course the problem was, once they have left, the people remaining would have more food to eat. Would they actually increase the consumption or could you tax them to keep their consumption constant? There were lots of debates about that.

One of the most interesting ideas which was never adopted very sadly, as an alternative to the Mahalanobis Plan, was by my own teacher Brahmanand, that basically development should proceed first with producing consumption goods and consumption goods will then generate labour mobilisation and that labour mobilisation will lead to production of other consumption goods and so on. But that was thought to be too right wing; the Left idea was first produce machines to produce machines to produce machines. Anyway, this whole body of ideas – and I'm sticking mainly to the Indian experience – was unfortunately rewarded with early success. I'm saying 'unfortunately' because the real difficulty with development in India did not become clear till the second decade or 1960s. The First Five-Year Plan was marvellous, 18 per cent growth rate over five years, sort of 3.5 per cent on an average. Second was even better, 23 per cent growth rate over five years and so between 3.5 per cent to 4 per cent growth rate for ten years and India had not had a growth rate like that for at least a century. So everybody was happy. Then the difficulty started mounting up because by and large what was happening was that dormant resources were being better utilised to begin with.

The Second Five-Year Plan ran into a resource crunch. Foreign exchange ran out but still it went through all right. The second decade was characterised by the Three Twos: death of two prime ministers, two wars and two famines. Resource shortage became a very serious problem and then it became obvious to people that putting resources into agriculture was not just a matter of transferring surplus. Real people actually live there and they had to think about development in terms of different sections of people living in different regions. Even so, the idea was very much on the production side, how did you raise agricultural production. There was a great belief in state farms, collective farms and all that. If you ever want to read books on agriculture written by people who have never seen a plough, read Lenin on agriculture. Lenin had never seen a plough. It's a brilliant book but nothing whatsoever to do with agriculture. Kautsky had written a book on agriculture as well and he had this mad idea that there are only two ways of developing agriculture, one was the American way and the other the English way. It was mind boggling but people took that sort of stuff seriously. So the idea was that only large farms were productive and for that therefore land had to be pooled. Panditji believed very much in cooperative land pooling because the land holdings had become very small and the fragments had to be pooled. That idea was put to rest by the Research Programmes Committee of the Planning Commission producing a report in the mid-1950s with one of the most powerful empirical results there has been that show that small farms were more productive than large farms. The agony of the left was spewed across the pages of the *Economic Weekly* and later the *Economic and Political Weekly* for the next fifteen years. Lots of people were more or less saying this cannot be true because theory tells me it cannot be true, there must be some empirical trap here because large farms must be more productive than small farms. Anyway, it went on and on but the empirical result was robust.

So the idea of the Green Revolution and all that starts from there. Don't worry about land pooling; find out where farms are more productive and give those farmers more money. Put more resources into agriculture and that will increase the food surplus. So development theory begins to ask questions about how do people invest, where does investment have real results and so on. Of course Indian development thinking, not now but so much in those days, was influenced by the Soviet Union which was very powerful. It was argued by the Left based on Russian history that if you are only going to regions where agriculture is successful and giving more money to them then you are doing what Stolypin did under the Czar's regime (I'm not going to tell you who Stolypin is, find out, you can Google). All this *a priori* thinking was thought to be contributing to development, but luckily for India, what happened was the discovery of high yielding seed varieties; technology plus the political compulsions of doing something about a failed agricultural policy compelled C. Subramaniam and other people to see that you had to make India self-sufficient in food. At that time India was relying on PL-480 shipments from America and it was pretty humiliating. But what nobody said at the time was that the Green Revolution was the *largest private sector success story* in India. Because the participants were all small self-employed firms. They were called farmers, they were small firms and they were self-employed and they were reacting to incentives which had been created through either input price subsidisation or output price subsidisation. The most remarkable story of that is that lessons learned in agriculture were not transferred to industry because people actually do not think of agriculture as an industry. Agriculture in the 1950s was not considered to be productive at all. It was supposed to be suffering from the surplus labour. Some argued that agriculture was productive but the zamindars were taking away all the surplus. Abolish zamindari and it will be all right. We abolished zamindari but productivity was still not very high. Productivity had to be raised. Now, the idea that productivity had to be raised began to then engage itself with behaviour. How do you raise productivity? You have to give people incentives and how do you give incentives? There began to be an exploration away from formulae and input-output tables to looking at where are the sectors of low productivity and high productivity. How could you get the high productivity people to give even higher productivity and then worry about the low productivity people.

Yet, not only in India but across the so-called developing world the first few decades of development [after independence] were actually better than before but they were not actually a success. This is when the world became aware that there is something called 'poverty'. That poverty is actually a problem of development. It's quite astonishing, if my memory serves me correctly, that the first and the second Five-Year Plans do not mention 'poverty eradication' as a goal. Poverty reduction was not formally a goal in either the first or the second or the third Five-Year Plan. Because the idea of development was to build the nation and at least in India Nehru had said explicitly to Marie Seton that he wanted this big public sector investment to make India militarily strong. He wanted to have domestic arms production and not foreign. That's why he was having this Mahalanobis Plan. Of course building up military strength is a perfectly legitimate objective of national policy. I'm not saying he shouldn't have done that, what I'm saying is that the idea that poverty had to be reduced doesn't actually figure in a lot of the literature on development till the late 1960s and early 1970s. By which time the developed countries had started talking about poverty. Poverty in America and poverty in Britain became the subject of books in the 1960s. In 1970s when McNamara became president of the World Bank (he was absolutely a hateful creature because of Vietnam) he was the first president of World Bank who said the objective of the Bank was to do something about reduction of poverty. And it is quite interesting how the whole development thinking shifts all sorts of gears after that.

From the 1970s onwards you begin to have the idea that the central problem is not about growth rate as such but about reducing poverty. If you can show that high growth rate is related to abolishing poverty that's fine. What it also did was that it removed the illusion that somehow poverty would be reduced by pure redistribution. Developed countries' experience of poverty showed that despite continuously high growth rate because of Keynesian policies, a welfare state and a progressive taxation policy, poverty persisted in rich countries. Of course poverty was ubiquitous in poor countries. What could you do to reduce poverty? Then began this very interesting deflation of hopes, which was really very healthy. The idea was that poverty elimination was actually a very difficult task. Poverty levels were measured in terms of a certain number of calories per day per person and you convert these calories into money expenditure – and you are familiar with this – into 32 rupees per day. The amount of calories required to sustain a person was measured only for the prison population. Just like Dadabhai Naoroji said in 'Poverty and Un-British Rule in India' that people have inadequate housing standards and adequate housing standards are defined by how much a prisoner is to be allocated in a British jail in India. President Roosevelt decided that whatever the calories were required for prisoners Americans have to have 500 more. So the calories required to sustain a poor person were decided by Roosevelt arbitrarily by adding 500 to the calories required by prisoners.

Even by that crude measure elimination of poverty anytime soon became starkly unrealisable and so we developed the idea of 'Basic Needs'. That development planning had to do something about basic needs. People have big quarrels about what they were, how basic were the basic needs. What is happening here across the way is that from things-oriented thinking it becomes a people-oriented thinking. People are still an abstraction because people are thought of in the large. They are thought of in terms of consumption levels.

A very big change occurs during 1970s because, say from 1945 to 1975, the story was that if poor countries don't have enough resources they needed foreign aid. This foreign aid was all part of the Cold War strategy. It had to be government to government, there is no other way to get in any capital. You had to calculate how much foreign aid was needed and so on. The oil crisis by which oil prices quadrupled completely changed the situation whereby 5 per cent of GDP of the developed countries was transferred to oil exporting countries. And those oil exporting countries were sparsely populated, most of them didn't know what to do with the money so they left it in the banks of some Western countries. And Western banks decided the only way they could pay any interest on its deposits was by lending it out and the most wild lending of money to developing countries followed in the

1970s. The whole situation completely changes the ideas about capital availability and it is very interesting that in banks you had loan desks in which people were told just make loans as large as possible and just get rid of this money! There was amazing inflation, negative interest rates and developing countries were getting money like there was no tomorrow. All sorts of completely unviable public sector industries were started because government has the money and they have to do something about it. And then the whole thing crashed when monetarism came and interest rates went up everybody was left with debt. One thing became clear, that there was a possibility of moving money from one side of the world to another side of the world through kind of private sector operations. This was still private loans to public governments. Then of course the debt crisis happens, especially in the developing countries, raising the question, is development just a problem of resources in some kind of abstract way – money, finance, debt and interest etc. But the importance of international linkages was established.

Another very important event happened due to the oil crisis – the oil crisis of 1973 is a crucial event for development thinking and development facts. In causing the Oil crisis of 1973, the immediate event was the Arab-Israeli war. But by then the developed countries had had nearly two decades of full employment and in those countries, especially the European countries and also in America, powerful trade unions had emerged and basically the real wages of industrial workers was going up year on year and of course government was guaranteeing full employment but limits had been reached. What was inflation was really a hidden war between the workers and their employers in terms of the fight over income shares. As workers' share got larger and larger and as employers' share got smaller and smaller, profit rates begin to suffer, a classic Marxian kind of cycle. The pressure on profitability became inflation, because employers want to sack workers and of course because full employment was to be maintained government had to spend money to hire them but not by setting up industry somewhere else. It was at that time in the early 1970s that Western capitalists decided that they would quit the shores of North East America or western Europe and travel eastwards. So the whole phenomenon of newly industrialised countries of Asia, the Asian Tigers and next batch of Asian Tigers, arises because it is classic Marx and Engels Communist Manifesto prediction – capital has no nation, no morality, and so forth.

Western countries, led by USA and UK, decided to relax the rules about capital mobility. They went for deregulation and more free market policies. Capital left Western countries and went to China, Indonesia, Malaysia,

Taiwan, wherever it was more profitable to go. So you begin to redraw the geography of where the manufacturing is. In the 1960s and 1970s everybody thought the North is not going to be very helpful and monopoly capitalism would obstruct the development of the Third World. This was the argument of Paul Baran in his book *The Political Economy of Growth*. South-South cooperation is what people hoped will solve the problems. In 1968 in a Santiago conference of United Nations Industrial Development Organization (UNIDO), it was thought that if a 25 per cent share of world manufacturing trade could be from southern countries that could be a great objective in twenty years time. Nowadays nobody would take it seriously. Nowadays you would say if 25 per cent is exported by developed countries they would be lucky and that has happened because of a combination of factors and that again changed the thinking in development. In the 1950s or 1960s big countries like Mexico, Brazil, India had distrusted foreign trade. They wanted tariffs, protection, import substitution industrialisation and all that. Because of the experience of colonialism, foreign capital was distrusted as much as foreign trade. Latin Americans also had their own sort of compulsions. There was a very influential thesis advanced by Raúl Prebisch, a great Latin American economist and Hans Singer, a British economist, which argued that terms of trade of primary products producers have a secular decline and therefore if you are in primary producing things, you will never have enough money to be able to buy industrial goods, you will have to manufacture them at home. That whole strategy collapsed with the emergence of South Korea and Taiwan and Hong Kong and so on. Because they had a very different strategy, they had suddenly grown by relying on export markets. They got the money and they exported manufactures aggressively. They didn't have sufficiently large domestic markets. What domestic market could Taiwan have? Suddenly development thinking begins to change; that the way out of poverty lies in getting capital from abroad, using your domestic labour in manufacturing sectors with fairly conventional technologies where there is not very much learning to do, there is no R&D required and you take cost advantage of cheap labour and go for it. Suddenly what you have is developing countries become interested in reform of the GATT (General Agreement on Trade and Tariffs) and they want greater access to developed country markets, *they* want free trade. You know the Uruguay round of GATT changed the equation because for a long time developing countries were saying to developed countries, we want to have nothing to do with your free trade, you go and cut tariffs if you want. In the Kennedy Round, Tokyo Round, we just want protection. Suddenly the whole dynamic changes and you have a group of emerging Asian countries which are fast growing. It was not either a State versus market question. The State was as important in Korea as it was in India or Mexico but the State was smarter in Korea than it was in India or Mexico. The State said we will give you a subsidy, we will give you money but you've got to prove yourself efficient if we give you a subsidy. And how do you prove your efficiency? Well, you get someone else to buy your products other than your own domestic consumers. That proves your efficiency, if a foreigner buys your goods. You can always appeal to patriotism and sell domestic consumers dubious products but will a foreigner buy it? That is a real test of efficiency and that's what the Koreans and Taiwanese were doing.

By the time the end of the 1970s comes the whole context of development thinking is very different. Suddenly possibilities open up. So-called developing countries can do anything. I remember that when South Korea start having double-digit growth rates people were suspicious; most people of a progressive tendency distrusted South Korea because it was part of the Cold War American empire. Of course the progressive people were Mexican, Brazilian and so on. First the Progressive people couldn't believe the numbers, they said they were cheating. And then China changed and that was the most significant event in development thinking. My own private theory is that Deng Xiaoping, when he finally got his chance, looked at Taiwan and more or less said this cannot be happening in my lifetime. These guys were failures, they ran away, renegades, terrible people. They were supposed to kind of collapse and come back to us on bended knees, and how come Taiwan is one of the fastest growing countries in the world? And not being stupid he actually jettisoned all his life's thinking and decided what I have been taught is wrong and what my enemies have been telling me is right and therefore I switch. One of the greatest examples of creative thinking in the world's history, quite astonishing. Why should a veteran Marxist, hardliner, been on the long march and gone through several purges, in his blue overalls, suddenly cut loose? That is what I think created a whole new firmament. At the same time, in developed countries macroeconomics Keynesianism was losing out, monetarism was rising. Keynesian economics lost all reputation because it had no cure for inflation and income policy did not work. I can't even begin to tell you how hard it was for us Keynesians in the West.

The next assault was the shift to free market thinking in the West, ideas of incentives and so on. In a sense what was happening in Korea and Taiwan was not actually a free market economy working but a different model of development which was more reliant on consumer goods markets in developed countries. Not that they believed in free markets, they believed in regulated market with government intervention but the success was selling in a market private consumer goods, cars or whatever. Development thinking at that stage was also beginning to move towards the idea that maybe development strategy was about how to do things by getting inputs from anywhere. The Japanese were actually very successful in this, they were the first people to prove that the kind of input-output thinking that was there until then was no longer necessary. Thus if you want a steel mill, it was thought that it is not very good to just have your own steel mill but you have to have your own iron ore and your own coal and have integrated large scale industry. US Steel is one of those examples. The Japanese had no coal or iron ore and they made a successful steel industry by basically getting things from elsewhere. It is called just-in-time inventory. Certainly it had become possible because technology had advanced through container shipping and communication satellites, computer aided design and management. Same thing with Asian countries. Asian countries decided they could borrow capital, they have the labour and off they went and so national self-sufficiency oriented idea of development also lost out. When the Chinese started importing foreign capital, who could defend national self-sufficiency?

The other aspect of what was happening is that the aftermath of debt crisis in Latin America was very hard, with the IMF battening down on them saying, you can't do this, you can't do that, adopt free markets. The fact that these nations were indebted compelled them really to adapt themselves to a very harsh fiscal policy and they were looking for how to think about development in a different way. And this is where the human development idea came from. I was part of the team, along with two of the speakers in this Institute of Social Sciences, Amartya Sen and Mahbub ul Haq. That's how the whole idea of human development was born. That you should forget about growth rate, forget about capital output ratio, forget about input-output tables, development is not any of that. It has got to do with life expectancy, health, education and later on what Amartya said, with human capabilities. Poverty not in terms of calories, poverty in terms of capabilities. What should people be expected to be able to do and why don't they have resources to do it and how can you organise it so that they do? So it is partly through the adversity of Latin American countries and partly through the adversity of developed countries when capital was leaving them, that thinking in development changes. And the human development story has now become so routine in India that every state and every district and maybe every *mohalla* [hamlet] has its own human development index. Yet the interesting thing is that it shifts the focus of development from nation state and macro to the quality of people's lives. What was interesting in the Indian case was that through the halcyon days of socialist pattern of society nobody talked about primary education or literacy at all. Steel production was the most important thing to do. Steel production, heavy machinery, heavy electricals, all sort of things, but not a single person talked about health or primary education or the gender issue. All those issues suddenly came to life in the 1990s. It was all about governance and accountability and transparency, life expectancy, morbidity, maternal mortality rate, infant mortality rate. I mean they were always there but you go back to the first, second, third and fourth Five-Year Plans, there is absolutely no mention of these. Somehow, through various actions and of course some brilliant thinking it finally comes to the idea that development has really got to do with the quality of people's life and basically of the Bahujan Samaj, the majority of the people. That is what has to be looked at. And very surprisingly the first person to talk about 'aam aadmi' (the common man) in Lok Sabha was Lal Bahadur Shastri. In a brilliant speech; he says what I see are all these plans and models. Are we actually improving the lives of the ordinary people who live in a small room in an urban area or of the peasants? Well, he was not there for a very long time and we had to wait another thirty years before this *aam aadmi* again emerges on the scene.

The interesting thing is that the way thinking about development changes is partly through the role of the material forces, changes in the outside world like the developed economies lost their industries and had to find some other solutions. Developing countries got into debt. Some of them used the State action imaginatively to get into export-oriented markets and you know India was one of the last countries to change in that respect. But it also changes due to new ideas such as human development or capabilities. It is now almost accepted universally that the measure of development in a country is the quality of life of its people. The disagreement is, or the alternative vision is, what will bring about that outcome.

Is there a conflict between growth and development which is a hot topic nowadays? I would argue not; have liberal economic reforms, high growth rate and then you can manage redistribution if you have revenues to redistribute. You can't have static economy and then insist on redistribution; that kind of redistribution never happens. We have a very peculiar notion in our mind of the economy being like a harvest – you harvest, then you thresh out the grain, then you divide the grain between different people's shares. That is not the way an economy functions; output is produced and distributed simultaneously. Then you have to tax people to raise surplus and then you have all these incentive problems. Even in developed countries with progressive taxation they have managed redistribution more by tilting the public spending towards the poorer classes than progressive taxation. So it is a combination of taxation and spending with spending having more importance. One of the disagreements is how much you need to sustain high growth rate. Secondly, to sustain high growth rate how much should the State take away. For example, I believe that high deficits are not a good thing, taking away money from the people for irresponsible fiscal policy is self-defeating. There are differences on how much foreign capital is required and so on. But there is no doubt that at the end of fifty years of development thinking, we are absolutely sure that there is no other measure of development except the people whose development you are pursuing. And for those people there are issues like gender which would now be unthinkable of obliterating from development indices. I recall that gender had become a big issue of development in 1995 when there was a UN conference on gender. I remember sitting in New York, myself, Amartya Sen, Mahbub ul Haq and various other people and inventing the gender equality measure and then all the human development measures were filtered through a gender perspective. That kind of change has come about through a variety of experiences. We will probably get more nuanced, more focused on diverse individual experiences and then ask ourselves, okay, even the human development index is not good enough because it is too general, can we calibrate it more, for example, to take care of disability or take account of old age, because old age is very important. Can we do something to specifically measure how well a society is doing by way of the disabled or by the elderly and things like that. There cannot be a single poverty measure, it is silly to have a single poverty measure. Not every person needs the same number of calories. Again and again development thinking becomes much more oriented towards outcomes. Outcomes are measured basically through quality of people's lives. In the next fifty years, which some of you will have to suffer, I think development thinking will get better. Thank you.

* * *

Question and Answer Session

Question: *Since the FDI proposal was turned down in Parliament the newspapers have been writing editorials saying this is the end of the world. If only FDI came in, if only the insurance sector was opened up, the economy would grow. I don't see the economics of this, in terms of the kind of money that is going to come in or the kind of employment that is going to be generated. I do not understand why such a huge fuss is being made about economic reforms because I believe that the problem in India today is that we are not doing things with the money we have. I think the fundamental problem is wastage, it's not about reforms. If we could run government properly and do things in a proper way, these so-called reforms can play a role on another plane. Would you agree with that?*

Lord Desai: No, of course not. I have been arguing for the last twenty years against that, partly because these are not two exclusive things. I entirely agree with you that there is a lot of wastage. But we passionately believe that governments are better than markets and we go on giving more and more money to the government who is wasting it and then in crisis we give *more* money to the government. So one problem is: there is wastage. Even today when the Food Security Bill is being discussed, the friends of the public distribution system (PDS) say we must support the PDS, the loss has come down from 54 per cent to 41 per cent – this is Jean Dreze in *The Hindu* a couple of months ago. Where would you see the madness of somebody saying I must insist on using a system which has only 41 per cent waste? I pay 40 per cent tax, in the UK that is, because I'm supposed to be a better-paid person. You are imposing tax relative to a high rate of income tax on the poorest people of India and that is supposed to be socialism. Thank you very much!

Secondly, when you say money comes, it is not just money which comes but new technology and new organising principles that come. For example there are large multinationals in the US, UK and so on which supply the corner stores, which are the equivalent of our Kirana stores. There is no reason why there should be apartheid, these multinationals are only supplying their own people and not a Kirana store. If they organise the supply chain properly they could supply the corner stores. The fear is that if they organise themselves in India, India will be ruined, it will be in a foreign trap, the East India Company will come back again – read Somnath Chatterjee's speech in Parliament in 1991. Through the forty years before 1991, the growth rate was 3.5 per cent. And not only that, health and education were neglected, poverty had not come down as rapidly as since 1991.

Yes, we should reduce wastage, that's quite right. But who is going to bell the cat? The system gains from wastage. The political system is financed through wastage of the public sector. This debatable black money, the whole political system lives on domestic black money. We know that. You know, the Election Commission in the Tamil Nadu election found something like 87 crores in cash in one truck of [a contestant]. I mean, how does the system not be actually shocked about this? And they debate black money in Parliament! My view is that, yes, we should reduce wastage. Wastage is always bad, in any economy. I don't think you've gone shopping in a large wholesale or vegetable market. I occasionally go to one. Look at the rats, rats sitting around with the fish being sold, mangy cats and dogs all over, puddles of dirty water, dog shit as well, what an unhealthy thing we suffer. We don't need to suffer. I don't need foreign capital to get rats out of markets. I also feel there is a more technical issue of the gap between the farmers' plight, what the farmers get and the price that consumers pay. If your middle bits are insufficient you end up paying the price for that.

* * *

Question*: I'm surprised at the omission of the ecological question in your speech and the question of the 'limits to growth'.*

Lord Desai: I consider the ecological question not to be a development question because it spans the whole world. The ecological question is a global question. There are a variety of ways of looking at the ecological question. Partly whether it is the stock of emissions which is the problem, which is mainly generated by the rich countries or the flow of the emission which is going to be done by the developing countries. All the battles from Copenhagen on are about this. Over the fifty years of development thinking very little was devoted to that aspect. Even today it is not an integral part. It ought to be, perhaps. And when it is done some of the issues are going to be similar but equally capable of diversity. One idea is that the whole world should come together and write down a beautiful global compact. Very technical areas of economics which I will not bore you with have shown that you cannot construct a social welfare function even for a homogeneous economy because people have diverse tastes. And if you try to do that you can only do it by assuming that people are completely identical and have identical tastes. But people value things diversely. The difficulty of Copenhagen and Cancun and Durban is that the issue is not global warming. If we talk about global warming you look at that single global number and environment is not a single global problem. It is a differentiated local problem, in different areas. Very often, what are needed are different local solutions for particular problems which may not be relevant to a global level solution. I'm very pessimistic about a global compact of the Kyoto-Durban kind. I'm very hopeful that people will do things, particularly locally. If you have flooding in Mississippi or in Queensland, or you have local famine, you've got to devise local solutions. As much as there is a relationship between ecology and development it can be furthered by local thinking at a fairly specific level and not get involved in a global discussion.

* * *

Question: One issue that is disturbing me is the issue of patents. In the pattern of economics is the production again going to shift back and will there then be a reorientation in which we will be mere supplicants of their products?

Lord Desai: What is interesting is that in London or the West they are terrified that the tectonic plates have shifted and development has gone away from them. The best prospect is that the European Union will have, maybe, between 0 to 1 per cent growth rate for the next fifteen years; they'll be lucky if it is not negative. I'm very serious. Obama is going around saying I'm really worried about the Indian educational competition or the Chinese competition. When I come to India I realise that people are seriously worried about the West still – but the West is very worried about India and China. It is not an unrealistic position. Just as in the 1970s the manufacturing moved out, what happened in the big crisis of 2008–10 is that developed countries had thought that they could not rely on manufacturing but started relying on services, financial and other services. In America the average wage of a manufacturing worker has not gone up for thirty-five years and families sustain themselves because two members of the family work. What in 1950s and 1960s a person working in a car company in Detroit could afford, a TV, a fridge, a car and so on, now two members work for and because they are working in the service sector which is lower paid they have to borrow money. This whole borrowing collapsed. So the sustainability of this Western standard of living is in serious danger.

The way I put it, is that capitalism in the West is geriatric and the dynamism in capitalism is out here. This is where things are happening. You know, people always say in Britain, we have lots of patents but no development. The real development, the 7, 8 and 9 per cent growth rate will happen here. Look at growth rates in Africa – in the last ten years they are fantastic and a place like Myanmar is going to explode in development. Look at Vietnam – who would have thought about it when I was marching on the streets about Vietnam in the 1960s that Vietnam would be one of the most rapidly growing economies. That is a perspective too much weighed down by the past. And I should add, a lot of people filing patents in the West are not actually Western-born. Because their education system is universalistic and admits everybody, you know, the Chinese, the Indians. A lot of the people in Silicon Valley are Indians. Another way to put it, I think, is that nation states don't develop, people develop. I always say about human development that if somebody moves from, say, poor India to US, his life expectancy doesn't go up by twenty years. His life expectancy is the same, more or less, so even the human development numbers can be misleading because it can be too macro. If that is the case let us do something about it. Response should be, let us beat them. Who would have thought that India would be an IT hub? Why is India an IT hub? Because IT was never part of the Planning Commission strategy of industrial development *(laughter)*. Why is Bollywood a success story? Because films were not even thought to be an industry, they never gave any money for films, and that's why they are a global success.

* * *

Question: *Is there a distinct form of Indian development thinking? You mentioned so many models, and the debate over these different ideas on development thinking.*

Lord Desai: The answer is somewhat mixed. I think what is true, partly because of Amartya Sen, we are argumentative, we write too much and talk too much. There has been more explicit thinking about development by Indians and by foreign experts given Indian data than for almost any other country. Some day someone will write the book which I absolutely have no time to write, about how India is unique to the development experience not because India developed fast but because India became a laboratory of people trying out their theories. For example, the whole notion of surplus labour – whether it exists or not, all that, which is what I started learning my development economics with, was very much fashioned with India in mind. Partly because China was not open to such thinking and experimentation for the first forty years, and partly because India was the only other large poor ex-colonial country where there was a sufficient number of very, very bright people in civil services, politics, academia – the number of people Nehru was receiving in the 1950s reads like a galaxy of international names. They wrote things, were heard, because Indians are very receptive. I'm not sure it actually helped because my picture of India is, after the first decade of 1950s, it floundered for the next three decades. Really badly floundered. Surjit Bhalla said its only because India has extremely clever people that these disastrous policies did not ruin the country. Somehow we made this totally impossible policy work. Or at least they did not break up the country.

It is quite remarkable that between roughly 1965 and 1990 India is not an example of good development policy strategy in terms of both overall growth rate or poverty removal. Mrs Gandhi picked up the slogan 'Garibi Hatao' (Remove Poverty) and all that and I hesitate to say this, but when Mahbub ul Haq wrote *The Poverty Curtain*, this idea, I'm sorry to say, originated in the World Bank. The first estimates of Indian poverty were not done by the Planning Commission or by the Government of India. It was Dandekar and Rath, two economists in the Gokhale Institute of Politics and Economics in Pune who were the first to give estimates on poverty. I remember the storm that broke out. Nobody could believe that so much poverty exists in India. Fifteen rupees per month or something like that. India doesn't really have the example that other people should follow. India is still stumbling around, partly because of the consensus building in our political system and partly because of its diversity – there is no single solution for all of India anyway, and its development experience is very diverse. For example, in the last ten years I would say, India is the test for the idea that governance matters. Governance matters more than anything else in the world. We didn't think about governance in the first fifty years of development thinking. So India is still a very good place to study, both for what to do and for what not to do. But it is not actually an example for a successful development strategy.

***

Question: *Your main argument, that we have moved over the last fifty years from things-oriented development to people-oriented development, that, I think, is not right, because this is a process which has been there even before 1961, the period which you are covering. For example, when Marx writes in Economic and Philosophical Manuscripts or even in China, in 1949, it was a 'People's Democratic Revolution'. They spoke in a different language, the language of contradictions between working class and peasantry, between mental and manual labour, and so on, but the concern for people was there. After the Second World War, the golden age of capitalism was possible because of the existence of a socialist block. And also because of the successful anti-colonial struggles. I think this Human Development Index in India is merely trying to lend a human face to the inhumane neo-liberal policies. It's nothing more than that.*

Lord Desai: I'm glad there's disagreement – I like disagreement.

* * *

Questions and Comments:

1. *I want to know whether the Lok Pal bill will give us anything sustainable regarding our economic system.*
2. *I agree with your view. Development thinking is changing and changing for the better. The change in progressive thinking in terms of development should be captured by changes in the way we govern ourselves. I believe only the decentralised form of governance can capture such thinking.*
3. *The quality of leadership is also very important because if the leadership is not interested in development, development won't take place. If leaders are co-opted into the (prevailing) system how can the system be changed?*

Lord Desai: No, it's peoples fault that there's no development!

* * *

Questions and Comments:

1. *Do you think that India can be poverty-free? And if yes, at which rate of development can that happen?*
2. *A simple layperson's question – America, Europe have (high) human development indices but why do they have all these bailout packages in the last so many years?*
3. *The government failure theories in 1990 built a case for liberalisation but despite this we had large-scale massive corporate fraud and corporate scams. But when the discourse of governance was being put forward fingers are pointed against the non-governance in/by governments. Fingers are never pointed at the misgovernance in the corporate sector.*
4. *We had a 'Hindu rate of growth' and then went for liberalisation. We had 8 to 9 per cent growth rate and even now it stands at 6 to 7 per cent. These large flagship programmes – Bharat Nirman and MNREGA show that government have not left people on their own. But despite this, we see the inefficiency where 83 per cent of our countrymen are living at merely Rs. 20 per day.*
5. *We seem to push a particular idea of development thinking that everything has to open up, economic reforms, open market and so on. On the other hand we seem to show that we don't really believe in it because we have huge funds invested in NREGA and the Food Security Bill. Isn't there a contradiction between these two? Doesn't this need attention? What does this finally display in terms of our own development thinking?*

Lord Desai: I am going to cluster the questions here – one was the question, will India be poverty-free? Another question, which Jaya Jaitly put, was in the contradictions in development thinking and practice with MNREGA, etc. Another was, does the old model not still have the maximum wisdom, i.e., the Left model of development? There's a very strong belief that somehow the true model is still a Left model and somehow the liberalisation model is full of scams and contradictions and corruption and so on. Then the question on the Lokpal bill.

On Poverty

On poverty, let me put it this way, and I am not just making it up on the spot. The definition of poverty in India ranges over such large numbers that you either have poverty of 24 per cent or of 80 per cent. It's not that anyone's being dishonest, but there are genuinely different views of development, like the 'calorific view'. The calorific view of development says, here are the calories, this is the food basket, translate the food basket into money, then add a little bit for shoes and clothes, and that is the poverty level. There's a long tradition of doing that.

Then, either you say like Tendulkar, no, let's have a little bit more added. All people can, say, live at $1 per day. Then there is [Arjun] Sengupta. The thing is that the notion of development is both absolute and relative; it always has been in the literature. Absolute notions are food-based notions, period. That you are poor if you can't have that many calories. There is no ambiguity about any other thing. If you have uncertainty in poverty measures you've got to be crude. Then there is a view that that's a very bad view of poverty, that the notion of poverty is, what in the view of the society, everybody should have something of. Make that list and see who cannot afford the things on that list. The famous economist Peter Townsend wrote a big fat book on poverty in the UK; he asked fifteen questions to everybody – one of the questions was: what do you have for breakfast, do you have eggs and beacon for breakfast or do you have one big meat meal in a week or 'Sunday roast' as it is called, and so on? And then he said, people who can't have that, or one or more of those things are poor, because they are not fully participant in the community life. Now that is a very different notion of poverty.

Then there is Amartya Sen's version of poverty, which arose from a debate with Peter Townsend, and Amartya said, don't be commodity minded, don't get stuck in commodities, think of what you would like people to be able to do. What are the set of capabilities people ought to have? And do they have the resources to use those capabilities? For example, everybody cannot be of the same calorific standards; or, if I'm disabled, I'm paraplegic, it may require four times as much money to make me mobile compared to you. If I get four times as much money, I'm not richer than you, I'm just as poor as you are, but my poverty level is different from yours.

In India there is this very interesting debate about Rs. 32 per day and these people couldn't explain where that Rs. 32 came from, but it came from the whole Dandekar-Rath tradition. I think the best way to define this is for the majority of people in the society to say we consider these sorts of things, it may be dal-roti every day, twice a day, whatever it is, what is the community's thinking of not being poor? (In India this has not happened yet). What does it cost? And how many people cannot afford this? It may be different by regions. It will be definitely different by gender, and it may also have elements like disability, area where you live and so on. If you live in Kashmir you may have a very different notion of poverty than you would have if you lived in Kerala.

Poverty is a very politicised subject. The idea is that if I can prove that 99 per cent of India is poor I'm more progressive, more left-wing than you are. If you go down on the percentage, you are a capitalist agent. Exactly as I used to say at the beginning of the 3rd Five-Year Plan especially, everybody who said there should be more money in agriculture was thought to be either a fascist or a capitalist agent, because agriculture was right wing and industry was left wing. Those are silly kinds of notions. I mean, India has sufficient resources for someone to say, let's get this poverty question very differently. If you are genuinely interested, you would say that people ought to have adequate livelihoods. And what does it take to get people adequate livelihoods? There was a man called Charles Booth in London, a businessman, in the 1870s. He was walking around in East End of London and he found lots of children wandering around. He asked why aren't you in school? (England didn't have free primary education till the twentieth century). And, they said, our families can't afford the money to send us to school. It was 4 pence a term or something then. So he started enquiring into the standard of life, the incomes of their families. How much did they spend on food, clothes, etc. His question was motivated not by calories but by children's access to education. So, for example, in your poverty level you must have whether children are getting an adequate education or not. About health access, etc. things like that. A lot of poverty is not about whether families can more or less meet everyday needs but if there is an accident, if somebody falls sick and can't go to work, they are wiped out.

From that point of view, I would say that no society should ever claim to be poverty-free. Because there is actually no limit to how much you can make people better off.

I do not believe that there will ever be a completely equal society. Okay, I am 71 years old and I have given up all hope of egalitarianism. But I do strongly believe that every society should try and reduce poverty as much as possible and not actually accept a limit, that this is good enough for the poor, but I would not live on that.

On MNREGA

Now, this MNREGA and so on. It's very interesting, there is a very basic contradiction in Congress thinking. It comes from the past. The liberalisers have discovered that there are ways of getting high growth rates. Basically, the corporates are growing very fast, exports are growing, all sorts of nice things are happening. That fills up the government's coffers. Government's revenue collection has been nothing like this in the past. They have got permanent account number (PAN) cards[1] and all that. But, the other people in the same party, they hate all this. They think all this high growth is terrible, high growth does nothing for the poor people. I don't know if they believe that only low growth does better for the poor people – because they are the guardians of the Low Growth Rate Society. That is where their dynasty had invested their energy in, the dynasty that was involved in the Hindu rate of growth.

They basically believe that the ideal government should subsidise everything and distribute money to the poor as quickly as possible. But it must be done in a way which doesn't enable the poor to get out of poverty. You must keep the people in poverty, and preferably, where they live. They will be allowed to live where they live, partly because then, they'll vote for you. The whole MNREGA in my view (I mean who am I to complain about people getting work 30 days, 100 days, a year or whatever it is, it would be cruel not to sympathise with that), but it is designed to keep people in that place doing work which more or less, has no value added but it prevents migration.

On Migration

I think migration is a good thing, partly because I migrated myself (*laughter*). I believe in full liberal migration all over the world and I think if people want to get out of poverty, very often one of the biggest weapons people have used is to up and go somewhere else. Why do you think the 'people of Indian origin' so-called, are in the Caribbean? Why are they in South Africa, in East Africa, in Malaysia? Why are there poor begging UP-walas in Maharashtra that Rahul Gandhi just discovered? Why, because they were miserable in UP, that's why they went there.

One-third of the European population in the nineteenth century migrated to North America. So migration is a way of getting out of poverty. It is a self-help strategy. But no, we can't allow that. That is, I think, the central contradiction.

---

1 Cards issued by the Indian Tax Office that are needed by non-resident Indians if they are investing in India or submitting tax returns in India.

On the Food Security Bill

And then this Food Security Bill is the next contradiction. If you allow public distribution system there is 41 per cent wastage. Now, I have been arguing for direct cash transfers. You want to remove poverty? Figure out what it requires and give the cash to whoever you think is poor. And you know what people say? 'You can't trust how they will spend the money'. Poor people don't know the value of money and you know the value of money? What kind of nonsense is this? The poor person understands the value of every penny and they spend it very carefully. They may be poor but they are not stupid. But cash transfer is thought to be not possible. I thought of this idea when I first asked a question in Parliament – there was US$50 billion in total foreign aid in those days, there were also a billion poor in those days. That's $50 per poor person with one dollar a week, why don't you just give people one dollar a week? If their income is less than one dollar a day, that very person will get at least 14 per cent addition to their daily income. And everybody can get larger than that.

Anyway, cash transfers I think has radical possibilities. It will not be done because you will lose control. Those six paises they get – where did the 94 paises go? It won't happen, because you would lose control over the money.

So, I still believe that high growth rate generates public revenue and if the public revenue was efficiently used, you'd get a much better bang for the buck in curing poverty, heath and all those things. Because the implementation, both the purchasing and the providing of public services is done by the public sector, we get an inefficient outcome. Public sector should purchase these services but not necessarily provide them. Either though decentralisation – that's one way – or through some other way. They ought to give up control, which they can't give up. So that is my long answer.

On the question on bailouts, basically, what was happening, in building an economy, manufacturing used to be 26 to 27 per cent of the GDP, and now it is 10 per cent in UK, for example. Manufacturing no longer employs many people, it has become high-tech and so an ordinary unskilled or semi-skilled worker has to have long terms of unemployment or work in the low-paid services sector. And, that has led to the crisis of living standards. That's led to borrowing, and the financial revolution has made possible construction of a huge credit mountain on a small cash base.

Now, that whole thing collapsed in 2008. For the Western countries right now, for the last three years, no way out has been found, of restoring the growth rate. There's lots of debate about it and because both governments and households are in debt, governments don't have the money to spend, and if you have the money to spend, households will not spend it because they have to pay back their debts.

In a sense, the Western model of living standards is becoming untenable and people are looking for a new model. The West doesn't feel mighty and powerful, like, in somewhere like India. There is a real, real scare right now going on. Certainly in the Euro zone countries. At least 15 out of the 17 Euro zone countries are not going to get back to their pre-crisis living standards of 2007 till 2025, if they're lucky. It's a deep, deep crisis in the Western economies. And it's not a crisis of capitalism because capital is alive and well, in Asia, Latin America and Africa. The great transformation in the world, the shifting of tectonic plates which started in the 1970s and continued, and its entirely a Marxist phenomenon, entirely predictable by Marxists because it's in the Communist Manifesto. Capital moves where it finds its highest profitability. That's the nature of capitalism.

Everybody has been saying, the great socialist revolution will come back. It won't, you should read my book on this. I'll tell you why – because it was premature socialism from a Marxian perspective. The Preface to *A Contribution to the Critique of Political Economy* says that 'No social order is ever destroyed before all the productive forces for which it is sufficient have been developed, and new superior relations of production never replace older ones before the material conditions for their existence have matured within the framework of the old society. Mankind thus inevitably sets itself only such tasks as it is able to solve, since closer examination will always show that the problem itself arises only when the material conditions for its solution are already present, or, at least in the course of formation.'[2]

Capitalism has not lost its energy. And the premature socialism of the Soviet Union collapsed in ignominy, without a single gun being fired. It collapsed because of economic inefficiency. In 1960 Khrushchev had said, we will bury you under a mountain of commodities. We'll produce more steel, more cement in the next twenty-five years. And you know, he was right. But it was the same steel, and more innovative steel had been developed in the West. It was the same cement, but better building materials had been found in the West. They went on doing the same thing again and again and again. It was a complete waste of time, because economics is not about production, it is about productivity.

---

2   Karl Marx, *A Contribution to the Critique of Political Economy* (Lawrence and Wishart, London; 1971) p. 21.

How much more productivity can you get one day to the next, by using better techniques, by skilling people better, by using better management, and things like that. And that's why capitalism has survived. And what's more, it's not a matter of being Christian or of Western values, nothing like that. Anybody can do capitalism. It's the easiest thing to do. Save hard, work hard and re-invest profits. That's why China is such a giant success. In 1965 the great man Henry Kissinger once said, if India and China could feed themselves there would be no problems left in the world. Less than fifty years ago this was said, and look where the world is now. And why is China so developed? Not because of the great People's Democratic Revolution. That was a disaster, and led to the largest famine ever in the world in which 40 million people died. Seriously, the biggest famine certainly in the twentieth century, perhaps ever, and all because of the Great Leap Forward. The 'People's Democratic Revolution' wasn't actually about people at all. People's name was used and misused, and people were traduced. I get very angry when I'm reminded of this because India, bourgeois, petty bourgeois, weak India, managed to get along without having such a famine of that sort at all. We did have two harvest failures in 1964–65 and 1966–67, but India didn't have the kind of deaths that China has had. Why? Because it was a miserable petty bourgeois democracy. It was not a 'people's democratic revolution'.

I think we have got to give up these illusions. I absolutely have no compunctions about saying, thank heavens, the world has cured itself of that socialism. We may get another socialism yet. But *that* socialism is, thank god, gone. Except in North Korea. I'm not at all apologetic about liberal economic reforms. I am old enough to remember what it was like – corruption was not invented in 1991 in India. Let me hasten to add, in 1946, Nehru said to, I forget to whom, maybe Sardar Patel, that the Congress fellows in UP were so corrupt that they have violated every article of IPC already and they have just been elected! I'm not making it up. This is 1946, before India became independent.

It's in the very interesting biography of Chaudhary Charan Singh by Paul Brass. You read that and you will see how Charan Singh was fighting against corruption.

The point about the misgovernance of corporations is entirely correct, but there are two things – regulatory structures are to be better and there is good Western example of better regulatory structures, and they have to be administered without political interference. Just take a British example – we have just had a report published on Monday on the failures of the Royal

Bank of Scotland on which the British tax payer had to give £84 billion or something like that. They wanted to prove they are pro-business. There is now written evidence that both Gordon Brown and his office were saying to the FSA, please don't be so hard on the banks. So it's one thing to have regulatory structures but you also need to have non-interference by political classes of all parties. What that does is that you have to review regulations again and again. Secondly, you really have to have very watertight ring fencing of the way those regulatory structures operate to keep them immune from political interference.

What is very interesting now is what the Security and Exchange Commission in the US is doing. In the last year there are a number of examples of heavy fines being imposed on Goldman Sachs, on Citibank, etc. Four years ago you sold this fraudulent package of mortgage securities to so-and-so; now pay US$200 million – for example, the trial of Rajaratnam. That is the kind of system you need. Americans hate being cheated and when their legal system gets going, it is merciless. Had the Royal Bank of Scotland thing happened in America, they would all have ended up in jail. All these guys need to end up in jail because they have defrauded the public.

Also if there is a real capitalism no bank would be saved, nobody needs to be saved in capitalism. These are deluded beliefs that people's welfare lies in saving banks. Banks do nothing for people's welfare. They may exist to make profits, if they don't make profits they should shut down.

About the Lokpal Bill. I think I'm surprised about the Bill. India has not lacked laws against corruption. There is a belief and you have to respect that there is some kind of overarching ombudsman sort of facility and then there is a debate whether the Central Bureau of Investigation (CBI) should be under it or not. Whether CBI should be under or not under, my opinion is that it has to be autonomous and free of political interference. In India there is confusion that because India is a democracy it entitles elected people to have infinite power to intervene in anything. That is not true. Mrs Gandhi started this very false doctorate of mandate, that because I have the mandate I can do anything I like including getting the Judiciary hassled. In a democracy there are strict limits on what the elected legitimate government can do and there have to be areas which are ring fenced because I think it is later on today or tomorrow that there is a judgement coming out against Jacques Chirac, who was president of France. He's been tried for fraud he committed when he was mayor of Paris and probably he may not go to jail but he will be convicted. That is a kind of thing you need, you need to have regulatory structures which are independent of political influence. I don't know whether the Indian parliamentary system is capable of giving up that much of power. Ok, we've got a good electoral commission which is alright but CBI is not independent and we have to see whether an independent Lokpal can be constructed. I should also say, actually it doesn't have to be done by 27th December 2011. There is no sacrosanct rule about the date that Anna Hazare wants it to be done. Law making is very, very difficult. I know something about this. Every comma, full stop and every sub phrase counts because lawyers will take you to court to get out of jail. So, formulating law is a very complex matter. Unfortunately, the Indian parliamentary system has got its own set of practices which is to 'avoid vote taking'. In the British political system, government would have a bill, there will be a clause, opposition would make an amendment, it would be debated and be voted upon. Indian parliamentary system is afraid of voting. So, everything has to be decided before the bill comes before parliament. This is a new trend. There's a nice paper by Liberty Institute as to why this has happened. That's a structural problem of the parliamentary system. There is paralysis of decision making unless everybody is in the same room and everybody has agreed to the package and then the package is voted through at a nod.

Acknowledgement

This chapter was originally delivered as the Closing Ceremony Address at the Silver Jubilee Celebrations for the Institute of Social Sciences, which was followed by a Q&A session, in New Delhi on 15 December 2011. Reproduced with kind permission of the Institute of Social Sciences.

Part 3

Indian Economy, Politics and Culture

Chapter 12

THE ECONOMIC POLICY OF THE BJP

Meghnad Desai

(1994)

The Bharatiya Janata Party (BJP) is the opposition party in the Indian Parliament and as such forms the shadow government of India. Its number of seats in the Lok Sabha rose from two in 1984 to eighty-six in 1989 and finally 119 in 1991. The BJP had also formed governments in four states – Uttar Pradesh, Madhya Pradesh, Himachal Pradesh and Rajasthan. These governments were dismissed by the President of India in December 1992 following the destruction of the Babri Masjid in Ayodhya and on evidence of the implication of BJP in that destruction. In the recent mid-term elections in these four states plus Delhi, the BJP has been returned to power in Rajasthan and Delhi though it lost Himachal Pradesh and Madhya Pradesh to the Congress and Uttar Pradesh to a conjunction of BSP and SP, two left parties representing backward castes.

Despite this reversal, the BJP remains the only credible alternative as a national government. Thus its economic policies are of interest to anyone interested in the prospects of the Indian economy. As is well known, the Indian economy is undergoing a process of structural reforms with liberalisation and integration into the world economy as prominent themes. Although the pace of economic reform has been uneven, it is clear that as long as the present government stays in power, economic reforms are irreversible. One of the questions at issue in examining the BJP's policy is its attitude to economic reform. As an ostensibly right wing but nationalistic party, the BJP combines (as any political party does) contradictory elements of liberalisation and dirigisme. The policy of the BJP is however neither a seamless cloth nor is it frozen in aspic. Factions within the party have differing views and the policy emphasis shifts over time. In this paper, I shall attempt to examine the economic policy of the BJP, discernible from its own documents.

Much of the literature on the BJP concentrates on its political stance, especially its Hindu nationalism as reflected in its slogan of Hindutva. There has been an upsurge in the study of the BJP and of the Sangh Parivar in general since the Babri Masjid's demolition. Important though the issues raised in this literature are – secularism, communalism, nationalism – they are not my concern. In its economic policy, the BJP allows no role for any specific Hindu or Hindutva element. Thus for example it does not espouse any notion of Hindu economics, as some of its followers, for example champion Vedic Mathematics (Jayaraman 1993). It is possible therefore to discuss the economic policy of the BJP without reference to its Hindu 'fundamentalism'.

Sources

Before going into the subject of this paper, it is appropriate to say that there seems to be no available treatment of the economic policy of the BJP to my knowledge. The BJP itself has published a pamphlet, 'Humanistic Approach to Economic Development (A Swadeshi Alternative)'. I have also referred to economic policy resolutions at various National Executive Meetings and the Election Manifesto for 1991 'Towards Ram Rajya'. Besides these, the BJP regards as a fundamental document, a set of lectures by its past president Deen Dayal Upadhyaya entitled 'Integral Humanism' (Upadhyaya 1965). [I have not yet however as of now consulted the 1986 Policy Statement].

The Economics of Economic Nationalism

The BJP is a right-wing nationalistic party. Until recently, it tried to maintain an image of a secular rather than a religious party. In the last three years, there has been a real tension within the party among elements which want to emphasise the Hindu face and those who want to maintain a secular nationalistic face. Be that as it may, the BJP is also often labelled a fascist party. It seems however that as far as economic thinking is concerned, there is no parallel between the corporatism of Italian fascism or the totalitarianism of German fascism and the economics of the BJP. Thus it would be fruitless to drag in the European literature on the economics of fascism. The economic thinking of the BJP has to be analysed within its Indian context.

In the broader context of Indian economic nationalism, there has always been the Nehruvian left-wing version and the Gandhian right-wing version. The contrast between the two runs across the role of the state, the importance of large versus small industries, the degree of centralisation, the reliance on Western as against indigenous models, the modern machine oriented versus the traditional handicraft production etc. These two strands coexisted uneasily within the Congress – and to some extent permeated official economic policy [eg in the restriction on machine textile sector to the advantage of handspinning/weaving sector]. During the brief regime of the Janata coalition 1977–79, it was the right-wing Gandhian economic nationalism which was much on display.

There is also another strand of right-wing economic nationalism. This could be labelled the big business economic nationalism. The Swatantra Party represented this strand with an acceptance of large scale industrialisation, foreign (Western capitalist) model but with an emphasis on the private sector rather than government. The Bombay Plan of 1946 was a preliminary version of this strand of nationalism.

It used to be thought that the Jan Sangh, the forerunner of the BJP, represented neither big business nor the Gandhians but the small shopkeepers. It was normal to characterise it as a petty bourgeois party. I am not aware of any hard documentation for this but do remember it being frequently asserted as obvious. It was also very protectionist and used to believe in the virtues of low imports.

What this brief outline of different economic tendencies points to is that a 'right-wing nationalist party' has no precise economic profile. Indeed being right wing may mean market oriented and internationalist which will conflict with being nationalist. Right-wing thinkers sometimes are anti-market and conservative, wishing to uphold the traditional social order. There is, in British terms, a difference between a Whig and a Tory though both are right wing. Socialists pride themselves in being internationalist but in economic matters are anti-market, protectionist and nationalist. In their aversion to the entry of foreign capital, a Nehruvian socialist will ride in tandem with a BJP follower.

A separate set of dividers will be along the centralist/decentralist orientation in which again the conventional Right/Left divide does not fit neatly.

Gandhians are right-wing decentralists but European fascists were right-wing centralists though recently on the European Left, a fashion has broken out for decentralist communitarian economics. Right and Left divide best along property ownership/redistribution lines with Leftists more keen to abridge private property ownership and use taxation/confiscation to redistribute income and wealth progressively. Right-wing thinkers treat private property as sacrosanct and even if they may deplore inequalities, they would rather rely on voluntary agency to effect redistribution. Gandhi with his idea of private property as trust is very much in the right-wing mould.

The BJP is in this sense an eclectic combination of right wing and nationalist elements. By the 1991 election, it had acquired an inclusive set of right-wing beliefs and once the economic reforms process was embraced by the Congress Government, it also moved decisively into the anti-internationalist camp. Reading the Humanistic Approach, we sense that by 1992, the BJP had staked a claim for the Nehruvian self-reliance, anti-foreign capital ground. While criticising the Licence-Permit-Quota Raj, the BJP emerges not as a free market, competitive libertarian party but a conservative nationalist dirigiste party. The best way to substantiate these claims is to follow the published sources.

The key document is the Humanistic Approach (HA hereafter) pamphlet. It brings together arguments put forward in earlier National Executive Economic Resolutions as well as the 1991 Election Manifesto. It is fifty-four pages long and has fifteen sections. It is a document that lays out a general philosophy as well as particular policy options on individual sectors agriculture, industry, infrastructure etc. As in all political documents written especially by opposition parties, there is more promise than is likely to be fulfilled, more criticism of the government than spelling out the hard choices that the party may have to face if and when it is in power. But this is the normal course of political rhetoric.

Significantly, the BJP starts off by claiming that its economic approach flows 'from our national heritage and from the concepts of Mahatma Gandhi's *Ram Rajya* and Pandit Deen Dayal Upadhyaya's *Integral Humanism*' (p. 7, emphasis in the original). Given the attitude of the RSS (Rashtriya Swayamsevak Sangh) towards Gandhi about other matters, it is remarkable that the BJP now claims the Gandhian mantle. The influence of Upadhyaya is much more direct. Perusing 'Integral Humanism' a pamphlet embodying four lectures delivered by Upadhyaya, one senses that his ideas are at the origin of the BJP's economics when it says it 'believes in a new social and economic order which is non exploitative, competitive and harmonious and which provides full play to the individual initiative and dignity' (ibid.).

The Upadhyaya pamphlet reveals an interesting and not wholly consistent jumble of ideas. The Indian ideal is said to be holistic and the Hindu way of fourfold goals which form Purushartha Dharma is said to define individual aspirations. There is an awareness of Marxism and of Western liberalism but a determination to reject both as too partial. There is an aversion to the market-oriented system prevailing in USA and a conservative critique of capitalism is attempted. In this respect, there is a parallel between Gandhi's *Hind Swaraj* and Upadhyaya's *Integral Humanism*. There is a vague desire for a third way but without any hard economic reasoning to back it up. It may be helpful to quote extensively from the last and fourth chapter of the pamphlet to give a flavour of the ideas.

> Both these systems, capitalist as well as communist, have failed to take account of the Integral Man, his true and complete personality and his aspirations. One considers him a mere selfish being lingering after money, having only one law, the law of fierce competition, in essence the law of the jungle; whereas the other has viewed him as a feeble lifeless cog in the whole scheme of things, regulated by rigid rules and incapable of any good unless directed. The centralisation of economic power is implied in both.
>
> ...
>
> Both therefore result in de-humanisation of man...
>
> We want neither capitalism nor communism. We aim at the progress and happiness of "man", the integral man. (pp. 76–77)

The sentiments expressed in the paragraph above are not untypical of many green, 'new economics', small is beautiful followers. Of course lacking any economic theory of how people behave or how things can be produced, allocated and distributed, much of this kind of thinking remains on the plane of the rhetoric. As happened with Gandhism, in the practical realm of economic affairs, these schools of thought live with the existing system and are thus conservative though they sound radical.

But such idealistic dressing up can be ignored. Its significance for our purposes is that there is no invocation of any old Hindu philosophy of economics as the correct one, no Vedic production system to worship.

Upadhyaya's thought is in line with many conservative and (in my view) muddled thinkers who are terrified by the market as well by planning.

Once we are past the idealist packaging, the BJP's economic policy is said to be based on '(t)he spirit of the Swadeshi and self reliance'. Right at the onset 'the growing resentment and resistance of many socially conscious groups and citizens of the country to operations of multinational companies in the country' is recorded sympathetically. Integration into a global economy, we are told, 'should not mean obliteration of national identity and predominant sway of powerful economic forces from outside'. Thus 'India must liberalise, industrialise and modernise – but it must do so the Indian way'.

This message of Swadeshi and the Indian Way looks politically attractive. Indeed, one doubts if the 'left forces' in India would disagree with this outline. However, what is lacking in the document is any appreciation of the economic consequences of following a severe Swadeshi path. Given India's indebtedness as well as the globalisation of the world economy during the recent years, it is necessary to understand that a strategy rejecting and restricting the entry of foreign capital imposes a severe burden on a domestic economy. [I have outlined some of these problems before. See Desai 1993]. The BJP's economic programme doesn't face up to this set of constraints and indeed in many ways makes inconsistent demands.

Indebtedness, both domestic and foreign, is clearly a major problem for the Indian economy. The BJP makes great play of criticising the government for getting into these debts. In a special pamphlet issued, presumably in 1992 (but like some other BJP documents, carrying no date), 'Towards a Debt Free India' (TDFI), the BJP blames the Nehru-Mahalanobis (NM) model. In fact, it is the 1980s dash for rapid economic growth with foreign borrowing, a tacit departure from the NM model that caused the indebtedness. This is not a rhetorical point since the NM model is as much based on self-reliance as the BJP advocates.

The BJP is acutely alarmed about the internal debt as much as the foreign debt. It was the growth of revenue deficit during the 1980s which allowed internal debt to go up from Rs. 310 billion in 1980–81 to Rs. 1700 billion in 1991–92, or 52 per cent of GDP. Foreign debt has grown from 10 per cent of GDP in 1980–81 to nearly 40 per cent by 1991–92.

The BJP asserts 'if we decide on a steadfast approach of reduction in foreign loans over the next 5 years, it is not a difficult job' (TDFI p. 9). Of course a *reduction* in foreign loans still *increases* the foreign debt. If anything can be said about the BJP's policy on debt, it is that it fails to understand that while there is some connection between internal and foreign debt, they require different policies.

Most of BJP's policies are directed towards reducing internal debt. There are general exhortations to convert deficits into surpluses, to liquidate existing debts by selling the holding of private sector equity in the hands of government financial institutions, leasing out surplus land, privatising of public sector undertakings etc.[1] But correct as these policies are, how do they reduce foreign debt? The 'Debt Free' pamphlet says:

> Instead of writing demeaning letters to the IMF and the World Bank begging for loans, let the Finance Minister draw up a programme for reducing the debt in a phased manner, cutting down on budget deficits and doing away totally with revenue deficits. Even the American Congress, which represents the richest society in the world, is asking for constitutional ceilings on budget deficits, after being burdened with huge debts. The BJP has also called for similar ceilings... (TDFI p. 10)

It is quite obvious from the quotation that the BJP confuses ceilings on internal debt with those on foreign debt. The reference to the American Congress is rather piquant and it is clear that the deterioration of the US capital account has escaped the BJP's notice. The reduction of internal debt by cutting budget deficits is alright; indeed, the IMF, much reviled by the BJP, insists on it. But the reduction of foreign debt requires cutting of the trade deficit by increasing exports above imports and/or by acting on capital account. It is here that the inflow of foreign equity investment whether direct or portfolio is a crucial step. Since much of India's foreign debt was incurred in the form of bonds or short run commercial paper, inflow of equity investment may help relieve the payments problem. A foreign debt denoted in equities has its risk shared between the lender and the borrower. The present Indian debt concentrates all the risk on the borrower. This was, however, the result of the mistaken belief that the Indian government would be better able to control the influx of foreign money if it borrowed abroad rather than let in foreign multinationals. National autonomy has costs attached to it and neither the Congress in the 1980s nor the BJP in the 1990s is willing to be able to face up to this hard fact.

---

1 However, as we shall see below, the BJP is opposed to any cut in agricultural subsidies on water and electricity which they consider to be the 'natural rights of farmers'.

It is in the question of entry of foreign capital that the BJP is most in line with the previous Nehru-Mahalanobis type policies. Thus, on foreign capital, HA says:

> Opening up of the country to external competition should be on selective basis and strictly keeping in view interests of the domestic economy – industry, materials, local talent and labour force. However the party realises that there is scope to welcome foreign investment and technology in areas where domestic efforts have been weak – energy conservation, pollution control, coal washery technology to name a few. The BJP's attitude is guided by the following principles:
>
> - Foreign investment should be allowed in high-tech, export-oriented and import substitution areas
>
> - Consumer goods should not be open for foreign investment
>
> - Existing multinational companies in the area of consumer goods industries will have to dilute their control within time frame to be evolved. In such cases, preference will be given to existing Indian employees in transfer of equities. (HA p. 23)[2]

This set of policy guidelines is of course precisely what was the official Congress policy. The problem with them as in many discussions of the issue of foreign capital in India is that the BJP sees India in a powerful position to be able to choose what type of foreign capital it would like. In the globalised world of the 1990s, countries are competing to attract foreign capital to their shores and this competition includes developed countries like the UK as well as developing countries – China, Vietnam, Malaysia etc. It is a peculiar mark of insularity of such nationalist thinking in India which will not accept this competition as a fact or as applicable to India. Then, of course, Indians complain that foreign capital refuses to come to India!

The solutions proposed to the external debt problem in the chapter on Balance of Payments in HA make this confusion obvious. Thus, despite the fact that the external debt problem is liable to be exacerbated by continuing borrowing from commercial banks or Non-Resident Indians (NRIs) on a no risk sharing basis (ie as debt rather than equity), the BJP promises that

---

[2] I should say that in the copy of HA that I was given, the last paragraph has been cancelled out but is still readable. I compared this against other copies with the NCSAS and the paragraph is retained. I am not sure whether this is a recent modification in BJP which is being signalled exclusively to me.

'the scheme would be drawn to attract substantial portions of (NRI) savings' which it estimates at US$100 billion. It also advocates discriminating in favour of industrial units set up by NRIs which can only discourage direct investment by companies which are not NRI yet foreign.

The trade policy of the BJP is vague and exhortatory. Export promotion boards are promised for each export commodity: 'Corporate sector would have to fulfil its export obligation especially if its production is import intensive'. It advocates import restrictions for non-essential imports and thinks this is a rational import policy. The current climate of free trade in which other developing economies are hoping to gain by GATT provisions (Uruguay Round) is clearly not to the BJP's liking. Of course, any trade restrictions actually adopted may violate GATT principles and lead to a denial of MFN treatment for Indian exports. The damage caused by such denial of MFN treatment would be serious and worsen the debt problem.

There is a similar lack of consistency in the internal debt reduction policy. Thus while in the chapter on fiscal policy in HA and in TDFI, much is said about reducing the revenue deficit, the proposals scattered throughout HA are to raise government expenditure. A particularly dramatic example of this is also available in the Economic Resolution of September 1991 at the Thiruvananthapuram meeting of the National Executive of the BJP. It is worth quoting extensively from this document to show how the BJP straddles both sides of the issue:

> The Government resorted to slogan mongering of liberalisation with an ulterior motive to attract foreign loans. It played cruelly with economy of Agriculture Sector by slashing the subsidy and further trying to differentiate between functionally non-differentiable farmer community by restoring the subsidy partially. The Executive Committee not only demand full restoration of subsidy to the farmers and early finalisation of agricultural policy which should include among others availability of good seeds in sufficient quantity at reasonable rate, providing water resources, electricity and like at reasonable rate, loans at concessional rates of interest are facilities akin to industries be provided. (BJP September 1991)

The Election Manifesto for May 1991 'Towards Ram Rajya' (TRR) says in its Charter of Rights of Kisan:

> Ensure abundant supply of water and energy, *the farmers have a natural right on these basic inputs* (emphasis in the original, TRR, p. 12)

There obviously seems to be no realisation that subsidies on fertilisers, water and power add to the burden of the large deficit since they amount to selling these inputs at commercially loss-making prices and the losses of the public sector agencies selling them will be part of the internal debt. The additional fact that undirected subsidies encourage excess input use as well as having adverse distributional effects is another blind spot.

In the section on taxation measures in HA, the BJP is for raising the income tax exemption limit, corporate tax exemption to employment-oriented industries in non-municipal areas, abolition of octroi duty (with an exhortation to 'persuade state governments to make good the loss to municipalities'). There is not a single revenue raising proposal but only revenue reducing ones.

Markets or Intervention

The BJP combines a rhetoric of attack on the Licence-Permit-Quota Raj with a large list of measures which involve setting up government boards, subsidies, legal restrictions on corporations etc. Indeed, the balance in the party's thinking is interventionist of the 1960s and 1970s type rather than towards internal liberalisation. In no particular order of importance, I list the interventionist policy items from HA's section on the Industrial Sector:

- A separate Ministry for Handicrafts and Village Industries
- National Artisans Development Bank to be set up
- An agency to provide marketing assistance and intelligence for small industries
- A Board for revival of sick small scale units on the lines of the Board for Industrial and Financial Reconstruction
- Certain areas of industrial production to be reserved for the small scale sector; entry of large industry and multinationals not to be permitted
- Differential rates of interest for small scale sector as well as extra tax benefits and credit facilities

This is combined with pleas for the relaxation of licensing for the sugar industry, simplifying the procedure for setting up of new units in the large scale sector, disinvestment from public sector enterprises and sale of their equity to the public (but one presumes not foreign public). Having taken a pro-privatisation stance on public sector units in its section on the industrial sector, when it comes to exit policy in the subsequent section on Full Employment and Industrial Relations the BJP is very close to the left parties:

> Factories may be closed down only with a golden handshake and that too only when sickness is terminally manifested and so decided by the appropriate authority. (HA p. 25)

Conclusion

The BJP is an opposition party and as such it follows the normal practice of such parties to be strong on promises and short on costing of the delivery of such promises. It promises full employment, price stability, poverty removal, the uplift and levelling up of each individual and section of society etc. It is wedded to modernisation, liberalisation, industrialisation but in a self-reliant Indian way. It would like to lower internal and foreign debt, restrict the inflow of foreign (but not NRI) capital, protect agricultural subsidies, cut income taxes etc.

There are questions to be asked. Is this a coherent strategy? Is it feasible given India's indebtedness? Will it actually solve the problem it sets out to tackle? Before answering these questions, let me add once more that party political documents are by their nature designed not to be intellectually coherent or internally consistent. They are propaganda documents. They are also not infallible guides to what the party would do if by chance it were to be elected to office. These things are true of all political parties not just the BJP. Thus relying on political programmes and pamphlets is a somewhat treacherous exercise.

With those caveats, let me say that the BJP has no realistic idea of what a Swadeshi policy may imply in terms of a fiscal burden if India's internal and foreign debts were to be paid back. The party seems to understand internal debt better than the foreign debt problem. But even its policies of cutting internal debt are inconsistent with its reluctance to cut subsidies or increase taxes. It doesn't see the connection between the inflow of foreign capital and India's ability to pay back foreign debt. It does not face up to the fact that restricting the influx of foreign capital will increase the burden of debt repayment. An export surplus will have to be created over and above the amount necessary to cover imports. A budget surplus may help in this process though the connection is not one to one. It would be realistic to predict that when and if the BJP were to come to power, it would not be able to restrict the inflow of foreign capital since the budgetary consequences of this choice would be severe. (It was the unacceptability of cuts in domestic consumption designed to pay back foreign debt that finally brought the Polish communist system down). Nor would it be desirable for the flow of foreign capital to be so restricted.

But there is also the clear indication that the BJP has adopted the standard Government of India rhetoric on intervention and dirigisme as its own preferred model. Now it can be argued that India's problems arose precisely because suitable though the NM model was for the 1950s and 1960s, it was not abandoned in the late 1970s in favour of an open economy approach. This was the choice made by the Asian Tigers. Even if the NM model had been appropriate in the late 1970s, it is definitely outdated by the 1990s, as much due to globalisation as due to an increasing sophistication of the Indian economy. The partial abandonment of the NM model in the 1980s led to the influx of foreign borrowing and a rise in the growth rate of GDP from 3.5 per cent to 5.5 per cent. It was, however, due to only a partial rather than a total abandonment that the debt crisis hit the Indian economy in the 1990s. Other developing economies, especially the Asian Tigers – China, Indonesia, Malaysia, Thailand – have all abandoned protectionist, dirigiste economic policy. It leads neither to growth nor to economic justice. The BJP clearly has not appreciated this fact. (See Desai 1993 for a critique of Indian economic policy.)

The BJP emerges from this examination as a conservative, interventionist party, high on populist rhetoric but unable to form a coherent strategy to implement its chosen strategy or indeed to see its undesirability. But then in that it is probably not much different from the left parties in India.

References

Bharatiya Janata Party (1991a) 'Towards Ram Rajya: MidTerm Poll to Lok Sabha: Our Commitments'. (Pamphlet) (May).
Bharatiya Janata Party (1991b) 'National Executive Meeting in Thimvanthapuram (Kerala): Report'. (Pamphlet) (September).
Bharatiya Janata Party (1992a) 'National Executive Meeting in Bhopal (Madhya Pradesh)': Report. (Pamphlet) (August).
Bharatiya Janata Party (1992b) 'Towards a Debt Free India'. (Pamphlet).
Bharatiya Janata Party (1992c) 'Humanistic Approach to Economic Development (A Swadeshi Alternative): Economic Policy Statement, 1992: Our Commitment to Antyodaya'. (Pamphlet).
Desai, Meghnad (1993) *Capitalism, Socialism and the Indian Economy* (EXIM Bank, Bombay).
Gandhi, M. K. (1908) *Hind Swaraj*.

Jayaraman, T. (1993) *Science and Secularism* (Madras, Tamilnadu Science Forum/Frontline).
Upadhyaya, Deen Dayal (1965) *Integral Humanism* (New Delhi, BJP).

Acknowledgement

First publication: Desai, Meghnad (1994) 'The Economic Policy of the BJP', Discussion Paper 1, Melbourne, National Centre for South Asian Studies, January, pp. 1–11. Republished with kind permission of the National Centre for South Asian Studies.

Chapter 13

INDIA'S TRIPLE BYPASS

Economic Liberalisation, the BJP and the 1996 Elections

Meghnad Desai

(1996)

I have been asked to deal with three things: what has happened to economic reform in India since 1991, where does the Bharatiya Janata Party (hereafter BJP) stand on liberalisation and what do the economic policies look like in the lead-up to the April 1996 elections.

The major thrust of liberal economic reform in India has now spent itself and while the reforms are irreversible the analogy is that of a bullock cart stuck in the mud: it is irreversible but that doesn't help very much. It's not going anywhere. It's not going anywhere because, as a lot of us have said, there are clearly tremendous democratic pressures in India. India is a federal polity with regular elections – and we are going to have national elections very soon in April 1996. In the current pre-election climate I see no political party, and no faction within any political party, which will take a positive view on liberalisation. I think this is unfortunate.

I think it is wrong. But it is my view. A consensus view has emerged in India that yes a lot of reform has happened, the economy has liberalised and it is not likely to go back to the pre-1991 or the pre-1980 Indian economy (people forget that a lot of reforms happened in the 1980s and of course, there was another set of reforms in the 1990s). I don't think there is any danger of going back to the 1970s but by the same token there is going to be a great difficulty in pushing forward reforms in the one or two major areas in which it has not fully realised itself.

The reason is that the popular political perception is that the reforms have, by and large, not helped the poor. They have not generated extra jobs and they have basically benefited a very small minority. Therefore, it is a task of a political party which wants to win political elections to go on a different platform which would say reforms are all right, but we must modify them, we must moderate them, we must qualify them and look after this other dimension. It is significant that in the national Cabinet, except for Dr Manmohan Singh (Finance Minister) and now the Commerce Minister Mr Chidambaram, there is no minister who is positively for economic reform and willing to argue its case up and down the country.

The case for reform, a case which I argued back in 1993 (Desai 1993), is that fast and radical integration into a globalising economy is India's best imaginable anti-poverty programme. Everything India did before 1991 failed to attack poverty. It is not true that before liberalisation happened, India was a socialist heaven. Indeed in all the statistics one can think of such as literacy and life expectancy, India was behind the average of all developing economies and therefore, despite the claim to be a democratic socialist republic, it was not actually doing very well compared to merely capitalist countries like Indonesia and Malaysia in terms of the anti-poverty programme or health or well-being of its people. So I think that nobody has been able to say that all that rhetoric is convincing.

The reform process has been slower than one would like to see partly because the old vested interests have been very hard to keep down. So all those subsidies continue and all those old burdens on the fiscal budget continue and state chief ministers are not stopped from getting into fiscal adventurism of the most gross nature (such as giving away rice at Rs. 2 per kilo). I don't care if they do it provided they raise enough taxation to pay for it. The point of saying that the deficits are bad is not to say that deficits are inflationary – I am not saying that – but by and large the burden of taxation in India falls on the poor. And to the extent that government expenditure is not retrenched, the poor go on paying the extra burden of taxation. Taxation in India is not progressive. Taxation is not progressive almost anywhere in the world but if you examine it carefully in India it certainly isn't.

The reform process has indeed helped the economy, much more than the sceptics said it would. Exports are growing very rapidly but the overall economic growth rate is stuck at 5 per cent, perhaps it is 6 per cent in 1995 as the government claims. But by and large India has not been taken even into a high, single digit growth rate of 8 or 9 per cent let alone Chinese type growth rates of 11 or 12 per cent. And because India is a democracy one has to understand that this in some sense is a choice which the people have made. And that if people make that choice one has got to respect it. If the perceptions of the political parties who are in touch with the people are that this is what is happening that is indeed what will happen. I expect that between now and six months after the elections of 1996 are over, there is not going to be any great dramatic gesture in terms of reform. A lot of small technical things which can escape the scrutiny of the Lok Sabha will go on. Technical reforms which the Finance Ministry, the Reserve Bank of India or various other bodies like the stock exchanges can put through, will go through. And a lot of those things are going through. Those reforms which have already been implemented have generated a dynamic in terms of what the businesses are doing. These will go on and that will create further opportunities in India. But the analogy I would give is that of a person who has followed a very unhealthy lifestyle in terms of eating, drinking and smoking and has a triple bypass. For the first six months or so he does what the doctor tells him. You know India had a triple bypass in 1991 and the doctor came and said you must do such and such. Of course the doctor said it not because the doctor happens to be evil but because doctors say this in the interest of the patient. But after a while the patient thinks 'ah...who is the doctor? What does he know. I am alright'. And you go back to the old habits. This is basically what is now happening. Now basically it looks to India as if it is all the IMF's fault that we had to liberalise – no fault of our own at all and the fact that the place practically went bankrupt is all somebody else's fault.

But I think that none of this is a new thing. You can study previous episodes of radical economic policymaking in India. I have recently published a paper in *India Briefing* by the US Asia Society in which I analyse this history (Desai 1995). You go through the last thirty or so years and see that each radical experiment has had a shelf life of about three to four years. After that it loses momentum. You can look at the Nehru-Mahalanobis experiment of the Second Five-Year Plan in 1955, then the Green Revolution, on to what happened to Mrs Gandhi's 'garibi hatao'[1] followed by the Janata government experiment and so on. This happens to radical policy reform because eventually if you cannot create a sufficient coalition of interests which see themselves benefiting from economic reform (I mean a numerically large coalition of interests), then eventually a combination of old interests which have been hurt by the reform plus those people who are not

---

1   Garibi hatao – literally 'poverty out' or abolish poverty.

benefiting and those whose hopes have been dashed, will eventually stop the reform. So what we will see in the forthcoming elections is that nobody will actually come out strongly against economic liberalisation as such. Liberalisation has joined ice cream and motherhood as something everybody has to swear by, but everyone will qualify economic liberalisation in two respects: exit policy and entry policy.

The exit policy, by which we mean the reform of public sector enterprises, is necessary. Whilst there are some profitable public enterprises there is an unacceptably large number which are loss-making. But the workforce in the public sector companies are the protected sector of the Indian working class. They represent about 8 per cent of the labour force, they enjoy special favours and they are especially well organised. I don't think there exists a political party in India which will touch it this side of the election and perhaps not the other side of the election. But what am I saying – after all I am standing here in Melbourne and all the local newspapers are full of battles between the ACTU and CRA. Who am I to talk about the justice of trade union claims in Australia? China has a very similar sort of problem even without trade unions. China has also for a long time, despite its rapid economic growth, carried a large State sector which is considerably less efficient than its village and town enterprises or its private sector. Thus I think it is unlikely that a dynamic exit policy will be pursued by any government that is likely to emerge after the next election.

Let me briefly indulge in an election forecast. Needless to say a lot of other people will have other forecasts. I don't expect any single party to emerge with a majority sufficient to form a government in the next election. I don't think anyone will disagree on that. What people will have differences on will be the identity of the largest single party. I will stick my neck out and say it is going to be the BJP. And I would say that despite what has happened in the Gujurat recently, which considerably tarnished the BJP's reputation as a clean party. The BJP has about 120 seats now and it will possibly get between 180 to 200 seats. Other people say this is madness and we have been taking bets ever since I arrived in Melbourne. I am going to be inundated with champagne bottles, I can tell you. Congress will be the next largest party – I imagine it will get between 140 and 160 seats and then there will be a variety of other parties. It is conceivable that the BJP will form the next government of India if it can string together a coalition with lots of small regional parties. Its tactic in Uttar Pradesh of supporting the BSP, a backward caste party which is normally anti-BJP, is a sign that at least the most sober part of the BJP (which is not always necessarily in control) wants to project itself as a minority-friendly, certainly not a minority-hostile, political party. I believe that no political party can come to power in India without having some sort of pro-minority stand. There are far too many minorities – it pays groups to define themselves as minorities in Indian democratic politics and people have to come to terms with the backward castes, dalits and Muslims and the regional influences. Therefore I think that the BJP has been trying to give signals, not entirely with the full approval of its membership because there are differences amongst them, but the BJP certainly has been down-peddling the Hindu bits of its image since earlier events. It may not be possible for them to find sufficient strength to form a government, but I believe that they will do that in 1996.

There is another possibility that the Congress will form the next government with the National Left Front (hereafter NLF) coalition of parties. Such a coalition will have to take a much more cool view of liberalisation because the NLF parties are not very pro-liberalisation. Certainly on the exit policy, nothing will happen.

Regarding the entry of foreign capital a lot has already happened – there has been a lot of legislation and there is not going to be any reversal in that. India is by and large a very law abiding place and if people want to change something they have to get a new law passed so I don't think that they are going to do anything sudden. The Enron case, in which the newly elected BJP–Shiv Sena government in Maharashtra tried to cancel the power contract, was shocking to a lot of people not because the stance was right or wrong but because it was done in such an arbitrary and extra-legal way. This is what shocked. Now you can see the Enron thing unravelling itself and the Maharashtrian government finally found out that there is money to pay for this sort of indulgence. And so now they are renegotiating the Enron deal. Apparently nobody had told them that these things are binding commercial agreements.

A Congress-NLF coalition will definitely be cool on the exit policy and it will be unenthusiastic but not obstructionist on entry policy. Much will depend on who stays on as Finance Minister. If Manmohan Singh stays we may have some guarantee that sanity will continue. Otherwise I do not give any such guarantee. If the BJP forms a government there is likely to be a modification on the entry policy. Those of you who have been following the BJP's policy will know that it has been all over the place since liberalisation started. Historically it was a very anti-dirigiste party. It was against all this permit-licence raj. It argued the case for the private sector. But the BJP is not a free market party. While it is against planning it is always going on about how pure capitalism is no good; pure socialism is no good either, they want something in the middle. Whatever that is. More important than that, since liberalisation started the BJP has moved itself into the arena vacated by the Congress. By and large it stands for an autonomous, self-sufficient, foreign capital-free development of the Indian economy. What I would call the Nehru-Mahalanobis model. The fact that that model has planning and restrictions is conveniently forgotten by the BJP. But that's what they now say they want – liberalisation but with an Indian image. Yes we will globalise but not at any cost; we will continue to have an Indian stamp. If you look at the BJP's various statements it is quite clear that they have not actually thought through very carefully what are the possible consequences of following a self-sufficient path in terms of taxation and other sacrifices. I do not think it's a feasible path. And I don't think that the BJP realises what is going on. But I believe that when in power they will more or less do what has been done so far with one important caveat. For a long time they have been backtracking on the foreign capital issue except for the matter of foreign capital in consumer goods industries. The BJP takes the view that we only want foreign capital in high technology areas and in areas where we 'need' foreign capital. We do not need foreign capital in the consumer goods industries they say. This is taking us back to the Janata Dal government of 1978-79 when, if you remember, we had problems with Coca-Cola. This is an interesting variant of the Gandhian-small-industries-local-industries stream of right-wing economic nationalism in India in which there is not so much interventionism in a planning sense but it is very much a protectionist position against foreign capital.

Now two things have happened which gives credence to this idea. One is, of course, the agitation against Kentucky Fried Chicken (hereafter KFC) in Bangalore. This was very much on a *Swadeshi*[2] platform. The same forces which opposed the Cargill Seeds office also have put obstacles in the way of KFC. In Delhi the local government is BJP run and when KFC opened recently, they had their licence revoked on health grounds. I don't want to go into the merits of whether KFC is actually worth eating or not – I've never eaten KFC so I don't know. The argument that there are health hazards in KFC, if it were true, should be systemically applied to non-foreign consumer goods being sold. If all the kitchens in all Delhi restaurants were examined (and not all the tandoors are always empty either) one would not

---

2   *Swadeshi*, literally 'of one's own nation', was originally based on an anti-British tactic by Tilak and then later Gandhi to boycott British imports and encourage Indian products.

find that KFC was the most unhealthy product available. But because it is foreign, it will be opposed. What I am saying is that this is the reality. You can't get on your high horse and say how can they do this? If these are the perceptions nothing can be done.[3] Nobody from the central Cabinet has got up and said how dare you do this – they didn't say anything about Enron and they didn't say anything about KFC. For small partisan advantage the Rao government is substantially compromising India's ability to obtain foreign capital in the future. What will happen is that the BJP will try to discourage the entry of foreign capital in the consumer goods industries – they cannot actually stop it because the legal situation is what it is. What I hope will not happen, and I can give no guarantee that it will not happen, is that they will not actually try to throw someone out. Even what has been done in Delhi is clearly not an action that a party aspiring to national office should lightly undertake. But then the BJP has a problem in that the national high command cannot always control its state units and so this thing has been allowed to happen. When Mr Advani[4] was recently in London he tried to say that the BJP was absolutely for foreign capital and how dare you say anything else. By and large he is trying to project a pro-foreign capital image. I think there are problems within his own party. There are people there who actually do have very strong feelings against foreign capital and the Indian Left is not likely to differ from the BJP on that question.

And so the pro-liberalisation enclave is surrounded from all sides. What I think will happened, because legal changes have already occurred, is this – there will be no change in the law but the climate may change. I'm not speaking on behalf of the government of India so I don't have to be upbeat on this. I'm merely making an analysis and my analysis is that to the extent that the BJP can keep the RSS[5] under control and under the *Swadeshi* banner, they will be able to have just a change of climate but not a change of policy. But clearly there is going to be a modification of the terms under which foreign capital will be admitted. This is extremely bad news. I do not think that there is a great nationalist path that India can follow that

---

3   In the event, the Delhi magistrates ruled the action against KFC as illegal.

4   Lal Krishna Advani was the leader of the BJP in the Lok Sabha and thus leader of the opposition. In January 1996 he resigned while facing corruption charges.

5   Rashtriya Swayamsevak Sangh (National Volunteer Corps) is a para-military pro-Hindu movement started before independence by the leaders of the Hindu Mahasabha. A member of the RSS, Nathuram Vinayak Godse was convicted for the assassination of Gandhi. The RSS has flourished in the last twenty-five years and is a fellow traveller of the BJP.

will do better for the people than the path of globalisation. If it were possible they had forty years to do it and they failed to do it. Therefore I don't see that the nationalist path will suddenly become the solution. But even in India's large scale private sector boardrooms there is not yet a complete willingness for liberalisation – and why should there be? Who likes competition? Who doesn't enjoy protection and high tariffs and subsidised industries which the large private sector has been enjoying? There are very few, positive, pro-globalisation forces which are pushing India forward. I don't see much further happening except for one, perhaps technically very important change – this would be complete liberalisation of the rupee on capital account, something which I have been urging for some time. I think that the Reserve Bank of India dipped its toe into the water and the rupee slipped down and I think the rupee will go down a little further. Not like a peso crisis but it will go down in the next year. So it will be some time before liberalisation of the rupee on capital account happens. But it will be necessary. That will happen if the Congress is part of the next government. It will not happen if the BJP is part of the next government.

* * *

Question and Answer Session

Question: Why are you so pessimistic about economic liberalisation when India has this huge middle class of 300 million people?

Lord Desai: I am wildly for liberalisation. I'm very interested in how the size of the middle class is very elastic. If you're selling India it is 300 million, otherwise it is 100 million. None of the statistics are accurate within 50 million. My view is that if India can only grow at 5 per cent and historically it has not grown at more than that, the promise of liberalisation will not have been fulfilled, since the fruits should be that India should grow at 8, 9 or 10 per cent. While export growth has been very high and manufacturing growth this year has been very high, the hesitancy and the slowness with which this liberalisation has taken place has meant that the fruits of liberalisation have not come as rapidly as they should come. Growth will generate the best anti-poverty programme possible. I'm happy to hear that 9 million jobs have been created but amongst the politicians out there no political party is going to come out and say that the reforms are fantastic, let's have more of them rather than less of them. All they are going to say is reforms are there, but our poor have not been helped, we need a third way. We must preserve India's independence. The ground which the BJP was occupying is again crowded in. I have a quotation from Mr Advani last week – he attacked Rao's economic reforms saying that they had opened the country to foreign investment but had brought in little for the great majority of Indians. That is where the consensus is going to form. I think it happens to be false but we're into perceptions, we're not into facts. If the political culture of all Indian parties is going to take that stance and reform is going to be technical, IMF led and not Indian, then there are problems. I wish it wasn't the case. I hope I could be more optimistic but I go around the world spreading gloom and despondency. That's my bag. I'm not a salesman. I'm an economist.

Question: *How do we explain that the middle class which has benefited most from the recent economic reforms in India is also the backbone of the BJP and it is the middle class which is voicing concern about economic imperialism? How do we explain this and do you think that the growing middle class will ultimately persuade these parties to change their agenda?*

Lord Desai: I think that the middle class is the backbone of every party in India – not just the backbone of the BJP. But I don't think that the middle class is going to be very politically articulate in pushing for reform. I've seen no sign of it. For a short time when Rajiv Gandhi was prime minister we saw some genuine interest amongst the middle managers and the technocrats for reform but right now there is no political personality on the Indian scene whose leadership and career reflect that dynamic of the x million Indian middle class. The middle classes, if they have their videos and TV, are very happy and don't feel like going out into the streets and doing anything further. There is this very strong view that somehow India will be able to combine liberalisation and national self-sufficiency in a great magic potion which nobody else has done so far. I think this is a delusion because foreign capital doesn't have to come to India – there are lots of other places for it to go to. We've now signed GATT so we can't restrict imports. They can't restrict manufacturers – if they don't manufacture in India they'll manufacture in Vietnam and export to India. And in having signed GATT Indian politicians are fooling themselves if they think people are lining up on India's doors just because of 300 million consumers. They can't just write their own ticket. There is no such thing.

References

Desai, M (1993) *Capitalism, Socialism and the Indian Economy*, Exim Bank Lecture, Bombay, January.

Desai, M (1994) *The Economic Policy of the BJP*, Discussion Paper No. 1, National Centre for South Asian Studies, Melbourne, January.

Desai, M (1995) 'Economic Reform: Stalled by Politics?', in Philip Oldenburgh (ed.) *India Briefing: Staying the Course*, New York, The Asia Society & M E Sharpe, Inc.

Acknowledgement

First publication: Desai, Meghnad (1996) 'India's Triple Bypass: Economic Liberalisation, the BJP and the 1996 Elections', Discussion Paper 2, Melbourne, National Centre for South Asian Studies, March, pp. 1–10. Republished with kind permission of the National Centre for South Asian Studies.

Chapter 14

COULD THE INDIAN ECONOMY DO BETTER?

Meghnad Desai

(2012)

Governor M. Narasimham, Dr. S. K. Rao, the family of Mr. K. L. N. Prasad and distinguished guests:

Thank you all very much for inviting me to come to Hyderabad and give this lecture. This is only my second visit to Hyderabad. My very good friend Prof. K. Krishnamurty was teaching here. And this is my first visit since his sad demise a few months ago. So for me, it is also a visit to pay my tributes to him. And of course, I should take advantage of this occasion to say something about the topic at hand.

I think as Governor Narasimham has said in his opening remarks, it is a rhetorical question to which the answer is obvious. I doubt that any such optimists are left who could say, well, India cannot do any better than this. There was a debate not all that long ago, when people were saying that, India could actually have a double-digit growth. But 9.5 per cent was as well as one could do, and therefore we must not aspire to anything higher. Now, as we are struggling to not slide down much below 7 per cent, clearly questions have arisen about India's growth path.

I think there are two kinds of issues involved. One is a very short-run issue, which is exercising all of us. And that is the current malaise in governance and in government. While it is no surprise to us that there is corruption, I think what people much more regret is the lack of decisiveness in policy. And how even when many people in the government and the majority outside are convinced that certain steps ought to be taken, the government seems to belatedly take them and then withdraw from those decisions.

Indeed, Finance Minister Pranab Mukherjee has openly talked about what he would like to do but he cannot do because they (the Congress Party) do not have the numbers. It is quite an astonishing thing! This is the first time, as far as I can remember in the history of Independent India, that in a coalition government, the leading party has a strength of 200 plus (208) – higher than the number of seats any party in a coalition has won since Prime Minister Narasimha Rao's government ended. And the largest party in the coalition actually says that they are helpless. Even Prime Minister Deve Gowda's coalition government did not get to this sorry state whatever else they may have done. I think, partly, this is a self-imposed paralysis. The paralysis of caution, the paralysis of a people who are risk-averse – the Congress Party specially is very risk-averse. All they want to do is to get to the finishing line first in the 2014 elections and, I presume, to pray for a miracle; but something may turn up before that.

But at another level, it is a structural problem. A structural problem which has been brewing for a while and has now come to a head. That is, despite twenty years plus of coalition governments in India, the rules by which a coalition government should be conducted have not been finalised or understood. Currently, the UK has for the first time in peacetime a coalition government since God knows how many years. When the Conservatives and the Liberal Democrats met to decide whether or not they should form a coalition government, there were intensive discussions for three days. Both sides had already read each other's manifestos and mapped out what areas they would be willing to concede and not willing to concede because a coalition was being considered between two parties that are unlikely to be in a coalition from what the people expected and required. The Liberal Democrats were quite surprised that the Conservatives had read their manifesto from day one. They had anticipated a coalition and prepared for it. The intensive discussions resulted in a formal detailed document, setting out where there are agreements and where there are disagreements. And that document is an official policy document of the coalition, to which both the opposition and the government can refer.

UPA-II has taught us a lot. In their case, there is no such document; there is not even an implicit agreement as to what are the common areas of policy. Not only that, another structural problem in a coalition government is that the cabinet government rules are suspended because above the cabinet, there is a higher circle of the coalition in which the leaders of the parties in the coalition sit. They conduct negotiations among themselves as to who shall be the ministers delegated by each party leader. If the UPA coalition leader had been the prime minister, we would not have had this diarchy or duality of power that we currently have. So that when Telecom Minister A. Raja had to be suspended, Mr. M. Karunanidhi was not talking to Dr. Manmohan Singh; he only talked to Sonia Gandhi, and similarly with Mamata Banerjee.

The NDA was a better-run coalition. During the NDA government, the coalition Convener was George Fernandes. Prime Minister Atal Behari Vajpayee was above the coalition leader. In the UPA, the coalition leader is above the prime minister.

These short-term problems are in some sense structural. India is not going to see in the reasonably distant future, a strong one-party majority government. In my view, it is not likely to see in 2014 even a dominant party, by which I mean a party with more than 100 seats in a coalition government. I very much suspect that we are going to have a third-front coalition government, which will not have a majority but which will have outside support from one or the other national parties. We will have a government reminiscent of the V. P. Singh/Deve Gowda type of regimes, but probably with a bigger coalition. Since those days, we have political leaders who have been state chief ministers with considerable success and India's polity has become more federal. So we will get a government that will not be a majoritarian, decisive government, but it will be functional, unlike the present government, which is not functioning.

Some of these issues are a matter of politics, party strength and so on. But, there is a serious lack of consensus in the country about India's record of globalisation, the balance to be struck in terms of the gains and losses, and the way we ought to go forward from here on.

My own beliefs have not been in doubt. I will very quickly summarise them. I think the economic changes since 1990–91 have been a good thing for the country. It raised our growth rate considerably and in a sustainable way. The growth rate before that was 3.5 to 4 per cent, the 'Hindu rate of growth'. The growth rate in FY 2010–11 was 8.5 per cent. Doubling of the growth rate in just over a decade is not an insignificant achievement. I also happen to believe that although inequality may have grown, poverty has come down. I know this is a contentious statement, but whether you take the National Sample Survey standard or the Tendulkar standard, or the dollar a day standard, on whichever standard, if you compare 1990–91 to 2011–12, the percentage of people below the poverty line, however it is defined, has come down.

In my book, *The Rediscovery of India*, I summarised the data until about 2008. Every time somebody mentions a poverty level of 'x' rupees, everybody goes into a tizzy. I feel very angry because India has a very long and strong tradition of measurement of standards of living, of doing the National Sample Survey work, of calibrating living standards, and debating about the poverty level. This work is not something that has recently been undertaken by the Office of Dr Montek Singh Ahluwalia, Deputy Chairman of the Planning Commission. This has been going on for forty years. And MPs at least ought to know that the tradition of poverty measurement in India is a glorious and very good tradition. I do not think people falsify data or cut corners. You may not like the result because you may not like the reality. There is also a tendency to award a prize to whoever says India is poorer than before. This tendency has been encouraged by the Congress Party of all people. The Congress Party has been around for sixty years, there have been fifty years of intense poverty, and to say that India's poverty level is higher now than ever before sounds crazy!

But, I want to say that India can do better. I would like to concentrate entirely on what to do about poverty. Because I think that is the central issue. Eventually, any growth programme is not about the rates of growth, per capita income or catching up with China. It is really about: Does human life get better in the growth process or not? Otherwise, you are wasting your time. During the first thirty years after independence, we were much prouder of our dams, factories and machine tools, the amount of steel output, and so on. That's okay; it gave us great pride. But eventually, it is about whether people are better off than before. Are they getting a better education, are they becoming healthier, are they getting more to eat? That is the question.

The central question of poverty can be related to a central failure of the development strategy, both before and after liberalisation. And that is the failure to industrialise at a rapid enough rate so that the surplus population in agriculture can have gainful employment. What we have seen since 1991 is an amazing growth of the services sector, which now contributes something like 56 to 57 per cent of the total national income. There is stagnation or some decline in the share of manufacturing in GDP, which is around 16 per cent right now; it used to be about 20 per cent. Manufacturing employs only about 13 to 15 per cent of the labour force. And then there is a vast section of the people in the rural sector. The agricultural sector's contribution to GDP is around 20 to 25 per cent. The percentage of Indian people living in rural areas is about 60 per cent. So, roughly speaking, the contrast between productivity in the services sector and productivity in the agricultural sector is 9 to 1. That is basically why there is poverty: it is because people are in low-productive occupations. Eventually, a country cannot pay its people higher than its average productivity. You can cut costs here and there, but that rule holds.

In ancient India, there were very rich rajas, and of course we are in Nizam's Hyderabad. Their wealth was fabulous, but ordinary living standards were not anywhere near close. So, the disparity was always there. The real challenge of development is how do you raise average productivity. Historically, the only way found has been to move people from agriculture to industry, or from rural areas to industry. Manufacturing is a remarkable thing in which people can get year-round employment, even for people who are unskilled manual workers or semi-skilled manual workers; and of course, you can train them for other things. India's manufacturing is predominantly medium to hi-tech products. It is hardly absorbing unskilled or semi-skilled workers; it is mostly absorbing skilled workers. Historically, all the Five-Year Plans have left behind the largely unskilled manual, semi-skilled manual people with limited literacy. A large part of the labour force in the informal sector is unemployed or under-employed. This has been going on since the first plan period. I think, it is astonishing that this persisting under-employment has not been seen to be the major reason for poverty. People have been giving all kinds of other reasons for poverty; they do not understand that, eventually, India has failed to industrialise. And you do not have to be China to do it; Indonesia has done it, Malaysia has done it. So, it is not rocket science.

India's response lately has been of two kinds. One is to set up special economic zones (SEZs), following the Chinese example. And more recently, there is the new manufacturing strategy. I want to argue that both these policies are misguided; they are not serious attempts to industrialise. The reason for that is very simple. Currently, the one asset you can own or capture which has the highest rate of return, apart from politics, is land. Basically, SEZs are land scams. People are keen on SEZs. They submit an application, get an allocation, hang on to the land, and after four years say, Sorry Sir, my project failed. They can make more money just holding on to the land than by doing anything else that I can think of. The idea is that land is a binding constraint to manufacturing. That is why you need SEZs. Setting up SEZs is a slightly dishonest idea. In these zones, companies are allowed to break the labour laws, they are allowed to deviate from the labour laws. Of course, the government completely denies that labour laws have been an obstacle to industrialisation. At the same time, they offer incentives to companies to go to SEZs or to a national manufacturing activity area. The problem with our labour laws is not so much that they do not permit hire and fire, but that India has very peculiar laws which do not allow a company to go bankrupt. If you cannot go bankrupt, you cannot be in business. You have got to have a rule that permits speedy bankruptcy, so that people can come in and go out. If you do not allow companies to go bankrupt, then people will be reluctant to set up companies. There are the tragic stories of Delhi Cloth Mills, which Dr Vinay Bharat Ram has narrated in his book, *From the Brink of Bankruptcy: The DCM Story*, about how long it took them to unwind. Or, in Bombay, the financial nerve centre of the country, the unwinding and shutting down of the textile mills and finally releasing the land for alternative work processes took something like twenty-five years.

I think the nation needs a serious debate about this. We need to industrialise rapidly. Industrialisation is a sure-fire way, much better than the National Rural Employment Guarantee Scheme (NREGS), to give people full-time employment. It is not for 100 days a year. It would be for 250 days per year of employment, which is full-time. And, it will transform the economics of the rural areas. If we want to industrialise, we have to have an open discussion as to whether land is a substantial obstacle. I do not think land is a substantial obstacle. Land is wrongly perceived to be a constraint. I do not think India needs industry in the middle of nowhere. Industries should be set up in small and medium-sized towns, on the edge of small and medium-sized towns. Industry ought to be set up so that people do not have to move too far away from their roots. Their housing is a problem. How do you create a community for workers in a SEZ? It is alright for the owners, but what about the workers? How are you going to create communities for them? There is considerable discussion about setting up infrastructure in SEZs. I have not come across any discussion of how you are going to create communities for the people who work in SEZs. If you want to create communities for workers, do what every country in the world has always done. I know they are called slums, but everybody has started by having slums on the edge of the city. Later on, the housing and amenities have improved, things are more right.

Rather than establishing SEZs or new manufacturing areas, the government should offer incentives to people even with respect to labour laws to set up industry in small and medium-sized towns and not in metros. They do not have to be clustered together, with 100 factories in the same compound. The factories can be scattered, which would be much better for all sorts of pollution. India can opt for a decentralised multiple location solution of setting up low-tech manufacturing industry, such as the one adopted by Indonesia, Malaysia and China, be it textiles or leather products. It can employ people who are currently either idle or in low productivity jobs in rural areas. This will enable India to enhance its rate of industrialisation, increase its share of manufacturing from 16 to 25 per cent, which is a key economic objective. Such a strategy can also generate a substantially great amount of employment; and that employment will come from rural areas. Capital is not a constraint; capital will be available. There is no dearth of capital, either from domestic sources, or from foreign sources. It is a misperception that land is a constraint. The so-called land constraint is due to the under-selling of land in SEZs and basically setting up a land scam. If India is to continue to set up SEZs, the land should not be sold; it should be put on rent or leased out. Then, nobody can make capital gain out of hanging on to the land. Because the government will never be able to tax it efficiently. So, we need to aim for a manufacturing growth rate of 15 to 20 per cent; it is not unthinkable. It is going to require an investment-GDP ratio in terms of manufacturing investment of not more than 10 to 12 per cent. There is infrastructure investment to be done by the government, which would be another 10 per cent or so; this is a ballpark figure.

The constraint is not so much of policy as of economic determination and political will, of having decided upon what the solution to the problem is; that it is an implementable solution and that the implementation is going to benefit not the people who are going to get concessions for setting up industry in SEZs, none of them deserve any concessions, but will benefit ordinary people who are going to find employment. So the national manufacturing strategy has got to be employment-oriented; it has got to be locationally diverse, and not concentrated. There ought to be an incremental growth in industrialisation in a variety of areas around the country, which will deliver sustained high economic growth. Then, the idea of a double-digit growth rate will not be beyond India's capacity. This will also lead to a reduction of the labour force in agriculture and non-agricultural rural activities, and an increase of the labour force in manufacturing. The services sector is doing quite well. So, this is the kind of scenario that I would strongly advocate.

Domestic Indian investors can borrow money abroad. It is not a question of a drastic change in taxation policy or anything like that. In a new climate of federalism where many States want to do things, you could say that the national manufacturing strategy is what the States do. Any State should be allowed to set up industries wherever they like, as long as they are located in small or medium-sized towns. If we can do these things, then a variety of constraints are relaxed and we may be able to do better. Obviously, there are several other things I could say about India doing better. But the other things which need to be done, like health or education, will be easier to do if at the centre of our strategy, there is productive employment for the majority of workers in India. Unless you generate sustainable livelihoods, things will not improve substantially.

I do not want to complain about poor people getting 100 days of work a year. But I do not think that is a sustainable way of generating livelihoods. Because you are not doing anything productive by engaging in those 100 days of work. You are just digging a hole and filling it up again for all practical purposes. It is a Keynesian way of income generation. Distributing income is a good thing, but India's problem is not a Keynesian one. India has a very different kind of problem. In a sense, you could even embark on the national manufacturing policy without necessarily having to rescind the NREGS.

That having been said, I want to take just a few more minutes to talk about whether or not it will happen. The difficulty in convincing people of this policy is a very strong misconception that promoting industrialisation by in any way moderating or changing the rules about hiring and firing and bankruptcy is the wrong way. All these years, because we have been much more interested in protecting jobs, we have not created sufficient employment. A very famous kind of paradox is that the more jobs you protect, the less employment you create. Eventually, you are defending existing jobs and not allowing the creation of new ones. And protection of existing jobs creates certain barriers to anybody prospectively thinking of starting a factory.

In Western countries, within my lifetime in the UK, we have been through this. We learned to abandon trying to protect jobs and have tried to create employment because we had a severe employment crash in the 1970s and 1980s. And, we are now back at fairly high levels of employment, apart from the recession, but with a flexible labour market and labour force activity of 75 per cent. This level of labour market activity is possible because flexible labour markets have been allowed to exist without in any sense creating exploitative labour practices. So, this can be done. The debate has to be much more open and much more political about whether that is the right way to go. Or, currently, what is called progressive policy is to leave the composition of the output frozen as it is, and pass on subsidies only to the rural sector. So, the anomaly of the rural sector not getting anything out of growth is corrected.

From approximately 2006–07 onwards, the policies of UPA-II have very systematically directed large sums of money to the rural areas through NREGS and other programmes. The idea being that rural areas have not gained much from liberalisation; therefore, money ought to go there. Roughly speaking, urban growth creates income and generates revenue; and the revenue has to be spent in rural areas, which have far less growth. Therefore, the fruits of growth are spent to keep people in the rural areas, where they are poor. But, this discourages mobility. NREGS discourages mobility. In a sense, the policy is to keep the poor poor, but make poverty tolerable.

Poverty can be tolerable because there is the *kamadhenu* (the sacred cow in Hindu mythology that grants all wishes and desires) of liberal economic growth. I think, this *kamadhenu* has stopped yielding as of the last quarter of 2011–12. If the growth rate is not seriously raised again, this way of tackling poverty, or at least alleviating the poverty problem, will not be open to India. Things are urgent. And an effective government will have to not only start a public debate about this, but actually change policy so that we use the revenue generated by growth in an economically efficient way – not so much to alleviate poverty but to get the poor out of poverty, which is a very different kind of goal. You can only get the poor out of poverty by giving them work which will generate enough income to get them out of poverty. Redistribution is not a permanent sustainable answer.

I will stop there. Thank you.

Acknowledgement

This speech by Lord Desai was the K. L. N. Prasad Memorial Lecture delivered at the Administrative Staff College of India (ASCI), Hyderabad, on 7 April 2012. First publication: Desai, Meghnad, 'Could the Indian Economy Do Better?' *ASCI Journal of Management*, vol. 42, no. 1, 2012, pp. 113–121. Republished with kind permission of *ASCI Journal of Management*.

Chapter 15

HINDUTVA'S MARCH HALTED?[1]

Choices for the BJP after the 2004 Defeat

Meghnad Desai

(2005)

Introduction

Two things are true about the 2004 general election in India. First, that they attracted worldwide attention, perhaps for the first time spontaneously and not because of some violent incidents that could have occurred. Second, because just about no one anticipated the results.[2] The day before the results were announced, the *New York Times* summed up the feelings of many forecasting that the National Democratic Alliance (NDA) would come in but with a reduced majority (Wildman 2004). This was the way most newspapers in India interpreted the successive rounds. As the exit polls came out, they were greeted with scepticism when they showed a large shortfall in the NDA's strength. Many had written off the Indian National Congress Party (INC), and 'India Shining' looked like the winning formula it was meant to be. A range of pre-budget sweeteners had been announced by the

---

1 Editor's note: this chapter was originally published as Chapter 13 in *Coalition Politics and Hindu Nationalism*, edited by Katharine Adeney and Lawrence Sáez, Routledge Advances in South Asian Studies. New York, Routledge, 2005. All references to other chapters here refer to chapters in *Coalition Politics and Hindu Nationalism*.

2 During the conference on 'Coalition Politics and Hindu Nationalism' held at the Institute of Commonwealth Studies, James Manor cautioned against automatically assuming that the NDA would win the 2004 general election.

Finance Minister Jaswant Singh from early January onwards. When the INC denounced them as doing nothing for the common man, few thought it had landed a blow.

The NDA's surprise defeat and the INC's return to power raise a number of questions. One of them is about the nature of social science and its usefulness. If everyone gets the forecast wrong, why should we trust social scientists / India's experts? In what follows, I shall first address that question. The second, much larger question, concerns the choices facing the Bharatiya Janata Party (BJP) in light of its defeat. In the title to this chapter I deliberately echo the question that Eric Hobsbawm asked of the British Labour Party after its election defeat in 1979 – rephrasing thus – '*Hindutva*'s march halted?' Had the BJP/NDA coalition won, there was little doubt that the BJP would have become the natural party of power, much like the INC used to be in the first ten years after independence. It would have moved into a hegemonic position in a Gramscian sense and controlled the discourse along its own ideological tramlines. School textbooks would have forever changed children's views of Indian history and minorities would have had to come to terms with a precarious state of existence, henceforth under suspicion of their loyalty. When this did not happen the question about BJP's future choices becomes urgent as much for the party activists as for students of Indian politics. The latter part of this chapter addresses that issue.

Uses of Social Science

What use are all the articles written about India, all the polls and surveys conducted, if virtually no one could predict the 2004 election outcome? Here I would like to make an econometrician's distinction between predictions and forecasts. Forecasts concern what would happen tomorrow or at some specific date in the future. The model at hand is cranked out, relevant values of the exogenous variables are fed in, and out comes the forecast values of the endogenous variables. An exit poll or an opinion poll tells us such a tale. Prediction is about questions of 'What if?'. If you alter some particular exogenous variable, what are the likely effects on the endogenous variables of interest? Prediction uses the structural information in the model to lay out the various likely effects, only some of which may actually come about. This is said not to evade the problem of failure of forecast. There still remains the question do experts know anything useful?

To answer that question I shall review the essays included in this volume [*Coalition Politics and Hindu Nationalism*]. The initial drafts were written in early 2004, before the results of the elections were announced. Their objective analysis of the NDA's performance did not concern itself with the issue of its re-electability. However, the analyses yielded insights about the NDA's policymaking challenges, largely at national level. Likewise, the post-election discussions of the results interpreted them at first as people's protest about the limited rewards of economic reform for the poor, of the need to manage globalisation more equitably. After more reflection some people instead interpreted the results as revealing no national message, but as an outcome of state-level forces which led to a surprise national outcome. This emerged clearly in articles written by Yogendra Yadav and colleagues from the Centre for the Study of Developing Societies (CSDS) which appeared on one of India's leading newspapers, *The Hindu*, on 20 May 2004. There, the defeat was attributed to a fatal choice of dropping DMK, siding with AIADMK in Tamil Nadu and the reversal in the fortunes of TDP in Andhra Pradesh that accounted for a substantial part of the loss of the NDA's fortunes. The Trinamul Congress was humiliated as the Left's fortunes brightened in West Bengal and then losses in Gujarat were a severe blow to the BJP.

Now this set of events tell us that the nature of the NDA coalition was itself a force in the election, over and above the individual electoral fortunes of the parties. This is discussed in Alistair McMillan's analysis of coalitions, both at a theoretical and at an applied level.[3] As he remarks '[r]ather than simply analysing coalition formation, coalition theory must also address the strategic incentives in maintaining or terminating coalitions in the light of the developing political context'. Quite so, since the BJP made a mistake in breaking with a local opposition party in Tamil Nadu and aligning with a governing party late in the life of the coalition. Given the strong anti-incumbency tendency of Indian electorates – some things are constant in Indian politics – this was a predictable own goal. Nevertheless, McMillan, as well as Jenkins, Zavos and Adeney bring out the federal nature of India's polity whereby people primarily choose a state government, but coalition politics determines what the national ruling coalition will be like. This interplay of state and federal politics, at both the executive and the party

---

3   Alistair McMillan, 'The BJP Coalition: Partisanship and Power-sharing in Government', Chapter 1 in *Coalition Politics and Hindu Nationalism*, edited by Katharine Adeney and Lawrence Sáez, Routledge Advances in South Asian Studies. New York, Routledge, 2005.

levels, is similar to a nested game, which McMillan cites as a possible analytical tool for studying coalitions.[4]

There are also insights in this volume about the BJP's conduct prior to the 2004 general election. While it relied on sophisticated TV commercials and Short Message Service (SMS) text messaging, the BJP appears to have ignored the rural and the poorer urban voter. James Manor's chapter[5] shows how the BJP's organisation is not at all strong, but quite thin, especially in rural areas. The INC was able to exploit this weakness by directing its leader, Sonia Gandhi, to large rural meetings. After the election, it was reported by many papers that the BJP had been sanguine about its chances and had failed to get its troops out for election work. In addition, there had been a reluctance of the Rashtriya Swayamsevak Sangh (RSS) cadres to come out. Manor warns us against assuming that RSS[6] always does the BJP's bidding or vice versa. This is an insight that will be useful in asking questions about the choices facing the BJP.

Nevertheless, between the RSS and the BJP, there are also differences about ideology. As Zavos[7] and Manor[8] point out, for the RSS *Hindutva* matters and its agenda is one of Hindu nationalism. The BJP, on the other hand, wants to win power and hold on to it. This requires coming out of the ghetto and making alliances. Thus, it was the alliance of the Jana Sangh with Jaya Prakash Narayan's *andolan* (movement) in Gujarat in 1974 that made the party respectable for the first time since the assassination of Mahatma Gandhi (for which the RSS and vaguely Hindu nationalist forces were blamed). Efforts of this type, as Jaffrelot points out,[9] were the

---

4   Alistair McMillan, 'The BJP Coalition: Partisanship and Power-sharing in Government', Chapter 1 in *Coalition Politics and Hindu Nationalism*, edited by Katharine Adeney and Lawrence Sáez. Routledge, New York.

5   James Manor, 'In Part, a Myth: The BJP's Organisational Strength', Chapter 3 in *Coalition Politics and Hindu Nationalism*, edited by Katharine Adeney and Lawrence Sáez, Routledge Advances in South Asian Studies. New York, Routledge, 2005.

6   The RSS cadres (and the youth cadres of the Bajrang Dal) have been a critical support base for the BJP for they work inside the crucial rural and urban electorates which the BJP has identified as crucial for winning elections.

7   John Zavos, 'The Shapes of Hindu Nationalism', Chapter 2 in *Coalition Politics and Hindu Nationalism*, edited by Katharine Adeney and Lawrence Sáez, Routledge Advances in South Asian Studies. New York, Routledge, 2005.

8   James Manor, Chapter 3 in *Coalition Politics and Hindu Nationalism*.

9   Christophe Jaffrelot, 'The BJP and the 2004 General Election: Dimensions, Causes and Implications of an Unexpected Defeat', Chapter 12 in *Coalition Politics and Hindu Nationalism*, edited by Katharine Adeney and Lawrence Sáez. Routledge, New York.

incipient attempts by the Jana Sangh at coalition building. It means tackling bread and butter issues, not just the ideological ones. In the state-wide elections held in late 2003, the BJP tried a *roti/kapda/makan* (food/clothing/shelter) strategy, and reaped dividends. This encouraged it to play the same card in the 2004 general election. This not only kept its coalition partners happy, but it was a way of casting its appeal wider. Indeed by attracting many ex-INC members to its fold on the eve of the election, including Muslim members (Najma Heptulla, for instance), the BJP was launching itself as the true successor of Nehru's Congress Party. But this action alienated its core ideological support, which wanted a commitment on *mandir* (temple) issues. It is no surprise that the post-election reactions by the Vishwa Hindu Parishad (VHP) have been not entirely sympathetic. But this is precisely where the party lost its ideologically minded cadres. The British Labour Party, for instance, is undergoing a very similar experience. If and when an ideological party widens its appeal to garner more votes, it stands to lose the support of its more fanatical supporters. This is a classic democratic compulsion. The BJP has tried to become an inclusive party, like the INC, and thus weakened its hold over the Hindu nationalist core.

Governing also involves dealing with day-to-day challenges. Since the balance of payments crisis of 1991 successive governments have had to rethink what they said about the economic reforms while in opposition, mostly since reforms are no longer a matter of choice. The only choice is the pace of reforms and an occasional twist one way or another. India needs to display a willingness to attract foreign direct investment (FDI) and for that end demonstrate good governance. Thus, privatisation is urgent and reforms of the labour market necessary. This is a story, which again meshes in with the federalist theme as Rob Jenkins[10] points out. Of course, reforms do not please the ideologues of the RSS and the BJP; hence the dilemma of governing and keeping faithful to one's beliefs raises its head again. The success of the BJP/NDA in managing the economy (by the end of its tenure the growth rate of GDP was over 8 per cent) alienated its core support, since it was soft on liberalisation and the entry of foreign capital.[11] By pointing out in its 'India Shining' commercials what it had done, the NDA Government also reminded its supporters of facts which were not to their liking. Hence, the 'India Shining' campaign did not only alienate rural voters.

---

10   Rob Jenkins, 'The NDA and the Politics of Economic Reform', Chapter 9 in *Coalition Politics and Hindu Nationalism*, edited by Katharine Adeney and Lawrence Sáez. Routledge, New York.

11   Rob Jenkins, Chapter 9 in *Coalition Politics and Hindu Nationalism*.

The story of the BJP/NDA Government, as it unfolds in the various essays in this volume, is that of continuity rather than change. Whatever its rhetoric, the BJP is as much of a centralist political party as the INC. It wants a militarily strong India with a high status on the world stage. Thus Kundu,[12] as well as Chiriyakandath and Wyatt,[13] point out that the nuclear decision and the alliances with the US and Israel are driven by the *realpolitik* of India's ambitions to be taken seriously as a regional power. But at the same time, no 'national' party can ignore regional and caste forces in its policies. In a coalition with such parties that rely on caste, region and religion for their appeal, this is doubly so. Therefore, while an analysis of foreign policy and national security reveals continuity, it is in the domestic policy arena where we would expect local and contemporaneous pressures to differentiate the NDA's government's policy from other governments.

However, here again the brute facts of coalition building point to the limits of what any dominant party in a coalition can do. The facts of life in India compel any coalition to accommodate regional and caste parties. These parties are, by and large, non-ideological, their principal focus being rent seeking for sharing with their clientele. So provisions for minorities and for particular states, the need to direct more revenues to the states with each successive Finance Commission are the common concerns of every coalition. Now that the INC is in power, it will have to play to the same tune as BJP had to as head of the NDA coalition. Subrata Mitra deals with the issue of minorities,[14] while Katharine Adeney discusses in detail the BJP's attitude about the federal constitution.[15] They each show how the BJP had to come to terms with minorities and states, despite its centralist and monist view of Hindu society.

The reality is that neither of the two largest national parties – INC or BJP – can by itself come to power. Indeed in the 2004 general election, their combined strength in the Lok Sabha fell from 293 seats in 1999

---

12   Apurba Kundu, 'The NDA and National Security', Chapter 11 in *Coalition Politics and Hindu Nationalism*, edited by Katharine Adeney and Lawrence Sáez. Routledge, New York.

13   James Chiriyankandath and Andrew Wyatt, 'The NDA and Indian Foreign Policy', Chapter 10 in *Coalition Politics and Hindu Nationalism*, edited by Katharine Adeney and Lawrence Sáez. Routledge, New York.

14   Subrata Mitra, 'The NDA and Politics of "Minorities" in India', Chapter 4 in *Coalition Politics and Hindu Nationalism*, edited by Katharine Adeney and Lawrence Sáez. Routledge, New York.

15   Katharine Adeney, 'Hindu Nationalists and Federal Structures in an Era of Regionalism', Chapter 5 in *Coalition Politics and Hindu Nationalism*, edited by Katharine Adeney and Lawrence Sáez. Routledge, New York.

– 182 for the BJP plus 111 for the INC – to 283 seats in 2004 – 138 for the BJP and 145 seats for the INC – as did their vote share. India's politics is becoming more fragmented, more devolved and less majoritarian. This requires living with federalism. Katharine Adeney shows that, despite the BJP's ambivalence about linguistic states and its preference for a strong unitary India, the BJP has had to come to terms with regionalism and cope with the challenges of adapting and reforming the structure of the federation.[16] One strategy to strengthen the centre against the regions is to break up the larger states into smaller units. Nevertheless, as big states are divided into smaller states, the number of small parties with a strictly local focus is going to rise, and the fragmentation of politics will increase. But, if this is the case, then a larger question is raised. Can the BJP ever realise its dream of a *Hindutva*-based government in India?

The Halted March of *Hindutva*?

The defeat in 2004 is not just sad for the BJP; it is tragic for the party. Through the 1980s and 1990s, it has struggled to acquire a national status. Far from being a minority, extremist pariah party, it has commanded national attention and international respect. From the irresponsible behaviour of some of its leaders as part of a howling mob bringing down the Babri mosque in 1992, it rose to come to power (briefly) in 1996 and again in 1998 and 1999. Its strength was confirmed at 182 parliamentary seats in two general elections (1996 and 1998). This was a contrast from the Jana Sangh polling approximately 50 seats (much as the CPI/CPM used to). In 2004, it had the chance to move up 182 seats to the sunlit uplands of 200 seats and above. Had the BJP broken through to 225 seats, then it could have dominated the next coalition, or even ruled alone with outside support (much as Narasimha Rao managed to do between 1991 and 1996). Winning another five-year term would have been an immensely significant step for the BJP's programme of gaining cultural hegemony. What Murli Manohar Joshi wanted to do, as Marie Lall has argued in her piece[17], was to change the Indian view of history so as to demonise Muslim rule forever more. Five more years would have given the BJP ideologues a real stranglehold on history and social science disciplines.

---

16 Katharine Adeney, Chapter 5 in *Coalition Politics and Hindu Nationalism*.
17 Marie Lall, 'Indian Education Policy under the NDA Government', Chapter 8 in *Coalition Politics and Hindu Nationalism*, edited by Katharine Adeney and Lawrence Sáez. Routledge, New York.

The new Congress-led government has shown the importance of this by moving on the school history textbooks issue immediately.

However, the setback from 182 to 138 parliamentary seats is serious, despite the fact that in terms of share of the vote the BJP did better than the INC. The question is, 'Will this mean the end of the road for BJP's dream of ruling India as a single party and of installing a *Hindutva* Raj forever or is this just a blip, *reculer pour mieux sauter* (to back up so as to better leap over), and the BJP will bounce back next time?'

Through the 1990s, the BJP had a difficult trapeze act to perform. It wanted to be known as the party for Hindus and this required them to be strongly anti-Muslim, not simply anti-Pakistani. It also had to convince the voters that it could be a responsible party capable of competently ruling India. For the latter it needed to not only manage the economic reforms but also to build a coalition with disparate forces. Its Hindu phase led to Advani's *Rath Yatra* (chariot procession) of 1992 and the demolition of the Masjid at Ayodhya. Its more extreme supporters have moved from anti-Muslimism to sheer xenophobia, so that all non-Hindu religions are demonised. Attacks on Christian missionaries were the latest expression and weapon in the struggle. While Narendra Modi did not foment the post-Godhra riots in 2002, he did nothing to curb them and was re-elected later that year. This told one section of the BJP that coming to power via mob riot was, if unattractive, at least an effective option. There was much talk of a 'Modi strategy' for winning mid-term state elections in Himachal Pradesh and elsewhere after Modi's triumphal re-election. This section of the party is the traditionalist core of the BJP whose favourite ideologue is Hedgewar and whose custodian is Advani.

The other face of the BJP is not as a Hindu party, but as a nationalist party, believing in India emerging as a strong nuclear power able to strut on the world stage with its weapons rather than any message of *ahimsa* (non-violence). It wants to show competence in government. This BJP wants a high status in world politics for India; it wants rapid economic growth with the latest technological gizmos. It wants India to rival China and contain Pakistan. Its favourite ideologue is Savarkar and Vajpayee is its face.

In possessing this Janus face, the BJP is not unusual. Ideological parties of the Left or the Right also face such a perpetual problem. The core supporters want to change the world, the pragmatic office seekers merely want to manage the world better than other parties have done. The ideologues want to take to the streets, mobilise the masses, bring down the old order, and usher in a new era. The pragmatists want to move in the corridors of power, raise real resources and achieve set targets. The very success of the pragmatists ruins the chances of the ideologues since the world is not ruined but improved.

Thus far, the BJP has managed to keep the two factions together since it wanted to achieve power. Having tasted power and made inroads in the cultural sphere, it badly wanted to continue in power. Indeed, the ideologues let the pragmatists have the front line roles in the election in the hope that their strategy would win another term to sharpen the ideological struggle. Now with a defeat, recriminations are breaking out as to who was responsible. There has already been a skirmish around the issue of Narendra Modi. Vajpayee was quoted as having said that Modi needed to be removed if the BJP was to win national confidence. The ideologues shot this down pretty quickly. Instead, they were quick to blame Arun Shourie who as the minister for (under another name) privatisation was outstandingly successful. However, Shourie was not ideological enough for the RSS. On the other hand, the ideologues overreacted to the prospect of Sonia Gandhi becoming prime minister. BJP leaders, such as Uma Bharti and Sushma Swaraj, took this almost as a personal affront and instead of behaving like rulers of states; they behaved like the mob that destroyed the Masjid twelve years ago. In the event they were wrong-footed by Sonia Gandhi who stepped back from taking the position of prime minister.

In opposition, the BJP will have difficulty keeping the ideologues down, unless there is a real prospect of a return to power soon. The party faces a problem of competing generations. The 'old guard', composed of Vajpayee, Advani and Joshi is moving on, and the 'new generation' of Pramod Mahajan, Arun Jaitley, Narendra Modi and Uma Bharti are waiting to take over. The ideology/pragmatism divide stretches across the generations. Unlike the INC, the BJP does not currently rule in many states, though it gained a few in the 2003 state assembly elections. Narendra Modi and Uma Bharti are ideologues, rather than pragmatics. However, the pragmatists were not totally marginalised since they were able to secure Arun Shourie a seat in the Rajya Sabha.

The BJP and Its Choices

The critical problem, however, will not be solely one of managing factions or the transition from one generation to the next. The structural problem facing the BJP is whether a party based on *Hindutva* can command a large enough vote share to come to power on its own.

The choice is between a sharp ideological and Hindu focus, which will test the hypothesis that since the majority of the voters are Hindus then a party based on Hinduism should eventually command majority support. The example, often cited by BJP ideologues, is that of Israel which bases itself on the strong racial/religious identity of Jews. Hinduism is, however, nothing like Judaism. It is pantheistic, lacks a single church or even a single book. It has no priesthood that is universally accepted. Hindus worship different gods and have various practices all of which pass as correct. There is no confession and no necessity to go to the temple every day or even once a week.

Hinduism is not a single religion. It is neither unitary nor indeed unifying. Intra-faith rivalries between devotees of Vishnu as against Shiva are frequent, though not lethal like Shia-Sunni battles. During an attempt in 2003 by the Shankaracharya of Kanchi to settle the Ayodhya *mandir/masjid* (temple/mosque) dispute, the secretary of the VHP questioned his bona fides saying that the Shankaracharya was a Shivaite and the temple was dedicated to an avatar of Vishnu! If the VHP itself takes such a fragmented view of Hinduism what hope is there for ordinary citizens of uniting under the banner of Hinduism?

The founders of the RSS were aware of this problem. Indeed every effort at reforming Hinduism in the wake of the ideological challenge of British and indeed Western Imperialism has been at recasting the old religion in the image of a monotheistic creed such as Christianity. The movements of Brahmo Samaj, Arya Samaj and indeed Vivekanand, were efforts at sanitising if not semitising Hinduism, so that it would have one God, one Book. The exalted status that the nationalist leaders, such as Aurobindo, Tilak and Gandhi conferred on the *Bhagavad Gita* by writing commentaries was one such effort. Nevertheless, that approach proved too highbrow for the masses. Initially the RSS eschewed religion and emphasised social regeneration of Hindu society.

But Hindu society is also not a unity. Even in its idealistic conception, it is a structured hierarchy that rejects egalitarianism. The caste structure has evolved from a four-fold *varnashrama* (castes) to multifarious *jatis* (subcastes) but it still retains not only the distinction between the upper (twice born) castes and the lower castes, but also the untouchables-*harijans* or *dalits* who are outside the pale and yet part of Hindu society. What would be regeneration of Hindu society for an upper caste RSS man would not be the same for a lower caste or a *dalit*. For the *dalit*, it would be the abolition of the hierarchy, which would constitute reform or regeneration. Hence,

Ambedkar's decision to leave the Hindu fold altogether after a lifetime of fighting for reform and embracing Buddhism.

The upper castes are not numerous enough to hold power in a democracy by themselves. As Westernised urban elites, they had a head start soon after independence, but they were also members of the INC which meant that they were able to retain power. The pressures of democratic elections soon valorised the caste divisions and made jatis into vote banks. A party hoping to come to power had to recruit lower castes and dalits as well as Muslims. The INC did this effectively until the late 1980s. Then the Mandal Commission (1980–2008) split the Hindu vote along upper and lower caste lines. The BJP's moment came then.

The agitation for the Ram temple in Ayodhya was a stroke of genius. Instead of the abstruse philosophy of the *Bhagavad Gita* the unifying symbol of Ram was upheld; known from the epic mythologies as an ideal person and popularised by Gandhi no less in his favourite *bhajan* (prayer), Raghupati Raghav Raja Ram. Here was a unifying symbol for Hindus, of upper as well as lower castes. If the *Hindutva* programme could be recast along the Ram bhakti lines, there was indeed a rainbow at the end of that dream.

The destruction of the *masjid* damaged the BJP's reputation, but it recovered by putting Vajpayee forward as its sober face and it was able to come to power as the leading member of a coalition. However, the provocative act of destroying a mosque had antagonised many smaller parties and thus the temple issue had to be put on ice. Had its ideologues displayed patience until single party rule by BJP became a reality, it may have been possible for the BJP to build a temple at Ayodhya. As it was, the BJP could not deliver what its impatient ideologues wanted and there was a distinct cooling between the various parts of the *Sangh Parivar*. In light of this history, both the VHP and the RSS were less than enthusiastic when the general elections were held in April 2004.

The structural question is, thus, as urgent as ever. Can *Hindutva* be Hindu based and still win a majority or does it have to be reshaped as nationalism first with less of an emphasis on Hinduism? Of course, there have been attempts to say that *Hindutva* is not about Hinduism, but about India and Indianness. The destruction of the Babri Masjid devalued that defence forever. As all can see, *Hindutva* is anti-Muslim even before it is pro-Hindu. So while the temple issue excites the ideologues of BJP, there is no hope of convincing the electorate that *Hindutva* is an inclusive philosophy.

Thus, Hinduism is a risky gambit for majority power. At best it can make BJP the largest party in a coalition, but not strong enough to meet the ideologues' demands. That was the lesson of the last government. Mere competence in governing and raising the growth rate of GDP – policies which would be almost 'secular' also did not help. How can BJP then shape its strategy so that it can win a majority on its own?

Hindutva or Hindu Democracy?

In choosing Israel as their ideal country, the ideologues of *Hindutva* have missed a vital ingredient. Judaism is a non-proselytising religion, like Hinduism, but it is also exclusive and guards its frontiers fiercely. It has also the recent experience of the worst tragedy of modern times in the Holocaust. Its need for a protective approach to its identity is well understood. Hinduism is inclusive but, by and large, it has suffered no grave tragedy. The Partition of India was a traumatic event, but it was an Indian tragedy not a solely Hindu one despite efforts on the part of RSS and others to claim so. Muslims remain in India as do Sikhs, Christians and others, India is not so much a secular society as a multi-religious one. The Indian slate in colonial times ran a regime that did not interfere in religious practices and discouraged, much to its chagrin, the Anglican Church from proselytising. The Indian state continued that after independence, though secularism was added in the title of the Republic only in the mid-1970s by Indira Gandhi.[18]

The Partition of India, as well as Nehru's own attitudes, made religious affiliations in political parties a disadvantage. Speculations about the possibility of a Hindu socialism, which flourished in the 1940s and early 1950s, were soon laughed off the court. Yet at the same time as India's independence, the recovery in Europe was aided by the revival of Christian democratic parties. In Germany and Italy, Christian democracy played a crucial role in stabilising and consolidating democracy after years of fascism. Christian socialism is a hardy plant in British politics (Stafford Cripps was a Christian socialist, for example). Zionism at its origin was a socialist movement. The idea that religion and politics cannot or should not mix is a very peculiarly Indian idea shared by 'progressive' elements. The BJP has not countered this idea by pointing to the European experience with Christian democracy. It has not even shown any awareness of Christian democracy.

---

18 Article 25 of the Indian Constitution provides for the free profession, practice and propagation of religion.

This is not the occasion to give a full account of Christian democracy, but suffice it to say that it has adapted Christian ideals for the Cold War era of liberal democracy. Christian democracy was always anti-communist, but also very much in favour of business treating workers fairly and in a spirit of communal harmony rather than class struggle. Christian democracy was a social as well as a political movement. It adapted itself to the secularising forces in European life by underplaying the formal religious elements in its make-up and bringing out the social relevance of religious values. It was a conservative but socially inclusive movement. For around forty years after 1945, it was the bulwark of Italian democracy and it is still alive as a powerful force in German politics.

It may be that the BJP may yet learn from the Christian democratic experience or it may fall foul to its own contradictions. It is not my purpose to solve the BJP's problems. The only point of discussing Christian democracy is to expose a successful model of combining religion with politics. If Christian democracy can flourish in a secular Europe there is no reason, in theory at least, why a Hindu democracy cannot flourish in India.

Conclusion

The defeat in the 2004 general election puts the BJP at a crossroads. It has to reconcile itself to never coming to power as a single party and hence implementing its *Hindutva* dream by stealth or not at all. In either case, a *Hindutva-based* India remains a distant prospect. It could, however, build a vote winning strategy by following the example of Christian democratic parties that downplayed religion as such but took its ethical message into the social sphere. Will it be *Hindutva* or Hindu-Lite for the BJP?

References

The Hindu (2004) 'How India voted: Supplement', *The Hindu*, 20 May. Online. Available at: http://www.hindu.com (accessed 21 May 2004).
Wildman, A. (2004) The New York Times, 13 May.

Acknowledgement

First publication: Desai, Meghnad (2005) '*Hindutva*'s March Halted? Choices for the BJP after the 2004 Defeat' in *Coalition Politics and Hindu Nationalism*, edited by Katharine Adeney and Lawrence Sáez, Routledge Advances in South Asian Studies. New York, Routledge, pp. 254–263. Republished with kind permission of Routledge.

Chapter 16

TWIN TROUBLES

Meghnad Desai

(2008/2009)

India and Pakistan are twins separated at birth. What was once a large and single economy until 1947 was split into two when the division of spoils took place at the time of Partition. Later, in 1971, it was split into three when a third country – Bangladesh – was born. Twins that become triplets are a rare medical occurrence, but an equally interesting economic development is the fact that South Asia has gone the opposite way from the path followed by the European Union, where a single market was created out of many (often mutually hostile) nations.

The two countries can also be contrasted in terms of the mode of governance each adopted after 1947: democracy for India and a mixture of democracy and dictatorship for Pakistan, secularism for India and a religious state for Pakistan. India also claims to be a socialist republic, something that Pakistan has never pretended to be. Finally, the two have fought many bitter battles and both have nuclear capability.

Yet for two countries that were once one and are neighbours, the extent of ignorance about each other that India and Pakistan share is unique. Most Indians think – indeed some openly say – that Pakistan's economy is a failure and the country is a basket case. Granted that today India's success as an economic power house is undeniable yet, as recently as ten years ago, the Pakistanis were equally snooty about India's economy. As it happens, there is and never has been much difference between the two countries if one studies their respective economic records.[1]

---

1   See my *South Asia: Economic Stagnation and Economic Change* written in 1997 on occasion of the fifty-year anniversary of independence of both countries, reprinted

* * *

In 1947, India was the larger, the more industrialised, the better educated and more 'bourgeois' society.[2] Pakistan, especially its western part, was better endowed in terms of land, and had a better agricultural and irrigation system. In terms of population, India is seven times (West) Pakistan but in area terms, India has only four times as much land. In 1947, India had a well-developed entrepreneurial class that had successfully launched many industries, such as steel and textiles. Pakistan, in contrast, had no industrial development and no industrialists. In the civil service as well, since India inherited the bulk of civil servants, Pakistan still needed British civil servants to stay on for a few years after independence.

Even so, there was not much difference between the two in economic terms. In terms of per capita income, India was ranked 55th and Pakistan 57th in a United Nations (UN) study of national income published in 1949, which also ranked Indonesia 67th, South Korea 68th and China 69th. Since both India and Pakistan started with a huge problem of resettling refugees, there was little growth in the first few years. However, India devalued the Rupee along with the Sterling in 1949 while Pakistan did not: a fact that was later to prove a costly mistake. Initially, India made a good start with economic development in the 1950s. Pakistan, on the other hand, had a difficult start since it had to set up industries from scratch. Both countries followed an Import Substitution Industrialization (ISI) strategy, but India neglected its private sector and boosted its public sector development instead. Conversely, Pakistan used State aid to build up private sector industrialists, but this ended up by creating a virtual monopoly where about twenty families owned most of Pakistan's industries. The 1960s were better for Pakistan during Ayub Khan's rule, which brought generous US aid. In India, on the other hand, industrial progress became slower in the 1960s.

We must remember that for the first twenty-four years of its existence Pakistan had an eastern wing – East Pakistan – which became Bangladesh after 1971. West Pakistan had a higher growth rate than East Pakistan. In the 1950s, West Pakistan grew at around 3.5 per cent, which was twice

---

    in *Development and Nationhood: Essays in the Political Economy of South Asia* (Oxford, Delhi, 2005).

2   See Aitzaz Ahsan: *Indus Saga* (Roli Books, Delhi) for a cogent argument that what became Pakistan and India were two different social formations, one feudal and other commercial-bourgeois. He cites this rather than religion as the basis for the division.

the rate of East Pakistan's growth. Per capita growth was negative in the East and around 1 per cent in the West. In the first half of the 1960s, West Pakistan grew at 7.2 per cent (4.4 per cent per capita) and East Pakistan at 5.2 per cent (2.6 per cent). Pakistan's economic performance improved once it shed East Pakistan, even though the argument of Bangladeshis was that West Pakistan was exploiting East Pakistan. Between 1965 and 1980, Pakistan grew at 5.2 per cent, while India plodded at a slow 3.6 per cent. This lead continued during the 1980s as Pakistan grew at 6.3 per cent and India followed at 5.5 per cent.

By 1997 – that is fifty years after independence – Pakistan was ahead of India in terms of per capita income. Pakistan was placed at 120 while India at 143 was just one place ahead of Bangladesh ranked at 144. During the same period, South Korea was ranked 37, Indonesia 92 and China 111. It was in the sixth decade after Partition, that India began to outstrip Pakistan in economic growth. The table that follows shows how far ahead of Pakistan India has reached in the last five years. The reason for this extraordinary growth is not just that Pakistan's economy has stagnated in this period, but that India has enjoyed a remarkable rate of GDP growth.

Table 16.1. Comparative Growth Rates
GDP Growth Rates 2003–2008

Year	India	Pakistan
03/04	8.5	4.8
04/05	7.5	7.4
05/06	9.4	7.7
06/07	9.6	6.9
07/08	9.0	6.4

By 2007, the relative positions of India and Pakistan had become reversed. India was ranked 122 in World Bank per capita income (US$) ranking with an income of $1,012 and Pakistan was 131 with $884. China ranked 99 with $2,485, Indonesia 108 with $1,918 and South Korea 28 with $19,983.

The economic structure of the two countries is also remarkably alike. India splits its national income between agriculture at 18 per cent, industries at 29 per cent and services at 53 per cent. Pakistan's numbers are 20 per cent, 27 per cent and 54 per cent respectively. The two countries have always received similar ranking in the Human Development Index as both are placed in the 'Low' Human Development category. In the rankings for 2008, India was placed at 132 and Pakistan at 139 with China at 94, Indonesia at 109 and South Korea at 25. Life expectancy is almost the same in both India and Pakistan: 64 years in India and 65 in Pakistan. According to the 2008 Human Development Report, Pakistan scores in terms of access to safe water with 91 per cent of households compared to India's 86 per cent but as recently as the first half of the 1990s, India was ahead with 81 per cent to 60 per cent for Pakistan. Pakistanis have better access to sanitation facilities than their Indian cousins – 59 per cent to India's dismal 33 per cent. India is better in contraceptive care and in prenatal care with 47 per cent to 28 per cent and 60 per cent to 43 per cent, respectively. However, there are more doctors per capita in Pakistan than in India: 68 doctors per 100,000 while India has just 51 doctors per 100,000.

Where the statistics for poverty are concerned, Pakistan does better than India with only 23 per cent of its population below the mandatory US$1.25 level, compared to India's 41 per cent. Again, Pakistan has 60 per cent and India 76 per cent (all figures rounded) where the statistics for those below US$2 are concerned. In comparison to these, China has 16 per cent and 36 per cent in the two categories and Indonesia 21 per cent and 54 per cent, respectively. India also has a higher degree of income inequality than Pakistan. The Gini coefficient, which measures inequality, has a value of 37 per cent for India and 31 per cent for Pakistan (Human Development Report 2008).

What makes the big difference in our perceptions is the absolute size of India's economy. Since India's population is around seven times that of Pakistan, in terms of total GDP, India with US$1.17 trillion ranks as a giant in the global arena (Pakistan: US$143.6 billion). India is 12th and Pakistan 46th in world GDP rankings. Together, the two countries would move up two ranks above Brazil and be placed just under Canada. Indeed, throughout its history people have been beguiled into thinking of India as a rich and prosperous country because the area was so large, and because her rulers, whoever they were, had immense wealth. The truth is that India's ordinary people were always poor. And, after sixty years of independence, this continues to be the case in both countries.

* * *

There are several conclusions to be drawn from these bald comparisons. As a region, South Asia has not been an economic success story compared to other Asian countries. The countries of South Asia are laggards rather than leaders. Moreover, in the long run of fifty to sixty years, the relative performance of the two countries is very similar with the ratio of their per capita incomes being not much different from unity. Now one then another goes ahead, but they are similar in being behind the rest than being much ahead of each other.

The question that stares at us then is why has economic development in South Asia been so slow in tackling poverty? One reason is the top-down elitist nature of the development strategy adopted. In both countries, capital intensive organised industries were given large subsidies, but these did not generate much employment. The military-industrial sector developed faster than the consumer-civilian sector. While both countries have a nuclear weapon and can launch missiles at each other, 47 per cent of Indian children under five years are underweight as are 38 per cent of Pakistani children. The formal or organised labour market absorbs only around a sixth of the labour force; the rest survive in the informal sector. The formal sector has health and tenure protection, guaranteed inflation indexed wages while the informal labour sector has none of these cushions. The real burden of this duality falls on the rural sector which is the largest in terms of the proportion of population that depends on it but the lowest in terms of its contribution to income. This means that the agricultural worker has low productivity and hence low wages/income. Both countries have failed to generate a manufacturing transformation of their economies; services have a similar 50 per cent plus share in total income.

The second reason is a shocking neglect of education. South Asia (apart from Sri Lanka) lags behind Sub-Saharan Africa in literacy and educational enrolment. India may have improved its primary and secondary school enrolment, yet it has still not guaranteed universal primary education. It is these dismal literacy statistics that reveal the real secret of the slow rate of progress in improving mass welfare. The adult literacy rate is in the mid-60s for both countries while female literacy is merely 48 per cent (66 per cent of the male literacy rate) in India and 35 per cent (53 per cent of the male rate) in Pakistan. This represents a gross waste of human resources for which the governing elites of the two countries are solely responsible. China, Indonesia and South Korea have female literacy in the high 70s low 80s. South Korea adult literacy stands at 98 per cent, while China and Indonesia register 86 to 87 per cent on this score.

***

This essay has many more numbers than it has text. But the message is stark. There is not much difference between India and Pakistan when it comes to economic performance except that in the last few years India has at last gone ahead of Pakistan in terms of its per capita income. Both countries neglect their human resources by failing to provide education or sanitation or health. Life expectancy is in the mid-sixties and the extent of child malnutrition is shocking. Yet both India and Pakistan boast of nuclear bombs and sophisticated defence arsenals. The sad truth is that societies choose what they want to spend their scarce resources on. In the case of India and Pakistan there is a remarkable consensus on this: both have chosen weapons over human welfare.

It is as if these fraternal twins were identical after all.

Acknowledgement

First publication: Desai, Meghnad, 'Twin Troubles' in *The Great Divide*, *India International Centre Quarterly*, vol. 35, no. 3/4, Winter 2008 / Spring 2009, pp. 96–105. Republished with kind permission of *India International Centre Quarterly*.

Chapter 17

BHAGAVAD GITA

Outlines of a Secular Critique

Meghnad Desai

(2013)

The *Bhagavad Gita* is a central text of Brahmanism.[1] The German philosopher William von Humboldt called it 'the most beautiful, perhaps the only true philosophical song existing in any known language'. When the Atom bomb was first tested in the deserts of New Mexico, J. Robert Oppenheimer who led the project recited the first line of the verse 11.32[2] from the *Gita* to invoke the terrifying sight unfolding before him.

The *Gita* is perhaps the best known book of India and as S. Radhakrishnan puts it 'the most influential work in Indian thought'.[3] Unlike the *Vedas* and the *Upanishads*, the *Gita* is short and concise, a book of just 700 verses that one can compactly carry in one's pocket and even memorise in its entirety as many have done.

---

1   I use the word Brahmanism rather than Hinduism because I think it better represents the nature of the religion both because of the centrality of the notion of Brahman and the apex position of the Brahmins. Max Weber the famous German Sociologist in his book *The Religion of India* says 'Only in recent literature have the Indians themselves begun to designate their religious affiliation as Hinduism. It is the official designation of the English census for the religious complex also described in Germany as "Brahmanism"'. (Weber, *The Religion of India*, p. 4)

2   *Kalo'smi lokakshayakmt'pravruddho lokan samaharmmihah pravruttah* (The Blessed Lord said: I am the Time-Spirit, destroyer of the world, arisen huge-statured for the destruction of the nations). Aurobindo's translation of verse 32 first line of the 11th *Adhyaya* of the *Gita*.

3   S. Radhakrishnan. *Indian Philosophy*, vol. 1 (Oxford India), p. 510. Humboldt quote is also on the same page.

Of course what makes the *Gita* sacred is that presumably the Supreme Lord himself in his avatar as Krishna recited it for the benefit of his friend Arjun. It is because of this unique characteristic of having divine authorship that the *Gita* has become the best known and the most commented upon text over the centuries. Its status was confirmed by Shankara's commentary in the ninth century CE. While Shankara refers to commentaries before his own,[4] his is the first and most authoritative commentary. Indeed Swami Vivekananda thought Shankara may even have written the *Gita* himself. Thus, he says in his *Thoughts on the Gita* '(T)he book, *Gita*, had not been much known to the generality of people before Shankaracharya made it famous by writing his great commentary on it... Some infer that Shankaracharya was the author of the *Gita* and that it was he who foisted it in the body of the *Mahabharata*' (*Complete Works*, vol. 4: 102–3).

The Modern Life of the *Gita*

The modern life of the *Gita* begins with the enterprise of Warren Hastings to have it translated into English. Sir Charles Wilkins (1750–1833) who did the translation made it possible for those who could not read Sanskrit to access the message. Soon after, the fashion of translating the *Gita* into European languages grew till Max Weber was able to say that the *Gita* had been 'Translated into almost all the languages of the earth.' (Weber, 361), Wilkins opened the door to the global popularity of the *Gita*.[5]

Yet the best read version of the *Gita* was by Sir Edwin Arnold. 'The Song Celestial' published in 1885 was to influence the young Mohandas Karamchand Gandhi when he reached London three years later. The *Gita* became a weapon in the independence struggle when after the partition of Bengal in 1905, a militant movement broke out across India, most especially in Bengal, Maharashtra and Punjab. Young people formed a society called 'Anushilan' which was dedicated to a violent overthrow of British Rule. Khudiram Bose who was hanged for the killing of two English ladies died with the *Gita* slung across his neck on the gallows.[6] When the offices

---

4   Shankara mentions critics as Vrittika but not by name. Baudhayan is often cited as a possible earlier commentator but his manuscript has not been recovered as yet.

5   Malinar, op. cit., gives a detailed account of the many translations in German and the debates which followed.

6   This and other details on the use of the *Gita* by 'terrorists' is from Bhiku Parekh (1989/99) *Colonialism, Tradition and Reform: An Analysis of Gandhi's Political Discourse* (Sage Publications. Delhi).

of the Dacca (now Dhaka) Anushilan Samiti were searched, a dozen copies of the *Gita* were found. Members of secret societies dedicated to a violent overthrow swore on the *Gita*.

Questioning the *Gita*

Most people who take part in listening to lectures on the *Gita* or sometimes even read the *Gita*, do so uncritically. Just to recite or listen as many do is, by itself, supposed to give you *punya* – good marks with God. One need not question or even try to understand the contents of the work. Suffice it to know that at the beginning of the Mahabharat war, Krishna the God-charioteer told Arjun what the *Gita* now contains. The divine association is a guarantee of the truth and the sanctity of the text. As it is, it is a difficult, often confusing book which suddenly launches into new topics in the midst of other matters, has largely redundant Manichean sections attacking lower castes and non-Aryan people and at times is baffling. If you take it all as the saying of a single Divine persona, then you have to perform intellectual acrobatics to make it sound consistent. This is why commentators have disagreed among themselves and found whatever they wish to find. Tilak found in it a message for militant action while Gandhi, an apostle of nonviolence, accepted a text which is a long persuasion to go out there and kill all.

Yet, there are a few critics who differ from the majority of readers about the merits of the *Bhagavad Gita*. Kosambi and Ambedkar are two worth quoting. Kosambi in his essay 'Social and Economic Aspects of the *Gita*', fires an opening salvo:

> The *Gita* has attracted minds of bents entirely different from each other and from that of Arjuna. Each has interpreted the supposedly divine words so differently from all the others that the original seems far more suited to raise doubts and to split a personality than to heal an inner division. Any moral philosophy which managed to receive so many variant interpretations from minds in widely different types of society must be highly equivocal. No question remains of its basic validity if the meaning is so flexible (12).[7]

---

7   D. D. Kosambi (1962) 'Social and Economic Aspects of the *Bhagavad-Gita*', in *Myth and Reality: Studies in the Formation of Indian Culture* (Popular Prakashan, Bombay), 'Myth' hereafter.

Ambedkar starts with the same question as Kosambi does.

> One is forced to ask why there is such divergence of opinion among scholars? My answer to this question is that scholars have gone on a false errand. They have gone on a search for the message of the *Bhagvat Gita* on the assumption that it is a gospel as the *Koran*, the *Bible*, or the *Dhammapada* is. In my opinion this assumption is quite a false assumption. The *Bhagvat Gita* is not a gospel and it can therefore have no message and it is futile to search for one. (T)he *Bhagvat Gita* is neither a book of religion nor a treatise on philosophy. What the *Bhagvat Gita* does is to defend certain dogmas of religion on philosophic grounds... It uses philosophy to defend religion.
>
> ...
>
> (T)he dogmas which the *Gita* defends are the dogmas of counter-revolution as put forth in the Bible of counter-revolution, namely Jaimini's *Purva-Mimansa*. There ought to be no difficulty in accepting this proposition. If there is any it is largely due to wrong meaning attached to the word *Karma yoga*. Most writers on the *Bhagvat Gita* translate the word *Karma yoga* as 'action' and the word *Jnana yoga* as 'knowledge' and proceed to discuss the *Bhagvat Gita* as though it was engaged in comparing and contrasting knowledge versus action in a generalized form. This is quite wrong. The *Bhagvat Gita* is not concerned with any general, philosophical discussion of action versus knowledge. As a matter of fact, the *Bhagvat Gita* is concerned with the particular and not with the general. By *Karma yoga* or action, the *Gita* means the dogmas contained in Jaimini's *Karma Kanda* and by *Jnana yoga* or knowledge it means the dogmas contained in Badarayan's *Brahma Sutras*...It is to lift the *Gita* from the position of a party pamphlet engaged in a controversy on small petty points and make it appear as though it was a general treatise on matters of high philosophy that this attempt is made to inflate the meaning of the words Karma and Jnana and make them words of general import. Mr. Tilak is largely to be blamed for this trick of patriotic Indians.[8]

Dr Ambedkar raises several issues in this critique. Of course by counter-revolution, he means the fight waged against Buddhism by Brahmanism

---

8   'Krishna and His *Gita*', in Valerian Rodrigues (ed.), *The Essential Writings of B.R. Ambedkar* (Oxford India, 2002), 193–204.

in which the *Bhagavad Gita* becomes a weapon. This fight was waged over more than 1000 years between the sixth century BCE and the ninth century CE when Shankara wrote his commentary. Not much has been written about this war between Buddhism and Brahmanism, and the traditional version of ancient Indian history erases all mention of Buddhism and pretends that Brahmanism was the most tolerant of all religions. There was a philosophical as well often a physical battle between the champions of Brahmanism and Buddhism.

The Place of the *Gita* in the *Mahabharat*

The *Gita* is read as a separate, standalone text. But, within the *Mahabharat*, it is a part of the *Bhishma Parvan*. When reading the *Gita* on its own, we get the impression that on the first day of the *Mahabharat* war, as the armies are assembled, there is Arjun depressed and shaken. Then, in front of the waiting armies, Krishna launches into his long exposition of philosophy of the paths to attain moksha. At the end of the 700 verses, Arjun is convinced and decides to fight.

The *Bhishma Parvan* however presents a very different picture. After all attempts at preventing war fail, as described in the *Udyog Parvan*, the *Bhishma Parvan* starts on the tenth day of the war, not the first one. Sanjaya who has magical powers to see into the past, present and the future *(pratyakshadarshi sarvasya bhutabhavyabhavisyavit)* comes to Dhritarashtra the blind King to report that Bhishma is dead.

In the sixteenth *Adhyaya* of the *Bhishma Parvan*, Sanjaya begins to describe in great detail the armies arranged on either side on the morning of the first day. The eighteen armies, eleven of Duryodhana and seven of Yudhishthira are ready once again. In the seventeenth *Adhyaya*, Bhishma is reported by Sanjaya to have said:

Adharmah ksatriyasyaisa yad vyadhimaranam grhe

Yad ajau nidhanam yati so'sya dharmah sanatanah. (Bhishma, 17.11)

It is a breach of the Law (*Dharma*) for a baron (*ksatriya*) to die of sickness at home, and his everlasting Law is it to find death on the battlefield. (Van Buitenen, 50–1; bracketed insertions are mine)

In the twentieth *Adhyaya* we begin again with Dhritarashtra asking as to which were the troops to greet the sunrise – his son's led by Bhishma or those led by Bhīma. Sanjaya gives a long description of the armies.

The warriors in both armies exulted, and in both rose a fragrance of flowers and incense. The first clash of the massed, marshalled troops that slowly and proudly advanced was magnificent, and the sound of music mixed with peals of conches and drums and the noise of roaring elephants and churning troops was deafening. (Van Buitenen, 68–9)

It is at this stage that Dhritarashtra asks once again the famous question with which the *Bhagavad Gita* proper starts

Dharmakshetre Kurukshetre samaveta yuyutsava

Mamaka pandavaschaiva kim kurvat vada Sanjaya. (Bhishma 23.1. Bhagavad Gita 1.1.)

When in the Field of the Kurus, the Field of the Law, my troops and the Pandavas had massed belligerently, what did they do, Samjaya? (Van Buitenen, 68–9)

There are several things to notice about this famous opening *sloka* (verse). This is the first and the only time the expression *Dharmakshetre* is used, thus elevating a war over a fraternal property dispute into a sacred encounter. Why would Dhritarashtra call it a *dharmakshetra*, thus admitting the justness of the claim of his nephews? Then again the question that the blind King asks has been asked by him twice in the previous *Adhyayas* already and answered by Sanjaya. Why do we now need the blind King to ask again what Sanjaya has already told him?

The answer has to be that whatever was the original course of the narrative, someone wanted to make a standalone text of the eighteen *Adhyayas* which form the *Gita*. The introductory question and Sanjaya's reply which then takes up the next twenty verses allow us to ignore all that has gone before in the *Bhishma Parva* and focus on Arjun's problem. This is no proof but a strong indication that the *Gita*, if not inserted into the *Bhishma Parva* as Vivekananda suspected, at some later stage was so rearranged that it could be extruded so as to be read separately.

Sanjaya repeats much of what he has already said to Dhritarashtra in 23.2–20 (*Bhagavad Gita* 1.2–20) but then in 23.21 (*Bhagavad Gita* 1.21) Arjun requests Krishna to place his chariot in the middle of the two armies (*senayorubhayor madhye*).

But then once the chariot is moved to the middle of the two armies, Arjun begins to have what can only be called a nervous breakdown: his body begins to shake, his mouth is parched, his limbs collapse and his favourite bow Gandiva slips from his hands as his skin burns. In short, he is in a funk. Thus he raises the fundamental issue: What is the point of war? I don't want victory, nor kingdom nor pleasures.

Krishna begins very much as one would expect any coach or mentor to do. He rebukes him and tries to shame him into action. Yet Arjun is unmoved and in distress submits to Krishna seeking instruction from him *(shadhi maam tvam prapannam)*, Krishna replies to him laughing at first *(prahasan)*. Then from 2.11 onward begins the *Gita* proper as many have come to see it. This is the beginning of Krishna's exposition of his response to Arjun's grief. The response can be described as twofold to begin with. The first response is what I would call Irrelevance of Agency. This occupies 2.11 to 2.30. Then there is a sudden change in the response and Krishna tries Humiliation of the Ego (2.31–38). This latter response is much more in line with what any good coach would do while the first is at a higher philosophical level.

When these two responses are done, I believe the *Gita* proper should have ended. What follows from 2.39 is another switch in theme. The text catches up with 2.30 and goes down philosophical byways and highways for the next sixteen more *Adhyayas*. Why should this be so?

Radhakrishnan gets to the heart of the matter when he says, 'It is possible that Arjuna might have had pointed advice from his friend Krishna which the poet (i.e. the author of the *Gita*) worked up into the poem of seven hundred verses.'[9] What is implied is that there was an author other than Krishna who found the original short text and then elongated it into a 700 verse poem. We shall see later why this is a very plausible idea.

Irrelevance of Agency

This is the first and what may be called Vedantic response. Krishna tells Arjun that in fact he will not be the author of his actions if he does fight and kill his relatives. Life and death are delusions that Arjun suffers from. He neither kills nor is he killed. Those he thinks are going to die have had their destiny already determined independently of what Arjun might or might not do. He has to wise up since the Wise know what is not what.

This is then a 'get-out-of-jail free' card from the Lord himself. You don't kill and are not killed. The body is transient and the soul cannot kill or be killed. So there are no consequences of human action. One can regard this

---

9   S. Radhakrishnan (1923/1999), *Indian Philosophy*, vol. 1, (Oxford India), 523.

as a deep doctrine as many do or as a fantastic escapism. Dr Ambedkar, being a lawyer, was unconvinced:

> To say that killing is no killing because what is killed is the body and not the soul is an unheard of defence of murder. This is one of the doctrines which make some people say that the doctrines make one's hair stand on their end. If Krishna were to appear as a lawyer acting for a client who is being tried for murder and pleaded the defence set out by him in the *Bhagvad Gita* there is not the slightest doubt that he would be sent to the lunatic asylum (Ambedkar, 197).

Humiliation of the Ego

But starting with 2.31, Krishna changes tack. The next argument is what I label Humiliation of the Ego. This is a conventional argument in which Krishna uses the logic that Bhishma has already been quoted above as using. Arjun had objected that killing and destruction of the kin group could be *adharma* (1.39). This could lead to sin (1.36). Krishna now changes tack and talks of *svadharma* which overrides any general concern for *dharma*. Svadharma for a Kshatriya is to fight and not brood over consequences of killing.

I reckon this short passage of eight verses 2.31–38 is much more likely to appeal to Arjun's own sentiments. He has been brought up as a Kshatriya (warrior), aware of his duties and his obligations. In the earlier *Adhyayas* of *Bhishma Parvan* the discourse of the blind King and of the Grand Sire Bhishma, is very much embedded in the culture of the family in *Kshatradharma*, a trap out of which Dhritarashtra knows neither his sons nor his nephews can escape. This is Arjun's duty explained in terms of the here and now rather than from the point of view of higher philosophy of the nature of the soul.

It is quite likely that the 'pointed advice' that Radhakrishnan thought Krishna may have given to Arjun is contained in 2.31–38. Nothing more would be needed to make Arjun fight. To be told that if he does not fight, his rivals would not credit him with higher wisdom but cowardice would be enough to rouse him. To be told even more pointedly that he could not lose either way would reinforce the message. To be told that it was sinful not to fight and no sin to fight clinches the moral argument as far as a Kshatriya like Arjun is concerned.

I would therefore suggest that Arjun's *Gita* is 1.21–46 and 2.1–10 and 2.31–38; forty-four *slokas* in all. It would make a perfect 23rd *Adhyaya* in Bhishma Parva. It is my argument that the *Gita* as it finally came to us is a result of many additions to what could have been a small original fragment, if there was one at all.

Gita as a Multi-authored Text

The idea that the *Gita* may be a multiple authored book is not new. Indeed it began with the first translation of Charles Wilkins' *Gita*.[10] Von Humboldt in reviewing Schlegel's Latin translation was 'aware of the possibility that the text had been composed by more than one author over a considerable period of time…(H)e regards the first eleven chapters as the "original" ones' (Malinar, 16). Deussen another distinguished Sankritist divided the text into three thematic units, (1) ethics (Chs 1–6) (2) metaphysics (7–12) and (3) psychology (13–18). The French scholar Charpentier believed that what follows 2.38 'can in no wise have belonged to the original epic text' (23–25).

The most cogent argument for multiple authorship was made by the Maharashtrian scholar Dr Gajanan Shripat Khair. His book *Quest for the Original Gita* was published in 1969 and a revised edition was issued in 1997.[11] Khair does not seem to be aware of any of the literature from which I cited earlier. He has arrived at his contention entirely on his own analysis which makes the coincidence of his ideas with those of previous scholars all the more remarkable.[12]

He divides the *Bhagavad Gita* into three parts – *Trikala Gita* as he calls it. According to him:

> The First Author wrote most of *Adhyayas* 1 to 6. The period of writing was of the Older Upanishads and pre-Buddhist, around 600 BCE. The principal philosophical issue is Sannyasa and the solution is *Karma yoga* (126 verses or 18 per cent).

> The Second Author wrote portions of *Adhyaya* 8, *Adhyayas* 13 to 15, 17 and portions of 18. The period was contemporaneous with the Buddha and the philosophical authority is Old Upanishads as before. The problem is

---

10 Malinar, op. cit., is a good source of the debates about the text of the *Bhagavad Gita* in Germany.

11 G. S. Khair (1969/97), *Quest for the Original Gita* (Somaiya Publications, Mumbai).

12 Malinar does mention Khair but does not give his ideas any more room than she does those of the others (27–28).

karma – choice (as Khair describes it) and the solution is *sattvikatva* (119 verses or 17 per cent).

The Third Author is the editor and the final arbiter of the document. He wrote the entire *Adhyayas* 7, 9–12, 16 plus interpolated in the *Adhyayas* the two others wrote. The problem is 'diverse creeds' and the answer is bhakti. His authority is the New Upanishads and his period is 300 to 200 BCE. (455 verses or 65 per cent). Note that while Khair has a tripartite division of the *Bhagavad Gita*, his analysis is more subtle than that of Deussen as he argues that the third author mixed up the different parts which disguises the divisions.

If we are to take this classification as a working hypothesis, it would seem that the *Gita* gets settled into its final shape at the time when the battle between the Buddhists and the Brahmanists is at its most ferocious. Of course, Kosambi puts the final rendition of the *Gita* much later to the Gupta period rather than the highpoint of the Buddhist period as Khair does. The ideas common to Kosambi and Khair are that (a) there are multiple authors and (b) that the text evolves over time as it responds to different circumstances prevailing as per the struggle between Buddhism and Brahmanism while Khair alone contributes the idea that (c) the Third Author adds to and edits the text to give it a sort of unity.

This makes sense if we see that the First Author is not joining a battle against Buddhism but expounding the Upanshadic doctrine in a concise way. It is like a catechism for young students. Once we are beyond 2.38 Arjun becomes only a vehicle for expounding what has to be taught. Hence, we begin with a mention of Sankhya in 2.39 and other philosophical issues follow.

The Second Author is a contemporary of Buddha if we are to take Khair's dating seriously. He is also a didactic writer expositing what has to be learnt. His style is dispassionate. He uses words such as *jnanin, munih, yatih, yogin* but sparsely. This is also a teaching text, meant for select audiences.

It is the Third Author who addresses the ordinary people who have little time and inclination for philosophical subtleties. As Khair says, 'His main audience is the common people and the neglected persons, who were deprived of opportunities of spiritual and moral salvation. Traders, merchants, atheists, worshippers of ancestral and popular gods – this was his audience' (51) since by this time the need to spread Brahmanism as widely as possible to counter Buddhism's popularity is urgent. The second or third century BCE which Khair gives as the likely date is the high point of the spread of Buddhism with Ashoka having given royal patronage to

Buddhism. The champions of Brahmanism had to fight back. The *Gita* with a popularised section moulded along with the earlier parts was to be the weapon. The date suggested by Kosambi of 150–350 CE would be even more suitable because under the Guptas, the Brahminical fightback had Royal patronage.

Khair's virtue is that he proposes a plausible hypothesis of how the different layers were integrated into a seamless whole which gives the impression of an integral text which most readers of the *Bhagavad Gita* take it to be. The idea that there was an author who was also the last one in and who edited the entire text by his interpolations to weave the separate texts into one is the missing link in the discussions of the experts who wrestled with the problem before he came along. Above all, his virtue is that he arrives at his conclusion unprompted and uninfluenced by the previous literature. He is a homespun amateur reader of the *Bhagavad Gita* who stumbles upon his discovery all by himself and proceeds to construct a theory of why the *Bhagavad Gita* should be as it is – choppy and seamless at the same time.

We can conclude, however, that apart from Arjun's *Gita*, there may have been three other *Gitas*. Ignoring the interpolation attributed by Khair to the Third Author, we can say that the three *Gitas* were:

1. The Veda-Vedanta *Gita* or *Karma Yoga Gita* of the First Author mainly across *Adhyayas* 2 to 6
2. The Samkhya *Gita* or *Jnana Yoga Gita* of the Second Author *Adhyayas* 8 (part), 13, 14, 15, 17, 18 (part)
3. The *Bhakti Yoga Gita* of the Third Author *Adhyayas* 7, 9–12.

Indeed, the role of the *Bhagavad Gita* as a weapon in battle between Brahmanism and Buddhism is well explained by Pande (1994):

> The *Bhagavad Gita* is an evolving response which deals with the conflicts between Veda and Vedanta and then with the challenge posed to Vedanta by Buddhism. Its shift to Bhakti is thus the climax of the battle between Brahmanism and Buddhism.

Indeed, as Pande further has observed, 'The *Bhagvad Gita* represents a progressive adaptation of the Vedanta to the challenges of the *Mahajanapada* Age'.

Conclusion

What seems to be a cautious conclusion from the discussion above is that:

a) There are probably multiple authors of the *Bhagavad Gita* as shown by stylistic changes and the frequent shift of subject matter.

b) There was probably an original short sharp lesson for Arjun by Krishna assuming that these were historical characters as described in the *Mahabharat*.

c) The periodisation of the three other segments follows the pattern of pre-Buddhist, contemporary with Buddhism's early days and lastly in the period when Brahmanism was reviving.

The purpose of essaying such a secular or humanist critique of the *Gita* is not to delve into the religious ideas of Buddhism as against Brahmanism. The important point is that the battle between the two was waged on the social terrain as much as the religious one. Buddhism rejected *varna* distinctions, challenged the hegemony of Brahmins and the necessity of ritual performance. It doubted the existence of a God and of the soul. Its challenge to the Brahmanical social order was the most profound revolutionary challenge to the old order. Urban groups mainly Vaishyas and Shudras joined Buddhism in large numbers. For around 500 years between the death of Buddha and the advent of the Common Era Buddhism shaped the social order in parts of India north and south.

The recapture of the initiative by Brahmanism which took place during the first 700 years of the Common Era, was achieved as much by the religious and philosophical debates as by the contest for patronage from one or the other King (Verardi op.cit.).

When Buddhism was defeated and left India for other Asian regions, the caste society was re-established firmly in India. Buddhism was wiped out from the historical memory of India till James Prinsep inaugurated the rediscovery of Buddhism by his decipherment of the Brahmi script. We now know much more about Buddhism and its place in Indian history but that is no thanks to Brahmanism which suppressed all memory of the challenge. When Ambedkar chose to reject Brahmanism for himself and his followers he chose Buddhism. This as much as anything else demonstrates the radical challenge of Buddhism.

The *Bhagavad Gita* was the most effective instrument in this struggle. It offered a simple, easy to read or recite, source of philosophical ideas of Brahmanism. It lent authority to these verses by attributing them to Krishna whose *bhakti* became a powerful instrument for winning over the masses to the cause of Brahmanism.

All this happened over a thousand years and more. We still lack a proper history of the rise and fall of Buddhism and the decline and renaissance of Brahmanism. Further analysis of the *Bhagavad Gita* may yet help in this task.

References

Khair, G. S. *Quest for the Original Gita*. 2nd edn. Mumbai: Somaiya Publications, 1997.
Kosambi, D. D. Myth and Reality: Studies in the Formation of Indian Culture. 2nd edn. Mumbai: Popular Prakashan, 2005.
Malinar, A. *The Bhagavad Gita: Doctrines and Context*. Cambridge: Cambridge University Press, 2007.
Minor, Robert. *Modern Indian Interpreters of Bhagavad Gita*. Albany, New York: State University of New York Press, 1986.
Pande, G. C. *Life and Thought of Sankaracharya* Delhi: Motilal Banarasidass, 1994.
Radhakrishnan, S. *Indian Philosophy*, 2nd edn. New Delhi: Oxford, 1999.
Radhakrishnan, S. *The Bhagavad Gita*. New Delhi: Harper Collins Publishers, 2010.
Rodrigues, Valerian ed. 'Krishna and His *Gita*', *The Essential Writings of B.R. Ambedkar*, (Oxford India, 2002), 193–204 (2010)
Verardi, Giovanni. Hardships and Downfall of Buddhism in India. New Delhi: Manohar, 2011.
Vivekananda, Swami. *The Complete Works of Swami Vivekananda*. 29th impression. Kolkata: Advaita Ashrama, 2009.
Weber, Max. *The Religion of India: The Sociology of Hinduism and Buddhism*, 2nd edn, translated by Gerth, Hans and Don Martindale. New Delhi: Munshiram Manoharlal, 2007.

Acknowledgement

First publication: Desai, Meghnad (2013) '*Bhagavad Gita*: Outlines of a Secular Critique' in *Civilizational Dialogue: Asian Inter-connections and Cross-cultural Exchanges*, edited by Sharma, Anjana. New Delhi, Manohar, pp. 165–175. Republished with kind permission of Manohar.

GLOSSARY

ACTU – The Australian Council of Trade Unions, the largest affiliation of trade unions and workers in Australia.

AFL-CIO – American Federation of Labor and Congress of Industrial Organizations.

AIADMK – The All India Anna Dravida Munnetra Kazhagam is a Dravidian party founded in 1972 and based largely in Tamil Nadu and the Union Territory of Puducherry.

AoA – Agreement on Agriculture. The Agreement is an International Treaty signed during the Uruguay round of GATT discussions in 1994 and focuses on the reform of international agricultural trade and domestic agricultural policies of the member countries.

APEC – Asia Pacific Economic Cooperation came into effect in 1989 amongst the major Pacific Rim Countries.

ATO – Alternative Trade Organisations.

ATTAC France – Association for the Taxation of Financial Transactions and for Citizens' Action is a global anti-globalisation movement that focuses on questions of financial equity at the level of citizens, states and regions.

BCCI – Bank of Credit and Commerce International.

Bharat Nirman – A program to promote rural infrastucture by the business sector; it gives awards in recognition of achievements.

BJP – Bharatiya Janata Party is the political arm of the Sangh Parivar, a group of Hindu nationalist organisations that promote India as the land of Hindus (i.e. Hindu Rashtra). Its origin dates back to the early years of Indian independence when the same kind of Hindu nationalist interests called themselves the Bharatiya Jana Sangh (est. 1951).

Boer War – Was fought from October 11, 1899, to May 31, 1902, between Great Britain and the two Boer (Afrikaner) republics – the South African Republic (Transvaal) and the Orange Free State. The Boers or Afrikaners were the descendants of Dutch settlers.

Brady Bonds – 'Named after US Treasury Secretary Nicholas Brady, who in association with the IMF and World Bank sponsored the effort to permanently restructure outstanding sovereign loans and interest arrears into liquid debt instruments... Principal and certain interest is collateralized by U.S. Treasury zero coupon bonds and other high grade instruments. Creditor banks exchanged sovereign loans for Brady bonds incorporating principal and interest guarantees and cash payments. Debtor governments had their principal, interest and interest arrears reduced. Countries involved in the Brady Plan restructuring: Argentina, Brazil, Bulgaria, Costa Rica, Dominican Republic, Ecuador, Mexico, Morocco, Nigeria, Philippines, Poland, Uruguay. Potential future candidates for Brady Plan restructuring: Ex-Soviet Union (Vnesheconobank), Nicaragua, Panama, Peru' (Emerging Markets Companion 1996–9).

BSP – Founded in 1984, the Bahujan Samaj Party or the Majority People's Party was formed by the dalit movement in India. It traces its origins to the work of Ambedkar in the 1930s and stands for the interests of the *dalits* or former 'untouchables'.

BRICS – Refers to five new emerging economies: Brazil, Russia, India, China and South Africa.

Glossary

CAP – Common Agricultural Policy. The CAP was the first major step taken by the European nations after World War Two in 1962 to move towards mutually beneficial economic policies. Such policies were designed to prevent future European wars. The CAP, above all other concerns, subsidises the income of European farmers. Given its large farm sector, the CAP was essential as a way of securing France's involvement in the development of the European Union.

CBI – Central Bureau of Investigation, the chief anti-crime investigative body in India.

The Club of Rome – traces its history to 1968 when it was set up as a 30 member discussion group so that international scientists, industrialists, economists and others could better inform themselves about global events and their impact on humanity. It describes itself as an organisation of individuals who share a common concern for the future of humanity and strive to make a difference. Their Secretariat is based in Switzerland and it has national associations in some 30 countries.

CRA – One of the largest mining companies in Australia now called Rio Tinto.

CSDS – Centre for the Study of Developing Societies (New Delhi).

Dalits – Former 'untouchables' castes, also known as 'scheduled' castes, because the Indian Constitution sets aside 'reservation' for them in parliament, schools, colleges and government services in general.

Derivatives – Futures, puts, options and other financial instruments which are derived from others, such as commodity prices, shares and bonds. Derivatives are often used as insurance against unfavourable movements in the underlying instruments. In portfolio investments derivatives are used to achieve a specific risk/return profile.

DMK – Founded in 1949 as part of the Dravidian movement, the Dravida Munnetra Kazhagam is an Indian political party based in the state of Tamil Nadu and Union Territory of Puducherry.

EC – European Community.

Enlightenment – Refers to the Age of Enlightenment and the ideas of this eighteenth century philosophical and intellectual movement which promoted reason, progress, liberty, tolerance, the separation of church and state and constitutional government.

ERM – enterprise risk management.

EU – European Union.

FDI – Foreign Direct Investment describes the investment by private individuals and firms in the domestic enterprises of foreign countries. FDI can take the form of either financial investments, the transfer of technology and or the transfer of expertise. The foreign individual or firm receives a partial share of the total equity value of the entity in which it invests.

FLO – Fairtrade Labelling Organization International.

FSA – The Financial Services Authority in Britain. It was a quasi-judicial body responsible for the regulation of the financial services industry in the United Kingdom between 2001 and 2013. It was founded as the Securities and Investments Board in 1985.

FSU – Former Soviet Union.

FTAA – Free Trade Area of the Americas. Negotiations to set up FTAA occurred over four years (1998–2002) to create a free trade zone between north America, south America, the Caribbean nations except Cuba. In the end it was not set up.

Futures – Financial instruments constituting a hedge against the uncertain fluctuations in the price of a commodity, or currency or exchange rate.
G7 – The seven largest, advanced economies of the world consisting of Canada, France, Germany, Italy, Japan, the United Kingdom, and the United States.
G19 – Globalisation in the 19th century.
G20 – Globalisation in the 20th century.
GATS – General Agreement on Trade in Services.
GATT – General Agreement on Tariffs and Trade.
GDP – Gross Domestic Product, one measure of the total output of a country.
GMO – Genetically modified organism.
GNP – gross national product.
HA – Humanistic Approach to economic development.
HDR – Human Development Report.
HIPC – Highly Indebted Poor Countries.
HSA – Hemispheric Social Alliance.
IFAT – International Federation of Alternative Trade.
ILO – International Labour Organization.
IMF – International Monetary Fund.
INC – Founded in 1885 as part of the Indian nationalist movement, the Indian National Congress Party claims to stand for secularism and tolerance in India.
INPEG – Initiative Against Economic Globalisation.
IPC – The Indian Penal Code, which is a comprehensive law first codified in British India in 1860.
ISGN – International Southern Group Network. Set up in 1984 in Cameroon as the Southern Networks for Environment and Development (SONED). Renamed in South Africa in 1994. It promotes cooperation and mutual aid between movements, alternative development centres and NGOs in the Third World countries.
ITO – International Trade Organisation; although it never came into existence, it was a precursor to the WTO.
IWW – Industrial Workers of the World.
Lokpal bill – The bill sought to establish an ombudsman to investigate cases of corruption. The bill was finally passed in 2013, more than 40 years after it was introduced to the Indian Parliament.
Luddites – Luddites were part of a 19th century movement that opposed machines and factory production; they often wrecked machines. In today's usage 'Luddites' refers to anti-industrial and anti-technology movements.
MAI – Multilateral Agreement on Investment.
MIF – Multilateral Investment Framework.
MFN – most favoured nations.
MFN rules – These rules mean that all countries belonging to the same agreement or group benefit equally from special arrangements made between two member partners: e.g. if one country grants a special favour to another, the same special favour applies to all members of the group.
MNC – Multinational corporation.
MNREGA – Mahatma Gandhi National Rural Employment Guarantee Act.
MPP – multi-party parliaments.
MST – Landless Workers Movement in Brazil.
NAFTA – The North American Free Trade Agreement, which came into effect in 1994 between Canada, Mexico, and the United States.

Glossary

NATO – North Atlantic Treaty Organization.
NDA – Founded in 1998 by the BJP, the National Democratic Allianceis a centre-right coalition of 13 Indian parties.
NGO – Non-governmental organisation.
NIC – newly industrialised country.
NLF – National Left Front.
NM model – Nehru-Mahalanobis model.
NREGS – National Rural Employment Guarantee Scheme. The history of legislative intervention in generating rural employment in India dates from the 1980s and focuses on various kinds of local public works programs. In 2005 the Government of India introduced the NREGS which was subsequently revised and extended as the MGNREGS.
NRIs – Non-Resident Indians.
OBC – other backward classes. This refers to castes that are 'backward' as measured by eleven socio-economic factors but not part of the Scheduled Castes and Scheduled Tribes of India. The benefits of reservation were extended to OBCs by the Mandal Commission set up in 1979. In 1980, the Mandal Commission recommended the extension of affirmed action to the OBCs, including the reservation of 27 per cent of jobs with the central government and public sector undertakings.
OECD – Organisation for Economic Co-operation and Development.
OPEC – Organization of the Petroleum Exporting Countries, founded in Baghdad in 1960.
OWINFS – Our World is Not For Sale. Describes itself as a loose grouping of organisations, activists and social movements which grew out of international campaigns against the WTO and MAI.
PAN cards – Permanent Account Number cards are cards issued by the Indian Tax Office which non-resident Indians need to have if they are investing in India and submitting tax returns in India.
PDS – Public Distribution System.
Portfolio investment – The purchase of debt, equity and other financial instruments. Equity portfolio investments usually stop short of obtaining management control in a particular enterprise. The goals of portfolio investments vary from growth to income to value preservation against adverse shocks.
QUAD – Refers to the Quadrilateral Security Dialogue which is an ongoing, informal strategic dialogue between the United States, Japan, India and Australia.
Quad countries – United States, Japan, India and Australia.
RD – Research and Development.
RSS – The Rashtriya Swayamsevak Sangh or National Volunteer Association serves as the ideological base of the Sangh Parivar, which is politically led by the BJP. The RSS was formed in 1925 by Keshav Baliram Hedgewar, in Maharashtra.
SEATINI – The Southern and Eastern African Trade Negotiations Institute.
Shiv Sena – A right wing, Hindu nationalist party which was formed in Mumbai in 1966 by a political cartoonist called Bal Thackeray. At first it was a local chauvinist formation that promoted the interests of Maharashtrians but later it adopted Hindu nationalist ideas in competition with the BJP.
SME – small and medium-sized enterprises.
SRI – Socially responsible investing.

Swadeshi – *Swadeshi*, literally 'of one's own nation', was originally based on an anti-British tactic by Tilak and then later Gandhi to boycott British imports and encourage Indian products.
TDP – Telugu Desam Party, set up in 1982 by N. T. Rama Rao and based in Andhra Pradesh and Telangan states.
TINA – 'There Is No Alternative'.
TJM – Trade Justice Movement. Set up in 2000, it is a British coalition of more than 80 organisations that campaigns for fair and just trade.
TNCs – trans-national corporations.
TRIPS – the Agreement on Trade-Related Aspects of Intellectual Property Rights; it was signed in 1995 by the members of the WTO.
TWN – Third World Network. This is is an independent non-profit international research and advocacy organisation involved in issues relating to development, developing countries and North-South affairs. It was set up in Penang, Malaysia in November 1984 during the International Conference on 'The Third World: Development or Crisis?', organised by the Consumers' Association of Penang and attended by over a hundred participants from 21 countries.
UAF – universal adult franchise.
UN – United Nations.
UNCED – United Nations Conference on Environment and Development.
UNCTAD – United Nations Conference on Trade and Development.
UNIDO – United Nations Industrial Development Organization.
UP – Uttar Pradesh, the largest and most popularist state in India. Not to be confused with UPA, etc.
UPA / UPA-II – The United Progressive Alliance, a coalition of centre-left political parties in India formed after the 2004 general election. It is chaired by Sonia Gandhi because the largest member party of the UPA is the Indian National Congress. UPA-II refers to the second ministry led by Manmohan Singh after the general elections of 2009.
VHP – Vishwa Hindu Parishad, a critical branch of the Sangh Parivar that helps the BJP to recruit members, especially international supporters. Its recruitment campaigns include devising and introducing new school text books.
WSF – Third World Social Forum.
WTO – World Trade Organization.

INDEX

Advani, Lal Krishna 249, 251, 269, 270
African countries, and globalisation 129
   poverty 200
agency, and the *Bhagavad Gita* 287–8
agrarian reform, China 176–7
   India 177, 179
Agreement on Agriculture 102–3
agricultural achievements, China 173–4
agricultural productivity 178–9, 203, 205
agricultural subsidies 102–3, 124, 138
   impact on developing countries 84
alternative trade organisations 96–7
Ambedkar, B.R. 284–5, 288, 292
American middle classes, and globalisation 132–3
American parochialism 31
anti-capitalism, history 54
anti-capitalist alternatives 64–9
anti-capitalist movement 34–72, 75–114
Anti-Corn Law League 79, 82
anti-Muslimism, India 269, 270, 272
Aristotle, on money 36
Arnold, Sir Edwin 282
Asian countries, capitalism 119
   economic growth 15, 119, 120
   impact of globalisation 129
Asian financial crisis, 1997–8 45–6, 47–9, 51, 52, 149
Asiatic Mode of Production 173
asylum seekers, and globalisation 126, 128–9
asymmetries of power 13, 15, 16, 18, 27
Atlantic Charter 3
authorship, of *Bhagavad Gita* 289–91
Bangaladesh 68, 200, 275, 276, 277
bank bailouts 226
Bank of Credit and Commerce International 16
banking, regulation 226
Baran, Paul. *Political Economy of Growth* 118, 208
BCCI *see* Bank of Credit and Commerce International
Bello, Walden 39, 56–7, 71
Bhagavad Gita 271, 272, 281–93
Bharatiya Jana Sangh 232, 266, 268

Bharatiya Janata Party xii, 182, 262–74
   economic policy 230–41, 246–50
Bharti, Uma 270
Bhishma Parvan 285–7
BJP *see* Bharatiya Janata Party
BJS *see* Bharatiya Jana Sangh
Boer War 3–4
Bombay University vi
border disputes 30
Brahmanand, P.R. 203
Brahmanism 281
   and Buddhism 284–5, 290, 291, 292
Bretton Woods institutions 10, 13–14, 16, 21, 39–41, 43, 71
Brexit vii–viii
   and Trump 133–4
British rule, in India 169–70
Buddhism, and Brahmanism 284–5, 290, 291, 292
budget deficit, India 196
Burns, Arthur F. 141
Bush, George H.W. 134
   and New International Order 3, 30
capital, free movement 126
capital flows 10–11, 58, 60–1, 63
   and equity 26–7
   history 42–3
   lack of regulation 16, 21, 63
   and trade 84
capital markets, liberalisation 124–5, 207–8
capitalism, Asian 119
   birth of 42
   as cause of war 22–3
   and civil society 34–72
   and globalisation 21, 158–61
   recurrent cycles of 150–1
   and social democracy 146, 152
   variant forms 154
Carson, Rachel. *Silent Spring* 28
caste system 172–3, 271–2, 292
Castells, Manuel, on globalisation 158
Chavez, Hugo 76
Chiapas insurgency, 1994 65
China, attitude to foreigners 170–1
   economic growth 167–8, 175–83, 191–8

economic predictions 183–6, 193–4, 195
history 168-9
political economy 166–89
political uprisings 173, 186, 197
rise of xi, 119
Chindambaram, P. 244
Chirac, Jacques, trial 226
Christian democracy 273–4
citizenship, passage to 126–7
civil rights movement 8–9
civil society, definition 17
and financial institutions 39–41
and global capitalism 34–72
and global trade 76–114
and trade strategies 111
see also non-governmental organisations
Clovis, Sam 136
coalition governments 254–5, 264–5, 267
Cold War, end 3, 4, 5, 7
colonisation, and capital flow 42–3
commercial banks 10–11, 12
commodities trading 80, 84
Common Agricultural Policy 90, 102, 124
communism, collapse 7, 45, 119, 224
comparative advantage, theory 78–9, 81, 84
Congress Party *see* Indian National Congress Party
corn laws, abolition 79
corruption 225–7
reduction 185-6
credit, US politics of 137–8
Cultural Revolution 179, 197
debt crises, 1980s 12–13, 43–4, 207
debt crisis, Latin America 210
debt reduction 157–8
India 235–6, 237–8
debt write-offs *see* international debt write-offs
deficits, US politics of 138–9
deglobalisation 20–32, 57
deindustrialisation 11
Delhi Cloth Mills, bankruptcy 258
democracy, and globalisation 26
Indian 187, 196–7
spread of 8–9
Deng Xiaoping 175, 180, 192
depoliticisation, of Indian economy 188

deregulation, of financial markets 11, 45, 158, 207–8
Desai, Meghnad, biography vi–viii
developed countries, consumption pattern 161
employment rates 160, 207
hegemony 154, 159
investment rate 161
living standards 223–4
productivity 161
taxation policy 161, 212
see also superpowers
developing countries xi
access to medicines 104, 112
and capitalism 118, 224
industrialisation 81, 84, 121
and welfare state 122
and the WTO 101–4
see also newly industrialised countries; Third World countries
development economics xi
development paths, China 175–83, 191–8
India 175–83, 191–8, 217, 256–7
development thinking 199–227
India 216–7
diasporas, and fundamentalism 30–1
and globalisation 24–5
Eastern Europe, economic growth 120
ecological crisis, and capitalism 154
ecology, and development 214–5
economic nationalism, India 232–4, 248–50
economic reform, China 180–1
India 181–2, 213, 230, 243–6, 266
economic refugees, treatment of 129
economic regulation, and global governance 18
economic sovereignty 9, 12, 13
economics, rethinking of 150–1
education, China 178
India 178, 196, 279
Pakistan 279
ego, and the *Bhagavad Gita* 288
Eisenhower, Dwight D. 141–2
election prediction 263
emerging economies *see* developing countries; newly industrialised countries; Third World countries
empires, dismantling of 5, 6, 7, 24, 30
employment, and globalisation 123

Index

environmental constraints 3, 16
environmental degradation, as global problem 28–9, 154
environmental policy responses 16, 28–9
equity, increased prominence 26
Eurodollar market 11
European Union, agricultural subsidies 90
fair trade movement 78, 96–7
Fairtrade Labelling Organization International 96–7
fascism, defeat of 119
federal polity, India 171, 188, 197
film industry, India 216
finance, as dominant force 35
    see also money
financial crisis, 2008 x
financial institutions, and civil society 39–41
financial markets, and Brexit 133–4
    liberalisation 35, 50–1, 61
financial orthodoxy, disregard for 135
financial sector, processes 35–6
financial services industry 35
financial system, regulation 145
First World War 22–3
fixed exchange rates 43
FLO *see* Fairtrade Labelling Organization International
Food Security Bill (India) 223
foreign aid, and poverty reduction 206–7
foreign capital, in India 237, 248–9
foreign direct investment 45, 46, 58–9, 61, 63, 84, 158–9, 182, 266
    lack of regulation 50
free market, and developed countries 209–10
    and globalisation 59
free trade 24, 28, 31, 32, 208–9
    civil society support 79
    as imperialist strategy 81
    objections to 78, 81
    and politics 80–1
    supporters of 85–6
Free Trade Area of the Americas 76, 108–10
Fukuyama, F. *The End of History and the Last Man* 5
full employment, developed countries 207
fundamentalism 30–1

Gandhi, Indira 175, 180, 181, 187, 226, 273
    Gandhi, Rajiv 187, 251
    Gandhi, Sonia 270
gasoline price, US 158
GATS *see* General Agreement on Trade in Services
GATT *see* General Agreement on Tariffs and Trade
GDP *see* gross domestic product
gender, and development 212
General Agreement on Tariffs and Trade 17, 18, 84, 159, 208, 238, 251
General Agreement on Trade in Services 35, 53, 106–7
German reunification 158
global capitalism 35, 153–4
    isolationist response 56–7
    supporters of 59–61, 85–6
global civil society 17
global corporations 14–15, 16, 159
global governance 2–18
global interdependence 12
global trade, civil society and 85–99
    imbalance 101–2
globalisation ix–xi, 9, 10, 15–16, 20–2
    alternatives to 64–9, 93, 98–9
    and free market 59
    and global governance 18
    and industrialisation 121–2
    and migration 124–6
    obstruction of 124
    opponents of 34, 54
    and poverty 118–29
    and sustainable development 153–63
GNP *see* gross national product
Gold Standard 10
Goldwater, Barry 134
governance, definition 19
Grameen banking 68
Great Leap Forward 176, 179
Green Revolution 177, 180, 204–5, 245
gross domestic product 156
    India 278
    Pakistan 278
gross national product 156, 162–3
growth rate decline, developed countries 223–4
Haq, Mahbub ul 210, 212, 217
Harrod, Roy 201

Hastings, Warren 282
Hemispheric Social Alliance 110–1
Hicks, John, on income 155, 162
Hindu nationalism xii, 188, 231, 249–50, 262–74
Hindu social structure, India 172, 178
Hinduism 271, 273
  see also Brahmanism
Hindutva *see* Hindu nationalism
Hobson, John A. 23
Hong Kong, economic growth 208
house prices, and wealth 151
human development indices 177–8, 212
  India 210–1, 218, 277–8
  Pakistan 277–8
Hume, David 36
Hurd, Douglas, and New Imperialism 3
IBRD *see* World Bank
IFAT *see* International Federation of Alternative Trace
IMF *see* International Monetary Fund
immigration restrictions, effects of 128
imperialism, as cause of war 22–3
INC *see* Indian National Congress Party
income, definition 155
  per capita 174, 176, 180, 192
    India 276, 277
    Pakistan 276, 277
  and sustainable consumption 162
India, economic development 201–2
  economic growth 167–8, 175–83, 191–8, 253, 255–61, 277
  economic predictions 187–9, 193–4, 253–61
  elections of 1996 243, 246–50
  elections of 2004 262–74
  history 169–70
  as multi-religious society 273
  Partition 272, 275
  political economy xii, 166–89, 230–41, 243–50, 253–61, 276–80
  as regional power 267
  rise of xi–xii, 119
India–Pakistan relations 275
India Shining campaign 262, 266
Indian National Congress Party 254, 256, 262, 263, 267–68, 272
industrial capitalism 38
industrial economy, state intervention 147, 209

industrialisation, China 176
  and globalisation 121–2
  India 174, 176, 194–5, 257–9, 276
  Pakistan 276
industry incentives 258–9
inequality, India 278
  Pakistan 278
inflation 11, 12, 207
infrastructure, US neglect and investment 140, 141–2, 143
Initiative Against Economic Globalization 39
Institute of Social Sciences (New Delhi) 199
International Bank for Reconstruction and Development *see* World Bank
international bankruptcy mechanism 62
international debt write-offs 44, 50, 58, 62–3
International Federation of Alternative Trade 96
International Monetary Fund 13, 39–41, 45, 46, 58, 149
  and Latin America 210
  opposition to 57, 71
international trade, actors and interests 82–3
investment, regulation of 106
Islam, in India 178
Islamic fundamentalism 30
isolationists, and globalisation 56–9, 90–2, 93
IT industry, India 216
Jaitley, Arun 270
Jana Sangh *see* Bharatiya Jana Sangh
Japan, economic growth 121–2, 192
  industry model 210
  productivity growth 160
jobs, displacement 27–8
  protection 260
Johnson, Boris 134
Joshi, Murli Manohar 268, 270
Jubilee 2000 50, 71
just-in-time model 122, 210
Kautsky, Karl 23
  on agriculture 203–4
Keynes, John Maynard 39–40
Keynesian economics 5–6, 11, 26, 122, 147, 150, 201, 209
Keynesian politics x, xi

Index

Khair, G.S. *Quest for the Gita* 289–91
Kissinger, Henry, on China and India xi, 118–9, 191, 225
Klein, Lawrence vi
Kondratieff wave 25
Kosambi, D.D. 283, 290
Kudlow, Larry 136
Kumar, Dilip vii
labour, free movement of 126
labour market, flexibility 260
  regulation and restrictions 127
Laffer, Arthur 136
Lakdawala, D.T. 199
land pooling 204
land reform, China 174–5, 192
  India 175
Left, future of 146, 149
Leftist theory, failure 147
Lenin, V.I. 23
  on agriculture 203
Leninism, defeat of 4, 5, 119, 146, 153
LETS schemes *see* Project LETS
Lewis, W. Arthur 202
liberalisation, of Indian economy 243–6, 248, 250–1
Liskova, Katerina 39, 41, 71
List, Friedrich 81
literacy rates, India 279
  Pakistan 279
localisation 57
Lokpal Bill (India) 226–7
London School of Economics vi–vii, ix
long waves theory 25
longevity, and the welfare state 123
Lula da Silva, Luis Inacio 76
macroeconomic models, distrust of 150
Mahabharat, and the *Bhagavad Gita* 285–7
Mahajan, Pramod 270
Mahalanobis Plan 202, 203, 205, 235, 245, 248
Mahathir 76
Mahatma Gandhi National Rural Employment Guarantee Act 219, 221–2
MAI *see* Multilateral Agreement on Investment
Manafort, Paul 136
Mandeville, Bernard 36
manufacturing industries 6, 11, 27, 81, 215

India 194, 257–9
  relocation, to Asia 207
    to developing countries 120–1, 138, 147, 159, 208
Mao Tse Tung 175, 179, 201–2
market, as threat to democracy 64
market economy, transition to 4
market prices, role of 157–8
Marx, Karl, and globalisation 23
  on money 37
mathematical achievements, India 173
Mauss, Marcel, on money 37
May, Theresa 134
McNamara, Robert 205
Meltzer Report 40, 48, 60
mercantilist, Trump as 132
micro-lending 68
middle class, India 251
MIF *see* Multilateral Investment Framework
migration 124–9, 222
  management 128
MNCs *see* multinational corporations
MNREGA *see* Mahatma Gandhi National Rural Employment Guarantee Act
Mnuchin, Steven 136
modernisation 175–6
Modi, Narendra xii, 269, 270
monetarist policy 11
monetary policy, US 143
monetary transactions, objections to 36
money, alternatives 67
  contrasting views of 38, 42
  and modernity 37–8
  and morality 36–8
Moore, Stephen 137
moral attitudes, and money 36–8
Mukherjee, Pranab 254
Multilateral Agreement on Investment 51–3
Multilateral Investment Framework 106
multinational corporations 21
multi-party parliaments 8
Naoroji, Dadabhai 200, 206
nation states 6–7, 8
  and capitalism 55–6
  and migration 126
  and political sovereignty 9

National Democratic Alliance 255, 262, 263, 264
national economies 10
National Rural Employment Guarantee Scheme 258, 260, 261
National Volunteer Organisation *see* Rashtriya Swayamsevak Sangh
nationalism 29–30
  as cause of war 23–4
  as threat to anti-capitalist movement 112, 114
NDA *see* National Democratic Alliance
Needham, Joseph 173
Nehru, Jawaharlal 175, 179, 192, 193, 201–2, 205
Nehru-Mahalanobis experiment *see* Mahalanobis Plan
neoclassical economics 147, 148
neo-liberalism, and liberal democracy 55
  and reformists 64
newly industrialised countries 5, 11, 216
  Asia 207
  see also developing countries; Third World countries
non-government–government cooperation 112
non-governmental organisations 9, 16, 26, 39, 54, 61
  and the MAI 51–3
North American Free Trade Agreement 65, 108–10
NREGS *see* National Rural Employment Guarantee Scheme
nuclear capability, of India and Pakistan 275, 279, 280
nuclear energy, cost of 157
OECD *see* Organisation for Economic Co-operation and Development
oil price rise, of 1973 10, 43, 132, 138, 157, 206, 207
  of 1979 11
one-party rule, and capitalism 184–6
OPEC *see* Organization of Petroleum Exporting Countries
open economies x, xi, 5
  in Asia 120
Organisation for Economic Co-operation and Development 5, 6, 51
Organization of Petroleum Exporting Countries 10, 11, 12

Our World is Not for Sale network 91
Oxfam, fair trade pioneer 96
  and trade advocacy 94–5
Pakistan, economic growth 276–7
  political economy 276–80
Pakistan–India relations 275
Partition, of India 272, 275
patents 216
Perot, Ross 134
Peso crisis, 1994 45
Pettifor, Ann 39, 41, 71
philosophy, Indian 173
post-industrial economies 6
poverty, developed countries 205, 206
  as development problem 205
  and globalisation 118–29
  increase in 55–6
  India 278, 279
  measurement 206, 212
    India 217, 219–21, 256
  Pakistan 278, 279
  reasons for 200–1
  and the welfare state 122–3
poverty reduction 200, 205–6
  Asia 120
  and globalisation 129
  India 255, 256–7, 261
  and migration 125
  strategies 123, 223, 244
power balance, shift in 15
Prague protests, 2000 39, 71
private enterprise, India 187–8
productivity, and capitalism 224–5
Project LETS 67, 68
protectionist, Trump as 132
protest movement 93, 98–9
public debt, India 235–6
  Trump's attitude to 132, 134–5
  US 139–40
  see also international debt write-offs
public health, India 196
  and TRIPS 104
public sector reform, India 246
Raj, K.N. 201
Rao, Narasimha 181, 187, 192–3
Rashtriya Swayamsevak Sangh 233, 249, 265, 270, 271, 272, 273
redistribution of wealth 211–2, 261
reformists, and global trade 92–3, 94–5
  and globalisation 61–4

refugees, flow of 4
resource shortage, India 203
Ricardo, David. *Principles of Political Economy and Taxation* 79
right-wing popularist, Trump as 132–3
Romney, Mitt 134
Roy, Arundhati 114
Royal Bank of Scotland 225–6
RSS *see* Rashtriya Swayamsevak Sangh
rule of law, China 185
Sanders, Bernie 133, 140
Schumpeter, Joseph A. 23
SEATINI *see* Southern and Eastern African Trade Negotiations Institute
Seattle protests, 1999 64, 69, 71
self-reliance 58–9
self-sufficiency 58–9
  and money 36, 38
Sen, A.K. vii, 210, 212, 216, 220
Shourie Arun 270
Simmel, George, on money 37
Singh, Charan 179, 225
Singh, Manmohan 181, 187, 244, 247
Smith, Adam, and money 36–7
  Wealth of Nations 79
social democracy, and 2008 financial crisis 145–52
  and capitalism 146
  and globalisation 147
social justice movement, and trade 78
social stability, India 172–3
socialism within capitalism 146–7, 148
socialists, and First World War 22–3
socially responsible investing 68–9
Soros, George 39, 41, 71
South Korea, economic growth 176, 192, 208, 209
Southern and Eastern African Trade Negotiations Institute 112–3
Soviet Union, collapse 3, 4, 54, 224
  influence on China 174
  influence on India 174, 202, 204
special economic zones 257–9
stagflation 11, 12
state capitalism 184
state power, and globalisation 56
state subsidies, and industry efficiency 209
subnationalisms, of India 187

superpowers, and free trade 86
  as globalisation leaders 86
surplus labour 202–3, 205
sustainable development, and globalisation 153–63
sustainable economic growth 154–6, 162
Taiwan, economic growth 176, 208, 209
tariff barriers 10, 81
tariffs, elimination and reduction 103
taxation, India 213, 244
  and redistribution 212
taxation policy, of BJP 239
technological achievements, of China 173
technological innovation, and capital flow 11, 15, 21, 35, 158
textile industries 173, 176
  collapse in India 181, 258
Third World countries x
  debt 50–1, 57–8, 59, 62, 157
  market access 95
  see also developing countries; newly industrialised countries
Third World Network 112
Tobin, James 16, 63
Tobin tax 63
trade, activism history 79–84
  alternative positions 98–9
  and civil society 76–114
  as engine of growth 78–9
  liberalisation, need for 124
  and poverty reduction 94–5
  regulation, reformist approach 92–3, 94–5
  Trump's attitude to 137–8
trade issues, information gathering and dissemination 111
  lobbying 111–2
Trade Justice Movement 92
trade policy, of BJP 238
Trade Related Aspects of Intellectual Property Rights Agreement 104, 112
trade unions, declining membership 148
trade wars 24
traditional societies, and money 38
transition to democracy, China 186, 193–4, 195
transnational corporations *see* global corporations
TRIPS *see* Trade Related Aspects of Intellectual Property Rights Agreement

Trump, Donald x–xi, 131–43
　supporters 137–8, 140–1
UNCTAD *see* United Nations
　Conference on Trade and Development
unemployment, in developed countries 160
unipolarity 31
unitary polity, China 172
United Kingdom, economic decline 7
United Nations 6–8, 17, 18
United Nations Conference on Trade and Development 12
United Progressive Alliance 194, 196, 254–5
United States, hegemony of 7–8, 31, 32
　presidential election 2016 131
　and the WTO 90
universal adult franchise 8
University of Pennsylvania vi
UPA *see* United Progressive Alliance
Upadhyaya, Deen Dayal, *Integral Humanism* 233–5
usury, objections to 36
Vajpayee, A.B. 269, 270, 272
Vishwa Hindu Parishad 266, 271, 272
wages, erosion 27–8
　stagnation, in US 140, 143
Ward, Barbara 16
wastage, India 213–4
wealth, nature of 151
Weber, Max 282
welfare state 122–3
　and aging population 123, 127–8
　and territorialism 126
Wendt, H. *Global Embrace* 14
Western countries *see* developed countries
Whittlesey, Charles vi
Wilkie, Wendell 134
Wilkins, Sir Charles 282
women's suffrage 8
World Bank 13, 39–41, 205
　opposition to 57, 71
World Development Movement War on Want 92
world economy, and globalisation 3–4, 5, 10, 17, 153
World Social Forum 75–7, 94, 98–9, 114
World Trade Organization 35, 77, 78, 84, 90, 92–3, 99–112, 113–4
WSF *see* World Social Forum
WTO *see* World Trade Organization
Zapatistas 65–6, 71